Trial by Fire and Battle in Medieval German Literature

Studies in German Literature, Linguistics, and Culture

Edited by James Hardin
(*South Carolina*)

Trial by Fire and Battle in Medieval German Literature

Vickie L. Ziegler

CAMDEN HOUSE

Copyright © 2004 Vickie L. Ziegler

All Rights Reserved. Except as permitted under current legislation, no part of this work may be photocopied, stored in a retrieval system, published, performed in public, adapted, broadcast, transmitted, recorded, or reproduced in any form or by any means, without the prior permission of the copyright owner.

First published 2004
by Camden House

Camden House is an imprint of Boydell & Brewer Inc.
668 Mt. Hope Avenue, Rochester, NY 14620, USA
www.camden-house.com
and of Boydell & Brewer Limited
PO Box 9, Woodbridge, Suffolk IP12 3DF, UK
www.boydell.co.uk

ISBN: 1–57113–291–0

Library of Congress Cataloging-in-Publication Data

Ziegler, Vickie L.
    Trial by fire and battle in medieval German literature / Vickie Ziegler.
      p. cm. — (Studies in German literature, linguistics, and culture)
  Includes bibliographical references and index.
  ISBN 1–57113–291–0 (hardcover : alk. paper)
    1. German literature—Middle High German, 1050–1500—History and criticism. 2. Ordeal in literature. I. Title. II. Series: Studies in German literature, linguistics, and culture (Unnumbered)

PT187.Z48 2004
830.9'3552—dc22

                                                  2004005050

A catalogue record for this title is available from the British Library.

This publication is printed on acid-free paper.
Printed in the United States of America.

Contents

Preface	ix
Acknowledgments	xi
List of Abbreviations Used in Endnotes	xiii
Introduction: Historical Background	1
1: Decoding the Codes: Treason in the Late Medieval *Karlsepik* — Der Stricker's *Karl der Grosse* and the *Karlmeinet*	21
2: The Ordeals of Tristan and Isolde	114
3: Saintly Queens under Fire in the *Kaiserchronik* and in Heinrich und Kunegunde	146
Coda: Der Stricker's "Das heisse Eisen" and Conclusion	168

Appendices:
I.	Der Stricker, *Karl der Grosse:* Plot Summary	175
II.	*Karlmeinet:* Plot Summary	179
III.	*Tristan:* Plot Summary	184
IV.	*Richardis:* Plot Summary	188
V.	*Heinrich und Kunegunde:* Translation	189
VI.	Comparison of Parallel Texts from the "Additamentum" and Ebernand von Erfurt	193
VII.	Der Stricker, "Das heisse Eisen" (The Hot Iron): Translation	195

Bibliography	199
Index	223

For Anthony,

"aller vröiden hêrre"

Reinmar der Alte, 168, 1

Preface

MEDIEVAL JUDICIAL ORDEALS, especially trial by fire or battle, conjure up vivid pictures in the modern imagination. Searing iron and clashing swords used in moments of high drama shape popular perceptions about the Middle Ages yet leave the reader without a context in which to understand this most dramatic of medieval judicial remedies. Ordeals were not the proof of first choice and were used only when other evidence was unavailable or ambiguous. Medieval people knew that the ordeal was an imperfect judicial process, just as we know that a jury trial may convict the innocent and let the guilty go free.

Literary texts provide us with some of the most graphic and detailed dramatizations of the use of the ordeal in the medieval legal system, since the ordeal brings forth a plentitude of moral and psychological issues. Because the conflict between good and evil stands at the heart of all epics, ordeals provide, both literally and figuratively, a battleground for this conflict and arouse great narrative interest. Lives and reputations are at risk in a high-stakes drama such as a trial for treason. The violence and the potential for destruction in a judicial duel parallel the intellectually combative and intentionally destructive verbal arguments frequently presented to the judge. Adultery in high places, then as now, affected the ruler's authority; the dramatic ordeal of the hot iron, with its purifying element of fire, concentrated official and private tension in a public event.

Law, like every other part of life that provides grist for the writer's mill, is bent and shaped to suit the demands of the narrative. Freed from the constraints of the court, the writer can pick and choose those parts of the legal process needed to shape the text. Because of this auctorial prerogative, the question of the degree to which a literary text can be used to understand a legal system has no neat, consistent answer. Although the degree to which a text reflects actual legal practice varies from writer to writer and from genre to genre, the texts analyzed in this study are all deeply rooted in contemporary legal procedures and perspectives, though some, such as the legends, reflect procedures and attitudes that had become or were becoming archaic. Further complicating the picture is the fact that literature may reflect actual practice in a way that law codes never could, because literature shows the application of the law in a situation that is supposed to occur in the real world. Unless the legal issue is portrayed in a way that is comprehensible to the reader, however, the law's function in the text will be misunderstood, obscured, or missed altogether.

Because Charlemagne (Karl der Grosse) was seen in the German lands throughout the Middle Ages as the great lawgiver, slightly more than half of this study deals with the Charlemagne literature of medieval Germany — specifically, with the trial of Genelun (Ganelon) for treason. Beginning with Priest Konrad's twelfth-century *Rolandslied*, with its strong ties to the *Chanson de Roland*, as a reference point, the study contains extensive analyses of Genelun's trial with the judicial ordeal in two later and little-known medieval German Charlemagne epics: Stricker's thirteenth-century *Karl der Grosse* and the fourteenth-century *Karlmeinet*.

The second part of this analysis will examine ordeals of fire and battle in legend and in courtly literature of the German Middle Ages; these genres also provide useful insights into the ordeal as a means of dispute settlement. This function of the ordeal is particularly apparent in ordeals by fire undergone by queens accused of adultery, which also involved treason. The ordeal of the hot iron enabled a public resolution of issues that could have led to a breakdown of the king's authority. Analyses of this type of ordeal include Queen Richardis in the *Kaiserchronik*, Queen Kunigunde in Ebernand of Erfurt's work, and Queen Isolde in Gottfried von Straßburg's *Tristan*. This section of the book also gives an example of a trial by battle in courtly literature, that between Morolt and Tristan, a trial that also involved vital questions about the authority of the king.

Medieval legal life in the German lands in the twelfth and thirteenth centuries flourished without a professional class of trial lawyers. This state of affairs may have led to a wider familiarity with legal procedures among the educated public; certainly writers of medieval German literature seem to have been well informed about the law, for legal references and situations involving legal issues abound. Because an understanding of these scenes in their legal and cultural context is vital to an accurate interpretation of the work in question, a brief background discussion of salient material about ordeals, judicial oaths, and dispute settlement will set the stage for the analysis of texts.

Acknowledgments

THE ORIGINS OF THIS BOOK GO BACK to my graduate school days, when I worked as live-in child care help for Professor Ellen Peters, then on the faculty of the Yale Law School. During the long trips from the outer reaches of Hamden to the Yale campus, Ellen told me a lot about her work; her enthusiasm for intellectual challenges of the law made a lasting impression on me.

A few years later, when Professor James Ross Sweeney and I were planning medieval studies conferences, he suggested a semester course, Crimes, Courts and Society in the Middle Ages, culminating in a conference. Asked to do one of the lectures for the course, I made the obvious choice of Isolde's trial by fire. Professor John Baldwin was one of the guest speakers for the course and conference; when I decided to expand ordeals into a book-length project, Professor Baldwin gave me much basic and valuable advice. My intellectual debt to him is apparent throughout this book. Professor Stefan Weinfurter of the University of Heidelberg made very helpful bibliographic suggestions.

As I read my way into background for the project, two libraries in Germany were particularly helpful: the Max Planck Institut für Geschichte in Göttingen and the Max Planck Institut für europäische Rechtsgeschichte near Frankfurt; Penn State's Interlibrary Loan Office showed extraordinary patience and skill as well. Professors Barbara Hanawalt and Juergen Eichhoff gave me valuable advice in the final stages of the manuscript, while Philip Winsor gave me the benefit of his years of experience as a senior editor of the Penn State Press. Student assistants who carefully helped with the mechanics of manuscript preparation include Alan Jalowitz, Brigitte Weinsteiger, and Adam Miyashiro.

To James Hardin and James Walker, Camden House editors, I would like to express my thanks for their interest in the book. Both are unfailingly helpful and encouraging; it has been a real pleasure to work with them. Philip Dematteis, the copy editor, immersed himself in a thorough and conscientious manner throughout, undergoing his own ordeal in the welter of sources and notes.

On a personal level, I would like to acknowledge the support of friends such as Jan Fleck and Anne Stevens; I owe a great debt to two other patient friends, also medievalists, Bridget Henisch and Elizabeth Traverse, innocent bystanders who were dragged through Charlemagne's judicial experiences and who offered valuable advice and much assistance.

A very special thank-you for support and encouragement goes to Anthony, who thought he had finished with trials by fire and battle in Prof. S. Thorne's law school class on English legal history.

V. Z.
January 2004

Abbreviations Used in Endnotes

ABÄG	*Amsterdamer Beiträge zur Älteren Germanistik*
CR	*Chanson de Roland*
DRW	*Deutsches Rechtswörterbuch*
FMS	*Frühmittelalterliche Studien*
HWBDR	*Handwörterbuch zur deutschen Rechtsgeschichte*
HZ	*Historische Zeitschrift*
JMRS	*Journal of Medieval and Renaissance Studies*
KG	*Karl der Grosse*, by Der Stricker
KM	*Karlmeinet*
MHDHWB	*Mittelhochdeutsches Handwörterbuch*
MHDWB	*Mittelhochdeutsches Taschenwörterbuch*
MHG	Middle High German
MLR	*Modern Language Review*
MNDHWB	*Mittelniederdeutsches Handwörterbuch*
PBB	[Paul's and Braune's] *Beiträge zur Geschichte der deutschen Sprache und Literatur*
RF	*Romanische Forschungen*
RL	*Rolandslied*
RSJB	*Recueils de la Société Jean Bodin pour l'Histoire Comparative des Institutions*
VF	*Verfasserslexikon*
VuF	*Vorträge und Forschungen*
ZfdPH	*Zeitschrift für deutsche Philologie*
ZSSRGGA	*Zeitschrift der Savigny-Stiftung für Rechtsgeschichte, Germanistische Abteilung*

Introduction: Historical Background

PROOF, A CORNERSTONE OF ANY LEGAL SYSTEM, archaic or modern, has always been a vexing problem in the long development of the rule of law. In medieval times, as we shall see, types of proof, such as eyewitness evidence, and means of establishing facts to prove something, such as inquests and hearings, were part of courtroom procedure; today's tribunals consider similar material. Early medieval legal life, however — not far removed from the practices of Franconian tribal law, where the ordeal was known, and not yet influenced by the great revival of Roman law in the twelfth century — relied, as well, on what we would call irrational proofs such as the oath, as it was understood at that time, and ordeal.

The heyday of the ordeal in medieval European society lasted from 800 to around 1200. Beginning with the Carolingians, who were strong proponents of its employment, the use of the ordeal increased markedly, in part because of government's advocacy of its use; new varieties of the ordeal, such as the ordeal of the cross;[1] and expansion into new areas.[2] While the ordeal, which had its European roots in Frankish society,[3] had attracted criticism from the ninth century onward, it had performed a useful judicial function for certain types of cases until clerical participation in it was forbidden by the Fourth Lateran Council in 1215, shortly after the probable date of composition of Gottfried's *Tristan*.[4] The unilateral ordeals, such as those of fire and water, suffered the most from this ban: since their efficacy depended on an unusual and verifiable reaction by the natural order, their demise was rapid.[5] In contrast, trial by battle, a bilateral ordeal that demanded no independent divine intervention to ascertain guilt or innocence, remained in place as a legal procedure in secular courts throughout the Middle Ages. Consequently, the evolution of these two types of ordeal is not congruent either in history or in the literary texts under consideration.[6]

In the primitive cultures in which the ordeal arose, nature was often identified with the deity. The original thought behind the ordeal was that nature could not tolerate a guilty being in its midst. The offender disturbs the divine order of nature and thereby that of the community and will be rejected by nature in any test.[7] As Christianity spread, God was seen to perform the function of nature. During the conversion of Europe, the ordeal functioned in early and high medieval society as a means of resolving otherwise intractable and unsolvable questions of guilt or innocence. Cases in which there were no witnesses or no credible witnesses still had to be settled; in such cases, God was called as a witness.[8]

Much has been made of the "irrationality" of the ordeal and the apparent steady progress of society toward more rational means of proof. This disentanglement of the ordeal from the context of medieval legal practice in which it had a definite place is anachronistic and distorts our understanding of the ordeal from the perspective of the historian, as well as that of the literary critic. Recent scholarly work on the settlement of disputes in early medieval Europe, the period in which the ordeal was most unquestionably popular, has shown that the courts had a variety of means for obtaining knowledge and discouraging potential perjurers, means that included both the rational and the irrational in twentieth-century terms. These methods included a kind of inquest; use of witnesses, both partial and impartial; as well as oath-helping and the ordeal.[9] The post-Enlightenment mind sees a contradiction between the use of witnesses to establish the truth, a practice sanctioned by reason, and the submission of the case to God, either through oath, oath helpers, lots, or ordeals, practices condemned by reason. This antithesis was simply not important in many places and at many times during the Middle Ages, since medieval man was quite comfortable both with his reason and with the belief that God could intervene directly in human problems.[10] The coexistence of both rational and irrational means of proof shows that medieval courts certainly embraced facts that could be established without divine intervention. Indeed, they turned to the ordeal, certainly the most dramatic of the so-called irrational proofs, only in special circumstances. We must, therefore, see the ordeal as part of a wide range of options for establishing truth and reaching a settlement.[11]

Ordeals were not the proof of choice in medieval courts: inquests, as well as the testimony of written evidence and witnesses, offered means of proof, as well.[12] Normal judicial procedure in the Middle Ages would also have required the oath as a means of deciding cases.[13] Like the ordeal, swearing an oath submitted the individual to God's judgment.[14] Underneath both the ordeal and the oath lay the concept of immanent justice, which presupposed divine intervention on a predictable basis in the conduct of people's lives.[15] The importance of the oath as a means of proof in medieval courts is hard for us to grasp; yet, if we look at the weight given today to sworn testimony, in which the name of God is invoked and which can involve criminal penalties if the testimony is false, we can catch a glimpse of the situation in medieval times. In the absence of strong political control by the state, the oath stood as the cornerstone of judicial proceedings. For this reason, much attention was paid to the repetition in the oaths of words and phrases that involved unseen powers. Such oaths helped to ensure the presence of deities, which changed from pagan to Christian in the course of time. The stakes were high; if the oaths were in any way insufficient, private warfare or feuds could ensue.[16] In the case of the oath, there was the possibility of both immediate and long-term reactions on the part of the Deity; immediate ones might include the impossibility of the oath helpers repeating the oath as demanded.[17]

Taking of oaths was an alternative to battle in pre-Christian times.[18] Someone knowledgeable in the law would state what penalties were involved; then the defendant would try to clear himself through an oath, trial by battle, or some other kind of ordeal.[19] Oaths were frequently given by the defendant, because it was his honor that had been affronted by the accusation.[20] The context in which this procedure functioned needs clarification for modern readers. While an oath in court today strengthens the statement of the swearer, it is still subject to the truth established by the court. The opposite situation obtained in medieval times. If the oath were sworn, then the judge was bound by it and was forced to end the legal dispute. The swearer became his own judge and gave his own verdict. Not the verifiable fact, but the oath was the truth. As in the case of documents and seals, the truth resided in the properly performed oath.

This Germanic understanding of the oath rested on the concept that law resided in form. Once an oath had been sworn in the correct way, its words had a magic force. Such an archaic understanding of the oath persisted into the High Middle Ages, even as the Church began to make headway with its ethical understanding of the oath. As the idea of truth in the oath came to include not only a guaranty for its long-term validity but also truth in a moral sense, the importance of form necessarily weakened.[21] The coexistence of the pagan and the Christian understanding of the oath appears in literature as well, in texts such as *Tristan* and *Engelhard,* and helps to explain the description of these oaths.

In medieval legal life a witness made a fact true by his willingness to put his life on the line, which was how swearing an oath was viewed. The fear of the awful consequences to one's person for giving a false oath lay in the belief that forswearing was a condemnation of oneself. In the taking of the oath the individual offered his own person as surety; he could, therefore, expect divine retribution on his person if he did not tell the truth.[22] Our literary sources, both legendary and secular, frequently bear out this belief. The major weakness of the oath in this regard was the fact that the mills of divine justice ground according to their own speed; punishment for swearing a false oath could come much later in the perjurer's life, well after the verdict that rested on that oath had had its effect.[23]

In order to remove, or weaken, the temptation to perjury, the involvement of the Church — in particular, the use of relics — became important. The swearing of oaths at the altar or upon relics was a well-known legal practice, common in property matters as well as in postulants' commitment to religious orders. The oath of the Christian at a saint's altar ensured that the saint would stand surety and not leave any attacks on his or her name, such as false oaths, unpunished. The saint did not diminish himself or herself by such participation in human affairs. On the contrary, the ability of the saint to intervene was seen as confirmation of his or her miraculous powers.[24] The religious dimension to the process could also influence the compurgators, who were not witnesses per se but supporters of the accused in regard to his or her character and case.[25]

Not only the demands of their consciences but also the heavy immediate penalties for perjury could make the task of a compurgator a burden never to be forgotten. A standard punishment for taking a false oath was loss of a hand. As an alternative to the amputation of their hands, Carolingian compurgators accused of perjury could be forced to the ordeal — often the ordeal of the cross — to demonstrate that they swore their oath without knowing the facts. Celestin III in the late twelfth century decreed that compurgators used purposely in cases where they could not know the facts were guilty of perjury if the party in question were guilty. While these measures seem harsh, they helped to ensure that the power of the oath to clear an individual remained convincing to the court and to society at large; otherwise, oath-taking would have had no legal standing.[26]

In spite of such measures, confidence in the ability of the oath to reveal the truth seems from the earliest records to have been tempered by a knowledge of the evil of which human beings were capable. Faced with various kinds of public disgrace and loss of position, privilege, or wealth, individuals with a bent to duplicity found fertile ground in the oath-taking procedure. The use of false oaths that were literally true posed a major legal and ethical problem during the entire Middle Ages. There were two sets of opinions on the matter of such oaths: according to one view, if the wording of the oath literally covered the facts, the oath was true. It was not important if the others present understood what was going on, because the oath functioned independently of the bystanders.[27] The Church rejected such an understanding: if the swearer gave his oath a meaning that no one else could be expected to comprehend, then onlookers could not take it into account in answering their subjective questions about the matter at hand. For adherents of the first point of view, the borderline between a true oath and perjury was an objective matter, divorced from inner motivation. For the other side, represented by the Church, the real truth could only be established by taking the individuals involved into account.[28]

The external, objective view that the Church rejected could have had its roots in the pre-Christian, magical understanding of the oath. Oath formulae were part of the world of magic, just as curses and blessings were.[29] All swearing was useless unless you had the right words and gestures; if you did, success was automatic and independent of your will, as well as of those around you. The only power that could be used to stop the effects of an oath was another, more powerful kind of magic. That is why you could not excuse yourself for breaking an oath you were forced to take: the oath was effective regardless of your own misgivings or rejection of it. The efficacy of the oath depended only on the precise completion of the necessary gestures and the exact repetition of the prescribed words.[30] Such formalism stood for the certainty and strength of the law; a law bound on these forms did not expect a dichotomy between word and will and had no internal or external monitors for it.[31]

This pre-Christian belief in the automatic, magical nature of the oath seems to reflect itself in the position that many medieval people took toward it in court. If a defendant, for example, did not want to make himself liable to divine punishment, he had two options: to change the formula stealthily and thereby vitiate the magic; or to speak the oath in such a way that it was literally true, while keeping the real intent and meaning hidden.[32] To falsify an oath in medieval times meant to destroy its efficacy through an alternative or stronger magic.[33] Modern sensibilities bridle at such an understanding of the oath; it seems external, merciless, and formalistic. Such a verdict is ahistorical, since archaic law did not take subjective considerations into account. With the Christianization of Europe, however, the focus moved from the external oath to the soul of the swearer. The Christian oath had a social frame of reference missing in the pagan situation, because the social nature of the Christian ethic demanded that an oath had to be subjectively true, as well, so that one's fellow human beings were not injured by it. God does not let himself be tricked by oath formulae, since he is the judge of all oaths. Whether in literature or in life, medieval courts were always on guard against these attempts at deception. We find such awareness appearing in literary accounts: the opponents of Queen Isolde do not want her to formulate her oath for that very reason.[34] In Stricker's *Karl der Grosse,* when Karl gives Genelun injunctions before Genelun's negotiating journey to the heathen, he warns the peer that he should not let himself be deceived either with cunning tricks or with oaths.[35]

Faced with an accusation for which an oath constituted proof, the individual could take the oath alone, or he could offer compurgators; the determining factors were the crime and the status of the defendant. A higher social status implied a large degree of public confidence in the validity of an individual's oath, in his "oathworthiness." Oathworthiness depended to a large degree on status and reputation. If an individual were known to be untrustworthy, he could not clear himself with an oath. People convicted of serious crimes, such as theft and perjury, were not considered oathworthy.

Another group that could not clear itself through oaths comprised individuals who either by birth or circumstance, through no fault of their own, were not oathworthy. This group had two main categories: foreigners and slaves. The stranger is not grounded in the community: there is no one to vouch for his character. Medieval society, with its intricate web of interdependent relationships, offered a rich matrix in which various facets of individual character came to light. The foreigner, such as Isolde in Gottfried's *Tristan*, is cut off from this network of family and other economic and social ties.[36] Such individuals have no oath helpers at hand.

Members of all three groups — the untrustworthy, the foreigners and the slaves — could be forced to the ordeal. Since ordeals seem to have been used as a last resort in medieval judicial procedures, the offenses involved were ones in which testimony and the swearing of oaths were not convincing or applicable and where there were no other means of discovering the truth. The types of crimes that frequently demanded the ordeal were sexual transgressions, where the hot iron or an ordeal involving fire was preferred; treason, often settled by ordeal by battle; and any crimes involving stealth, such as murder or theft. Heresy, too, could fall under this rubric, since belief may leave no traces. These were all areas in which a definitive result had to be obtained.[37]

Sexual offenses and treason seem to figure most prominently in the literary texts involving ordeals. Several factors combined to make these topics attractive literary themes: the nature of the offense; the high drama of the ordeal procedure, with the presence of clergy, relics, and, frequently, the princes of the realm; and the divine revelation of guilt or innocence. Consequently, our study demands a closer examination of these two means of proof, beginning with trial by fire. The natural ability of fire to purify plays a role in some ordeal rituals: for example, when Shadrach, Meshach, and Abednego pass through the fiery furnace, protected from harm by God's presence.[38] In the story in *Daniel*, Nebuchadnezzar caused the furnace to be heated to seven times its usual heat before the three Jews were thrown into it. The court then saw "how the fire had no power to harm their bodies."[39] This biblical account suggests that as a test of the power of the Hebrew God the furnace was heated to an extraordinary degree, a feature we find in the Kunigunde legend. The power of God suspended natural law even in the face of an extreme situation, where death was the only rational outcome. The belief expressed in this biblical passage, that God would protect the innocent in the face of certain danger, figures in ordeal procedure, as well.

For romantic improprieties, the ordeal of the hot iron seems definitely to have been preferred both in history and in literature.[40] It was particularly appropriate for women, because of their limited capacity for battle.[41] Accusations of adultery frequently forced medieval courts to resort to ordeals, since adultery is generally planned to occur when no witnesses are present. Even if there were witnesses, it was hard to get reliable testimony from them: their own bona fides were suspect, either because they cared more about the accused than they did the truth, or because they were afraid of reprisals.[42] Such ordeals generally were used when the case in question could be settled in no other way and when rational proofs had failed.[43]

In reality, those who underwent the ordeal of the hot iron were always burned. The bandages were taken off in a few days to judge whether or not the wound had healed: if the burns had subsided, they were acquitted; if the wound had festered, they were guilty.[44] The decision as to what degree of healing constituted innocence was ambiguous.[45] Since equality before the law is a modern ideal, to which exceptions are still frequently made, it should not be surprising that such standards were rather elastic in the time period under consideration. In the three ordeals involving accusations of adultery against queens that this study analyzes, the reputation of the individual played a significant role; it was a major consideration in deciding whether she should undergo the ordeal at all. In some cases, indeed, where the saintly character of the accused queens made the ordeal seem superfluous, the queens insisted on it for reasons that will become apparent in the discussion. Queen Isolde, on the other hand, had to undergo the ordeal because of the general (and accurate) opinion at court that she had been unfaithful to her husband. Reputation often determined the degree of severity of the ordeal, as well; in an unusual example, the plowshares for Queen Kunigunde were made hot enough to make any normal mortal quail, thereby underscoring the saintliness of a character able to survive such a test.[46] In these ordeals the victims are examined on the spot and judged, a state of affairs that has more to do with telling a good story than with fidelity to reality. Concern with rigging the ordeal was widespread; here our materials reflect reality, since three of them have references either to attempts to deceive or to prevention of trickery.

Another form of ordeal, trial by battle, was part of the warp and woof of the judicial fabric of the Middle Ages.[47] This procedure had its roots in Germanic times, when a fight was the remedy of choice for dispute settlement.[48] In the pre-Christian era, divine intervention was thought to occur on the side of the protagonist with the best magic and not on that of the party who was in the right from an absolute point of view.[49] In many of the Germanic tribal laws this ancient custom received a specifically Christian framework, becoming a judgment of God. In its first appearance in the Lex Gundobada, God proves who is in the right and whose oath is true. In contrast to the situation in pre-Christian times, the abstract idea of justice becomes important. The fight does not establish this fact but reveals it, since God intervenes on behalf of the right.[50] Like the ordeals of fire and water, it was used in instances where the truth could not be established in other ways. In contrast to these other ordeals, which involved the accused and the elements, the trial by battle demanded neither a direct response from the natural world nor an immediate sign of divine intervention.[51]

One of the major functions of the ordeal by battle was to combat wholesale perjury. When an oath was taken in court, the person who gave the oath was liable to defend it in a duel if challenged; therefore, one had to be extremely careful.[52] Ordeal by battle was frequently meant to underscore the religious implications of the oath, which also received emphasis through swearing on relics or the Gospels.[53] Defeat not only imperiled the soul's salvation in the case of a false oath but also involved loss of whatever was at stake in the legal case, as well as more serious considerations, including, depending on the time and place, the loss of property, a hand, legal protection, or one's life. Consequently, these fights were often bestially ferocious.[54]

While the intensity of the battle was not regulated, much else surrounding the judicial duel was. Though the actual content of the regulations can vary, they seem to deal with the same major areas: who was eligible to fight, rules surrounding the engagement, and, as we have seen, penalties incurred by the loser. Women, ecclesiastics, and those who were ill were allowed to use a champion. While there are a few examples of women fighting for themselves, the more frequent choice seems to have been subjection to the ordeal of a hot iron in situations where the accused man would have gone into combat.[55]

The judicial procedures for the stages of the ordeal by battle have survived in, among other places, French customals written down in the thirteenth and fourteenth centuries that reflect practices from earlier periods. The presentation of pledges, the authorization by the court and the oath before it, then the battle, seem to have been the three major parts.[56] Such combats did not generally take place on the spot but at a time in the future; a delay of four to six weeks was common in southern Germany. The protagonists had time to practice and to put their affairs in order, should the worst come to pass. They had to put up security for their reappearance; if the defendant did not show up, he was judged guilty. Generally, the battle stopped with the setting of the sun.[57]

Because the trial by battle was employed in cases where the truth could not be ascertained in any other way, it often appears in cases involving clandestine, as well as heinous, crimes.[58] The bond between offenses of a traitorous nature and the judgment of God through battle was so strong that Frederick II excluded accusations of treason when he abolished trial by battle for southern Italy.[59] In addition, it was used in cases involving treason, sexual license, and murder.[60] Because of their drama, these offenses figure most prominently in literary texts. In addition, this type of ordeal could function as a sort of controlled legitimization of vengeance or of a private war. In the course of the Middle Ages the boundaries between the battle as a legal procedure and the battle as a defense of personal honor became less clear.[61]

The ordeal by battle frequently led to death and certainly to bloodshed.[62] While God was expected to support the truthful combatant, no matter how strong his opponent,[63] there was still a certain amount of uneasiness. Those familiar with such struggles knew that many factors outside of divine intervention could determine the course of a fight. For these reasons, the trial by battle attracted criticism at a relatively early date, particularly from the religious establishment.[64] Attitudes were not consistent, however. While the Church continued to increase the distance between itself and the shedding of blood, ordeal by battle was a frequent recourse for monasteries and other religious establishments in legal disputes.[65] Much of the opposition from the Church came in regard to the direct participation of the clergy in trial by battle, which faced papal bans during the twelfth century.[66]

Yet, in spite of this ongoing antagonism from the Church, the ordeal by battle flourished during the thirteenth and fourteenth centuries in the secular world. While there was a conflict between the lords, who could adjudicate in cases of high crimes, and the aristocrats, who wanted to retain their traditional right to resolve differences through force, both tendencies worked to keep the judicial duel alive in the courts. The right to fight was the mark of a free man.[67]

Much of the opposition to the ordeal from the intelligentsia, which was primarily the clergy or those with a clerical education, rested on the belief that it forced God to act in situations where man, not God, demanded certainty. As this discussion has indicated, these objections hit the unilateral ordeals the hardest, since they required a direct intervention in the natural order, which was seen as a temptation of God. The anti-Christian element in the ordeal lay in the fact that it forced God to act in a situation in which he might not wish to do so, thereby affecting the Last Judgment. Many church officials felt the ordeal's roots were in superstition. The twelfth-century rebirth of interest in Roman law, which did not have the ordeal, and its tradition of rational proofs could only have strengthened this current of opposition, as did the clergy's distancing itself more and more from secular judicial proceedings during the twelfth century.[68]

Though the unilateral ordeal lingered on in some parts of Europe (it was employed in certain thirteenth-century German regions, in Navarre, and in some Italian towns),[69] it soon gave way to other methods of resolving difficult cases. Juries developed quickly after 1215 in England and some other countries, but the most significant change was the use of torture. In part as a reaction to the loss of one kind of proof, criminal procedure in Continental courts in the thirteenth century went from accusation followed by ordeal to inquisition followed by torture. Confession, the "queen of proofs," was the most certain evidence of guilt when divine intervention was no longer a possibility.[70]

This brief survey of historical writing on the ordeal has shown that the unilateral ordeals went into a marked decline during the thirteenth century, while ordeal by battle survived well into the fifteenth century as a judicial procedure, in spite of criticism leveled against it from various quarters. Ordeal by battle appears in a favorable light not only in the twelfth-century *Rolandslied*, written by Priest Konrad, but also in the thirteenth-century

Karl der Grosse; the fourteenth-century *Karlmeinet,* probably compiled by clerics in Aachen; and in *Tristan*. In the case of the ordeal by battle, the three examples in the *Karlsepik* display significant variations that seem to show individual differences, as well as changing societal currents and problematic issues. Since there was much clerical opposition to ordeals in general and specific objections to ordeal by battle, the literature in question could certainly have reflected a different point of view; but it does not. Instead, it reflects trends in the larger society.[71]

In contrast, the unilateral ordeal, in the examples from literature and legend analyzed here, undergoes a different development. In the legends the ordeal by fire, endured by saintly queens, remained fixed in a hagiographic amber for centuries.[72] These ordeals were essential elements that justified the veneration of their heroines, because the tests revealed the women's sanctity. In thirteenth-century secular literature the ordeal by fire, scathingly attacked by Gottfried, receives a burlesque treatment approximately twenty years after the 1215 Fourth Lateran Council in a short work by Stricker. This rather bawdy and satirical approach to the ordeal by fire was apparently still guaranteed to amuse in sixteenth-century Germany, where Hans Sachs used it in a *Fastnachtsspiel*.[73] The ordeal by fire, passing rapidly into disuse in real life in the thirteenth-century German lands, appears in these works in two stock treatments, that of the legend and that of comic literature, that in later related texts seem to remain fixed.

This situation should warn us against assuming monolithic attitudes toward the ordeal conditioned by our endemic cultural Darwinism, which likes neat, progressive development. There were many different and frequently conflicting attitudes toward ordeals in the German lands in the late twelfth, thirteenth, and fourteenth centuries, attitudes that are reflected in the texts chosen for this study. There is ample evidence that medieval people distinguished between bilateral and unilateral ordeals much of the time, while there are other contemporary voices at variance with these assumptions. There is strong evidence for firm clerical opposition to trial by battle, whether because of the shedding of blood, the inevitable deaths, or its unreliability; but there are also indications that other clerics were not unwilling to use it, particularly in the earlier Middle Ages, or to countenance its use. What has seemed important is to set aside any impulse to fit these texts into a preconceived interpretative structure and, instead, to determine what they, created as they were in the legal and literary context of their time, can tell us about the contemporary attitudes to the law that they reflect.

In so doing, our analysis will show how much such an inquiry can enhance our understanding not only of the work in question but also of changing cultural attitudes. The role of the feud in the treason trial of Roland's betrayer in the Charlemagne material provides a good example. Since the early twelfth-century *Song of Roland,* feud formed the cornerstone of the Ganelon/Genelun figure's defense, as it does in Stricker's work, where the defenders of the nobility's right to declare a feud come to represent the older — and, in Stricker's eyes, inadequate — compensatory justice. Those who condemn Genelun propound the newer penal approach to crime.

While the question of the right to feud as a means of dispute settlement dominates Stricker's work, the *Karlmeinet* hardly mentions it. The significance of this change in a traditional narrative such as the trial for Roland's betrayal raises questions of interest to social and legal historians, questions that can only be answered if the distinctiveness of each work becomes clear. Because these German texts are either unknown, not easily accessible, or both, this study will examine the differences at some length, so as to give a solid base to those in other disciplines who might be interested in the cultural changes these works reflect. As the great twentieth-century architect Mies van der Rohe frequently said, "God is in the details."

Notes

[1] This unusual ordeal first appeared around 758/68. Both parties stood up with outstretched arms as if they were on a cross; the first to drop his arms lost. It was forbidden by Louis the Pious in the ninth century. See Gerhard Köbler, *Bilder aus der deutschen Rechtsgeschichte von den Anfängen bis zur Gegenwart* (Munich: Beck, 1988), 81.

[2] Robert Bartlett, *Trial by Fire and Water* (Oxford: Clarendon P, 1986), 9, 12; see Gerhard Köbler, "Welches Urteil ist das Gottesurteil des Mittelalters," *Vom mittelalterlichen Recht zur neuzeitlichen Rechtswissenschaft: Bedingungen, Wege und Probleme der europäischen Rechtsgeschichte*, ed. Norbert Brieskorn, Paul Mikat, Daniela Müller, and Dietmar Willoweit (Paderborn: Schöningh, 1994), 89–108 (91–104); and Hermann Nottarp, *Gottesurteile* (Munich: Kösel, 1956), 103–88, for a survey of the use of ordeals in Germanic and early medieval German societies.

[3] Bartlett 7; he notes (103) that trial by battle appears in many Germanic law codes. For a detailed survey of the ordeal in Franconian society, see M. Pappenheim, "Über die Anfänge des germanischen Gottesurteils," *ZSSRGGA* 48 (1928): 136–75.

[4] There has been considerable debate on the reasons for the decline of the ordeal, most of which coalesces around two opposing positions. The first claims that the ordeal declined gradually because of widespread social change; representatives of this position include Peter Brown, "Society and the Supernatural: A Medieval Change," *Daedalus* 104 (1975): 133–51; Raoul C. van Caenegem, "La Preuve dans le droit du moyen âge occidental-Rapport de synthèse," *La Preuve, RSJB*, no. 17 (Brussels: Editions de la Librairie Encyclopedique, 1965): 691–753, esp. 697–725 and 749–53; van Caenegem, "Law in the Medieval World," *Tijdschrift voor rechtsgeschiedenis* 49 (1981): 13–46, esp. 14 and 31; van Caenegem, "Methods of Proof in Western Medieval Law," *Mededelingen von de Koninklijke Academie voor Wetenschappen, Letteren en Schone Kunsten von België, Klasse der Letteren* 45 (1983): 83–127, 97; see also Paul R. Hyams and Colin Morris, "Trial by Ordeal: The Key to Proof in the

Early Common Law," *On the Laws and Customs of England: Essays in Honor of Samuel E. Thorne*, ed. Morris S. Arnold et al. (Chapel Hill: U of North Carolina P, 1981), 90–126.

The other position holds that the demise of the ordeal was swift after clerical opposition to it coalesced around a pope sympathetic to such attitudes. The main representatives of this position are Bartlett and John W. Baldwin. Baldwin's works dealing with the decline of the ordeal include "The Intellectual Preparation for the Canon of 1215 against Ordeals," *Speculum* 36 (1961): 613–36; *Masters, Princes, and Merchants: The Social Views of Peter the Chanter & His Circle*, 2 vols. (Princeton: Princeton UP, 1970), I: 323–32; "The Crisis of the Ordeal: Literature, Law and Religion around 1200," *JMRS* 24 (1994): 327–53; and *Aristocratic Life in Medieval France: The Romances of Jean Renart and Gerbert de Montreuil 1190–1250* (Baltimore: Johns Hopkins UP, 2000), 203–13, 234–36. In his chapter "The End of the Ordeal and Social Change" (34–69) Bartlett discusses the theory of social change and his objections to it; his chapter "The End of the Ordeal: Explanations in Terms of Belief" (70–102) substantiates his theory in a detailed analysis of the relationship of the confession to the demise of the ordeal; the evolving theories about the two types of supernatural manifestation, the miracle and the sacrament; and the implications for the ordeal. For an earlier discussion of clerical opposition to the ordeal, see Nottarp 332–63.

[5] The *Sachsenspiegel* mandates only the ordeal of the hot iron for criminals who were not oathworthy and were subsequently accused; they could choose among the ordeals of the hot iron, hot water and a fight against a champion. *The Saxon Mirror*, trans. Maria Dobozy (Philadelphia: U of Pennsylvania P, 1999), Book I, no. 39 (80). By contrast, trial by battle is treated extensively: Book I, no. 43 (81); no. 48, no. 49, no. 50 (82), no. 51 (83), no. 62 (86), no. 63 (87–89; detailed rules of combat), no. 68 (90); Book II, no. 3 (93), no. 8 (94), no. 13 (96); Book III, no. 29 (122), no. 36 (123); no. 65 (133); no. 92, 141. See also Gerald Buchda, "Der Beweis im sächsischen Recht," *La Preuve, RSJB*, no. 17 (Brussels: Editions de la Librairie Encyclopedique, 1965), 519–46, esp. 533–46. Buchda summarizes all of the instances in the *Sachsenspiegel* in which trial by battle was used (536–37). Bartlett discusses the lingering presence of unilateral ordeals as well as trial by battle in the German lands in the high and late Middle Ages (130–31).

[6] Bartlett 2, 107–8, 120–22. Hyams and Morris note that after the Fourth Lateran, the use of trial by battle was not diminished and, in some areas, actually increased later in the century (101, 119–20). Buchda says that the judicial duel did not disappear from Saxon legal procedure until the beginning of the fifteenth century (537). See also Jean-Philippe Lévy, "L'Evolution des la preuve, des origines à nos jours. Synthèse générale," *La Preuve, RSJB*, no. 17 (Brussels: Editions de la Librairie Encyclopedique, 1965), 9–70 (27); Baldwin, *Aristocratic Life* 211–12.

[7] See Nottarp 15–17; see also van Caenegem, "La Preuve" 695–96; Jean Gaudemet, "Les Ordalies au Moyen Age: Doctrine, Legislation et pratiques canoniques," *La Preuve, RSJB*, no. 17 (Brussels: Editions de la Librairie Encyclopedique, 1965), 99–135 (100–107); Lévy 13–17; S. F. C. Milsom, *Historical Foundations of the Common Law* (Toronto: Butterworths, 1981), 4–5; Adalbert Erler, U. Kornblum, and G. Dilcher, "Eid," *HWBDR*, 5 vols. (Berlin: E. Schmidt, 1964–1998), I: cols. 860–70

(esp. Erler cols. 861–63); *DRW*, vols. 1–4 (Weimar: H. Böhlaus Nachfolger, 1936), II: cols. 1301–7; Michael Goodich, *Violence and Miracle in the Fourteenth Century* (Chicago: U of Chicago P, 1995), 54–55.

[8] See Bartlett 24–33, 135; Herbert Kolb, "Himmlisches und irdisches Gericht in karolingischer Theologie und althochdeutscher Dichtung," *Frühmittelalterliche Studien* 5 (1971): 284–303 (290). See also Baldwin, *Aristocratic Life* 203–4.

[9] See Wendy Davies and Paul Fouracre, eds., *The Settlement of Disputes in Early Medieval Europe* (Cambridge & New York: Cambridge UP, 1986), 214–22. See also Susan Reynolds, *Kingdoms and Communities in Western Europe, 900–1300* (Oxford: Clarendon P, 1984), 14; Bartlett 26. Milsom says that proof, not simple accusation, was central to medieval lawsuits and was the major task before the victim (285).

[10] Reynolds compares the modern acceptance of jury trial results, even though it is known that juries make mistakes, with medieval attitudes towards the ordeal. Medieval people generally accepted the results of the ordeal, whatever their individual opinions about it in a given instance might have been (36–37). See also Hyams and Morris 103.

[11] See Davies and Fouracre 221–23; Yvonne Bongert, *Récherches sur les cours laïques du Xè au XIIIe siècle* (Paris: Picard, 1949), 219.

[12] Bartlett 26. See also Köbler, "Welches Urteil" 104–5, where he cites 600 Franconian verdicts between 500 and 1000 that show ordeals in 10 cases with the trial by battle in the forefront. Stephen D. White discusses the ways in which litigants in the earlier Middle Ages in France frequently decided to avoid the ordeal even after it had been proposed in court: "Proposing the Ordeal and Avoiding It: Strategy and Power in Western French Litigation, 1050–1110," *Cultures of Power: Lordship, Status and Process in Twelfth-Century Europe,* ed. Thomas N. Bisson (Philadelphia: U of Pennsylvania P, 1995), 89–123. See esp. 90–101, where White discusses the use of the ordeal in conflict resolution.

[13] Hans Hattenhauer notes that in the oral legal culture that prevailed in Germanic Europe until the High Middle Ages the oath was the most important legal procedure: "Der gefälschte Eid," *Fälschungen im Mittelalter, Teil II: Gefälschte Rechtstexte. Der bestrafte Fälscher* (Hannover: Hahn, 1988), 661–89 (661). Heinz Holzhauer details the fluctuation in use of the oath with and without the judicial battle through the Middle Ages, with the oath alone gaining in popularity by the High Middle Ages; he cites Rudolf von Habsburg's pronouncement of 1290, in which the accused could refuse trial by battle through a *Reinigungseid.* The oath, which is also found in Roman law, probably owed some of the great prestige it enjoyed in the Middle Ages to both Roman and ecclesiastical influences: "Der gerichtliche Zweikampf," *Sprache und Recht: Beiträge zur Kulturgeschichte des Mittelalters: Festschrift für Ruth Schmidt-Wiegand zum 60. Geburtstag* (Berlin: De Gruyter, 1986), 263–83 (275–76). See Ian Wood, "Disputes in Late Fifth- and Sixth-Century Gaul," *The Settlement of Disputes in Early Medieval Europe,* ed. Davies and Fouracre (Cambridge & New York: Cambridge UP, 1986), 7–22 (16–18). Wood notes that barbarian law codes show early evidence of ecclesiastical influence (19). See Julius Wilhelm Planck, *Das deutsche Gerichtsverfahren im Mittelalter,* vol. 2 (Hildesheim & New York: Olms, 1973), II, 102–29 for a discussion of the different categories of judicial oaths: he distinguishes between the *Sicherungseid* and the *Entscheidungseid,* which includes the oaths of

innocence. See also Kornblum, "Eid," *HWBDR*, vol. 1, cols. 863–66 (cols. 863–64); van Caenegem, "La Preuve" 701–2; Bartlett 121.

[14] Bartlett 30. For a discussion of oath-taking in early Germanic law see Wood; see also Davies and Fouracre 14–18.

[15] In "La croyance en la justice immanente à l'époque féodale," *Le Moyen Age* 54 (1948): 225–48 Paul Rousset deals primarily with the eleventh and twelfth centuries but extends many of his comments to cover the later Middle Ages, as well. He comments on ordeals as a manifestation of the concept of immanent justice (234–41). See also Baldwin, "Crisis" 327.

[16] Karl Kroeschell, *Deutsche Rechtsgeschichte 2 (1250–1650)*. 8th ed. (Opladen: Westdeutscher Verlag, 1992), 45.

[17] Edward Peters, introduction to Charles Henry Lea, *The Duel and the Oath*, ed. Peters (Philadelphia: U of Pennsylvania P, 1974), 7. See also Bartlett, who says that the oath was more dependent on future judgment by God than on an immediate reaction (30). Oath helpers were people close to the accused, most often relatives, who would swear the oath, as well. Dobozy notes that "an oathhelper was a compurgator, one who strengthened a person's oath by swearing to his upright standing but not to the content of his oath" (193).

[18] See Lea 15–18, 65; Holzhauer, "Zweikampf" 275.

[19] Kroeschell, *Deutsche Rechtsgeschichte* 44–45.

[20] Wilhelm Ebel, "Recht und Form: Vom Stilwandel im deutschen Recht," *Probleme der deutschen Rechtsgeschichte* (Göttingen: Schwartz, 1978), 257–79 (268–69).

[21] See Hattenhauer, "Der gefälschte Eid" 666, 672–73.

[22] Hans Hattenhauer, *Das Recht der Heiligen* (Berlin: Duncker & Humblot, 1976), 73–75. Hattenhauer notes that legends contain frequent mention of punishment after perjury (75). See also Hattenhauer, "Der gefälschte Eid" 662. See also Ruth Schmidt-Wiegand, "Eid und Gelöbnis, Formel und Formular im mittelalterlichen Recht," *Recht und Schrift im Mittelalter,* ed. Peter Classen, *VuF,* vol. 8 (Sigmaringen: Thorbecke, 1977), 55–90 (55, 76); "Gebärdensprache im mittelalterlichen Recht," *Frühmittelalterliche Studien* 16 (1981): 363–79 (377); and "Prozeßform und Prozeßverlauf im 'Rolandslied' des Pfaffen Konrad," *Recht, Gericht, Genossenschaft und Policey: Studien zu Grundbegriffen der germanistischen Rechtshistorie. Symposion für Adalbert Erler,* ed. Gerhard Dilcher and Bernhard Diestelkamp (Berlin: E. Schmidt, 1986), 1–12, where she notes (11) that in addition to this gesture's role in an oath, it could also be a sign of anger.

Jutta Schmidt-Lornsen, "Der Griff an den Bart-wikingerzeitliche Bildzeugnisse zu einer bekräftigenden Gebärde," *Sprache und Recht: Beiträge zur Kulturgeschichte des Mittelalters. Festschrift für Ruth Schmidt-Wiegand zum 60. Geburtstag* (Berlin & New York: De Gruyter, 1986), 780–95 cites (791–92) an *RL* manuscript from the end of the twelfth century that depicts a scene from Genelun's trial. In this illustration Karl sits on the throne with crown and scepter in one hand and his beard in the other.

[23] See Holzhauer, "Zweikampf" 275–76.

[24] See Lea 25–29; Köbler, "Welches Urteil" 92, 105; Hattenhauer, *Recht der Heiligen* 67–69.

[25] For the role of compurgators, see Peters, introduction to Lea 7; see also Lea 64, 71–72.

[26] See Lea 64–65. While its value in the early twelfth century for difficult cases among ecclesiastics was generally accepted, the absolute nature of the oath opened the door wide to perjury. Around 1130, in a simony case involving a bishop, Pope Innocent II stated that conjurators need only swear as to their belief in the defendant's oath. Innocent III codified this order and thereby cut the ground out from under the compurgatorial oath. Where the compurgator was previously held to be as guilty or as innocent as the accused, now he had only to state publicly his conviction that an individual's oath was true; Lea 71–72.

[27] A literary example of such an oath occurs in Isolde's ordeal by fire in *Tristan*, in which she swears that she had lain in no man's arms except those of her husband and, of course, those of the poor beggar who rescued her when she fell into the river. Since the poor beggar was Tristan in disguise, her oath was literally true but false at the core.

[28] Hattenhauer, *Recht der Heiligen* 76–78.

[29] See Hattenhauer, "Der gefälschte Eid" 662; Erler, "Eid," *HWBDR*, vol. 1, cols. 861–63 (862); Kornblum, "Gerichtlicher Eid" col. 863.

[30] Hattenhauer, *Recht der Heiligen* 78–79.

[31] Ebel, "Recht und Form" 264–65.

[32] Hattenhauer lists two ways to falsify an oath: an ambiguous formulation and a stealthy change in the oath rituals ("Der gefälschte Eid" 662); see also R. J. Hexter, *Equivocal Oaths and Ordeals in Medieval Literature* (Cambridge, MA: Harvard UP, 1975), 1–2.

[33] Hattenhauer notes that the medieval meaning of *fälschen* differs from the modern German one, since the ethical content that dominates now was only present in a small way during the thirteenth century ("Der gefälschte Eid" 663–64). Basing his conclusions on usages in legal contexts, Hattenhauer suggests that *falsch*, which appeared as a loan word only in the twelfth century, had the meaning "unbeständig, unwirksam," while *fälschen* meant "kraftlos machen."

[34] Hattenhauer, *Recht der Heiligen* 76–82.

[35] "und nim des vil wol war, / daz dich niht triegen di heiden / mit listen noch mit eiden.": *Karl der Grosse von dem Stricker*, ed. Karl Bartsch (Berlin: De Gruyter, 1965), ll. 2124–26.

[36] Bartlett 30–32. For comments on determining who was eligible for taking an oath, see also Lea 38, 57–58, 63, 66; Kornblum, "Gerichtlicher Eid" cols. 864–65; Alexander Gal, "Der Zweikampf im fränkischen Prozeß," *ZSSRGGA* 28 (1907): 236–89 (249).

[37] Bartlett 24–27, 29–33, 106–9.

[38] Bartlett 21–22.

[39] Daniel 3:27, *The Revised English Bible with the Apocrypha* (Oxford: Oxford UP/ Cambridge: Cambridge UP, 1989), 768.

[40] Bartlett 19; Baldwin, "Crisis" 329. Richard D. Forsyth, Margaret H. Kerr, and Michael J. Plyley offer the anachronistic thesis that the ordeals were designed to spare the lives of the guilty. They suggest that women were sent to the ordeal of the hot iron because observation had confirmed that women were likely to sink in the cold-water ordeal: "Cold Water and Hot Iron: Trial by Ordeal in England," *Journal of Interdisciplinary History* 22 (1992): 573–95 (587). This thesis overlooks the fact that the ordeal of choice for settling questions involving sexual offenses was the hot iron. It also overlooks the symbolic value of fire in purification.

[41] Holzhauer, "Zweikampf" 278, n.66.

[42] James Brundage, *Law, Sex and Christian Society in Medieval Europe* (Chicago: U of Chicago P, 1987), 223–24. By the late twelfth century Church courts had taken charge of cases involving marriage and their verdict was considered final, although civil adultery trials were permitted by some decretists (319).

[43] Bartlett notes that the ordeal was frequently used when there were neither accusers nor other evidence but simply a suspicion (29; see also 26, 33).

[44] A. Erler, "Gottesurteile," *HWBDR* 1, cols. 1769–73 (col. 1770).

[45] Bongert 225; see Wolfgang Schild, "Das Gottesurteil der Isolde: Zugleich eine Uberlegung zum Verhältnis von Rechtsdenken und Dichtung," *Alles was Recht war: Rechtsliteratur und literarisches Recht. Festschrift für Ruth Schmidt-Wiegand zum 70. Geburtstag*, ed. Hans Höfinghoff (Essen: Item, 1996), 55–75 (60–61). Forsyth et al. discuss from a physiological standpoint burns and infections arising from contact with an iron object heated to the degree it could have been (589–94). Many instances have been documented of people who walked on hot coals, etc., who were not burned. While burn infections before the antibiotic era were frequent, the most common types, septicemia and pseudomonas aeruginosa, either seldom occur in individuals with burns small in area or generally do not appear before the fifth day after the burn (593).

[46] Robin Chapman Stacey, "Law and Order in the *Very* Old West: England and Ireland in the Early Middle Ages," *Crossed Paths: Methodological Approaches to the Celtic Aspect of the European Middle Ages*, ed. Benjamin Hudson and Vickie Ziegler, Penn State Proceedings in Medieval Studies, no. 1 (Lanham, MD: UP of America, 1991), 39–60. White suggests that the ordeal process could be influenced by the social standing of the person who proposed it (105). White also notes that ordeal results could be interpreted in different ways, giving rise to conflict, and that some litigants were unwilling to accept the results of an ordeal (99, 106).

[47] Discussion of the question of the relation of the ordeal by battle to the other ordeals appears in Bartlett 115–18; Holzhauer, "Zweikampf" 270–71; see also the entry for "Kampf," *DRW*, vol. 6 (Weimar: H. Böhlaus Nachfolger, 1967), cols. 1013–32, esp. cols. 1013–26.

[48] Bartlett 103–4. Ute Schwab discusses the use of the ordeal by battle among the Germanic peoples in "Die Zweikämpfer von Monkwearmouth," *Iconologia Sacra: Mythos, Bildkunst, und Dichtung in der Religions-und Sozialgeschichte Alteuropas [Festschrift für Karl Hauck]*, ed. Hagen Keller and Nikolaus Staubach (Berlin & New York: De Gruyter, 1994), 496–518 (514).

⁴⁹ See Lea 112–32; Kurt Georg Cram, *Iudicium Belli: Zum Rechtscharakter des Krieges im deutschen Mittelalter* (Münster & Cologne: Böhlau, 1955), 8–9. Holzhauer discusses the origins of the judicial duel, which seems to have been found in other cultures, as well: "Zweikampf" 265–74. See also G. Baist, "Der gerichtliche Zweikampf, nach seinem Ursprung und im Rolandslied," *RF* 5 [Festschrift Konrad Hoffmann zum 70. Geburtstag] (1980): 436–48 (437–38). Since the present analysis concerns itself primarily with the legal function of the trial by battle in its Western European context, particularly in the German lands, questions of origins and parallels in other societies lie outside its scope. The issue has been hotly debated; for a useful summary of nineteenth-century legal scholars' opinions on the original nature of the duel see Alexander Gal, "Der Zweikampf im fränkischen Prozeß," *ZSSRGGA* 28 (1907): 236–89 (238–41).

⁵⁰ Cram 11. Cram distinguishes, as does Nottarp (269–70), between a duel as *Entscheidungsmittel* and as *Beweismittel* and says that it was already a means of proof in the Burgundian law. For discussion of this distinction among German legal scholars, see Bartlett 114. See also Lea 103; Gal, who discusses the connection between a false oath and the judicial duel (238); Rousset, who notes that the combatants in a judicial duel are only the instruments of divine justice (239); Planck, *Gerichtsverfahren* II, 145–46; Erler says that it evolved from a means to a decision to a proof ("Gottesurteil" col. 1771); Heinz Holzhauer, "Zum Strafgedanken im frühen Mittelalter," *Überlieferung, Bewahrung und Gestaltung in der rechtsgeschichtlichen Forschung*, ed. Stephan Buchholz, Paul Mikat, and Dieter Werkmüller (Paderborn: Schöningh, 1993), 179–92 notes (192) that the earlier Germanic belief that fate would punish the person who was not in the right prepared the way for the Christian interpretation and survived as an undercurrent long into the Christian Middle Ages.

⁵¹ Bartlett 121–22: "the judicial combat did not claim or require a miraculous intervention in the physical elements. It claimed, in theory, that a weak, just man would defeat a strong, unjust man, but it did not anticipate a ritually-effected change in iron or water, the material of the world. It was the most natural as well as the least liturgical of the ordeals."

⁵² Bartlett 121–22. See Peters, introduction to Lea 7; see also Bongert 239.

⁵³ Lea 117, 166–67; Bartlett 105–6; Rousset 237; Hattenhauer, *Recht der Heiligen* 68–71.

⁵⁴ Bartlett 111; Lea 166–71.

⁵⁵ Lea 153–54; Bongert 241. Nottarp notes (294) that while fighting was generally considered a man's work, the redoubtable women of Bavaria were allowed to do battle.

⁵⁶ Jean-Marie Carbasse, "Le duel judicaire dans les coutumes méridionales," *Annales du Midi* 87 (1975): 385–403 (388).

⁵⁷ Lea 173, 178; see Bongert 243, 246 for comments on the French situation.

⁵⁸ Bartlett 106; *DRW*, vol. 6, col. 1014.

⁵⁹ Bartlett 107. See also Hermann Conrad, "Das Gottesurteil in den Konstitutionen von Melfi Friedrichs II von Hohenstaufen (1232)," *Festschrift zum 70. Geburtstag von Walter Schmidt-Rimpler,* ed. Rechts- und Staatswissenschaftliche Fakultät der Rheinischen Friedrich Wilhelms-Institut (Karlsruhe: Müller, 1957), 9–21 (11–12).

⁶⁰ Bartlett 106. The sensational nature of many of the crimes involving the ordeal by battle should not obscure the fact that it was used in a wide variety of cases, including property disputes and arson. See also Lea 128.

⁶¹ Marguerite Boulet-Sautel, "Aperçus sur le système des preuves dans la France coutumière du Moyen Age," *La Preuve, RSJB,* no. 17 (Brussels: Editions de la Librairie Encyclopedique, 1965), 275–325 (286); Peters, introduction to Lea 9.

⁶² See Henri Pirenne, *Historie du Meurtre de Charles le Bon, Comte de Flandre par Galbert de Bruges* (Paris: Picard, 1891), 93–95.

⁶³ The trials by battle in the *Karlsepik,* as well as in *Tristan,* bear out this belief. See ensuing discussion.

⁶⁴ See Nottarp 350–51; Dagmar Hüpper-Dröge, "Der gerichtliche Zweikampf im Spiegel der Bezeichnungen für 'Kampf,' 'Kämpfer,' 'Waffen,'" *FMS* 18 (1984): 607–61 discusses (648–49) clerical criticism of the judicial ordeal in the Burgundian law codes; Bernhard Schwentner, "Die Stellung der Kirche zum Zweikampfe bis zu den Dekretalen Gregors IX," *Theologische Quartalschrift* 3 (1930): 190–234; Kolb, "Himmlisches und irdisches Gericht" also mentions (290–91) the criticism of the ordeal by battle from the early Middle Ages onward. Such criticism centered on its judicial validity and its relation to Christian ethics. Theologians were against it, and the secular courts were in favor of it. Constance Brittain Bouchard, *Strong of Body, Brave and Noble: Chivalry and Society in Medieval France* (Ithaca, NY: Cornell UP, 1998) notes (129) that there were constant fears that the wrong person might win; she cites the example of Ganelon, who almost walked out of court a free man because everyone was afraid of his champion.

⁶⁵ See Hyams and Morris, who cite manuscripts from the mid-twelfth century or later that contain both the benedictions for the Church of York that were designed to support its champions fighting judicial duels and other examples indicating clerical support (114–15). See also Bartlett 94, 95, 121, 125. Bartlett notes that the weight of local custom forced ecclesiastical establishments either to defend themselves with the duel or to be present during a trial by battle (117); the dean of the cathedral in Hamburg was still prescribing ordeals in 1257 (130). See also van Caenegem, "Law" 14; Nottarp 271, 350. Baldwin cites an example of trial by battle from Gerbert's *Violette,* written c. 1227–29, in which clergy participate, indicating that the Fourth Lateran Council was unsuccessful in its attempts to prohibit clerical assistance (*Aristocratic Life* 211–12). See also Nottarp 351–52 on this point.

⁶⁶ Bartlett 116–22. See also Buchda, "Beweis" 531–32. Nottarp notes that in the case of a duel the secular judge, not a priest, decides on guilt or innocence (265). Misgivings about the trial by battle were of long standing: for example, an eighth-century Langobard king, Liutprand, had already expressed doubts about its validity, as did the Salian Franks (Nottarp 270). See also Bongert 229–30; Carbasse 385, 386–88, 393, 394, 396; and Hüpper-Dröge, who describes the objections of Carolingian theologians to the legal duel, as well as the objections against it in the Lombard laws (624, 627). Baldwin notes that since the council of Clermont (1130), trial by battle had been linked with tournaments and was condemned by important Roman and French councils of the Church. The Fourth Lateran Council of 1215

also reiterated the prohibition against the judicial ordeal in Canon 18, to little avail (*Aristocratic Life* 209).

[67] Bartlett 120, 124–26; Baldwin, *Aristocratic Life* 209.

[68] Bartlett 70–102; Nottarp 354–63; Gaudemet 123; van Caenegem, "La Preuve" 713–14; Baldwin, *Masters, Princes and Merchants* 323–32; Adolph Franz, *Die kirchlichen Benediktionen im Mittelalter*, vol. 2 (Graz: Akademische Druck- u. Verlagsanstalt, 1960), 313–26; Boulet-Sautel 292–94; Lévy 7–9, 26; Jean-Philippe Levy, "Le Problème de la preuve dan les droits savants du moyen âge," *La Preuve, RSJB*, no. 17 (Brussels: Editions de la Librarie Encyclopedique, 1965), 137–68, here, 141–43; Baldwin, "Intellectual Preparation"; Brown 308.

[69] Brown 317. Winfried Trusen, "Das Verbot der Gottesurteile und der Inquisitionsprozeß," *Sozialer Wandel im Mittelalter: Wahrnehmungsformen, Erklärungsmuster, Regelungsmechanismen*, ed. Jürgen Miethke and Klaus Schreiner (Sigmaringen: Thorbecke, 1994), 235–47 notes that secular courts were understandably reluctant to let go of ordeals in the courtroom without alternative procedures in place (238).

[70] See Edward Peters, *Torture* (Philadelphia: Blackwell, 1996), 40–54; Rebecca V. Colman, "Reason and Unreason in Early Medieval Law" *Journal of Interdisciplinary History* 4 (1974): 571–91, here, 578; John H. Langbein, *Torture and the Law of Proof: Europe and England in the Ancien Régime* (Chicago: U of Chicago P, 1977), 6–7, 76–77; Bartlett 135.

[71] Baldwin has found similar patterns: in "Crisis" he says: "the ordeal functioned in the literary texts in ways congruent to those found in other historical documents" (329); see also 350–51. See also *Aristocratic Life* 211, where he notes the effect of Fourth Lateran on ordeals in the genre of romance: ordeal by battle replaces ordeal by fire in a "wager" tale, Gerbert's *Violette*, written slightly more than a decade after 1215 (in 1227–29). Gerd Althoff, "Spielen die Dichter mit den Spielregeln der Gesellschaft," *Mittelalterliche Literatur und Kunst im Spannungsfeld von Hof und Kloster*, ed. Nigel F. Palmer and Hans-Jochen Schiewer (Tübingen: Niemeyer, 1999), 51–71 notes that even in literary sources, where one would expect that the temptation to depart from accepted rules of social interaction would be the greatest, the instances in which the characters play by the rules far outnumber the times they do not (56).

[72] Elizabeth Roth, "Sankt Kunigunde-Legende und Bildaussage," *Historischer Verein für die Pflege der Geschichte des Ehemaligen Fürstbistums zu Bamberg* 123 (1987): 5–68 gives a detailed discussion of the legend and accretions to it. The walk over burning plowshares in the presence of bishops was still appearing in twentieth-century religious sculpture in Bamberg (31).

[73] Der Stricker, *Verserzählungen I*, ed. Johannes Janota (Tübingen: Niemeyer, 1979), 37–50; Hans Sachs, *Werke*, vol. 9 (Stuttgart: Spemann, 1875), 85–95.

1: Decoding the Codes: Treason in the Late Medieval *Karlsepik* — Der Stricker's *Karl der Grosse* and the *Karlmeinet*

TREASON, IN WHATEVER AGE and under whatever conditions, cuts to the heart of the human condition, since it ruptures those bonds of trust on which we base our lives. The gravity of the deed explains its perennial appeal, particularly when it destroys not only trust but also lives, as is the case with those epics dealing with the betrayal of Roland, the nephew of the great Frankish emperor, Charlemagne. Turoldus's Old French *Chanson de Roland*, written around 1100, describes the ambush of Charlemagne's rear guard by Muslims in Spain — an ambush arranged in this work by none other than Roland's stepfather Ganelon, in collusion with Islamic rulers supposedly under Charlemagne's control. Forbidden by Charlemagne to head the delegation to the Muslims, Roland nominates Ganelon, known for his wisdom and valor. Ganelon, using the prerogative of the feud, determines to seek revenge and betrays Roland and the Frankish rear guard to the Muslims for a considerable sum of money. After Roland's death, he is brought to trial, complete with a judicial duel to decide his fate, and is executed.

The power struggles in this work — between Charlemagne and Ganelon, Charlemagne and his peers, the Carolingians and the Muslims, and Roland and Ganelon — plus the high drama of a trial for treason ensured its popularity as a narrative, as the late medieval German versions of this story attest. The *Chanson de Roland* is the most famous of the chansons de geste,[1] which have as their subject matter the legendary history of the Carolingian world. They were popular in the French territories from the eleventh to the fourteenth centuries. Charlemagne, of course, is the dominant figure, but the exploits of other knights, such as William of Orange, also figure prominently. Many of these works are cyclical narratives; two major themes predominate: quarrels between powerful lords and the massive battles of the Christian French against the heathen in Spain, the northern coast of Africa, and the Islamic East. Though they originated in French territory, they were immensely popular in the rest of Western Europe — including the German lands, as this study will show in the case of Charlemagne. Many of the major critical questions, such as the mode of transmission and the degree of dependence on oral tradition, will probably never be resolved, since the lack of concrete evidence precludes certainty.

The narrators of these stories generally call them histories, and some do present details that correspond in varying degrees to actual historical events, such as the ambush of Charlemagne's rear guard in the Pyrenees in 778. In the spring of that year Charlemagne had gone to Spain with two armies to assist the Muslim governor of Barcelona, Yaqzan Ibn Al Arabi [Suleiman], in a revolt he had begun against the emir of Cordoba, Abderrahman. This expedition offered the Carolingians a chance to gain additional territory to protect them from Saracen incursions from the south, and the opportunity to convert Muslims to Christianity.[2] The Saxons, however, started a revolt, and Charlemagne had to abandon his siege of Saragossa; by this time he had begun to believe that Al-Arabi was treacherous, so he took the latter hostage and went back to Pamplona, which he destroyed. Disregarding the oath by Duke Lupus of Gascony submitting to Charlemagne's authority, Gascons ambushed the Franks' rear guard, who on their way back home, in the Pyrenees had killed and robbed them. No contemporary account of this disaster mentions Roland; he had, however, been cited among the faithful paladins of Charles's court in a document dating from 772 to 774. Einhard's biography of Charlemagne mentions him as one of the retainers who was killed in this ambush, but Einhard may have included the name because a legend had already sprung up around Roland. Einhard's comparatively extensive account reflects the importance attached by the Carolingian world to this stunning attack, while his reference to treachery on the part of the Gascons provides great narrative opportunities that were to form the basis of the *Chanson de Roland* and the subsequent reworkings of the legend.[3]

A major characteristic of this genre encountered repeatedly in the medieval German versions of the Roland material is the tendency to depart from a source whose outlines were generally well known.[4] Our consideration of the trial of Genelun in the various German versions shows that the picture of Karl varies according to the concerns of the individual work in question, whether or not the new picture corresponded to the historical reality. For the medieval writer past and present were intimately connected; since the present was legitimized through its connection to the past, the past was changed to reflect the desired picture, dependent on the time, the place, and the predilections of the writer/compiler. Underlying all of these processes was the tendency to look at both past and present in terms of their connection with *Heilsgeschichte*, a tendency certainly apparent in our study with regard to the figures of Karl and Genelun.[5] The modifications in the trial of Genelun, as we shall see, provide vivid contrasts in attitudes toward the feud, the empire, crime, and appropriate punishment in works previously neglected.

This material first found its way into the German lands through the efforts of Konrad, a twelfth-century cleric whose *Rolandslied* became an essential part of the Charlemagne epics in high and late medieval German territories. To understand the German context in which the Charlemagne epics flourished it will be necessary to examine briefly the great emperor's reputation in this region. Karl der Grosse and his astounding achievements provided a linchpin for German historical and political references throughout the Middle Ages. In addition, that the emperor's reputation as the representative of the law was widely known in the German lands in the High Middle Ages is reflected in the phrase *karles reht*.[6] The myth-making was already well underway during and shortly after Karl's lifetime through the work of Alcuin, Theodulf, and Einhard, while, later in the ninth century, Notker der Stammler wrote his *Gesta Karoli*, which, even at this early date, presented a figure wreathed in legend.[7] Three emperors, Otto III (983–1002), Frederick I (1152–90), and Frederick II (1215–50), made extensive efforts to revere Karl as a model who set standards for their eras. Otto III made a pilgrimage to Karl's crypt and opened it in 1000; Frederick I canonized Karl in 1165, celebrating him as his own great predecessor; while Frederick II, along with a goldsmith, nailed the splendid sarcophagus for Karl shut in Aachen on July 27, 1215.[8] The Staufer emperors were, of course, happy to use Karl's position and reputation to justify their own imperial politics.[9] In the course of the first half of the fourteenth century, as the Bohemian King Wenzel took the name Karl IV, there was a great surge of increased emphasis on Karl's veneration, particularly in Aachen and Prague.[10]

There were two active historical traditions, the ecclesiastical and the imperial, both of which seemed to figure in the literary representations of his reign in the German Middle Ages.[11] These traditions fused in the image of Karl maintaining order in the secular world as the great guardian of the law, which was instituted by God.[12] For medieval emperor and subject, law and justice were indivisible; laws were valid because of their innate justice. Therefore, any initiative to enforce a just cause was directly linked with God and, consequently, had added power and authority.[13] This state of affairs was particularly compelling when God's anointed representative on earth and the highest earthly judge, the emperor, played a role. When the case in question involved treason against not only the empire but also against the Church, the stakes could not be higher, which helps to account for the popularity of the Genelun episode in the *Karlsepik*.

Both of these traditions, the ecclesiastical and the imperial, inevitably intertwined, appear in a series of three medieval German literary works about Karl: Priest Konrad's *Rolandslied* (probably written in Braunschweig around 1172), Der Stricker's *Karl der Grosse* (1215–30), and the Roland section of the *Karlmeinet* (probably Aachen, first half of the fourteenth century).[14]

Konrad's work, in contrast with the *Chanson de Roland*, takes on the qualities of a hagiographic legend.[15] Consistent with the ecclesiastical tradition, Karl appears as God's chosen ruler, the defender of the faith, and the patron of many religious orders. These tendencies continue in the two later works; Stricker's *Karl der Grosse* and the *Karlmeinet* build on the crusading zeal and some of the hagiographic aspects of Konrad's work, while Stricker's epic gives particular emphasis to Karl's imperial role, as well. Both of the later epics, as the analysis here will show, reflect either differently nuanced or changed attitudes toward major thematic elements such as Genelun's declaration of a feud against Roland.

Konrad made available for the first time to a German audience the connection between the Karl material and treason: the defeat at Roncevalles is linked with betrayal and discord in the Christian camp.[16] Legal procedures dominate in the latter part of the work, revealing in a series of scenes contemporary issues of conflicting loyalties and power struggles.[17] The trial scene proved to be a flexible framework for the two later writers, because the historical account of the events surrounding Hruodland's death left many spaces blank.[18] This state of affairs, combined with the plethora of material about Karl, gave writers in each era a chance to reinterpret the material to suit their respective cultures. Such a new formation necessarily resulted when narrative was taken from one cultural context, with its characteristic legal, political, and religious aspects, and put into another one with other attitudes.[19]

The major differences among these works and the insights that they offer into the milieu in which they appeared have been largely obscured because of an earlier erroneous critical opinion that the two later works were simply copied with minimal revision.[20] This attitude has caused them to be neglected as important sources of information about the ongoing influence of the great emperor in the German lands, as well as of changing cultural attitudes.[21] Stricker's work has begun to be recognized as an independent epic, which has its own political and cultural agenda with particular emphasis on the empire and on the veneration of Karl,[22] but the *Karlmeinet* has been largely ignored. This analysis will show, in the case of the treason trial of Roland's betrayer, Genelun/Wellis, how the two later writers transformed this scene to reflect their own concerns about the maintenance of imperial authority, the rule of law, and the cultural implications of treason and its punishment.[23] In their works the writers connect these concerns with the Karl material, giving them added weight and importance. Frequently, as is the case with Genelun, the betrayer of Roland,[24] the ordeal does not reveal the identity of an unknown perpetrator; rather, it confirms the moral and legal order of society against those who would destroy it for their own ends.[25] In Stricker's *Karl der Grosse* the Genelun section serves to deepen and expand the characterization of Karl not only as the defender of the faith and as a powerful emperor but also as the guarantor of the rule of law.

Familiar with contemporary legal procedures and issues,[26] Stricker builds on suggestions in earlier Roland material to make significant changes and additions to the events before the trial and to the courtroom scene itself. Set against the *Rolandslied* of Priest Konrad, Stricker's version is more concerned with the extension of imperial authority and the rule of law. The legendary Karl, renowned as the great lawgiver, is in this work repeatedly portrayed as rejecting the feud and the compensatory system of justice in favor of the rule of law and a penal approach. Legal issues also serve to characterize the archtraitor Genelun: he represents the profeud faction, the challenge to peace and justice. His advocacy of self-help judicial remedies reflects his amoral approach, which threatens the foundations of the social, religious, and legal order Karl represents.[27]

The establishment of a rule of law presented a continuing problem for medieval monarchs. This process arose out of the larger context of dispute settlement between the king and powerful vassals, a situation that was met with various approaches during the time between the Carolingians and the High Middle Ages.[28] Armed conflict between the king and his retainers was a constant of life in all of the medieval centuries; what seems to vary is the way in which these disputes were settled. During the Carolingian period conspirators were dealt with summarily: if they were not executed quickly, they could expect detention in a monastery or, as a special mark of imperial favor, blinding.[29]

With the collapse of the Carolingian dynasty, the special and uniquely powerful position of the emperor seemed to decline, probably because of the lack of prestige accruing to the early Ottonians.[30] Consequently, in the tenth century, conflicts between the king and the barons were marked by a carefully escalated series of reactions by both parties. Even after blood had been shed, total submission on the part of the rebellious vassal — that is, throwing oneself at the feet of the monarch — usually brought forth clemency on the part of the king, though he may have demanded a period of arrest or banishment. Frequently the offender received his old offices or rank. These vassals were, of course, members of powerful families.[31]

With the rise to power of the Salian Franks, this understanding of how things were done changed. Now, instead of negotiators on both sides working the matter out, the emphasis lay on the power of the monarch to punish.[32] Through the twelfth century the tendency to prefer solutions other than legal verdicts of guilt or innocence predominated. When such verdicts were given, they were frequently ignored. These rebellions were settled through property and financial restitution or armed conflict, which forced one side or the other to make such concessions.[33] This context helps us to understand the cultural background of Genelun's treachery and trial in the medieval German Charlemagne epics. When we see Genelun's family trying to make restitution of goods and service, we see a long-established practice in force. When we see Genelun's family ready to resort to force when Karl spurns the offer and prepares to condemn their relative, we see a centuries-old baronial behavior pattern.

Genelun's approach to dispute settlement is to declare openly that he is in a state of feud with Roland. Because Stricker pays much more attention to legal issues surrounding the feud, a brief background discussion seems useful. Central to the maintenance of imperial order was the regulation of the rights of feud, a practice rooted in the earliest traditions of the Germanic peoples.[34] Dating from a time when the family structure was responsible for many of the functions of a modern state, such as security, the feud could enforce order through its threat to the entire family. Frequently, however, the efforts to secure resolution of a grievance left few in the affected families alive to enjoy the peace. Efforts to restrict the feud were already afoot in Burgundian and Visigothic law codes and continued through the Carolingian era, again in Barbarossa's time, and in the repeated efforts in the *Gottesfrieden* and *Landfrieden* laws of the eleventh through the fourteenth centuries.[35] During the Salian period rulers frequently tried to end a feud or punish those who took part in one, sometimes by exile. Whether or not the monarch intervened was a matter of the exercise of political power left to his discretion and political instincts.[36] The continuing vitality of the feud in the German lands throughout the Middle Ages, as well as the use of force in other legal situations, compels us to realize that a violent deed only becomes a crime when the social milieu in which it occurs condemns it as such.[37]

Although feuds were fiercely waged, they seem to have operated under certain rules with official or familial intermediaries, who were almost always present. The conduct of the highly ritualized feuds of the fourteenth and fifteenth centuries, however, differed from what is known about the conduct of the feud in the eleventh.[38] Medieval rulers generally used two approaches in the regulation of the feud. The first dealt with the rules about feuding: who could do it and how it was to be done. The second was to advocate the use of the courts and criminal law in cases where recourse to feud was common.[39] In the Mainz *Landfrieden* of 1235 there is a passage urging the plaintiff to go to court before avenging the deed himself.[40] This law, written close in time to the composition of *Karl der Grosse*, parallels the content of those additions in Stricker's work that restrain the use of the feud — for example, in Genelun's escape and capture by Otto. Under attack by Karl, Otto does not allow his relatives to start a feud against Karl; and Karl refuses to accept Genelun's argument that he had a legitimate right of feud against Roland. Certainly the matter was a current one at the time in which Stricker was writing; what better way to counter the aristocratic tendencies toward self-justice than to show in an expanded text the fateful consequences of a feud and the avoidance of due process for Christianity and the empire?[41]

Written some fifty years after the canonization of Karl, Stricker's work begins with a discussion of good and evil in which he presents Karl as the ruler who has most advanced God's honor, sometimes through force, and as a saintly man whose intercessory help is readily available (*Karl der Grosse* 63–114).[42] This introduction casts a long shadow over the fate of Genelun, especially since Karl as a representative of good is contrasted implicitly with treacherous men (17–20). Such a judge can scarcely err.[43]

The beginnings of legal proceedings against Genelun occur shortly after the sound of Roland's Oliphant reaches the encampment of the emperor. Stricker follows both the broad outlines and in some cases the exact wording of Konrad; yet, even in this brief passage he sounds themes that resonate throughout for his treatment of the traitor Genelun — themes that are frequently implied in the *Rolandslied* but receive fuller treatment in Stricker's work. Unlike the figure of Karl in the *Rolandslied*, Stricker's Karl, while full of anguish, is not portrayed as temporarily bereft of his senses.[44] This difference in accent strengthens the portrayal in this scene of Karl as decision-maker, ready to move against Genelun.

Stricker's first characterization of Genelun as faithless sounds a theme that he develops strongly in the subsequent Genelun sections.[45] Stricker's Karl immediately connects Roland's death with a loss of reputation and distinction for him and the empire.[46] With this charge, Karl repeats a statement the angel made to him about Roland at the beginning of the work.[47] The context in which the angel makes this statement is a political one: the angel has just described for Karl the extensive territorial conquest that his nephew Roland will bring about (364–427).[48] Since God legitimized this conquest through his instructions and his gift of Durndart to Roland via Charlemagne, Dietrich's subsequent use of Durndart in the judicial duel is yet another clear sign that Genelun's side must lose. The presentation of Durndart from an angel is not in the *Rolandslied;* yet, it is but one of dozens of examples one could cite to show how well Stricker understood the earlier text's main thrusts. The divine imprimatur regarding Durndart and the territorial conquests reinforce the authority and importance of the empire, a much more significant motif for Stricker than for Konrad.

In contrast to Konrad, Stricker does not include at this point the charge of greed as motivation for Genelun's crime, as the *Rolandslied* does (6094–98), but instead emphasizes Roland's fidelity to Genelun, a motif absent from this section in the *Rolandslied*. Genelun's honor and reputation grew under Roland's efforts, just as Karl's did (*Karl der Grosse* 7144–50). The literary effect of emphasizing Roland's commitment to Genelun is to heighten the dastardliness of Genelun's betrayal.[49] To underscore Genelun's treacherous behavior, Stricker's Karl refers to David's punishment of evil men.[50] The implicit comparison of Karl with David can only heighten the legitimacy of Karl's firmness toward Genelun.

Karl's accusation of wrongful death begins the legal proceedings as a preliminary to the arrest of Genelun.[51] As affected relative, it is Karl's duty to accuse Genelun; as the judge in the case, he can order the latter's apprehension. The accusatory process is not limited to place; therefore, Karl could proceed with it in the army's encampment and did not have to wait until he returned to his court at Aachen.[52] Karl's statements in regard to Roland's death and Genelun's responsibility contain the necessary legal elements: the naming of the individual believed to be guilty and the circumstances surrounding the crime. His lament over the loss of Roland is followed by the accusation of Genelun, a charge made also by Naymis.[53]

Naymis,[54] just as in the *Rolandslied*, is ready to dispatch Genelun on the spot, but in both works he must wait for justice at court to take its course — reflecting, as Petra Canisius-Loppnow suggests, the widespread attempt at all levels of society to discourage the preference for self-administered justice, the right that everyone had to punish an individual caught in the act.[55] Moreover, insistence on a court proceeding during the eleventh and early twelfth centuries indicated that the monarch hoped for a stern punishment.[56] In Stricker's work, however, the justification for waiting reflects the protection that the judge was supposed to offer to the accused so that the manner of his execution would disgrace his family for generations.[57] The comparable passage in the *Rolandslied* lacks this emphasis on the position of important families, an element that Stricker stresses later in the scene relating to Karl's grief over Roland's death. Could Stricker be emphasizing, as he does during Karl's lament over his weakened position vis-à-vis the nobility because of the loss of Roland, the importance of holding powerful families of the realm in check, not only in battle but also through court proceedings that affected their reputations? Further evidence that Stricker's text presents a real power struggle between the emperor and mighty families comes from Karl's own recognition of his situation during the tense scene in the courtroom as he asks for advice about Genelun's fate.[58]

With Karl's pronouncement that Genelun must be tried and condemned to a dishonorable death, Genelun has lost his reputation.[59] *Êre* [reputation, fame, honor], which does not appear at this point in the *Rolandslied* text, occupies an important place in Stricker's work in this passage. All Karl's *êre* lay on Roland; Roland increased Genelun's stature and reputation; Genelun's crime has robbed him and his relatives of *êre* for generations. *Untriuwe* [infidelity, treachery], which appears at the beginning and end of this passage, results in loss of standing, symbolized by Genelun's ride on a donkey (7180–88).[60]

During Genelun's long and uncomfortable journey to justice, his trial by battle is already prefigured in all three versions by the duel between Baligant and Karl. While this fight is never described explicitly as a *judicium Dei*, there are definite legal references connected with a judicial duel, particularly in Stricker's work.[61] To whatever degree this battle was reminiscent of a judicial duel, it serves as a foreshadowing of the trial, just as the fight between Otto and Genelun does. Since Genelun/Wellis has aligned himself with the heathens, it is also another indication of his eventual fate.

Immediately prior to the trial section Stricker inserts a long passage detailing Karl's reaction to Roland's death that differs from the *Rolandslied* treatment in several significant ways, reflecting Stricker's emphasis on Karl and the empire rather than on Roland.[62] Stricker's version expands the brief account of Roland's value to the empire that appears in Konrad's work. The opening lines of Stricker's account of Karl's grief pick up and expand on references from the capture scene to the legal basis for the actions taken against Genelun: he first mentions the extent of Karl's *triuwe* toward Roland shortly before referring to Roland as Karl's *neve*.[63] Since the bond between a maternal uncle and nephew was considered in some cases to be even stronger than the father-son bond, Karl had familial duties, as well as political reasons, to engage himself in a legal matter on his nephew's behalf.[64]

The repeated emphasis on this close relationship in Stricker's version helps to motivate the attack on Genelun. Karl would have been expected to punish those responsible for a kinsman's death in any case.[65] His position as emperor, however, adds a political dimension to the search for justice. Karl's repeated reference to the relationship between himself and Roland has its parallels in the discussion of the importance of family to the maintenance of imperial power:

> du waere mîner ougen wünne
> unde ein trôst in dînem künne. (10565–66)

[You would be the joy of my eyes and a comfort in your family.]

> [Karl] ich bin nu ellende
> under mînen mâgen allen,
> sît du mir bist enpfallen.
> ich hân deheinen mâc nû,
> der mich gewaldes alse dû
> in mînem lande bewar.
> wir sîn mit dir verderbet gar,
> beide ich und al mîn künne. (10612–19)

[Even among all my relatives, I am now helpless and miserable, since you are lost to me. Now I have no kinsman who protects my power in my land as you would. Both my entire family and I have met disaster along with you.]

These lines make it clear that Karl depends on his family for military support to retain his authority and that the family's fate is determined by its ability to supply such strength. Since only Roland among all of his relatives could have provided the requisite strength,[66] Karl and his family face a considerable loss of power.[67] Military weakness can immediately lead to loss of territory, influence, and respect:

> die bürge die du mir gwünne
> unde mir mit dîner kraft
> die herren mahtest diensthaft,
> in Swâben unde in Franken,
> die beginnent nu harte wanken:

> des si ê niht entâten
> und mich mit vorhten hâten,
> do du in under di ougen saehe:
> den wirde ich nû vil smaehe.
> sine furhtent niht mê dîne hant.
> owe lieber neve Ruolant,
> nu verstu alsô von mir,
> daz du füerest mit dir
> mîn saelde und al mîn êre. (10620–633)[68]

[The castles that you conquered for me and the lords whom you made vassals in Swabia and Franconia, they will now begin to waver greatly. They did not do that before; they were afraid of me when you were looking them in the face. They will scorn me now; they do not any longer fear your hand. Alas, dear nephew Roland, as you leave me, you take with you my well-being and my power.]

This passage contains a detailed description of the political effects of Roland's conquest and his death. The increase in fortresses and vassals in Swabia and Franconia that comes about through Roland's strength begins to melt away. Roland's demise removes their fear of opposing Karl. For this reason, Karl's power and reputation [*êre*] also weaken.[69]

The connection between Roland's strength and Karl's authority appears in another passage where there are no apparent parallels in Konrad's text:

> owe lieber neve Ruolant,
> wie gar mîn dinc an dir stuont!
> swaz mir die vînde nû tuont,
> dazn richet niemen âne bete,
> als dîn vil reinen lîp tete. (10574–78)[70]

[Alas, dear nephew Roland, how completely my affairs depended on you! Whatever my enemies do to me now, no one will avenge it without a command as you, virtuous as you are, would have done.]

The significance of these sections for Genelun's trial might well lie in the fact that they make his crime that much more serious. There is a definite air of realpolitik in the midst of Stricker's Karl's grief.

The increased emphasis that Stricker gives to the political ramifications of Roland's death perhaps arises from the changed attitude toward murder apparent since the early decades of the twelfth century in city legal codes, *Friedensordnungen*, and later *Weistümer*. These codes tended to look at wrongful death more in the light of a crime against society, which society ought to struggle against and punish, than just a crime against a family.[71] While Karl mourns the loss of his relative, the dangers that Roland's death unleashes threaten not only Karl and his relatives but also the well-being of the entire empire. Perceiving weakness, other subjects, such as the Swabians, could become restive, while the silence of the peers during the trial of Genelun indicates the internal weakness caused by Roland's death. Seen in this context, Genelun's crime necessarily has far greater implications for Karl — and, therefore, the state — than the mere interpersonal quarrel that forms the basis of Genelun's defense. The seriousness of Roland's loss receives additional emphasis in Stricker's version through his addition of Genelun's flight and capture by Otto, a section that does not exist in the *Rolandslied* and was added by both Stricker and the *Karlmeinet* author.[72] This narrative adds significant support to several of Stricker's major themes. Otto, a prominent peer of the realm like Genelun, is accused of treason; rather than starting a feud with willing relatives, he clears himself and remains a loyal supporter of the emperor, who condemns Genelun.[73] Genelun's escape reinforces his guilt; the passage, therefore, gives Karl additional leverage in his effort to have Genelun punished for his crime.

During the consternation and confusion occasioned by Alite's death at the news of Roland's slaying, Genelun, with the help of his relatives, escapes (11287–324). Their intervention to help their relative foreshadows the considerable efforts that they make in Aachen to secure Genelun's release. Genelun meets merchants, of whom he asks a favor. Genelun says he has killed a knight who was for no reason his *vient* [enemy], a term that implies the existence of a feud; when individuals come seeking him, the merchants are to tell them that Genelun is too far away for them to catch him (11331–62). Otto, the leader of the imperial search party, decides that it is a waste of time to continue the chase, whereupon all give up. When they come back to court, however, they tell the emperor that they would have hunted Genelun had Otto allowed it (11363–94).

This series of events throws Karl into a rage; in a passage replete with legal terminology he tells Otto that he will deprive him of land, personal property, and knightly status because Otto has behaved as a very unfaithful vassal and must, therefore, be held as a traitor (11402–27). Karl bases this harsh decision on his belief that in the chase after Genelun, Otto has not served him as he ought to have done, resulting in a loss of imperial favor.[74]

The legal implications in this passage raise some of the same issues that appear in Genelun's trial: the loss of property and position. Because of his alleged treason,[75] Otto stands to lose "lehen, eigen unde swert." *Lehen*, of course, is the fief; *eigen* is his own inherited property.[76] *Swert* would refer here to his social position as a knight. Karl's threat to withdraw his *hulde* reflects legal realities within the feudal system. The concept of *Huldeverlust* [loss of favor and protection] as a reaction by the ruler was, of course, modeled on wayward humanity's relationship to God. It carried with it real penalties, such as loss of fiefs, offices, and presents and banishment from the court.[77] If the fiefholder were accused of a crime such as treason in the High

Middle Ages, the matter had to be brought before the *Lehnsgericht*.[78] The common punishment for treason in the Middle Ages was hanging, though drawing and quartering was also used.[79]

Karl's fulfillment of his threat would have left Otto financially impoverished and socially degraded. This context is important for understanding Karl's reason for not avenging himself physically on Otto.[80] Karl has already indicated that he will deprive Otto of property and social position; the only injury left that he could inflict would be corporal, as the text indicates.[81] Because of the range of legal meanings that Middle High German *laster* can have,[82] Karl's remark opens a wide range of possibilities, including an offense against human or divine law or a blameworthy act. There may also be legal reasons why Karl does not attack Otto. Because of what he perceives as Otto's apparent infidelity to him as Karl's vassal, Karl makes a formal declaration of his intent to abrogate his obligations to Otto and to punish him. He will deprive Otto of his feudal and alodial lands and his social status as a punishment for Otto's unfaithful service. Otto will be barred from court and from legal assemblies (11404-25). These actions, not physical punishment, are the appropriate remedy. Once again, Stricker reveals how familiar he was with legal customs of his day. *Huldeverlust* in the secular realm, modeled after the theological concept, presupposed a ruler who saw himself as the representative or the anointed of God, which Karl certainly did. In feudal terms the loss of *hulde,* which Karl declares to Otto, involves the loss of all benefices from the ruler, as well as any kind of legal help from the king or the right to be at court.[83]

Otto's relatives and supporters, interestingly enough, are, like Genelun's family, prepared to support their kinsman against the emperor. They want to start an *urliuge* against the empire (11459-63). The *urliuge,* which could mean all kinds of armed fights, including feud, was a legally recognized means of self-help available only to the aristocracy.[84] Their readiness to use force to settle the issue, as well as the family solidarity of Genelun's relatives, reflects the self-confidence of the great families of the empire at the time, a situation that makes Karl's previous lament about the loss of power and influence at Roland's death more believable. The parallels between Otto's followers and Genelun's are even more striking, since in both cases their lords are accused of treason. Unlike Genelun, however, Otto, who knows that he is innocent, refuses any kind of struggle against the emperor because that would indicate his guilt in the eyes of others.[85] Stricker emphasizes Otto's renunciation of his right to declare a feud, contrasting him with Genelun. As part of his extended polemic against the feud Stricker may have added the motif of the rebellious vassals, since Otto would certainly have had every right to attack Karl.[86] Instead, he urges his followers to serve the emperor in any way they can (11464-82).[87] Otto, like Karl in the trial scene, wants to resolve the conflict within the legal customs of the court. He asks for help in bringing Karl to the point at which he will listen to Otto's justification;[88] he is then quite ready to be judged in this context (11482).

Otto, like Karl, combines adherence to court customs and legal procedures with a strong faith in God. Before he rides out to apprehend Genelun, he asks God for aid in finding the fugitive and in proving his innocence of any sort of collaboration with Genelun in the commission of the latter's crimes (11483–90). His prayer is answered, because he sees Genelun try to escape; this eyewitness account proves the traitor's guilt.

As his horse gallops up to Genelun, Otto makes an accusation that combines both legal and theological considerations:

> weiz got du triwelôsez vaz,
> dune kumest nu niht fürbaz.
> verworhter lîp, vervluohter geist,
> des êwegen tôdes volleist,
> du muost den keiser gesehen,
> dir sol dîn reht von im geschehen. (11531–36)

[God knows, you faithless vessel, you are not going anywhere now. Lost individual, accursed spirit, accomplice of eternal death, you must see the emperor. Your verdict should come from him.]

Otto's attack on Genelun begins with the word *triwelôsez*, which, as we have seen, has legal implications. The centrality of *triwe* has already been apparent in Karl's lamentation over Roland, as well as in his attack on Otto. *Triwe* is necessary to the functioning of any society; in medieval life, however, it had a specific feudal context, as well as a moral one, a context that moved it into the political sphere, as well. A lapse in either public or private life endangered the offender's soul; here the word is associated with Genelun's treason and his flight, both acts of infidelity.[89] Further references to contemporary legal practices occur in the last two lines of the above quotation: here Stricker refers to the emperor's position as the head of the court, responsible for the law. Since Middle High German *reht* has such a wide range of meanings, including courtroom proceedings, verdict, purgatory oath, or the carrying out of a death sentence, absolute certainty is not possible; *urteilsspruch* would seem appropriate, however.[90] The theological aspects of this speech appear in 11531–34, in which Genelun is portrayed not only as a lost soul but also as a representative of eternal death, that is, the devil. Otto's verbal assault provokes a response from Genelun that contains words with legal meanings, reflecting the older law in that law and honor are intertwined.[91]

The fight between Genelun and Otto, like that between Baligan and Karl on another level, prefigures and foreshadows the duel between Pinabel and Dietrich. This doubling, a common device in medieval literature and one that has its roots in biblical exegesis, functions on several levels. The fight draws attention to Genelun's violent, aggressive nature, already in evidence in his scenes with Roland. Genelun loses, which foreshadows his eventual conviction and death. It underscores Otto's fidelity in contrast to Genelun's treachery: Otto knows that it is a fight to the death and still does not hesitate (11549–50). Unlike the duel between Pinabel and Dietrich, this combat is not a judicial one. God's interest in and intervention on the side of the right is not thereby excluded however: when Genelun is close to dispatching Otto and winning his freedom, God intervenes on the side of the "werde margrâv" [worthy margrave], not on that of the "ungetriwen man" [perfidious individual] (11575–81) Genelun. Since God assists the right side in a battle that is not part of a trial, where he would be expected to manifest his will, the reader expects his intervention on the side of Genelun's enemies during a judicial ordeal.

Genelun's capture results in the loss of both status as a free man and personal freedom. He must give up his sword, the sign of his knighthood as well as his passport to liberty. In such a case Otto would have apparently had the right to kill him; he does not do so but makes sure that Genelun has the chance to go to court, as the emperor wishes.[92] Once again we see in Stricker's text a firm rejection of personal justice. In addition, Genelun is strongly bound and tied to Otto and his two helpers, a practical as well as a symbolic gesture, and is brought to Aachen in this fashion (11586–94). This dramatic physical appearance, which would indicate to all who saw the convoy both the emperor's power and the rule of law, show how valuable gesture could be in communicating a legal situation to the community.[93]

Genelun's capture results in the restoration of Otto to imperial favor. His meeting with Karl contains four legal words, *versagen* (11604), *urkünde* (11611), *unreht* (11617), and *buoze* (11626), that underscore the legal, as well as the personal, difficulties that Genelun's behavior caused Otto. Stricker presents the terminology in a sequence that parallels the legal process as it unfolds. In the first instance the narrator describes Otto's loss of Karl's protection.[94] The second legal word, *urkünde*, used here in the sense of proof, appears in Otto's presentation of the captive to Karl.[95] *Unreht*, used by Karl in his admission that he made a mistake, has a legal meaning of violation of the law.[96] Otto leaves the amount of the damages (11626–27) to Karl.

Otto's response to the emperor is replete with the polite phrases one would expect, but he does not fail to use the legal term for reparations: *buoze*.[97] Material consideration for an offense had been a defining characteristic in the tribal legal codes; whether Karl's largesse here reflects Germanic tradition, or whether it is the response appropriate from an emperor in such a case, is unclear. In his insistence on legal procedure in Otto's case Stricker also emphasizes the devotion to due process in Karl's court, reinforcing the High Middle Ages' picture of Karl as a great lawgiver. Stricker's addition of the Otto incident to the Roland story, therefore, deepens the Genelun scene.

Genelun's treachery and evil nature receive extra emphasis, while the virtues of fidelity and fairness occupy a central position, supported by divine intervention, as they will be during the trial.

In contrast to Genelun's *untriwe,* Otto has become the model of faithful service.[98] Because of his exemplary virtue in this regard, Otto receives from Karl the commission to guard the archtraitor (11641–42). The rest of Karl's speech is full of legal terminology explaining why he is not proceeding according to the rules of the feud but is bringing Genelun to trial:

> swie ich im von schulden *vient* bin,
> ine wil niht *rihten* über in
> nâch *vientlîcher râche.*
> ich wil die vürsten zÂche
> *urteiles* über in frâgen
> vor allen sînen mâgen.
> dâ sol man hoeren unde sehen
> den *mort,* der von im ist geschehen. (11645–52)

[To whatever degree I am rightly his enemy, I will not judge him according to feud revenge. I want to ask the princes at Aachen to deliver the verdict in front of all of his relatives. There everyone should hear and see the treacherous killing that he has committed.]

Vient, vientlîcher are clearly used here in the context of the feud. Just as Karl renounces personal revenge in the case of Otto, so, too, he does here, insisting on the primacy of the courts. While *râche* in earlier periods was not a sharply defined legal term, it did appear in conjunction with the feud, as it does here.[99]

This remarkable passage, which comes at the end of the section on Otto as Karl gives Genelun into Otto's care to be brought to Aachen, has no parallel in the *Rolandslied* and is yet another indication of Karl's deep commitment to the rule of law. Stricker could be using this passage to inveigh against the feud, a major and frequently growing problem in the High and late Middle Ages.[100] His emphasis on the *urteil* supports this interpretation, since even in the later twelfth century court judgments rarely induced a powerful noble to abandon relatives, friends, or retainers.[101]

Instead of blood revenge, Karl proposes to ask the princes at court in Aachen for the *urteil,* which involved all decisions and proposals for decisions before the court[102] This procedure reflects contemporary legal practices in that the judge did not deliver the *urteil* but asked those who could act in the legal capacity of verdict finders to do so.[103] These people were not only expected to know the law applicable to the situation but were also expected to create respect for the verdict through the strength of their reputations in the community.[104] In addition, they had to be of equal birth to the accused. In cases in which princes were involved, only princes could find the verdict, as is the case in Stricker's work, where they are specifically mentioned as the appropriate group (11648–49).[105] The verdict must be given in the presence of Genelun's relatives: on the one hand, they have a right to be concerned about the fate of their kinsman, on the other hand, an open procedure might assure less unrest on their part about the fairness of the proceedings.[106] During this session those present should, according to Stricker, "hear and see the murder that he has brought about"; in his linking the charge of murder with Genelun's treachery, Stricker's Karl follows contemporary practice.[107] Since the murder will not be repeated, Karl is probably referring to the testimony and the judicial ordeal that will prove Genelun's guilt.

On arriving in Aachen, Karl summons his court (*gerihte*) and prepares to preside over it (11663–71). Prior to arrival in Aachen, Genelun was held under a kind of arrest that reflects the decline in his legal position; he received only enough care to remain alive (11655–59). These comments are not in the *Rolandslied* text and would seem to reflect the assumption of guilt on the part of the emperor and his adherents. At this point Stricker goes back to the *Rolandslied;* but he adapts freely and with obvious deliberation, since he changes some lines he takes over in important ways, leaves out others, and adds material. These changes occur immediately in Stricker's treatment of the plea of Genelun's family.[108] While in the *Rolandslied* it follows Genelun's defense (8760–70), here the plea occurs as soon as Karl opens the court (11670–706). As a portrayal of a logical strategy, Stricker's change has much to commend it. Everyone present knows that Genelun is responsible for Roland's death, as Genelun himself in his arrogant monologue predicted that they would. Consequently the best choice open to the relatives is to convince Karl that it would be to his advantage to keep Genelun alive, preferably before public accusation and the hardening of attitudes make retreat difficult. During the twelfth century such negotiations frequently took place immediately before blood was shed; here they occur shortly before the judicial duel.[109]

To achieve their ends Genelun's relatives in Stricker's work, as in the *Rolandslied*, do not address the theological dimensions of Genelun's behavior; to do so would only weaken their case.[110] Their plea in Stricker, more than twice as long as the corresponding passage in Konrad, contains two interesting additions. In the later work Genelun's relatives promise to assume responsibility both for Genelun's reparations and for his future service to the empire. In Konrad's work Genelun's family promise at the close of their presentation that Genelun will serve the empire (8769–70). In contrast, at the beginning of this passage in Stricker (11682–83) Genelun's family link his misdeeds to the welfare of the empire and its ruler:

Konrad's *Rolandslied*	Stricker's *Karl der Grosse*
si spraken: "uil groz sint sine sculde. uns ist harte misseschen: di tiuristen sin gelegen; nu ne mah si nieman wider gewinnen. geere dine kunlinge! Gestille, herre, dinen zorn: laz in zo dinen gnaden komen durh diner swester ere! des bite wir dih, herre. Genelun dienet dem riche imer mere uorchtliken." (8760–70)	swaz er wider dem rîche und wider iwern hulden hât getân, des sol er iu ze buoze stân mit lîbe und mit guote und mit willigem muote. dâ sul wir im helfen zuo, daz er des alsô vil getuo. unz wir iu an verdienen daz, daz wir iwern angestlîchen haz und iwern zorn gestillen. durch iwer swester willen und daz wirz iemêr verschulden, lât in komen ziwern hulden. die ze Runzevâl sint erslagen, die muoze wir leider verklagen. wir mugen si wider gewinnen niht: ez ist uns leit, hulfe ez iht. nu nemt die lebenden der für. ob Genelûn den lîp verlür, sô hetet ir deste mê verlorn. mâzet herre iwern zorn und lâzet Genlûnen leben. wir wellen iu dienen unde geben, unz wirz bringen an die vart, daz niemen baz verdienet wart. (11682–706)
"They said, 'His guilt is immense. We have endured much disaster. The best men are dead, but no one can bring them back to life. Think about your relatives! Still your anger and for your sister's honor, be gracious to Genelun. That we beg of you, lord; Genelun will always serve the Empire obediently."	"Whatever he has done against the Empire and in relation to your protection of him, he is legally responsible for reparation both with his person and with wealth and with a ready will. We will help him so that he in this matter will do so much until we in your eyes have become worthy through this service and have quenched your distressed hate and your anger. Because of your sister's wishes and because we would always be in your debt, let him receive your favor. Those who were slain at Roncevalles we must always mourn, but we cannot bring them back: if it would help, it is a sorrow to us. Now take the living instead. If Genelun lost his life, then you would lose even more. Lord, control your anger and let Genelun live. We want to serve you and give, until we bring it to the point that no one was better repaid."

In Stricker's work Genelun's relatives promise that not only Genelun's personal wealth and powers but also theirs are at Karl's disposal until he is no longer angry with them.

Stricker's portrayal of the manner in which they make their attempt seems consonant with contemporary custom on such matters in those cases in which they were used. Negotiators worked out a settlement, dependent on such factors as the seriousness of the transgression, the positions of the accused and the victim, and the strength of each party's case.[111] The weakness of Genelun's family's position is, however, the nature of Genelun's crime, which mitigates against such a negotiated settlement.

With that in mind, the relatives make a specific commitment to ensure that Genelun becomes a model of exemplary service to Karl. In their enthusiastic guarantees and assurances to the emperor, Genelun's relatives address the central issue of the defendant's loyalty to the crown. In this manner Stricker skillfully links Karl's earlier lament over the damage done to the empire through Roland's loss to Genelun's relatives' promise to bring forth service of the highest order from Genelun (11704–6).[112] To underscore Genelun's dedication they use a figure of speech related to body language in a legal context: the gesture of standing at the emperor's service reflects submission.[113] The relatives' potential role in strengthening the empire underscores the political power of great families that Stricker emphasized in Karl's earlier lament about the effect of Roland's death on imperial power.

While Konrad touched on this theme, Stricker expands it at strategic points in his version of the narrative. Compensatory service for Roland's death by Genelun to Karl can in no way expiate Roland's death. Karl's response to the expansive promise Genelun's relatives make on his behalf is that all of the gold of Arabia would not weigh heavily enough in the balance for him to accede to their request (11707–13).[114] Because Stricker makes the potential value of Genelun's and his family's service to the emperor a much larger issue than it is in the *Rolandslied,* Karl's extravagant rejection of wealth far larger than the resources of Genelun's entire family has a more telling effect than it does in the earlier work (*Rolandslied* 8773–78).

Since the implication is that this service compensates in some way for the losses incurred by Karl because of Roland's death, Karl's rejection of their offer, as well as any potentially larger ones, could also be a rejection of *Totschlagssühne,* the older legal remedy.[115] Connected as it was with the feud, the negotiation of damages between the two affected parties was part of an older legal system, which Stricker consistently portrays as being on the wrong side of the issue. As we have seen earlier, Karl consistently and anachronistically sides with newer legal practices.

The question of Genelun's guilt has a direct bearing on the portrayal of the trial by battle. In Stricker's work the escape scene has given definitive proof that Genelun is guilty.[116] This section, missing in the *Rolandslied,* leads, perhaps, to a most striking difference: the *Rolandslied* text states clearly that Genelun was brought before the court bound; *Karl der Grosse* is silent on this point. In the *Rolandslied* Genelun's relatives protest that he has not been convicted of anything; therefore, he still has all of the rights accruing to a man in his station and should not appear in such a compromising state (8734–38). This protest is not in Stricker's work. Two explanations for its absence have been advanced: that Genelun's flight removes all doubt about his guilt and that, therefore, such a protest is meaningless; or that Genelun appeared in Stricker's court scene without physical restraint.[117] The latter interpretation seems more likely, since a bound defendant could not speak for himself before the court, which Genelun does. Stricker, who is always careful about legal details, has apparently clarified an inconsistency in the *Rolandslied,* where Genelun does appear bound in court but also speaks in his own defense.[118] In Stricker's work no mention is made of physical restraint; so Genelun's defense of himself does not seem legally out of place, unless he had lost his rights because of flight.

Genelun's argument has as its core, as it has since the *Chanson de Roland,* the legal question of whether or not he was in a state of feud with Roland.[119] If he can convincingly make the case that his killing of Roland was justifiable because of the legally sanctioned practices that had grown up around the feud, then he is not guilty of murder, as Karl claims (11436).[120] By the early twelfth century the belief that the most serious crime was the taking of another's life began to dominate thinking about crime, replacing the attitude that crimes against property were the most serious. Karl's linkage of Roland's killing with the damage done to Christianity and the empire reflects this newer thinking. The strength of this linkage is much more apparent in Stricker's reworking of the material than in the *Rolandslied,* perhaps reflecting the growing acceptance of the premise that the killing of an individual was a crime against the entire society.[121] Because Roland's loss was, in Karl's view, a serious blow to the empire, Genelun's only hope for acquittal lies in convincing the court that Roland's death was justified in terms of the feud and was, therefore, not murder.

Although the distinction between *mort* and *totslac* was not always made in the Middle Ages, a leading indicator for murder was stealth in the carrying out of the deed. Intent, such as self-enrichment through another's death, was an additional factor that increased the gravity of the offense, as it does in Genelun's case. The question of the perpetrator's responsibility in the case of murder could have different answers. Even well into the Middle Ages Germanic tradition still survived in the tendency to assign *wergeld* as reparation for murder instead of punishment in the form of the death penalty. This remedy seems appropriate to Genelun's relatives. When the murder case was a serious one, however, as the murder of a peer of the realm and the emperor's nephew would have been, conviction was followed by the death penalty.[122]

Stricker's account, as usual, pays more attention to the legal context. Central to the question of whether or not a state of feud existed was the public statement of the accuser; in this regard, Stricker presents a more clear-cut legal situation because of the additions he makes. One of these appears directly after Karl has accused him of murder (11719). Stricker's Genelun answers the charge: he did not commit this crime of which he is accused. The twelve peers did, indeed, die because of his efforts, but he committed no murder, and the manner of their death was *unmortlîche* (11724–25, 11729).[123] With this introduction to his defense, missing in the *Rolandslied*, Stricker's Genelun then gives an explanation reminiscent of his counterpart in the *Rolandslied* in regard to the feud. His announcement was made "vor dem rîche / offenlîche" (11730–31).[124] As we have seen, an important part of the legal definition of *mort* was the element of secrecy. Genelun's insistence that he made a public declaration of his intent, in accordance with legal custom, means that his killing of the peers could not be murder. It was precisely this *diffidatio*, the formal notice of a quarrel, that legitimized any killing committed in the course of a feud and set it off from the violence of the thieves and highwaymen, who had neither legal standing nor reputation.[125] The apparent brazenness with which Genelun makes his case, while reflecting the knowledge that the best defense is a good offense, also is indicative of the aristocratic attitude that the feud was an inborn right.[126]

To substantiate his claim that a state of feud existed, Stricker's Genelun adds more legal ammunition to his defense than was present in the *Rolandslied*.[127] In the process he refers to events occurring before his mission to Marsilie that strengthen his claim that there was a feud between them:

Konrad's *Rolandslied*	Stricker's *Karl der Grosse*
er sprach: "herre, ez was mîn wille.	er sprach: ich hân deheinen mort
ich nelougin dir sîn niet.	begangen alse man mir giht.
der zwelve tôt ist mir liep.	Ine lougen aber des niht,
iz ist gewisse der mîn rât.	Ine habe daz erworben,
ich hete in ê widersaget	Daz die zwelfe sint erstorben.
ze dîner antwurte offenlîche.	Daz geschach ummortlîche.
daz erziuge ich mit dem rîche."	Ich hete in vor dem rîche
(8740–46)	Offenlîche widersaget
	Und hete ein michel teil geklaget
	Mîn leit daz si mir tâten.
	si heten mich verrâten
	und schuofen mich in den tôt.
	Daz ich daz rach, daz tet mir nôt.
	(11724–36)

Konrad's *Rolandslied*	Stricker's *Karl der Grosse*
[He said, "Lord, I do not deny that that was my intent. I wanted the death of the twelve peers and such was my counsel. But I had previously declared myself in your presence to be in a state of feud with Roland. The princes of the empire are my witnesses."]	[He spoke: Contrary to accusations made against me, I have done no murder. However, I do not deny that I arranged things in such a way as to cause the death of the twelve peers. That was not murder. Before the council of princes I had declared myself to be in a state of feud with them and had openly accused them of much of the wrong which they did me. They betrayed me and sent me to my death. It was necessary for me to avenge that.]

In precise legal terminology — *offenlîche widersaget, geklaget, leit* — Genelun explains the crime against him and his remedy. Since *widersagen* has the legal meaning of declaring a feud, the addition of the adverb *offenlîche* underscores the public aspect of this important legal procedure. *Klagen* was the appropriate legal term for an accusation, while *leit* was part of the judicial vocabulary for damages.[128]

This statement by Genelun perhaps has its justification in his series of angry replies to Roland's nomination of him as messenger in Spain. Stricker makes four significant additions that support Genelun's defense before the court. All of these changes have the effect of strengthening the public nature of Genelun's declaration and have direct links with his self-defense:

>dû hâst gerâten mînen tôt. (2008)

[You have counseled my death.]

>sîme stiefsun Ruolande
>tet er manegen starken fluoch. (2022–23)

[He cursed his stepson Roland vigorously and often.]

>ine wirde Ruolant niemer holt,
>sît er mir ie sô vîent wart,
>daz er mir schuof an dise vart (2066–68)[129]

[I will never stand in a relation of trust to Roland, since he had so much enmity toward me that he arranged for me to go on this journey.]

> Ruolant ist aber vil gemeit,
> daz er mich hin hât gegeben,
> sol ich behalten mîn leben,
> sô mir dirre mîn bart,
> in geriuwet disiu vart. (2178–82)
>
> [Roland is, however, very pleased that he has put me in this situation. If I remain alive, I swear by my beard that he will regret this journey.]

In the first passage Genelun accuses Roland of direct responsibility for his death. Genelun's charge that he was being sent to certain destruction weakens, however, in the light of an addition by Stricker: Karl forces the heathen emissaries to swear an oath that Genelun would not be harmed during his trip (2195–202).[130] There are no comparable passages either in the *Chanson de Roland* or the *Rolandslied*; in the *Chanson de Roland* Ganelon expressly says that he will have no safe conduct.[131] Weakening Genelun's justification for a feud might be one way of attacking the institution and criticizing the mores of a bad character, since Stricker's own attitude toward the feud seems largely negative. Certainly one of the socially destabilizing elements of the feud was the right of nobles to enter into a feud for the slightest of legal pretexts. While Genelun's declaration of a feud against Roland is of course essential to the story, it was not, legally speaking, his only option. Revenge, which was his goal, would have been available through the court, where trial by battle, originally a means of feuding within the confines of the court and its rules, replaced the feud.[132] Because he could have gone to court rather than betray his country, Genelun's insistence that he was being sent to his death rings somewhat hollow in the face of the oath the heathens must give and undercuts his legal defense.[133]

While Genelun publicly curses his stepson [2022–23], the most explicit declaration of a feud comes in the third of the above quotations, where Genelun speaks of Roland as *vîent* in regard to himself. *Vîent*, a legal term relating to feud, strengthens Genelun's claim on a right to revenge, which he makes in his speech before the court. Retribution crops up again in Genelun's speech to Karl shortly before his departure. Using the legal term *leit* (injury), Genelun says specifically that Karl did not hurt him.[134] The addition of *leit* to Genelun's self-defense before Karl's court reinforces the legal context in which his declaration of a feud occurred.

Stricker's Genelun assesses the main components of his defense well before Roland's death in his conversation with the heathen Blanschandiez as they travel to Marsilie. This speech, which has no counterpart in the *Rolandslied,* anticipates the legal and political realities that will confront Genelun at Karl's court after Roland's death:[135]

> welt ir im nemen sîn leben,
> daz ich in iu gerne wil geben:
> dar an fürhte ich Karlen niht,
> und sage iu wâ von daz geschiht.
> sînes dinges stêt an mir sô vil,
> daz er muoz volgen des ich wil,
> daz ez ze volgenne stêt.
> swie ez Ruolande ergêt,
> des trûwe ich doch wol hin komen.
> der keiser hât wol vernomen,
> daz ich im widersaget hân.
> ouch muoz er mich geniezen lân,
> daz sîn swester ist mîn wîp.
> dannoch erwer ich mînen lîp
> mit mînen mâgen harte wol.
> swaz ich ze suone geben sol.
> verliuset Ruolant sîn leben,
> daz wil ich allez gerne geben. (2433–50)

[If you will take his life, which I will gladly give you, I am not scared of Karl's reaction in that matter, and I will tell you why. He depends so much on me that he must do what I want, when it comes to that. Whatever happens to Roland, I will come out of it in good shape. The emperor certainly knows that I declared myself to be in a state of feud with Roland. Since I am his brother-in-law, he must let me survive. In addition, I can defend myself with my relatives. Whatever I might have to give in the way of reparations, if Roland loses his life, I will gladly pay it.]

In this remarkable speech Genelun assesses, in a cold-blooded and rational manner, the strength of the defenses he can muster when Roland's death is discovered. In the political sphere, the power of the great families, a recurrent theme in *Karl der Grosse,* works for Genelun: Karl's welfare is dependent on him (2437–38), and Genelun's relatives will defend him (2446–47).[136] Blood ties afford him protection, since he is married to the emperor's sister (2444–45). Not only his intimate relationship to the emperor but also his great personal wealth will shield him. Genelun is ready to pay whatever reparations are necessary, as long as Roland dies (2448–49). He believes that he has nothing to fear because of his public declaration of feud before the emperor (2442–43). In keeping with the consistent characterization of Genelun, no religious considerations arise to trouble him. He even seems oblivious to his own inordinate pride: he is absolutely certain Karl cannot survive without his advice (2437–38). Lacking any consciousness of Christian ethics,[137] this speech places him squarely in the world of Germanic tribal law, with its emphasis on blood ties, feud, and *suone*.[138]

Because Genelun is firmly convinced that he has followed the rules for a declaration of a feud with Roland owing to what he sees as Roland's betrayal, it follows that revenge is justified (11730–36).[139] The connection with feud leads us to another function that Genelun's character performs in Stricker's work: Genelun here embodies the old law, the earliest means of legal redress used by the Germanic peoples. As we have seen in the Otto section and in the pretrial treatment of Genelun, Otto and Karl have repeatedly inveighed against the feud, preferring to submit to the courts even though they had the right to do with Genelun as they wished.[140] Combined with the previous negative references to blood feuds and personal vengeance, the specific identification of revenge with Genelun is another means of attacking his personal ethos, an ethos that Stricker has found wanting in other contexts.[141] Stricker may have retained Genelun's speech not only because of its presence in the sources but also because of his obvious preference for courtroom procedure over the old system of personal and immediate justice. Genelun, the archtraitor and ally of the devil, represents, as well, the profeud faction.[142] This characterization sets him apart from Karl, the defender of the faith and the great lawgiver, who represents here the predominance of newer legal ideas. Genelun's great weakness, which this speech lays bare, is a common one for powerful people bent on evil deeds: blinded by pride, they think that they can get away with such deeds and do not consider the places where they are vulnerable to attack.

These newer ideas, represented by Karl, meet with much resistance from the princes. Just how deeply rooted the Germanic understanding of the feud was among powerful noble families reveals itself in the response of the peers to Karl after Genelun's speech. In answer to Genelun, Karl says that Genelun has, indeed, indicted himself. By not directly replying to Genelun's assertions, Karl implicitly discounts the argument that Genelun was justified in killing Roland because of a publicly declared feud. Instead, Karl accuses him of betraying the Christians to the heathens (11737–43). A war against the enemies of the Church enjoyed a unique status above and apart from all other armed conflicts, including those between kings. Genelun's decision to declare a feud in such a situation is in itself an attack on the Christian cause, as well as on the military security of the empire. This situation brings into sharp relief how fluid the boundaries between a legal feud and rebellion or revolution could be and what dangers feuds posed to the establishment of royal authority.[143]

Another reason for Karl's rejection of the defense position could be that he felt Genelun had no legal justification for the feud.[144] Southern German sources from the thirteenth century indicate that condemnation of actions arising from a feud as criminal was a claim that, among other things, there were not sufficient legal grounds for it. Otherwise, such charges would not have been leveled, because the aggrieved party would have had a legal right to do what he did. Acts of violence arising from unjustified feuds were among the first offenses that the developing penal codes addressed: manslaughter, murder, and abduction and rape of women.[145] Perhaps for these reasons Karl then asks what Genelun, in view of his guilt, owes Karl and the empire (11744–47). The response is a deafening silence. Mindful, as Stricker says, of the presence of Genelun's closest relatives, the rest of the court, to whom the emperor looks for support, do not dare answer for fear of putting themselves in mortal danger from Genelun's family (11748–54).[146] The conflict between the rule of law and self-help justice is nowhere more clearly expressed than in the deafening silence from the peers of the realm.[147]

To uphold due process Karl gives the princes a choice: they can help him uphold legal procedure and thereby enrich themselves, or they can take the part of Genelun and his family (11758–71). If they choose the latter course of action, he will lay down both his crown and his rank. If the power of Genelun's family prevailed, Karl's internal authority would be gone, open to challenge by any powerful block whose path he crossed.[148] The empire's skin is thin at this point, revealing the Germanic family structure still intact beneath it. Karl's earlier lament over Roland's loss and his dependence on relatives to maintain his power could show how much the political structure was still linked to blood relatives in the first half of the thirteenth century. Karl tends to identify himself and his family with the empire; but in the absence of a more highly developed political structure, older social organization shows through, threatening the attempts to establish a rule of law. If an emperor cannot punish the traitor who betrayed him with the enemy and caused his nephew's death, then he cannot protect anyone, and there is no reason for confidence in or fear of his authority.[149]

Karl's courage in making the power struggle a public issue disconcerts Genelun's relatives, who have only one goal in mind, however they reach it: to save Genelun's life (11775–81). Karl has rejected their expansive offer of reparations, has put Roland's death in the context of a crime against society, and now has offered to abdicate if Genelun goes unpunished. Their depressed response must arise from their realization that Karl has raised the stakes by pitting his authority against their potential threat. Karl's offer to give up the empire, which is less developed in the *Rolandslied,* presents Karl as a much more active and engaged ruler than the other two works do. The hedging, cowardly response of the nobles serves to enhance the portrait of Karl.[150] Not only two different legal points of view but also two power bases struggling for their existence make compromise impossible. The issue must be decided through the judicial duel.[151]

What Genelun's defense purposefully overlooks but Karl's accusation makes clear is that Genelun's secret treaty with Marsilie betrayed the empire. In the second of Karl's two speeches before Pinabel's challenge in Stricker, he links Genelun's crime with attacks on both Christianity and the empire, not simply against the Church. Stricker thereby underscores even more clearly the limitation of feud rights, which has been a consistent tendency in his adaptation. It was common practice for feuds to cease within the *Land* when the territory was in a state of war, which the empire certainly was.[152] The skilled legal arguments presented by both sides in this case, juxtaposed with the judicial duel, show a telling overlayering of newer and older concepts of judicial procedure.

The grounds on which the duel is fought are not about Genelun's role in causing Roland's death. The facts, in other words, are not in dispute. What is at issue, as the lengthy legal arguments have shown, is whether or not Genelun had a right to bring about Roland's demise. The ultimate question that lies behind the struggle in the court is whether the rule of law and due process will prevail or whether the older structure of feud, as self-help justice, will be validated once again. Stricker, as is his tendency throughout this scene, goes into considerably more legal detail than Konrad does: the duel scene in Stricker's work is approximately twice the length of the corresponding section in Konrad.[153] For example, in a greatly expanded section prior to Binabel's challenge (11775–92) he includes material reflective of some contemporary attitudes toward the judicial ordeal, that is, self-preservation. Pinabel's relatives have one concern: to save Genelun's life. As we have seen in the introduction, some medieval people preferred to trust in a strong arm rather than in God's intervention. Genelun and his family, who show throughout a singular lack of concern for their accountability before the Almighty, settle on Pinabel, as the strongest among them, to rescue their relative (11784–85). Consistent with this attitude is Pinabel's failure in his challenge to the court to mention God intervening on the side of the right.

Other examples of Stricker's predilection to expand legal information abound. For instance, while Konrad's Binabel devotes one line to the legal justification of his relative's behavior, Stricker's Pinabel structures his speech like a detailed legal defense, rejecting the charge against his relative.[154] He then explains why Genelun's deed cannot be considered murder, adding new and supportive information to his relative's self-defense: Genelun on three different occasions had declared publicly that he had a feud with Roland (11800–802). The only defense with any legal standing that Genelun has is the statement that he was in a state of feud with his stepson. He and his relatives interpret this claim to mean that any action resulting in Roland's death was permitted. Pinabel's public criticism in Stricker's work, as in Konrad's, concerns the interpretation of the law and not the facts of the case.[155] Karl and his party, however, rest their argument on the treason committed against the empire in Genelun's secret plot to kill Roland and betray the Carolingian army.

While Karl insists on the rule of law in the attempt to give Genelun due process, aspects of an older view of homicide, in which it was a private matter between the family of the deceased and the killer, still exist on Karl's side, as well. For example, Dietrich's offer to avenge Roland's death because Roland is his kinsman (11820–23) could reflect practices associated with the feud, transmuted into the judicial duel, as well as the older belief in the responsibility of the victim's family to respond to this attack on the family's power and importance. Combined with this attitude is the other one apparent here, the damage Roland's death has done to the cause of Christianity and the empire. This larger concern mirrors a tendency, apparent since the first decades of the twelfth century in decrees declaring truces and in city legal codes, to view homicide as an attack on society at large that cannot be countenanced.[156]

The importance of the rule of law in Stricker's work comes to the fore in Dietrich's challenge to Pinabel. While Stricker's scene is about the same length as its counterpart in Konrad's work, there are changes in points of emphasis, one of the most significant being the emphasis on *reht* and *unreht* in Stricker. *Rechte* occurs once in Konrad's account (8839), while Stricker mentions these words four times (11832, 11834, 11836, 11844). He contrasts the *unreht* that God made right in the case of David and Goliath, and the reality that he continues to intervene.[157] In so doing he raises the law to a high standing.[158] Dietrich closes his speech with a reference linking God to justice in the ordeal by battle:

> got müeze den kampf selbe sehen
> und lâze uns beiden reht geschehen. (11843–44)[159]

While Stricker's Dietrich emphasizes the active role of God,[160] his counterpart in the *Rolandslied* casts his challenge in a much more theologically oriented manner. References to God, Christ, and Christianity are more frequent,[161] as Tirrich portrays his judicial duel as part of the eternal struggle of Christianity against evil. Genelun's treacherous behavior has severely damaged Christianity and barred him from *cristinlichem rechte* [the rights of a Christian] (8839).[162] Tirrich's sword should establish the truth in Christ's name, since he is fighting against an opponent who is God's enemy (8833–43, 8852–53).[163] By contrast, and consistent with his other revisions, Stricker's Dietrich seems more concerned with linking God to the specific role of establishing justice and less interested in family ties and theological questions.

In both the *Rolandslied* and the *Karl der Grosse* Tirrich/Dietrich assumes that God will prove that Genelun is guilty through the judicial duel; there is, however, a small but significant change in the statements of Binabel in the *Rolandslied* and Pinabel in the *Karl der Grosse*. While Konrad's Binabel (8804) refers in a parenthetical way to God's presence in the proof through battle, Pinabel in Stricker's work never mentions God in his prediction that he will quickly show anyone who steps into the ring that Genelun is innocent (11803–6). The omission of any reference to God in Pinabel's speech also has the effect of resting the outcome entirely on Pinabel's gladiatoral skills, which figured in his choice to represent Genelun.[164] Stricker's change makes the sharp delineation between good and evil and the David/Goliath comparison between them more consistent.

Genelun's relatives' confidence in Pinabel in combat appears again in Stricker's section dealing with the hostages, where they express the belief that even if there were four of Dietrich, Pinabel would dispatch all of them (11878–81). Stricker, who spends three times as many lines on the hostage matter as Konrad,[165] devotes a great deal of space to the situation in which Genelun's relatives find themselves — material missing in Konrad's work. Karl's counselors advise him to take hostages among Genelun's supporters, as those individuals deserve to lose their lives for their hostility toward the empire. While much in Stricker's work reflects legal procedures of the early thirteenth century, the killing of Genelun's relatives who serve as hostages, already appearing in the *Chanson de Roland,* probably reflects practices of an earlier era. In Germanic/Franconian times the hostages whose cause was lost were generally killed, while in the Middle Ages the development of knightly codes of behavior and the influence of the Church led to better treatment for them. They could remain imprisoned for a while, then be ransomed.[166]

Faced with a powerful section of narrative that adds drama, even though it might have differed from current practice in such situations, Stricker seems to have adapted it to a major theme he emphasizes throughout this section: the relation of powerful families to the maintenance of imperial authority. Stricker adds at this point material that is missing in the earlier German work. His hostages accept the obligation with enthusiasm, give themselves into captivity, and state that they chose freely to die, swearing that Pinabel would be victorious (11863–81). These additions display a powerful family's solid and public opposition to Karl's cause. Because of this attitude, the emperor's counselors believe that the family deserves to be suppressed strongly (11855–62). Another source of the enmity against Pinabel and, by implication, Genelun's other relatives lies in the possibility that not only Genelun but also his family benefited financially from his deal with the heathens (12075–81). Here again Stricker links the welfare of the empire to the behavior of influential aristocratic families, as he has done throughout the section dealing with Genelun's apprehension and trial.

Literary portrayals of medieval ordeals often dispense with the customary waiting period, as is the case in both of these works. The battle takes place as soon as possible after the challenge. Other parts of the ceremony leading up to the ordeal are either missing, such as the oath (absent in Konrad, as well), or deemphasized.[167] In Konrad's work Karl leads all of his people, including the nuns, in prayer prior to the battle, masses are held, psalms are sung (8881–96). Perhaps reflecting the Church's repudiation of ordeals after the Fourth Lateran Council in 1215, Stricker shortens this section, leaving out liturgical references (11887–92).[168] Stricker's description of the preparations for the fight (11885–948) is somewhat longer than Konrad's (8873–913) and differs in its points of emphasis. Stricker devotes much more space to the protagonists, as well as to the royal ban on certain activities on pain of death. Not only the armor, which Konrad does not describe, but also Dietrich's comparative physical disadvantage (11910–14) receive emphasis. Dietrich's obvious weakness, which causes Pinabel's camp to be confident of victory, becomes a means for Stricker to underscore repeatedly the necessity for God's intervention (11911–21).[169] Both works contain an imperial ban on the participation of spectators from any social level in the battle on pain of death,[170] but Stricker adds an additional specific reason: that Karl wished to protect Dietrich from interference by Genelun's relatives (11922–25). This interdiction gives further evidence of the self-confidence and the power of prominent families. An additional reference to spectators, those who wished to join the fight out of affection or hate (11944–48), most probably reflects contemporary legal realities.[171]

Stricker's battle scene is two and one-half times the length of the comparable passage in the *Rolandslied* (*Karl der Grosse* 11885–12062; *Rolandslied* 8915–992). A significant difference between the two versions lies in the reappearance of Roland's sword, Durndart, as Dietrich's weapon in Stricker's work. Karl gave the sword to Roland; he now gives it to the man who is to prove the guilt of Roland's murderer, underscoring the sword's symbolism as an instrument of the law. Given to Karl by the angel, who wants Roland to have it, Durndart possesses almost reliclike status (11967, 11969). The angel tells Karl that whoever is wounded with Durndart will never become well again (375–76). Consequently, Dietrich's association with Durndart becomes an important factor in the trial by battle: not only is the sword holy (11967); it is also the sword of Dietrich's relative, the exemplary peer of the realm whom Genelun killed.[172] Its presence, therefore, adds to the transcendental quality that surrounds this struggle. The legendlike qualities that the presence of Durndart and the repeated comments about God's help add to this trial by battle are underscored, as in Konrad, by references to Pinabel as the accomplice of the devil.[173] As with the ordeals of Kunigunde and Richardis, the outcome is never in doubt; Stricker repeatedly invokes God's assistance for Dietrich throughout the battle.[174]

Dietrich himself emphasizes God's intervention and its connection with justice and the law at the end of the fight.[175] God's decision as to Genelun's guilt makes it possible for the emperor to ask his court for a decision regarding punishment. Stricker's Karl combines an interesting mixture of personal preference and binding legal procedure: he consulted those whom he wished to consult but whom he was legally obliged to consult (12093–95). The question he poses — what does the traitor owe the empire? (12095–96) — puts Genelun's crime in the context of damage to the larger body politic, which, as we have seen, is characteristic of the newer interpretation of murder as a crime against the social order. Konrad's Karl does not speak to this point; his court says only that the empire should be cleansed [*gerainet*] (8995), which has religious overtones. The earlier work does not reflect this more contemporary understanding of the legal implications of treason and murder. The plea to avenge the widows and children of the men who were killed (12099–106), which is also present in Konrad's work, probably comes from a more archaic understanding of murder as a crime against the family.[176]

To exercise his rights as a judge in capital crimes Karl, using a formula not present in Konrad's work, asks the court to give the judgment:

> des frâge ich iuch beide
> bî dem rehte und bî dem eide
> und bî mînen hulden dâ bî,
> welches todes er mir schuldec sî. (12111–14)

[For that reason I ask you, both in regard to law and oath and my obligations in the matter, what kind of death he owes me.]

While *hulde* carried a legal obligation of fidelity in feudal relationships and stood next to the oath, it also could refer to a general oath to perform the duties of the office faithfully. After his election, according to the *Sachsenspiegel*, the king was supposed to swear such an oath.[177]

In their decision to let Genelun be torn apart by horses, the nobles chose a means of death that, according to Stricker, was no longer used.[178] The gravity of his crime, however, justifies such an execution (12115–19). Stricker's comment about the archaic nature of this means of execution is, perhaps, an explanation to an audience that might have been surprised by the savage sentence. To clarify the situation further Stricker adds that the hostages, who were not hated as much, were simply beheaded; Stricker's audience would have immediately understood that such a death was more honorable.[179]

Stricker speaks explicitly of Genelun's death as revenge for the murder of Roland (12137–38). His account limits itself to a description of the way in which he was bound to the four horses and the spurring of the horses in different directions. In contrast to Konrad's version and the *Karlmeinet*, the detailed description of the wide territory over which body parts were distributed is missing.[180] Since Stricker has indicated that, for his age, such a punishment was relatively unknown, this omission may not be surprising.

Punishment does not stop with the Genelun figure, as it does in the *Karlmeinet*.[181] Karl, angered by Genelun's unrepentant death, transfers his anger to Genelun's relatives (12155–58). Publicly shamed and despised until their deaths, they must relinquish much so that the treason of their relative can be adequately punished (12159–81). This passage, the final example of Stricker's emphasis on Genelun's family, also reaffirms Karl's power in a telling way: he is able to disgrace an entire extended family with the highest of aristocratic connections. Genelun's family members, who had tried to save their traitorous relative through a time-honored approach of reparations to the injured party, must bow to the establishment of an imperial rule of law. Their dishonor condemns treason further; treason against the emperor was the work not just of one individual but of the entire family (12165–67). The Germanic custom of supporting one's relative through feud or appeals to the emperor has been turned on its head and used to reveal the power of the emperor to inflict, in the establishment of order, severe loss on relatives of an offender.

Karl's ability to increase good in the world, contrasted with Genelun's faculty for causing ripples of misery and evil, concludes Stricker's sentencing scene (12175–89). The work ends shortly thereafter with Karl's death and glorification: the last three lines of the work invoke St. Karl's help and protection (12204–6).[182]

Karlmeinet

Karl's role as a symbol of imperial power and justice continued to exercise an apparent fascination for upper-class individuals in the medieval German lands. Today the Rhenish late thirteenth-/early fourteenth-century compilation *Karlmeinet* is little known, but the 800 pages of edited text represent a considerable investment on the part of both writer and patron. The six-part work, a biography of Karl from birth to death, takes its name from the narrator of the first section.[183] Current critical opinion suggests that this monumental narrative was a product of the St. Mary's monastery in Aachen during the first half of the fourteenth century.[184] The anonymous monk who was the writer made significant changes and additions to the group of independent narratives about certain episodes in Karl's life. Book V, around 9,000 verses, in which the Roland material appears, contains, as we shall see, additions of varying length. There is no certainty as to how much of this material came from the monk who served as its final compiler and how much he simply took unchanged from those who had reworked the material previously. This analysis will contrast the changes in the *Karlmeinet* with the *Rolandslied* and with Stricker's work, with the underlying assumption that the compiler presented whatever material he had before him in a narrative that would be tailored to the taste and expectations of his audience.

The section that concerns us, where the Roland material appears, comes late in the text. While there is general agreement that the part of the *Karlmeinet* with which we deal — the trial of Genelun, who is here called Wellis — had as its source the *Rolandslied*, there is uncertainty about the writer's other sources.[185] Just as in the case of Stricker's approach to the material, the author shows himself capable of significant changes that seem to reflect concerns, preoccupations, and attitudes of his time.

For the *Karlmeinet* author, writing approximately a century later, the emphasis on family ties between Karl and Roland, feuds, political calculation, and detailed legal arguments from Wellis are of little interest. These changes, coming from 80 to 100 years after Stricker wrote, could certainly reflect changes in the judicial system and, quite possibly, urbanization, which was a major force for change in the northwestern Germanic lands around the Netherlands, which, of course, includes Aachen. As the authority of the empire increased, the predilection for private vengeance had to be curbed. The steadily increasing pressure to go to court to settle differences rather than resort to feud could lie behind the disappearance of the latter as an issue in the later work.[186] This omission seems significant, because of the long literary tradition of feud with Roland as the core of Genelun's defense.[187] While it was the center of Genelun's legal argument both in Konrad's work and in Stricker's epic, in *Karlmeinet* feud and the complex legal issues that surround it are never directly mentioned in the capture and trial scenes; Wellis's defense consists simply of a statement that he is not guilty of treason and any money he took from the heathen did not damage Karl.

The comparative lack of involvement by Wellis's family in the *Karlmeinet* stands in sharp contrast to both Konrad's and Stricker's works and changes the context quite dramatically. In Konrad's version the relatives emphasize the close kinship ties, while Stricker's account promises reparations from Genelun and his relatives. In the *Karlmeinet* no attempt is made by Wellis or his family to offer reparations for Roland's death as a substitute for capital punishment; such an offer would have been expected under the old legal system based on compensatory rather than penal justice. During the twelfth century such negotiations frequently took place immediately before blood was shed, such as before the judicial duel in this case.[188] When we see Genelun's family in Stricker's work trying to make restitution of goods and service, we see a long-established practice in force. In the *Karlmeinet* the family does not even make a statement in court, which contrasts sharply with the situation in Stricker's work and is a further reflection of the decline in usage and prestige of the Germanic system of compensatory law.

The real challenge that powerful families presented to imperial authority in Stricker's life of Karl is considerably diluted in the *Karlmeinet* version. The adapter is consistent in this regard in that he greatly weakens the kinship theme between Roland and Karl, as well. Kinship ties figure in only one passage in the *Karlmeinet* trial scene, a key event in all of the Roland material, when Pinabel defends his relative before the court prior to serving as the Genelun figure's champion. Pinabel is accompanied by a large number of armed family members and gives a firm and manly defense of his relative.

The nobles consider this defense and ask Karl to pardon Wellis. Karl becomes angry and says that he will fight Wellis himself before he does that. There is no more resistance from the nobles, and no serious threat to Karl's authority from Wellis's family is ever entertained. This scenario differs dramatically from Stricker's version, where Karl threatens to abdicate his throne if the cowardly nobles side with Genelun's family instead of with him.

Central to the concern of both Stricker and the compiler/writer of the *Karlmeinet* was the maintenance of imperial authority.[189] The trial of the Genelun figure and his punishment provide an opportunity for each writer to expand on this theme. In Stricker's work Karl upholds his authority and that of the rule of law in the face of a serious challenge by one of the great families anxious to exercise self-help justice. The dominant scene in Stricker's work for the power of the emperor to display itself is in the trial scene; the enactment of the verdict confirms the power established during the proceedings. In contrast, for the *Karlmeinet* author Karl's authority seems to exercise itself in the straightforward and unequivocal implementation of his judicial powers, as a discouragement to potential traitors. The frequent comments about the deterrent force of this execution bear out this interpretation. The significant addition the *Karlmeinet* author makes in the last part of the Wellis trial shows the reader how important the maintenance of order and imperial authority is for the emperor and how wide the range of powers that he holds over his subjects is.

These differences show up in the very first scenes involving Wellis. In the earlier part of the work, where a messenger must be chosen to go to the heathens, Wellis erupts in a series of angry outbursts similar to those in Stricker and in the *Rolandslied*. Wellis complains that Roland is sending him to his death so that he can have his stepfather's inheritance to the disadvantage of his son; he accuses Roland of forgetting *truwen* (440b, 39), cries repeatedly that Roland has done this to him and that he and the twelve will experience bad times because of Roland's action (A440, 25–A440b, 43; A440b, 60–64; A441b, 40–48).[190] While the legal term *vient* [enemy], present in Stricker, is missing, there is certainly a public display of enmity and a promise of harm to Roland and his followers. Yet, in a significant change from earlier versions, this open attack never becomes the basis of a feud defense for Wellis in court.

The chief objection Wellis makes is the same as that of his literary predecessors: the danger of the trip. Like Konrad and Stricker, the *Karlmeinet* author also includes material that shows that Wellis traveled under the emperor's protection: Karl's glove and staff (A441, 1–7). This writer shows an awareness of changes in legal custom, however, for he explains to his readers that this was at that time a sign of *vreden*.[191] As in the earlier versions, Karl in the *Karlmeinet* assumes responsibility for Genelun's choice as emissary — foreshadowing later legal problems for Wellis, who cannot convincingly blame Roland.[192]

Roland's reply to Karl about Wellis's accusations shows the *Karlmeinet* author's ability to read closely yet adapt. Because of Roland's mother's relationship with Karl, he would not take any action that would hurt her and upset the emperor. Karl has been good to him for a long time and has taken him into his council. The *Karlmeinet* Roland sharpens the issue of betrayal: where Stricker simply uses the word *untriuwen* ["infidelity"] (2081), the *Karlmeinet* text is more direct: were he (Roland) to become a traitor (*verreder*, A442, 8), that would upset Karl greatly, thus foreshadowing the outcome of Wellis's treachery (A441b, 50–442, 8). Like his predecessors, the Roland of *Karlmeinet* assures him of the absence of any predatory motives regarding his half-brother Baldwin (A441b, 62–65).[193]

Karl also mentions their family ties and implores the same angel that guided Tobias to protect Wellis (A442b, 66–67). The *Karlmeinet* author's choice of the reference to Tobias, which is not found in this detail or at all in the other versions,[194] could function on several levels. In the Book of Tobit, Tobit's son Tobias goes on a long journey to recover money that his father, fallen on hard times, badly needs. The archangel Raphael, in the guise of a relative of Tobit's, accompanies the young man, keeps him safe, and gives him important advice. The portrait of the trusting Karl, which the *Karlmeinet* author reinforces frequently, receives further emphasis when Karl implicitly compares Wellis to Tobias. Since the story of Tobias and the angel is an edifying one, with Tobias always trying to do the right thing,[195] Karl's choice of this comparison assumes that Wellis is just as faithful as his apocryphal counterpart. In addition, the biblical reference adds to the portrayal of Karl's piety.

The subsequent meeting and negotiations of Wellis with Blantschandis (A444b, 60–A448b, 68) closely follow the earlier works. The passage dealing with the comparison with Judas, however, offers useful insights into the consistency of the *Karlmeinet* author's adaptation and his characterization of Wellis. Immediately after the deal is made, the narrator begins a lengthy comparison of Wellis with Judas (A447, 30–54) that follows the relevant passage in the *Rolandslied* (1926–43) much more closely than Stricker's comparable passage in *Karl der Grosse* does. The postfigurative comparison of Genelun/Wellis with Judas goes point by point in the *Rolandslied* and *Karlmeinet* versions.[196] The typological frame of reference that these two works include for the Judas comparison is yet another example of the intensified religious emphasis common to both — though that emphasis is not identical, as this analysis will show. The *Karlmeinet* author even adds a pious exhortation to his readers in the middle of the Judas section, asking them to thank God that God wants to bring them to heaven (A447b, 42–45).[197] This difference in emphasis, which becomes important in the trial scene, reveals itself also in what the *Karlmeinet* author leaves out, such as the vehement and lengthy excursus about King David and the betrayal of two kingdoms, a further reflection of his comparative lack of interest in imperial politics.[198]

When Roland's mighty blast on the horn reaches the Franks, Duke Names tells Karl that Wellis has betrayed Roland (A458b, 52–57). Wellis is immediately bound, before any real evidence is presented.[199] Karl's reaction to Roland's death comes later, in the middle of the battle scenes, when he visits Runzevalen. The *Karlmeinet* author's account of Karl's grief is closer to the *Rolandslied* version than it is to Stricker's text; he gives a much shorter version of Karl's speech about the different regions of the empire and the consequences of Roland's death for political order:

> Ind nw geyn man enleuet,
> An den ich Rolant moege maessen.
> Zo weme sal ich mich nw verlaissen?
> Bedrouet is al myn kunne.
> Dy lant du myr wunnes,
> Sassen ind Swauen,
> Dat sy sich mir ergauen.
> Des waende ich dir noch dancken.
> Beyeren ind Vrancken
> Hait mich nw versme.
> Owy leder ind owe! (466b, 44–54)

[And now no man lives who would measure up to Roland — on whom can I depend? My whole family is threatened. Land you won for me, Sachsen and Swabia became subject to me. I had hoped to reward you for that. Bavarians and Franks have now treated me disgracefully. Alas!]

This speech touches on concerns expressed in both the *Rolandslied* and the *Karl der Grosse:* the preeminence of Karl's family and the loss of certain territories. When one compares the two sections, however, one is struck by the obvious similarity to the *Rolandslied* text (7536–45). Instead of dwelling on political considerations, as Stricker's text did, the *Karlmeinet* version expands the scene dealing with the Frank's recovery of their dead: there are almost 100 lines detailing Karl's extreme grief and the preparation for burial of the bodies of Roland, Oliver, and Turpin (A466b, 57–A468, 3). Karl frequently falls into transports of grief at Roland's death, reflecting a tendency of the *Karlmeinet* version to repeat or double significant thematic elements.[200] After the cursory mention of the empire in the first passage dealing with Karl's anguish at the loss of his nephew, his reaction remains on the level of personal loss and bereavement. The emphasis is on individual spirituality, not on the state of the empire.[201] This passage affords glimpses into the major concerns of the *Karlmeinet* author, concerns that give his text a different slant than that of either Konrad or Stricker. While Konrad's *Rolandslied* is a portrayal of a holy war against the Saracens, and Stricker uses the betrayal and trial to discuss important political problems about lordship and conflict resolution, the *Karlmeinet* author seems to have as one of his major concerns religious devotion. The burial of the dead Franks as martyrs to the faith adds further weight to the forces bearing down on Wellis.[202] The Franks now turn their attention to finding him; at this point the *Karlmeinet* author introduces his version of Otto's capture of the traitor. Otto wants to capture Wellis, because of whom he has lost the emperor's favor (A493b, 34–38). The *Karlmeinet* author forces his reader to infer what Stricker brought out in great detail: that Wellis has gotten away from Otto, who did not pursue him forcefully enough. Consistent with his changes in the trial scene, the narrator leaves out the assistance of Wellis's relatives, as well as the desire of Otto's family to declare a feud against the emperor, reflecting the *Karlmeinet* author's decreased emphasis on familial power politics.[203] While the *Karlmeinet* writer omits some parts of the Otto narrative found in Stricker's version, he provides just as bloody a battle between Otto and Wellis as his predecessor did. Wellis has no alternative but to fight to the death; displaying the calculating nature common to all of the Genelun figures, he surveys the field and assumes, like Stricker's Genelun (11541), that Otto is alone, increasing his chances of making his escape if he can kill his opponent (A493b, 60–63). He tells Otto that he is going to pay him back for his accusations and has no fear of him if he has come by himself (A493, 55–59). In contrast to Stricker,[204] there are no references to God's direct intervention or any other suggestion that this encounter is anything other than a fight to apprehend a criminal (A494, 20–25).

Battle fatigue, plus the intervention of two fresh warriors, bring Wellis to his knees, destroying his arrogance and leading him to surrender his sword; unlike Genelun, Wellis takes from this point onward a passive role in the proceedings (A494, 26–32). In sharp contrast to Stricker, the *Karlmeinet* writer lets us hear only once, and briefly, from Wellis (A516b, 39–45) until the end, when he reintroduces Wellis as the penitent traitor — an addition of his own. After the loss of his sword, Wellis is stripped of his armor, bound, and placed on a horse. A bound person cannot speak for himself in court, so from a judicial point of view the *Karlmeinet* author's imposition of silence on Wellis as he awaits his miserable fate would be in keeping with legal custom.[205]

The end of the episode involving Otto, in which Wellis is delivered to Karl and the emperor reconciled with his vassal, has close affinities with the corresponding section in Stricker. The sight of Wellis provokes an emotional outburst on Karl's part, parallel to the passionate outpouring of grief seen in earlier passages (A495, 3–9). He sends Wellis away, ordering him to be tortured.[206] Karl welcomes Otto back into his favor, apologizing for his behavior and promising various kinds of reparations because of the burden he has laid on him. Because the *Karlmeinet* writer has left out the detailed passages in Stricker in which Karl denounced Otto and threatened him with the loss of his position if Genelun were not returned, these charges are only alluded to by implication in this adaptation. Perhaps the author, who continually shows Karl in a favorable or positive light, did not want to portray him losing his temper vis-à-vis an innocent peer but only shows him apologizing.[207]

Otto in this version gives a speech that reflects extraordinary forbearance and forgiveness — unlike that of Stricker's Otto, whose response is positive but measured. In contrast, *Karlmeinet*'s Otto did not resent the suffering he endured; he would have regretted missing it and, indeed, has simply disregarded everything Karl said in anger, because that anger was necessary. Otto would have died of sorrow had Wellis escaped. Now, as God willed it, and as Wellis's sin demands, he has been found. Otto values Karl's goodwill and friendly disposition toward him more than considerable property without Karl's favor. As in Stricker's version, Otto makes no demands about compensation but leaves that to Karl's grace. The different accents in this speech reflect the idealizing tendencies apparent in this writer's work. Otto's speech presents a core element of Christian ethics — personal suffering in terms of a higher good — and idealization of Karl.[208]

While Otto was never directly threatened by Karl if he lost Wellis, others were. In the doubling tendency to which he seems to be disposed, the *Karlmeinet* author lets follow, on the heels of Otto's enrichment, a commission to another group of nobles to guard Wellis. This scene does not exist in Stricker, but the *Karlmeinet* author threatens the nobles chosen to guard Wellis with penalties more severe than those Stricker's Karl levied against Otto when Genelun escaped: if Wellis gets away, his guards will suffer the fate reserved for him unless they leave Karl's lands (A496, 24–A496b, 34).

Like the *Rolandslied* and Stricker's *Karl der Grosse*, the *Karlmeinet* contains a scene with Alda (Alite in Stricker's text), Roland's fiancée, who expires on hearing of his death.[209] The brief account in the *Rolandslied* (8685–726), in which Karl breaks the news of Roland's death to Alda, offers to marry her to Ludwig, hears her rejection of any other marriage, and watches her die, is contained in the two later versions. Stricker and the *Karlmeinet*, however, expand the section. Both include messengers to Gerart, the guardian of his niece Alita/Alda; their journeys to Karl; and the news of Roland's death and its effect on her (A495b, 64–A512, 14). Both expand the one line in the *Rolandslied* (8728) about her burial with other saintly women. This section in the *Karlmeinet*, which at first blush seems somewhat extraneous, takes up approximately 17 percent of the narrative that begins with the council discussing an emissary to the heathens and ends with Wellis's conviction and death. Why did this writer expand it to such an extent? In what way is it related to our central concern, Wellis's trial and the legal proceedings surrounding it? Are other thematic tendencies brought out here that figure in Wellis's guilt and condemnation?

A constant element in this writer's shaping of the Roland material has been the great personal grief of Karl over the loss of his nephew. This anguish plays a major role in his determination to have Wellis convicted of murder. Consequently, a scene such as this one — which, in effect, is a doubling of earlier scenes in which Karl and his men must deal with the news of Roland's loss — gives Karl several occasions for accusation of Wellis, threats of corporal punishment for him, and new outbursts of grief as he tells Oliver's uncle, Roland's mother, and others about the peers' deaths due to treachery.[210] These passages show the effect of Roland's loss on those nearest and dearest to him; Berte, Roland's mother, seems to be near death from the shock as Karl urges her to revive herself and dedicate herself to charitable works as a response to Wellis's treachery, increasing the reader's sense of Wellis's villainy (A508b, 66–A509, 4). They also fit in well with the tendency toward personal religious expression and meditation on martyrdom and suffering that characterized late medieval religious life in northwestern Europe.[211]

Alda's death, common to all the sources, lays another implied burden of guilt at the feet of the traitor who caused the misery that broke her heart. The *Karlmeinet* author expands this scene greatly from Stricker's account, including scenes from her dream,[212] mystical experience, and religious devotion. Just as in the dream, Alda goes to the cathedral in which the bodies of Oliver and Roland lie in state. Lying in a faint, she hears the voice of Oliver, who says that she will leave this land and go with him and Roland (A509, 19–509b, 54). Although her only request is for a priest to hear her confession, a bishop comes; his position could reflect both her high rank and her sanctity, as is the case with Kunigunde and Richardis. After gazing at the bodies of Oliver and Roland, she bids farewell to her family and dies (A509b, 60–510b, 66). In an unusual interpolation in the first person the author tells us that he understands that the angels came and took her soul to heaven (A510b, 67–71). Through its attention to Alda's pure devotion, this extensive description, not present in earlier versions, implicitly contrasts Alda's goodness with Wellis's evil, which destroyed her by causing Roland's death.

The repeated description of the transports of grief Karl suffers when thinking of Roland's death once again bring forth the intervention of the barons, who call Karl back to the business at hand (A511, 1–40). These gentle but firm reproofs, not present in Stricker's version in the scenes under consideration, seem to function as barometers of the range of Karl's grief and not as an indication of a character flaw or a veiled attempt by the barons to take over. The emphasis on suffering that characterizes both Alda's and Karl's reaction to Roland's death is yet another indication that for this author the death of Roland through treachery was in a major way an occasion to express deepened religious sensibilities, reflecting religious currents of the time and region.[213]

With Roland, Oliver, and Alda committed to the grave, Karl turns to the pressing matter at hand: the trial of Wellis. In an unusually detailed passage, which differs from Stricker,[214] the princes advise Karl that he bring Wellis to trial in France. What is new in this section is the detailed description of Wellis's loss of rights: he will not be allowed to defend himself (A512b, 42) and will lose everything he possesses:

> Ind heysch em verdeylen[215]
> Leyn, eygen, ind wyff,
> Huys, lant ind lyff
> Ind lantrecht ind ere. (A512b, 48–51)

[And cause him to be deprived of contract, property, wife, house, land, life as well as his rights within his region and his honor.]

Once again this author shows that he is well aware of legal issues, because he gives a detailed list of what will be taken from Wellis. The term *lantrecht*, which did not appear in this passage in Stricker, seems to show a different legal consciousness.

These detailed descriptions of loss of legal rights and property, occurring in a council of princes, foreshadow what is to come. Making the journey back to France, Karl places Wellis's treason in a special context related to failure on Karl's part to fulfill his duty to his people, since he lost so many men in Spain. He asks for their forgiveness, then says that Wellis must pay for his deed with his life (A513b, 56; 514b, 39). Once again, Karl in this work, in contrast to that of Stricker, seems primarily moved by his own personal failure rather than by reasons of state, that is, the weakening of the empire through the loss of valiant peers. Unlike Stricker's Karl, he goes to the shrine of St. Dyonisius directly before the trial, asking for the saint's help in avenging the wrong Wellis has done (A515, 1–13) — yet another element in the increased tendency toward personal religious devotion characteristic of this version.[216]

The doubling of scenes noted earlier in this work appears again before the beginning of the trial in regard to the question of Wellis's appearance in his own defense. In each case, Karl laments his loss and accuses Wellis (A514, 33–514b, 39; A515b, 55–67]). In the first instance, Salomon of Brittany urges Karl to let Wellis, because of his standing, speak in his own defense during the proceedings. In this presentation he reflects some concern about Wellis's rank and, therefore, his position in the empire — concerns that were much more dominant in Stricker but are greatly reduced in this version. Salomon notes that while Karl has the final authority (A514b, 44), Karl should preserve both his reputation and his power by dealing with Wellis in a manner commensurate with Karl's station by letting him appear before the court, since Wellis himself is of princely rank. If he cannot make a defense, then he can be broken on the wheel (A514b, 40–62).[217] A similar passage appears shortly thereafter, just before Karl makes his formal accusation in Louwen before the court. Otyneir, a prince loyal to Karl, requests that Wellis, who is, after all, the husband of Karl's sister and has a dear son, be allowed to speak before the court. Otyneir points out that while Wellis has lost his reputation, he is still of noble birth. His word deserves to be heard, just as Karl's has been (A516, 1–21).

If the reader contrasts the length and detail of these scenes requesting a hearing for Wellis because of his station with the mere five lines devoted to the presence of his family who did not want him killed (A516, 27–31), one is struck by the contrast with Stricker's account, replete with lengthy discussions about the value of Genelun's family to the empire and the offers of compensation. Birth and rank still matter in late medieval Germany — certainly in Aachen — but the power struggle between the authority of the emperor and that of great families seems not to be an issue here.

Neither in this scene nor in the later one when Pinabel challenges the court does there seem to be a serious threat to Karl's control. Perhaps the main function of the scenes in which Karl is urged to give Wellis a chance to speak is to show that every opportunity was given the defendant and that Karl can be shown always to have behaved in an exemplary manner. The first accusation scene is quite brief: Karl accuses Wellis of treason, and Wellis denies it.[218] In Stricker's version Genelun bases his defense on the nobles' inborn right to declare publicly that a feud existed and then to do whatever they wanted to the offending party. Shrewdly counting on his familial relationship to the emperor and the importance of himself and his relatives, Genelun expects political expediency to carry the day (2433–50).

Although Wellis's first refutation of the charge of treason is cut short by Gundeluff's accusation that a Moor told him that Wellis had betrayed the Franks for money, Wellis's subsequent denial of guilt before the first judicial duel contains no mention of a state of feud (A517, 21–517b, 43).[219] Wellis's claim of innocence angers Gundeluff. Charging Wallis with *untruwe* and *missedait*, he bases his indictment on the testimony of a heathen prisoner he captured. Wellis swore an oath to the heathen king for silver and gold to betray Karl's men, depriving the emperor of Roland and thereby sullying not only his own baptism but also Christianity (A516, 54–A517, 20). To prove the veracity of his charges Gundeluff challenges Wellis to a judicial duel:

> Got sal id an eme wrechen!
> Wylt hey dar weder sprechen,
> Id en sy de waerheit,
> So byn ich also gereyt,
> Dat ich mit eme vechte,
> Ind mit dem gotz rechte
> Wyl ich en bedwyngen
> Ind wyl en dar zo brengen,
> Dat hey mit synem munde geit,
> Dat hey dyne man verreit. (A517, 11–20)[220]

[God should avenge it on him. If he wants to contradict the charge, saying that it is not the truth, then I am prepared to fight with him and with God's law, I will subdue him and bring him to the point where he states with his own mouth that he has betrayed your men.]

Gundeluff's invocation of divine assistance at two points in this passage underscores both the nature of the battle — that is, that it is an ordeal — as well as the religious devotion of Karl and his followers.

As a powerful king, Gundeluff knows that Wellis cannot refuse his challenge, since Wellis is not a monarch and is only connected with the emperor's family through marriage.[221] Wellis refuses to be intimidated, referring to Gundeluff merely as "the Frisian" (A517b, 39). Wellis offers his glove and, with it, the battle, according to French custom (A517b, 44–46).[222] Hostages are given, as in the later judicial combat. Characteristically for the literary duels, the combat takes place shortly after the challenge. In this case the combatants and their parties retreat to *herbergen* (A517b, 56), where they arm themselves for the confrontation. Compared with the subsequent judicial duel, the preparation time and the preduel scenes are much briefer; there are no more oaths or statements.

The narrator assumes a great deal of confidence in the ability of trial by battle to reveal the truth: Wellis knows that it would be dangerous for him to fight, because he had done wrong, so he rides around on his horse in such a way as to make his relatives believe that he is practicing maneuvers to see if the horse is suited for battle. When he gets to a far corner of the field, he gives his horse the spurs, deserting his relatives and hostages (A518, 4–25). Narrative interest at this point seems to overtake legal reality. Although in contemporary legal practice Wellis would now be considered guilty as charged because he did not appear for the battle, the narrator treats his readers to another hot-blooded chase resulting in a fierce fight and a continually defiant Wellis (A519, 25–A520, 28).[223] Wellis is then bound and brought before Karl. Even in the late Middle Ages a bound defendant was considered guilty, though his right to defend himself had been expanded.[224] Wellis is now in a most difficult legal position.

The ensuing scene with Karl delivering the charges against Wellis to the assembly and demanding an *ordel* have some close parallels to Stricker's text.[225] The crimes Karl lists involve both breaking of promises and homicide.[226] Because of these accusations, Wellis was supposed to fight to clear his name, but he fled the scene: Karl's inclusion of Wellis's flight was undoubtedly meant to make it harder for the nobility to acquit him.[227] The most significant change the *Karlmeinet* text makes in this section, and it is a major one, is the excision of the alleged state of feud as the justification for the betrayal of the Franks. Except for a brief reference near the end of the trial scene, when the verdict is in and a legal defense no longer relevant (A530b,

54–65), this justification is gone. Consequently, the *Karlmeinet* contains no feud-based legal arguments by Wellis's family; nor does Wellis appear before the court at the appropriate point in his own defense, as he does in the two older versions.[228]

While the judgment finders discuss Karl's charge to them, Pinabel and his men arrive. The *Karlmeinet* author carefully constructs this scene to extract the most narrative tension possible. The medieval audience wants to know who Pinabel is so they will know how much power he has at hand: he is the son of Wellis's sister and a prince himself, facts that have legal relevance during the course of this scene. The display of raw force by Pinabel stops the judgment finders in their tracks. They explain their action in terms of deference to Pinabel's close family ties to the accused (A520b, 45–A521, 3).

Changing the focus back to Pinabel, the narrator emphasizes his good qualities, citing his sources: Pinabel is brave, generous, and honorable (A521, 5–8).[229] Since Pinabel's defense of his errant relative will rest in part on a character reference, his own reputation needs to be made known. The narrator skillfully presents this scene much as one of the judgment finders must have seen it: first the shock of Pinabel's arrival, the recognition of him, the fact he comes with a small army. Then, as the onlookers have time to survey the scene before them, they believe that Pinabel is known to be a man of good character, they observe how large and well-armed the troops are, and they see the presence of a sword in Pinabel's hand: all of these perceptions prepare the listeners for his speech (A521, 5–18).

Because the *Karlmeinet* author has deleted the feud as a justification for Roland's betrayal, he also changes the role of the Genelun figure's champion. The *Karlmeinet* Pinabel comes armed with two legal arguments, which were not in either of the two previous works. The force of these defenses will be amplified by the presence of his knights.[230] The first is a character defense, a common form of proof in medieval courts;[231] the second concerns the eligibility of the judgment finders. Pinabel projects an image of confidence and moral outrage: the manner in which he addresses the emperor reveals how powerful he believes his position to be:

> Here, dyt ys eyn ouel dynck
> Ind eyn groesse ungenade,
> Dat yr mit quadem rade
> Myme oemen desen laster doet. (A521, 22–25)

[Lord, that is an evil matter and a great injustice, that you with false counsel perpetrate such slander against my uncle.]

This passage is replete with strong language: *ouel, ungenade, quadem rade,* and *laster*.[232] These expressions reveal the depth of Pinabel's indignation, which matches the heights of his character defense of his uncle. Wellis is now a mature man known for his many virtues and for the honorable deeds of his youth; never has there been any attempt at treason during his life (A521, 28–A521b, 1). The charge of treason, which Pinabel addresses directly, cannot be true because there is no previous evidence that Wellis had ever done such things. This line of defense has grounding in the text, from no less an authority than Karl himself: in the scene in which Roland nominates his stepfather for the mission, he praises Wellis's experience and bravery (A440, 1–18), as do the nobles (A440, 20–24).[233] In the face of Wellis's anger and fear, Karl assures Wellis of his high standing (A440b, 67).

Pinabel's second line of defense rests on Wellis's reputation in the empire and the eligibility of the judgment finders. Karl has no peer of his stature, whether French, Lothringian, Bavarian, Flemish, Norman, or Burgundian. Pinabel demands that Karl allow him *gerichte*, which seems to be a request to have a part in the verdict regarding Wellis. His explanation following this request is linguistically ambiguous and introduces an element missing in the earlier trial scenes, *lantrechte*:

> Off yr versaget mir gerichte,
> Ich en laissen ys neit so lichte,
> Ich en kome ys in arbeyt,
> Wan ich byn here so gereit,
> Dat ich vur en vechte
> Na myme lantrechte. (A521b, 45–50)

[If you deny me my day in court, I will not take that lightly; I won't come into difficulties should that happen, because I came prepared to fight for him, according to the law of my land.]

On the face of it, the text does not allow us to determine if Pinabel is prepared both to do battle and to fight a judicial duel according to his *lantrechte*.[234] He asserts the equal standing, if not the primacy, of his *lantrechte* over against those of the empire.

While the introduction of *lantrechte* into the *Karlsepik* seems new, the cowardice of the nobles vis-à-vis a display of force from a powerful family is not. Struck both by Pinabel's openness and his strength of will (backed up, of course, by force), they ask Karl to acquit him (A521b, 61–A522, 9). The *Karlmeinet* Karl reacts angrily, just as Stricker's Karl did, but in a much-abbreviated passage (A522, 10–21). In contrast to Stricker's Karl, the *Karlmeinet* Karl does not threaten to abdicate: he says only that he would fight Wellis himself rather than let him go (A522, 17–18). The almost perfunctory manner in which this scene from Stricker is treated in the *Karlmeinet* adaptation is most striking. The *Karlmeinet* author has not only dismissed the feud as a legal defense and a political issue but has also dropped the power struggle between the nobles and Karl and Karl's threat of abdication. In these omissions there is a high level of consistency: whoever his patron was, and whatever his own origin and background were, the *Karlmeinet* author seems not to be interested in imperial power struggles. This state of affairs could certainly point to a writer in holy orders who was more interested in a good story involving the themes of treason, pain, and personal devotion.

The *Karlmeinet* author is, as we have seen, perfectly capable of adding material that interests him, as well as of embroidering incidents. In contrast to the two earlier Charlemagne epics, two older nobles accuse Wellis of treason and offer to do battle. In his use of two specifically legal terms, Oiger seems almost to function as a judge: the legal meaning of *erkennen* is for a judge to decide or to condemn someone to death, while *verdeilen* means to deprive someone of something — in this case, Wellis of his life — through a verdict.[235] Once again the *Karlmeinet* author reveals both his background knowledge of the law and his ability to make rather precise changes and adaptations.

> Ich erkennen Wellis gare.
> Hey is eyn verredere.
> Ich wil en offenbere
> Hee verdeilen syn leuen. (A522b, 44–47)
>
> [I condemn Wellis completely. He is a traitor. I want to deprive him of his life openly (that is, before the court).]

Oiger continues to function as the prosecuting judge when he criticizes Pinabel's defense, given in the face of Wellis's attempted flight (A522b, 41–61). The *Karlmeinet* author has shown a consistent tendency to put either good advice or Karl's opinions into the mouths of his closest retainers. If this author was writing in an urban environment, with a powerful noble patron, that could explain the repeated emphasis he gives them. Here, however, there may be another narrative reason for their inclusion. Karl rejects their service because of their age (A522b, 62–66), whereupon a *kynt*[236] [un-knighted lad], Dederich Lamp, offers to do battle.

Dederich differs from his counterparts in Stricker's and Konrad's works: there he is a blood relative of Roland and, therefore, would have been expected to fight.[237] The *Karlmeinet* Dederich has quite a different motivation. He is immediately introduced as "eyn vry man" [a free, privileged man] (A523, 5) and the son of a nobleman, probably a minor one. Reasons other than identification are in play here: standing was important in trial by battle.[238] After Dederich lost his father, he served Roland, who was going to knight him at Whitsun — plans foiled by Wellis's treachery (A523, 10–24). The verbal boldness of the young, inexperienced boy foreshadows his courage in battle: "Dat ordel wyl ich sprechen, / Dat eme verdeilt ys syn leuen" [I will deliver the verdict that deprives him of his life] (A523, 26–27). This passage also contains the proper legal terminology that describes the reasons why the trial by battle must take place.[239] As with Stricker's Dietrich, Dederich repeatedly invokes God's help, seeing God as the avenger of Roland (A523, 25, 31; A523b, 34, 36, 37; A524, 29).

Unperturbed by the fact that Dederich has not been knighted or tested in battle, Karl accepts his offer, repeatedly emphasizing that God has sent them this exemplary young man (A523b, 44, 50–51, 56; A524, 3–4). Karl's faith in God, consistent with the saintly aura with which this writer surrounds him, makes him certain that this rather questionable military quantity would carry the day. If the audience for this work was an urban one, the acceptance of an unknighted boy from a minor family must have been popular with them.

Dederich's challenge brings forth an arrogant and condescending answer from Pinabel, an addition of the *Karlmeinet* author. Calling Dederich a young fool, Pinabel includes in his speech a comment that appears in other ordeals by battle when one of the combatants seems vastly superior in strength: when you call for mercy, it will be too late[240] (A524, 26–28). In his reply Dederich moves from the legal considerations of his last statements to Pinabel's sinful nature, accusing him of arrogance and pride, which leads him to do evil in his attempt to save Wellis (A524, 29–A524b, 39). Once again, he asks God to be his aid.[241] In spite of his youth and inexperience, Dederich here behaves like the respected counselors of Karl's court, who have just offered themselves as champions.

Legal terms and considerations abound in the narrator's descriptions of preparations for the judicial duel. The narrator notes approvingly that the combatants offer surety with the gloves (A524b, 41–43). The taking of hostages receives much attention: Pinabel sends Wellis, two prominent peers, and others, as Karl demanded. Karl sets strong terms: he swears by his crown that he will treat them as traitors if they are so foolhardy as to take on the murder and the other sins of Wellis (A524b, 45–59).[242] The change in emphasis from Stricker's work at this point is remarkable, however. Instead of accepting any enthusiastic volunteers from among Genelun's highly optimistic relatives, as was the case in the Stricker work, Karl specifies which prominent family members he wants. No such conviction of Pinabel's ultimate triumph appears. The Stricker text says that any hostage who is willing to defy the empire in such a way deserves to die, giving a specific political justification, while the *Karlmeinet* author, though he mentions treason, places the reason for their suffering the same fate as Wellis in their support for his murder and other sins.[243] Deemphasis on imperial concerns and politics is, as we have seen, typical for this later work, as is the definite lack of emphasis and interest on the power of aristocratic clans.

The place in which the judicial duel was to occur was the occasion for some dispute. Pinabel wants the battle to take place right away, but Karl, once again in council with his nobles, decides to move the site of the duel to Aachen, because he can have his German princes at hand, of whose loyalty he is assured (A524b, 60–A525, 10).[244] This section is the only significant incident in the *Karlmeinet* version of the trial in which reference is made to the possibility of hostility breaking out between the supporters of the emperor and the members of Wellis's family. Possibly the narrative justification for the amount of detail the writer devotes to the long list of Karl's adherents, predominantly from central and northern German lands, is his predilection, apparent earlier in this work, for describing either a real or a potential battle (A525, 4–30). Certainly he builds on hints in the earlier *Karlsepik* immediately prior to the judicial duel that the potential for an outbreak of fighting between adherents of opposing sides was likely in this highly charged atmosphere.[245] In his own version of the preduel procedures, the *Karlmeinet* author once again draws some of his favorite nobles into arrangements to cover an eruption of combat, such as bringing a thousand armed knights into the area.[246]

The *Karlmeinet* author's portrayal of the battle scene has telling similarities with and differences from that of Stricker. Like Stricker, he pays attention to the legal context: Karl presides over his court, noting the agreement for the judicial duel and calling for hostages (A525b, 44–51). As in Stricker, Karl arms Dederich. In the *Karlmeinet*, however, the significance of this arming is different, because Dederich is not Roland's relative as he is in the earlier work, where he would be part of Karl's extended family. The arming of a minor, unknighted noble by the emperor would have been a welcome narrative element to a late medieval urban audience, just as would have been the choice of this individual who was at a lower level on the social scale. Other differences, which parallel the *Karlmeinet* version's earlier emphases, involve the role and prominence of the leading peers, especially Oyger, who functions as an adviser to Karl. The author seems to take every opportunity to put these nobles, particularly Oyger, in a positive supporting position.[247]

The *Karlmeinet* compiler also added to his account of the judicial duel an oath-swearing scene involving the relics of St. Patrick, a choice that has direct connections to Karl and Aachen. Consistent with the strong tendency in the *Karlmeinet* to private devotion and the cult of the saints, another new element in this scene is Karl's command to bring St. Patrick's bones onto the field for the swearing of oaths prior to battle:[248]

> Dat dede hey durch de lyste,
> Want hey wael wyste,
> So we dar vp ouel swoer,
> Dat hey vele sere mysvoer,
> Dat was en ouch kundich. (A526, 14–18)

[He did this for intelligent reasons, because he knew well that whoever swore badly (that is, falsely) on (the relics) went grievously astray, that was known to him.]

Swearing a false oath on the relics of a saint made the saint himself part of the legal proceedings: with his *auctoritas* and *fides,* he functions as a guarantor of truth.[249] He stands surety for events taking place long after his death; immortality is not unreality but a part of reality superior to human existence. In such circumstances a false oath becomes the means to condemn the swearer, who has misused the saint, thereby bringing retribution from higher forces on his head.[250] God does not delay in manifesting his displeasure in Pinabel's oath that Dederich is a liar and guilty of perjury. When Pinabel tries to kiss St. Patrick's relics, he cannot, because God will not allow it: the oath was not suitable.[251] In contrast, Dederich has no problem in venerating the saint in this way.

In the *Karlmeinet* version of the battle scene the author again shows his awareness of legal custom: the judges of the judicial duel he chooses are nobles of high station (A526b, 60–A527, 2).[252] The place of battle is clearly marked out: an open, smooth green field (A527, 22–25). In his final challenge to Pinabel, Dederich once again accuses Wellis of treason and murder and rejects a cowardly truce (A527b, 35–40). This section does not appear in either Konrad's or Stricker's work, while the midbattle offer common to the earlier versions, in which Pinabel offers Tirrich/Dietrich both homage and fiefs for a cessation of hostilities, is missing.[253] Since the major difference between the Dietrich figures is one of social standing, with the two earlier Dietrichs related to Karl and the *Karlmeinet* Dederich an orphaned scion of the lower nobility, the *Karlmeinet* author may have felt that such an offer on the part of Pinabel was incommensurate with Dederich's station.[254] Perhaps for these reasons the *Karlmeinet* author moves the exchange prior to the battle, with only a brief reference by Dederich to the cowardly truce.

The battle scene itself contains some changes from the earlier versions. Gone are the references to Durndart and the characterization of Pinabel as the devil's man that we find in Stricker. Instead, there is much praise of Kurtan and, by implication, its donor. Dederich even makes a speech to his sword (A528, 31–34). Pinabel, calling Kurtan the devil's weapon, gives a detailed account of its effectiveness, citing the loss of his good hand (A528b, 35–44). The other major change is the specificity of the *Karlmeinet* author about the various battle wounds. He mentions a wound in the side; another between the helmet and shield; the cutting off of Pinabel's hand, which falls in the sand; and the slashing of nose, chin, and beard (A528, 18–20, 23–24, 27–28; A529, 1–5). These examples parallel his morbidly precise descriptions of various forms of capital punishment in the quartering of Pinabel and in the verdict scene.

Pinabel's death occasions a lengthy section of praise to God by Karl, which has similarities to other prayers by the emperor in this work. He emphasizes God's grace and his own unworthiness, which remind us, once again, of Karl's saintliness. Karl describes God as the highest judge, who cannot tolerate injustice (A529, 17–40). In a connection to the passage where the relic for St. Patrick is brought out, the author notes that whoever swears a false oath subjects himself to God's anger and revenge.[255]

Pinabel's fate brings other changes and additions by the *Karlmeinet* author. Instead of the beheading found in the two earlier works, he is hanged, which was considered a more dishonorable death.[256] As is his wont, the author gives an unusually vivid picture of the disposal of the corpse, noting that Pinabel still wore part of his armor and was fastened on a gallows with ropes (A529b, 50–57). In this case, Pinabel's death both fulfills an earlier promise by Karl and foreshadows Wellis's fate (A529b, 50–62).[257]

Dederich, already the recipient of a greater share of Karl's largess than his station would allow him to expect, now receives even more honor and recognition: the young hero, weakened greatly by loss of blood, is brought to the palace at Aachen, where Karl kisses him on the mouth and orders him brought to his own quarters so that no medical treatment will be lacking. He then promises Dederich *lant ind guet*, because he desires to make him rich (A530, 4–19). The striking changes that the *Karlmeinet* author makes in the Dietrich figure — culminating in this great reward after Dederich's victory, which is not in the Stricker text — make a compelling case for arguing that the *Karlmeinet* author had a different audience, for whom he wanted to make the story more appealing. Certainly Karl's treatment of Dederich differs sharply from the two earlier versions, where the Dietrich figure, a blood relative of the emperor, does not receive any special mention. If the home of the *Karlmeinet* is, indeed, Aachen, we might suspect that this audience would include individuals of nonnoble birth who would enjoy seeing advancement based on merit.

The emphasis on Karl as the representative of God's justice on earth, which we have seen in the condemnation of Pinabel, continues in the sentencing scene when Karl goes to mass prior to the opening of court (A530, 25–31). Unlike his literary predecessors, this Karl accuses Wellis yet again, and Wellis makes a singular speech. This speech, which has no counterpart in the earlier versions, where the Genelun figure is mute after the judicial duel, is remarkable on several counts: it contains an admission of guilt, the stirrings of repentance, and the desire to die a good death.[258] These additions are important for an understanding of how the *Karlmeinet* author shaped his own version. After Karl has reminded him once again of his crimes — murder, treachery, and the death of his nephew — Wellis shows some regret and admits that Roland died because of his evil counsel:

> Here, ich en mach noch neit enkan
> Gelouen mynre *myssedait*.
> *Leyder* durch mynen *boesen* rait
> Lyt Rolant nw doyt.
>
> Id was mir alsulch *vngemach*,
> Dat ich id *vnsanffte* wrach
> An *vnschuldigen* luden.
> Dat *ruwet* mich huden,
> Dat ich dar an haen *mysdaen*.
> (A530b, 50–53; A530b, 63–A531, 1)

[Lord, I neither want to nor can believe my sin; unfortunately through my bad advice Roland now lies dead. . . . It [the trip to Marsilie] was such an injury to me that I avenged it in a rough way on innocent people. It grieves me greatly now that I have done wrong in this way.[259]]

Remorse was foreign to the two Geneluns in the earlier German versions, but the number of words in these passages that indicate wrongdoing or regret (see italics) make it hard to ignore Wellis's contrition.

The significance of this change for the different approach of the *Karlmeinet* writer can hardly be overstated; the subsequent analysis will suggest that currents in popular religion in the fourteenth-century northern German lands could have influenced this strikingly different end for the Genelun character. Between these two admissions of guilt and regret, Wellis makes only brief and indirect references to a feud:

> Ich dede id euer durch noyt,
> Ich endede id ane schult neit,
> Want hey schoff ind reit,
> Dat ich zo Marselis wart gesant
> Zo Zarragotzen in dat heyden lant.
> Dat dede hey durch de schulde,
> Dat hey vele gerne woulde,
> Dat ich dar verlore myn leuen.
> Dat enmochte ich eme neit vergeuen.
> Id was mir alsulch vngemach,
> Dat ich id unsanffte wrach
> An vnschuldigen luden. (A530b, 54–65)

[I did it, however, out of necessity, and not without reason, because he arranged things so that I was sent to Marselie in Saragossa in heathen territory. He did that for a reason, because he really wanted me to lose my life. I could not forgive him for that. It was so upsetting to me that I avenged it in a hateful manner on innocent people.]

The lengthy discussions of the declaration of a state of feud, replete with legal language, that play such a major role in Stricker's version are barely mentioned here, and, with the exception of the word *wrach,* no legal terminology is used.[260] With so little space devoted to it, the feud for this writer is obviously an issue of little importance.

For the *Karlmeinet* author, the main emphasis in Wellis's speech is on regret and reluctance to undergo the horrible corporal punishment that will surely follow. Throwing himself on God's and the emperor's mercy, Wellis admits that he has done wrong and greatly fears the torture that he must endure (A531, 1–5). This fear is further proof of his recognition of his guilt, since one does not fear punishment unless he is conscious of his guilt.[261] He believes that this punishment will benefit his soul:

> Id is recht, dat myn lyff
> Gearne de mysdait,
> Vp dat der selen werde rait. (A531, 8–10)

[It is just that my life is penance for my sin, so that it will go well with my soul.]

This attitude represents a striking new element in the Genelun figure's characterization, one that could reflect popular religious attitudes of the period, including the marked emphasis on confession and penitence.[262] The added importance attached to confession of one's sins reached a fever pitch in the fourteenth century; this tendency began after the canon *Omnis utriusque sexus* issued by the Fourth Lateran Council in 1215, in which the faithful were required to go to confession once a year at Easter. The increasingly heavy emphasis on this aspect of religious life among the laity can be seen in the lives of fourteenth-century saints and in religious literature; certainly, the clerics of the *Marienstift* in Aachen would have been intimately acquainted with these tendencies.[263]

Wellis's speech reflects an additional current in popular religion in the northwest German lands in the fourteenth century: dying a good death. Not only was achievement of this goal beneficial to the villain's soul, a concern that Wellis himself expresses (A531, 8–10); it also benefited those who suffered from his crimes, for whom he feels remorse (A530b, 64–66). The good death of the criminal removed the pain of the murderer's victims, who died unexpectedly, without last rites.[264] The state of one's soul, the necessity for personal devotion, which this writer consistently brings out, is far better served with the portrayal of a penitent Wellis hoping to die in God's grace than with the traditional Genelun figure, hateful and unrepentant to the end as he silently meets his inevitable fate.

For Karl and his nobles, however, the main value in Wellis's sentence and its execution is its potential to serve as a warning example, a deterrent to future crime. That belief comes to the fore again and again in the discussion of possible punishments. This addition, which comes at the end of the treason trial, consists of the plethora of punishments offered for Wellis. In the earlier *Karlsepik* of medieval Germany, the *Rolandslied* and *Karl der Grosse,* the only death sentence mentioned for Genelun is the traditional one for treason: being torn apart by horses; and Stricker even notes that that was not done any more (*Karl der Grosse* 12119). In sharp contrast, the *Karlmeinet* author lists an array of choices. Karl asks his princes to order a horrible death for Wellis, the boon companion of Judas (A531, 20).[265] He asks specifically that the punishment be extremely painful and arouse great anxiety, pain, and horror (A531, 12–18). As he has done before, the *Karlmeinet* author brings the peers of the realm to the fore, including two who figure frequently in the events at court, Oyger and Gerhart. These five princes then suggest, in some detail, public executions they feel would be suitable (A531, 24–A532b, 47). The range of possibilities begins with Gerhart's suggestions that Wellis should be pulled naked through the kingdom, beaten all the while, as a warning example to Karl's subjects.[266] Gerhart emphasizes the deterrent effect of such a punishment:

> Ind laist lude mede gaen,
> De en mit geyselen sere slaen
> Dat vleyse van den beynen,
> Dat de lude alle gemeyne
> Iamer on eme seyn,
> Op dat id numme moge gescheyn.
> Dat by spele sal hey der werlt geuen. (A531b, 39–45)

[And allow people to go along who beat him with switches, taking flesh from the legs, so that all may see his misery publicly, that it may never happen again. He should give the world this example.]

Since Wellis will never commit any more crimes, the obvious advantage of this type of death is the audience participation.[267]

Another lord suggests that he be burned alive; a more innovative Salomon proposes that Karl starve his lions and vultures for a few days, so that they are full of hunger and anger, then turn them loose on a bound Wellis. The explicitly gory description of dining activities by the animals, including the drinking of Wellis's blood, continues the marked tendency toward terrifying detail that characterizes this section. Oyger suggests that the traitor be put in prison for two days and taken out on the third, as if he were to be released. Then he should be given a meal of highly salted food with nothing to drink. An oven should be fired and Wellis seated inside, where he would die of thirst as Roland died in Ronceval. The last punishment suggested, which is the one chosen, is for him to be pulled apart by four horses, so that his flesh is scattered everywhere and devoured by animals. Count Otmar, who makes this suggestion, adds that people will talk of it for centuries to come:

> ... de was Iudas geselle,
> Dat man id zo wunder zelle
> Her na ouer dusent iaer! (A532b, 45–47)
>
> [He was Judas's companion, which people will consider in amazement for more than a thousand years!]

The need for an example to serve as a deterrent is quite obvious here, and it is emphasized even further in the description of Wellis's death. The horses cover a great deal of territory, including woods, boundary posts, and stony areas — presumably mountains — dispersing his body over a wide area, including shrubs, meadows, and thorny bushes (A532b, 64–A533, 2). The narrator comments that Wellis paid for his misdeed so severely that people always will tell it in amazement and repeat it as an example to all Christian people, so that God will keep them from such a thing through his great goodness and mercy (A533, 3–13).

Neither Konrad's nor Stricker's work contains such a gruesome excursus; whether the *Karlmeinet* author had another source or added this material on his own, he and his readers must have had a context for this grisly catalog, a context certainly not in evidence for Stricker's audience a hundred years earlier. This section, plus the novel appearance of a penitent Wellis, give the *Karlmeinet* quite a different cast. While the question of individual predilection must remain unanswered, are there any currents in early fourteenth-century Rhineland culture that could account for these rather striking departures? What symbolic aspects related to Wellis's crime would have been attached in the popular mentality to each of these punishments? There are suggestive answers in the areas of political authority, the criminal justice system, and popular religious culture that can all enhance understanding of this problematic text. We shall be looking briefly at the role of public executions in maintaining governmental authority, the increasing emphasis on corporal punishment in the criminal justice system, and changes in popular religious culture, including an increased emphasis on penance and on the agonies of the crucifixion of Christ, in order to suggest a framework for this unusual departure from the sources.

As we look back at the spectacle of public execution in the High Middle Ages, tendencies that continued well into the early modern period, we find a world so different from our own that it is hard to keep out anachronistic attitudes, such as the modern view that physical suffering must be avoided, whatever the cost. Medieval people knew that in the course of their lives they could expect to suffer unbearable pain simply because of the absence of anesthesia and lack of effective analgesics. The ubiquitous presence of pain had a religious dimension, as well. Christianity has always advocated a transformation of life's inevitable miseries into a path to holiness, a tendency that was markedly more prominent in the late Middle Ages with the voluntary mortifications of the flesh of many saints, including St. Francis. Pain was seen as a purgatorial force.[268] The spectacle of a body ravaged by pain or corporal punishment was an important part of public life, as well as of one's inner devotional life. In civic life this spectacle in the late Middle Ages would have been a public execution; in religious life meditation on Christ's crucifixion included an active imagining of Christ's suffering as one went through the Stations of the Cross.[269]

Not only the death itself but also the type of punishment prescribed had symbolic significance and was meant to convey various messages to the onlooker. Late medieval penal practice in the German lands sought to remove all physical trace of the individual convicted of capital crimes. Certain types of deaths and the manner in which one went to them were reserved both for certain crimes and for certain classes. The fact that many of the means of conveyance to the death and the death itself could involve infamy or the loss of honor played a role in the punishment of the victim and his family.[270] For example, being bound on the way to the site of execution was a source of infamy, particularly to an aristocrat accustomed to complete freedom of movement.[271] Decapitation, because it was swift and involved less violence to the body, was seen as the most honorable form of execution, while hanging was a common punishment for thieves.[272] Beyond these were the deaths reserved for archcriminals, and it is here we find those mentioned for Wellis. The torture-executions mentioned above, which involved a longer period of suffering, fall into this category. Burning was considered a disgraceful death because it involved the destruction of the body.[273] An execution that involved consumption of body parts by animals also belonged in the category of deaths of ultimate degradation. The body was denied Christian burial; was lowered to the realm of the animals, since it provided food for them; and was totally destroyed. Animalization in criminal cases almost always involved some kind of betrayal, as is obvious in the case of Wellis.[274] In the sentence of death through tearing apart by horses it is animals, not even the universally despised executioner, who perform the killing. No more telling indictment of Wellis and his behavior in the eyes of his peers could be given than this gruesome series of horrible punishments.

Although the preceding discussion has attempted to suggest aspects of a framework in which this section of the *Karlmeinet* could be understood, it has not dealt with the question of why the writer includes so much gruesome detail. In addition to the demonstration of the emperor's absolute power, there is another answer to this question that involves developments in art, literature, and judicial practices taking place in northwestern Europe and in the area of the Rhineland in which the *Karlmeinet* was written.[275]

Developments in art were influenced by the Passion narratives, which by the fourteenth century included a large lay audience reaching to the merchant middle class.[276] Characteristic of these late medieval accounts of the Passion are detailed descriptions of Christ's sufferings, which Thomas Bestul connects to the revival and broad dissemination of judicial torture arising from the increasing influence of Roman law and the decision of the Fourth Lateran Council in 1215 forbidding clerical participation in the ordeal. A fourteenth-century text, *Christi Leiden in einer Vision Geschaut*, serves as a particularly influential example.[277] The following excerpts from this text are representative examples that parallel in degree of physical detail the discussion of punishments in the *Karlmeinet;* the first occurs during the beating prior to the crucifixion, the second during the attempt to nail Christ to the cross:

> Darnach slugin en di anderin echte mit geiseln, die hatte Pylatus dün machin von rindes huden mit starckin kneufin unde warin dý uber gozzin mit blie, unde dý kneufe waren also groz alse eyn hassel nüz. Da midde slugen sie en alse sere, daz sie daz fleisch von deme gebeyne riezzin, daz die stücke des fleischis an dem libe hinge unde man das gebeine sach. . . .
>
> . . . sie namen yme dy rehtin hant unde zogin sie yme zü deme loche des astes unde slugen yme eynen neyl dar durch. Der neyl was stümp unde dryeckete unde die eckin warin scharp alse eyn meßir, unde furte yme fiele der hut und auch des fleischis durch das loch des cruces, unde slugen den neyl so faste, daz der knauff des neylis in der hant gebaugit stunt unde fulte die wonden so ful, das eyn bludes drü (e nyt dar uz mochte. Da namen sie da die andern hant unde zugen sie yme ubir des cruces este, da was die hant so ferre von dem loche, daz sie iz nyt yn mothte gelangen. Da namen sie eyn seil unde dadin yme eynen strick an die hant unde zogin yn so faste, daz die aderen unde die geliedere uz eyn andere gningin, daz die hant gereichete daz loch. (*Christi Leiden* 38, 42)
>
> [Thereafter they beat him again and again with scourges, which Pilate had made from cattle hides with strong knots, which were covered with lead and the knots were as big as a hazel nut. With these they beat him so much, that they tore the flesh from the bones, so that the pieces of flesh hung from the body and one could see the bones. . . . They took his right hand and pulled it to the hole in the branch (that is, the arm of the cross) and pounded a nail through it. The nail was blunt with three corners sharp as a knife and took with it much of the skin and flesh through the hole of the cross, and they pounded the nail so hard that the head of the nail was bent into the hand and filled it so that blood could not drip from it. Then they took the other hand and pulled it over the arm of the cross, but the hand was so far away from the hole that they could not make it reach. So they took a rope and put

it on the hand and pulled it so tightly that the tendons and the limbs separated, so that the hand then reached the hole.]

The probable Rhenish origin of this text, with its intense attempts to re-create Christ's Passion, parallels developments in the legal system in this region. Torture as a judicial procedure deeply affected the Rhineland, where it was well established by the end of the thirteenth century. These currents in the larger society would have increased familiarity with the spectacle of torture in the court system, which Bestul believes could have influenced the portrayal of Christ's suffering in the Passion, where contemporary, nonbiblical methods of torture appear in the narrative. Such parallels reflect a well-developed judicial mechanism ready to offer effective punishments for grievous offenses against the body politic.[278]

Located as he seems to have been at the center of religious life in Aachen, the *Karlmeinet* writer would have been surrounded by the explosion of Passion art and narrative. Could not the *Karlmeinet* text attempt to do verbally what contemporary Crucifixion art of the period did visually? To facilitate the desired inner perceptions, the gruesome details had to be spelled out, just as they were in art of the Passion. The *Karlmeinet* writer uses words to produce in the reader the abhorrence and deterrent effect both the narrator and Count Otmar mention at the end. The matter-of-fact character of their descriptions suggests a familiarity with such procedures on the part both of the author and of his audience.[279] Such familiarity contrasts sharply with Stricker's explanation and justification of Genelun's punishment to his audience and reflects the striking changes between attitudes toward corporal punishment in the two works, separated by about 100 years.

The *Karlmeinet* text suggests that the severity of the punishment will keep it in people's memory, so that they may pray that such a terrible fate will never befall them. Count Otmar predicts that it will be talked of for more than a thousand years. The chief value of such an execution lay not in the degree of cruelty and suffering inflicted on the guilty party but on its statement of imperial power and its deterrent effect. Displaying the awesome might of the state was the first goal; if that was effectively done through means that seem bestial to us, the cruelty was a means to an end, but not the end in itself.[280] As the inquisitorial aspects of a trial became more secret in the late Middle Ages, owing in part to the demise of the ordeal, which could function as a public inquisitorial process, the only part of the legal course of events that remained public and allowed the state to assert its authority was the spectacle of the completion of the sentence.[281]

In the context of presenting a life of Karl as exemplary emperor for the times and circles in which Stricker and the *Karlmeinet* author moved, these writers also use the Genelun/Wellis treason trial and ordeal as a means to emphasize ideas and issues that they saw to be important. Trial by battle could serve as a narrative structure to reflect contemporary concerns because it continued to be used in secular courts through the fourteenth century and beyond and could, therefore, function as a framework in which to address current issues. Therefore it is not surprising that Stricker's *Karl* and the *Karlmeinet,* written more than a century apart for different audiences, show marked variations in the account of the trial and the ordeal.

For Stricker, writing for a secular court, the paramount issue surrounding Roland's death and Genelun's treason was the implications for the might of the empire. This concern consistently shapes Stricker's presentation, from Karl's initial reaction about the rebellious regions to the emphasis on imperial justice rather than the recourse to feud. Self-help justice, private revenge with no interference from the reigning monarch, even though the victim was the emperor's nephew — this scenario is Genelun's impossible dream. His relatives, anxious to preserve his life and aristocratic prerogatives, continue in the response common to those who wish to settle a feud — the payment of reparations. In their stubborn and desperate attempts to save Genelun's life and redeem their reputations, they align themselves with him and his position, thereby sharing the opprobrium that Genelun, as a boon companion of Judas, must bear. Because of Karl's insistence that Roland's death was a blow to the might of the empire and the Church's earthly mission, those who insist on the justice of Roland's death in terms of feud rights are themselves condemned by their adherence to the system of self-help justice. Legal customs thus become a means of characterization in Stricker's work, with the profeud faction representing the forces of negative behavior that weakens the power of the empire. Karl's approach, that of court-imposed physical punishment for an offense against the body politic, is fused with Karl's responsibilities both for the empire and for the Church; the resort to the courts and the imposition of the death sentence is part of his positive characterization.

Karl's threat to abdicate if his conditions are not met shows how closely he links his imperial power with the imposition of the verdict: were he not able to enforce it, he could not exercise his authority to protect the empire. Not only Genelun but also his entire family has to suffer for his treason, reflecting the power Karl has as the highest judicial authority to inflict reparations — not as the result of a feud but as the highest judicial authority, charged with the maintenance of order.

For the *Karlmeinet* writer secular political considerations, such as power struggles between the nobility and the crown, receive a decreased degree of emphasis, with the virtual excision of the feud as a rationale for Wellis's defense. The significance of noble families also lessens in this later work: while Karl relies on the advice of individual peers, the role of Wellis's family in his defense is greatly reduced, while the Dietrich figure, a member of the lower nobility in this work, has no family ties to Roland as he does in Stricker. While the maintenance of imperial authority remains important, it appears more closely related to Karl's role as the representative of God's justice on earth, as evidenced in the frequent remarks about the deterrent effects of Wellis's execution. The connection of Karl with St. Patrick — whose relics, in a scene not found in Stricker's or Konrad's works, appear just before the judicial duel — further underscores Karl's religious authority in the dispensation of justice.

These changes could well reflect the concerns of a clerical compiler active in the northwest German lands at a time in which changes in judicial practice, including the growing use of torture and the tendency in late medieval German penal practice to remove all traces of the malefactor's body, fused with currents in art, literature, and theology reflecting an increasing emphasis on the events surrounding Christ's Passion. The detailed catalog of gruesome punishments, Wellis's remorse and concern that he die a good death, and the gory description of his end could mirror the civic and religious culture of a fourteenth-century northwest German city such as Aachen.

The *Karlmeinet* author and Stricker were both intimately acquainted with the law and its workings in their time. These works were, of course, written for patrons, whose own reasons for commissioning such lengthy biographies must remain hidden. What we do know is that the two works reflect different legal and cultural milieus and use the legendary prestige of Karl to propagate these attitudes to their readers. Earlier critics' summary dismissal of them as pallid and uninteresting translations must now be revised. These works have much to add to our understanding of late medieval German attitudes toward imperial authority, as well as evolving feelings about crime and punishment, and they deserve to be much better known by both Germanists and historians.

Notes

[1] Since the critical literature connected with the *Song of Roland* is vast, the following bibliographic references are designed only to point the reader to sources that will provide an introduction to the topic. For a general discussion of the genre of the chansons de geste and the *Song of Roland*, as well as an authoritative translation, see Gerard Brault, *The Song of Roland: An Analytical Edition* (University Park & London: Pennsylvania State UP, 1978), introduction 1–30; Edward A. Heinemann, "Chansons de Geste," *Dictionary of the Middle Ages,* vol. 3 (New York: Scribner, 1983), 257–62; Gérard Moignet, *La Chanson de Roland* (Paris: Bordas, Larousse, 1969), 5–19; Karl D. Uitti, *Story, Myth and Celebration in Old French Narrative Poetry, 1050–1200* (Princeton: Princeton UP, 1973), 65–127. More-recent studies include Dominique Boutet, *La chanson de geste* (Paris: PU de France, 1993) and Sarah Kay, *The* Chansons de geste *in the Age of Romance* (Oxford: Clarendon P, 1995).

² Documents close in time to the event suggest that Charlemagne may have been motivated, as well, by appeals from Spanish Christians for aid. See Brault 1, 3; Moignet 6.

³ *Einhardi Vita Karoli Magni*, ed. G. H. Pertz, G. Waitz, O. Holder-Egger (Hannover, 1911; rpt. Hannover: Impensis Bibliopolii Hahniani, 1965), 12–13; Brault 1–3; Moignet 11.

⁴ Moignet 5–11; Brault 1–3; Heinemann 258, 260. Boutet, *La chanson* says that the interplay between oral and written narratives plus the rewriting of earlier versions offers the most fruitful analytical approach (8–9). Two important older studies that emphasize oral elements of the narratives are Jean Rychner, *La Chanson de geste: Essai sur l'art épique des jongleurs* (Geneva: Droz, 1955) and Joseph J. Duggan, *The Song of Roland: Formulaic Style and Poetic Craft* (Berkeley: U of California P, 1973), while Madeleine Tyssens, *La Geste de Guillaume d'Organe dans les manuscripts cycliques* (Paris: Société d'édition "Les Belles Lettres," 1967) argues for written transmission. See also S. Nichols, *Formulaic Diction and Thematic Composition in the Chanson de Roland*, University of North Carolina Studies in Romance Languages and Literatures 36 (Chapel Hill: U of North Carolina P, 1961); R. Howard Bloch, *Etymologies and Genealogies: A Literary Anthropology of the French Middle Ages* (Chicago & London: U of Chicago P, 1983), 100–107. For a recent study that discusses the chansons de geste in their historical context see Dominique Boutet, *Formes littéraires et conscience historique: Aux origins de la literature française* (Paris: PU de France, 1999), 109–37.

⁵ Erich Köhler, *Ideal und Wirklichkeit in der höfischen Epik: Studien zur Form der frühen Artus- und Graldichtung* (Tübingen: Niemeyer, 1970), 5–6.

⁶ Einhard describes Charles's attention to Frankish law, *Vita* 33. See Robert Folz, "Charlemagne en Allemagne," *Charlemagne et l'Épopée Romane*, vol. 1, Actes du VIIe Congrès International de la Société Rencesvals (Paris: Les Belles Lettres, 1978), 98–101. Other evidence for Karl as the paradigmatic lawgiver of the Middle Ages abounds. See Sigurd Graf von Pfeil, "Karl der Grosse in der deutschen Sage," *Karl der Grosse*, vol. 4: *Das Nachleben,* ed. Wolfgang Braunfels and Percy E. Schramm (Düsseldorf: Schwann, 1967), 326–36: 326–27; Udo Von der Burg, *Strickers Karl der Grosse als Bearbeitung des Rolandsliedes* (Göppingen: Kümmerle, 1974), 155; and *Saxon Mirror* 17, 31, and 67, where the second prologue to the codex invokes Charlemagne along with Constantine as Christian rulers who advanced Christ's law. Frieder Schanze, "'Kaiser Karls Recht,'" *Verfasserslexikon*, vol. 4 (Berlin & New York: De Gruyter 1983) cols. 945–47, describes a song [*Meistergesang*] of 1493 that continues the tradition of Karl as a lawgiver. Ruth Schmidt-Wiegand, "Kaiserchronik," *HWBDR*, vol. 2: cols. 548–52 notes that in this highly influential work the main duty of emperors was the administration of justice (col. 549). For work on pictorial representations of Karl relating to the law, see Marianne Ott-Meimberg, *Kreuzzugsepos oder Staatsroman? Strukturen adeliger Heilsversicherung im deutschen Rolandslied* (Zurich & Munich: Artemis, 1980), 4 n. 7; Kroeschell, *Deutsche Rechtsgeschichte* 76. See also Norbert Ott, "Reich und Stadt: Karl der Große in deutschsprachigen Bilderhandschriften," *Karl der Große als vielberufener Vorfahr,* ed. Lieselotte E. Saurma-Jeltsch (Sigmaringen: Thorbecke, 1994), 87–111; 108–10 regarding the iconographic significance of the picture type *David rex et propheta,*

which is used in the *Sachsenspiegel*. Karl alone functions as the founder and guarantor of the law not only for Eike's collection but also for others, such as the *Schwabenspiegel* and city codes of the late Middle Ages; see, in this context, Dietlinde Munzel-Everling, "Sachsenspiegel, Kaiserrecht, König Karls Recht? Überschrift und Prolog des Kleinen Kaiserrechtes als Beispiel der Textentwicklung," *Alles was Recht war: Festschrift für Ruth Schmidt-Wiegand zum 70. Geburtstag,* ed. Hans Höfinghoff (Essen: Item, 1996), 97–111.

[7] Matthias Becher, *Karl der Große* (Munich: Beck, 1999), 118–19. See also Lieselotte E. Saurma-Jeltsch, "Karl der Große als vielberufener Vorfahr," in *Karl der Große als vielberufener Vorfahr,* ed. Saurma-Jeltsch, 9–17; André Moisan, "Le rayonnement de l'épopée de Charlemagne à travers l'Occident," *Cahiers de Civilisation Médiévale Xe–XIIe siècles,* 39 (1996): 373–77 gives a brief account of the early process of epic formation (374–75); Helmut Beumann, "Grab und Thron Karls des Großen zu Aachen," *Karl der Große,* vol. 4: *Das Nachleben,* ed. Wolfgang Braunfels and Percy E. Schramm (Düsseldorf: Schwann, 1967), 9–38; Gerhard Lohse, "Das Nachleben Karls des Grossen in der deutschen Literatur des Mittelalters," *Karl der Große,* vol. 4, 337–47, notes (437) that the opening of Karl's grave by Otto further increased interest in the legendary emperor.

[8] Karl Bertau, *Deutsche Literatur im europäischen Mittelalter,* vol. 1 (Munich: Beck, 1972), 74–77. Renate Kross, "Zum Aachener Karlsschrein," *Karl der Große als vielberufener Vorfahr,* ed. Lieselotte E. Saurma-Jeltsch (Sigmaringen: Thorbecke, 1994), 49–61 discusses the controversies surrounding the creation of the various sections of the Karlsschrein; for information about Friedrich II, see 55–56.

[9] Von der Burg, *Strickers Karl* 213, 223; Wolfgang Spiewok, "Karl der Große als Maezen und Literarische Figur," *Das Rolandslied des Konrad: Gesammelte Aufsaetze von Danielle Buschinger und Wolfgang Spiewok* (Greifswald: Reineke, 1996), 1–13; Becher 120. Saurma-Jeltsch, "Karl," 14–15 notes that in contrast to the French Charlemagne tradition, the German one makes him a saint. The canonization was performed by the counter-pope Paschalis III, which seems to have slowed its acceptance. Karl-Ernst Geith, *Carolus Magnus: Studien zur Darstellung Karls des Großen in der deutschen Literatur des 12. und 13. Jahrhunderts* (Berlin & Munich: Francke, 1977) notes that Stricker's *Karl der Große* is the first work in German in which clear reference is made to Karl's canonization (169).

[10] Munzel-Everling 111. By the late Middle Ages legends in which Karl was the central figure and the cult of Karl as a saint were firmly anchored in the lands between the Rhine and the Elbe; Zurich became a second Aachen, while Frankfurt and Nuremberg venerated Karl to extraordinary degrees. See Matthias Zender, "Die Verehrung des Hl. Karl im Gebiet des mittelalterlichen Reiches," *Karl der Große,* vol. 4, 100–112 (102–3, 105, 107). See also Danielle Buschinger, "Pouvoir central et principautés territoriales: Perspectives allemandes sur le monde épique à la fin du moyen âge," *Actes du XIe Congrès international de la Société Rencesvals* (Barcelona: Real Academia de Buenas Letras, 1990), 151–64 (153–54) for a discussion of Karl's political importance in fourteenth-century German lands.

[11] Folz, "Charlemagne" 77.

[12] See Ott-Meimberg, *Kreuzzugsepos* 7; Becher 120; Saurma-Jeltsch, "Karl" 11; Geith, *Carolus Magnus* 33, 263–64; Petra Canisius-Loppnow, *Recht und Religion*

im Rolandslied *des Pfaffen Konrad* (Frankfurt am Main & New York: P. Lang, 1992), 69. See the famous statement "God is Law itself" in the first prologue of *The Saxon Mirror* (67); Fritz Kern, *Gottesgnadentum und Widerstandsrecht im früheren Mittelalter: Zur Entwicklungsgeschichte der Monarchie* (Münster & Cologne: Böhlau, 1954) contains a discussion of the relationship of German rulers to the law (122–37).

[13] Marianne Ott-Meimberg, "'*di matteria di ist scone.*' Der Zusammenhang von Stoffwahl, Geschichtsbild und Wahrheitsanspruch am Beispiel des deutschen Rolandslieds," *Grundlagen des Verstehens mittelalterlicher Literatur*, ed. Gerhard Hahn and Hedda Ragotzky (Stuttgart: Kröner, 1992), 17–32 (21); Kern, *Gottesgnadentum* 124–25; Horst Fuhrmann, *Einladung ins Mittelalter* (Munich: Beck, 1987), 200.

[14] Ott-Meimberg, "Zusammenhang" notes (20) that because these stories were known to be historical, they differ from almost all other literary material in the medieval German lands; Helmut de Boor and Richard Newald, *Geschichte der deutschen Literatur von den Anfängen bis zur Gegenwart*, vol. 1 (Munich: Beck, 1949), 240–49; Bertau 462–70. The story in which Karl figures as a crusader has its roots in the tenth century, when Andre of Monte Soratte reported that Karl had made a pilgrimage to Constantinople and Jerusalem. At the beginning of the twelfth century, after the First Crusade, a monk from St. Denis wrote a report about Karl's pilgrimage. Both monks used these legends to explain the presence of important relics in their houses: for Monte Soratte, the bones of the Apostle Andrew; for St.-Denis, a nail of the Cross and the Crown of Thorns. The *Chanson*, which appeared in the twelfth century, suited the crusade mentality of the time. See Becher 119. Konrad also knew the *Kaiserchronik*, written in Regensburg around 1146, and cites it extensively; see Horst Richter, *Kommentar zum Rolandslied des Pfaffen Konrad, Teil I* (Bern: Herbert Lang, 1972), 328–29.

[15] See Friedrich Ohly, "Die Legende von Karl und Roland," *Studien zur frühmittelhochdeutschen Literatur*, ed. L. P. Johnson, H.-H. Steinhoff, and R. A. Wisbey, Cambridge Colloquium 1971 (Berlin: Schmidt, 1974), 292–343 (311); Karl-Ernst Geith, "Das deutsche und das französische Rolandslied: Literarische und historisch-politische Bezüge," *Kultureller Austausch und Literaturgeschichte im Mittelalter*, ed. Ingrid Kasten, Werner Paravicini, and René Pérennec (Sigmaringen: Thorbecke, 1998), 75–84 (75–77).

[16] Ott-Meimberg, "Zusammenhang" 23–24.

[17] The *RL* has attracted the lion's share of critical attention. Because legal questions in general and the trial scene in this work have been extensively analyzed, this study will only use the *RL* and related critical material as a point of reference. Canisius-Loppnow's excellent study contains an extensive legal analysis of issues surrounding Genelun's trial (211–70). For an earlier analysis see Ott-Meimberg, *Kreuzzugsepos* 163–210. Monika Schulz, "'Was beduerfen wir nu rede mêre?' Bemerkungen zur Gerichtsszene im 'Rolandslied,'" *ABÄG*, 50 (1998): 47–72 also discusses the trial scene in the older work.

[18] Writers of vernacular epics were free to portray it as they wished, causing a growth in the number of stories about this attractive and doomed hero. See Ott-Meimberg, "Zusammenhang" 22.

[19] Ruth Schmidt-Wiegand, "Prozeßform und Prozeßverlauf im 'Rolandslied' des Pfaffen Konrad," *Recht, Gericht, Genossenschaft und Policey: Studien zu Grundbegriffen der germanistischen Rechtshistorie. Symposion für Adalbert Erler,* ed. Gerhard Dilcher and Bernhard Diestelkamp (Berlin: E. Schmidt, 1986), 1–12 gives a description (5) of Konrad's approach to legal matters in his text that seems to be applicable to both Stricker and the *Karlmeinet* (*KM*) writer, as well: to resolve apparent contradictions and introduce different motivations through omissions and additions, according to each writer's obvious knowledge of the legal customs of his era. As an example of such a major change, she cites the role of the judicial duel in the *RL*, which, according to German custom, becomes part of the process of proof, of establishing the truth — a condition that obtained in older German law for cases of treason. While her remark pertains to the *RL*, it also has validity for the later intra-German adaptations.

[20] Fr. Konrad's work remained the major source for Stricker and the *KM* narrator-compiler. There seems to be general agreement that both later writers had other sources, but there is no certainty as to what these sources were. The relation of Stricker's work to the *KM* is also unclear, complicated as it is by the existence of virtually identical passages. See Von der Burg, *Strickers Karl* 224–81; Karl-Ernst Geith, Elke Ukena-Best, and Hans-Joachim Ziegeler, "Der Stricker," *VF,* vol. 9 (Berlin: De Gruyter, 1993) cols. 417–49 (col. 422); Hartmut Beckers, "*Karlmeinet*-Kompilation," *Die deutsche Literatur des Mittelalters: VF,* vol. 4, ed. Wolfgang Stammler, Karl Langosch, and Kurt Ruh (Berlin: De Gruyter, 1983) cols. 1012–28 (cols. 1012, 1021–22). He notes that like Stricker, the *KM* author makes a dramatic departure from Konrad after v. 8658, prior to meeting with Alda and the subsequent trial scene (cols. 1021–22); Udo von der Burg, "Konrads *Rolandslied* und das *Rolandslied* des *Karlmeinet*," *Rheinische Vierteljahrsblätter* 39 (1975): 321–41, gives a good summary of the history of critical problems about the relationship of the two works; R. Zagolla, *Der Karlmeinet und seine Fassung vom Rolandslied des Pfaffen Konrad* (Göppingen: Kümmerle, 1988) compares Fr. Konrad's work with a *KM* manuscript but does not deal with the trial scene; see his remarks about possible sources (277–78); Edith Feistner, "Karl und Karls Tod: Das 'Rolandslied' im Kontext des sog. '*Karlmeinet*': Biographische Zyklik und ihre Implikationen," *Wolfram-Studien XI: Chansons de geste in Deutschland: Schweinfurter Kolloquium 1988* ed. Joachim Heinzle, L. Peter Johnson, and Gisela Vollmann-Profe (Berlin: E. Schmidt, 1989), 166–84; Gertrud J. Zandt, "Bemerkungen zu einer Neuausgabe einiger Abschnitte des Rolandteils aus der *Karlmeinet*-Kompilation," *ABÄG* 30 (1990): 151–58; Susan E. Farrier, *The Medieval Charlemagne Legend: An Annotated Bibliography* (New York: Garland, 1993), 143 lists both Fr. Konrad and Stricker as sources for the *Karlmeinet*.

[21] Examples of this attitude include Dieter Haacke, "Konrads Rolandslied und Strickers Karl der Große," *PBB* 81 (1959): 274–94; Haacke believes that Stricker's work was written primarily for entertainment. Ohly, "Legende" 311–12 has a brief negative section on Stricker's version. Dorothea Klein, "Strickers 'Karl der Große' oder die Rückkehr zur geistlichen Verbindlichkeit," *Wolfram-Studien* 15 (1998): 299–323 sees Stricker's version as a hagiographic life (315–23); her account does not analyze the trial scene or compare it with Konrad's version. Ott-Meimberg, *Kreuzzugsepos*

4 says that with Stricker's *Karl* the literary interest in the Karl material in the German lands was finished.

[22] Critical opinion has finally begun to catch up with the high esteem in which the work was apparently held in the Middle Ages, when there were more than forty manuscript versions. Two fourteenth-century manuscripts, St. Gallen, Kantonsbibliothek Vadiana, Cod. 302 and Berlin, Staatsbibliothek zu Berlin, Preußischer Kulturbesitz, Ms.germ. Fol. 623, are far above the average illustrated manuscript in regard to the stylistic level, the expense of the paints, and the artistic quality. The St. Gall manuscript occupies a significant position in the history of upper German book painting. See Ott, "Reich und Stadt" 93–95.

For recent positive analyses, see Rüdiger Schnell, "Strickers 'Karl der Große': Literarische Tradition und politische Wirklichkeit," *ZfdPH* 93, Sonderheft (1974): 50–80 (51, 77–78); Canisius-Loppnow 34–38; Rüdiger Brandt, *Erniuwet: Studien zu Art, Grad und Aussagefolgen der Rolandsliedbearbeitung in Strickers "Karl"* (Göppingen: Kümmerle, 1981).

For other brief recent references to Stricker's *Karl*, see Schulz 71–72, no. 88; Spiewok 13; Sabine Böhm, *Der Stricker — ein Dichterprofil anhand seines Gesamtwerkes* (Frankfurt am Main & New York: P. Lang, 1995), 149–50. A useful recent overview of Stricker's work, Daniel Rocher, "Hof und christliche Moral: Inhaltliche Konstanten im Oeuvre des Stricker," *Mittelalterliche Literatur und Kunst im Spannungsfeld von Hof und Kloster,* ed. Nigel F. Palmer and Hans-Jochen Schiewer (Tübingen: Niemeyer, 1999), 99–111, gives a helpful brief account of Stricker reception, with occasional remarks about *Karl* (101–2).

An early discussion of the political ramifications of Stricker's work, Rudolf Köster, *Karl der Große als politische Gestalt in der Dichtung des deutschen Mittelalters* (Hamburg: Hamburger Verlagsanstalt K. Wachholtz, 1939), 39–43, suffers because of the political distortions of the time. Köster sees antipapal, pro-Hohenstaufen tendencies in Stricker's adaptation. See also Geith, *Carolus Magnus* 16.

[23] For example, Von der Burg, *Strickers Karl* 152–53 notes that while Stricker only added about 500 lines to Konrad's version in the first half of his own work, in the second half he added 1,400 — particularly in relation to Karl, Roland, and Genelun.

[24] See Friedrich Ohly, "Zu den Ursprüngen der Chanson de Roland," *Medieaevalia litteraria: Festschrift für Helmut de Boor* (Munich: Beck, 1971), 135–53.

[25] See Marguerite Rossi, "Le duel judiciaire dans les chansons du cycle carolingien. Structure et fonction," *La Chanson de geste et le Mythe carolingien: Mélanges René Louis,* vol. 2 (Saint-Père-sous-Vézelay: Musée archéologique regional, 1982), 945–60, for helpful remarks about the judicial duel's function in literary texts.

[26] Erudition is a hallmark of this nonaristocratic writer's work; see Karl Bartsch's introduction to his edition of *Karl,* where he notes that the name Stricker is synonymous with "poet" (1); John Margetts, "Die erzählende Kleindichtung des Strickers und ihre nichtfeudale orientierte Grundhaltung," *Das Märe: Die mittelhochdeutsche Versnovelle des späten Mittelalters,* ed. Karl-Heinz Schirmer (Darmstadt: Wissenschaftliche Buchgesellschaft, 1983), 316–43 (340).

[27] Otto Brunner's *Land und Herrschaft* (Vienna: Rohrer, 1965), originally published in 1939, is still useful for an understanding of the feud in medieval life (1–110). In 1992 Howard Kaminsky and James Van Horn Melton translated it as *Land and*

Lordship: Structures of Governance in Medieval Austria (Philadelphia: U of Pennsylvania P). Brunner notes that attempts to limit and ultimately abrogate the feud and self-help were a constant problem for the state throughout the Middle Ages (17, 32). See also Gerd Althoff, "Genugtuung (satisfactio): Zur Eigenart gütlicher Konfliktbeilegung im Mittelalter," *Modernes Mittelalter,* ed. Joachim Heinzle (Frankfurt am Main & Leipzig: Insel, 1994), 247–65 (247–48); Holzhauer, "Zum Strafgedanken" 179–92 deals with the feud and the issue of punishment (181–84).

[28] Historians of medieval Germany have analyzed this problem extensively in recent years. See Gerd Althoff, "Königsherrschaft und Konfliktbewältigung im 10. und 11. Jahrhundert," *FMS* 23 (1989): 265–90; Althoff, "Konfliktverhalten und Rechtsbewußtsein: Die Welfen in der Mitte des 12. Jahrhunderts," *FMS* 26 (1992), 331–52; Timothy Reuter, "Unruhestiftung, Fehde, Rebellion, Widerstand: Gewalt und Frieden in der Politik der Salierzeit," *Die Salier und das Reich: Gesellschaftlicher und ideengeschichtlicher Wandel im Reich der Salier,* ed. Stefan Weinfurter and Hubertus Seibert (Sigmaringen: Thorbecke, 1991), 297–325.

[29] Althoff, "Königsherrschaft" 277–78.

[30] Althoff, "Königsherrschaft" 288–89.

[31] Althoff, "Königsherrschaft" 265–76.

[32] Althoff, "Königsgewalt" 278; Althoff, "Konfliktverfahren" 337.

[33] Althoff, "Konfliktverhalten" 332–34, 351–52. Althoff notes that Barbarossa's suit against Heinrich den Löwen is often cited as an example of the rule of law in such matters (332). See also Eberhard Schmidt, *Einführung in die Geschichte der deutschen Strafrechtspflege* (Göttingen: Vandenhoeck & Ruprecht, 1965), 55–56.

[34] Here it is important to distinguish between the knightly feud and blood revenge; the latter is how Rudolf His describes the nonknightly feud of the countryside and town: *Geschichte des deutschen Strafrechts bis zur Karolina* (Darmstadt: Wissenschaftliche Buchgesellschaft, 1967), 59–62. See Schmidt 47–48. See also Ekkehard Kaufmann, "Selbsthilfe," *HWBDR,* vol. 4, section 2, cols. 1615–16; *DRW,* vol. 3, cols. 445–48.

[35] Schmidt notes that with the *Lütticher Gottesfrieden* of 1082 the truce of God movement reached the border of the empire (49–50). Between 1083 and 1085 it was established in the archdiocese of Cologne and in Saxony at Goslar and in 1085 at the great synod in Mainz, where most of the episcopate and Henry IV took part. During the investiture controversy, the *Landfrieden* began to predominate.

For a brief and informative survey of twentieth-century research directions on the feud and armed conflict among the upper strata of society see Reuter 299–301. See also Ruth Schmidt-Wiegand, "Mord und Totschlag in der älteren deutschen Rechtssprache," *Forschungen zur Rechtsarchäologie und Rechtlichen Volkskunde* 10 (Zurich: Schulthess, Polygraphischer Verlag, 1989), 47–84 (56).

[36] See Reuter 306–8.

[37] Dietmar Willoweit, "Gewalt und Verbrechen, Strafe und Sühne im alten Würzburg-Offene Probleme der deutschen strafrechtsgeschichtlichen Forschung," *Die Entstehung des öffentlichen Strafrechts: Bestandaufnahme eines europäischen Forschungsproblems,* ed. Willoweit (Cologne, Weimar & Vienna: Böhlau, 1999), 215–33 (220–21). In his introduction to this collection of essays, "Programm eines For-

schungsprojekts" (1–12), Willoweit discusses his German Research Council project, the rise of a public penal law, and the ruling methodological assumptions his project seeks to correct. Willoweit believes that the progression to the monopoly by the state of the right to punishment was much more erratic and inconsistent than earlier studies in legal history had suggested. Holzhauer, "Zum Strafgedanken" gives a brief summary of research on this point (179–81).

[38] See Reuter 300.

[39] Ekkehard Kaufmann, "Fehde," *HWBDR*, vol. 1, cols. 1083–93 (cols. 1083–91); Joachim Gernhuber, *Die Landfriedensbewegung in Deutschland bis zum Mainzer Reichslandfrieden von 1235* (Bonn: Röhrscheid, 1952), 13–14, 49; Brunner, *Land und Herrschaft* 35; Heinrich Mitteis, "Land und Herrschaft: Bemerkungen zu dem gleichnamigen Buch Otto Brunners," *HZ* 163 (1941): 255–81 (264); Althoff, "Konfliktverhalten" 332.

[40] Kaufmann, "Fehde" col. 1091.

[41] Mitteis observes that the limitations on feud rights did not run in a straight, irreversible line throughout the Middle Ages (264). The struggle against the feud could not succeed with mere prohibitions; rather, the state had to take positive concrete steps against it, such as the building up of a comprehensive system of justice.

[42] Line references to Stricker's work will appear in the text with the abbreviation *KG* where appropriate. The edition used is *Karl der Grosse von dem Stricker*, ed. Karl Bartsch (Berlin: De Gruyter, 1965). The lines in the introduction referred to here are 63–114.The edition used for the *Rolandslied* (*RL*) is Carl Wesle, ed., *Das Rolandslied des Pfaffen Konrad*, 2nd ed., ed. Peter Wapnewski (Tübingen: Niemeyer, 1967). The edition used for the *Karlmeinet* (*KM*) is the 1971 reprint (Amsterdam: Rodopi) of Adalbert von Keller's 1858 edition (Stuttgart: Litterarischer Verein).

[43] In Stricker's work pertinent differences from the *RL* that relate to the trial scene occur even at the very beginning. In contrast to Konrad, Stricker opens with an account of Karl's youth and the plan of his two half-brothers, Wineman and Rapote, to murder him — a plot foiled by Karl's vassal, Count Diepolt. When Karl returns to claim his inheritance, their remorse occasions his pardon. The two serve Karl and God thereafter with great fidelity [*triuwen*] (145–264). This short narrative section has the themes of betrayal and murder by relatives at its heart, just as the Genelun material does: "den vil mortlîchen sin" (168). The element of secrecy, as the subsequent discussion of Roland's death will show, was what set murder apart from manslaughter. Murder [*mort*] was also the term used to describe Genelun's crime. Karl's reaction to the treachery of his half-brothers, however, differs markedly from his reaction to Genelun's evil deed. In the light of Karl's reaction to Roland's betrayal, the reasons for this difference in behavior seem to lie in two areas: the brothers' reaction and the effect of their treachery. Unlike Genelun, they show repentance on Karl's return. While one may question the motivation for their regret, it contrasts sharply with Genelun's total rejection of remorse or guilt. The second reason for Karl's clemency may lie in the fact that no permanent harm was done, whereas Roland's death had a serious impact on the empire. Wineman and Rapote's misdeed seems to be treated more like a family matter, unlike that of Genelun, which damaged the state.

[44] *RL* 6075–76, "der kaiser begunde uor angesten swizen, / er chom ain tail uz sinen wizen" [the emperor began to perspire out of fear, / he became somewhat irrational] are missing in Stricker's description of Karl, though related passages occur in the *KM*. The only reproach to Karl (7134–36) comes from Genelun, who accuses the emperor of inappropriate reaction to fears about Roland. These lines could be interpreted as a further indication of Genelun's willingness to distort situations to his advantage.

[45] *Ungetriuwe* does not occur in the corresponding *RL* text; in Stricker it is immediately linked with treason: "zuo der vil grôzen riuwe / schalt in der ungetriuwe, / Genelûn der verrâtaere" [For this great misery, Genelun the traitor, the faithless one, reproached him] (7123–25). In addition, Stricker's Karl has already raised the question of *triuwe* [fidelity] in his commission to Genelun before his journey to the Muslims. Karl will make him richer than any prince, therefore he expects that Genelun will negotiate as a loyal vassal (2166–72).

[46] "du hâst mir alle die verlorn, / an den mîn êre elliu lac" [You have lost for me all of those on whom my fame totally rested] (7140–41).

[47] "an im [Roland] stêt elliu dîn êre" [On him rests all of your reputation] (433).

[48] Schnell notes the contrast with the *RL*, which mentions only the crusade against the heathens in Spain, while *KG* lists fourteen lands that must be conquered ("Strickers 'Karl'" 62). Schnell notes, as well, that the angel does not mention religious motivation for the conquest; indeed, the call for a crusade comes only after the lands are subjugated. (468–69) Schnell's interpretation of this passage adds support to the thesis that Roland's death has serious political implications for Karl in Stricker's account of the trial scene.

[49] Literary stepfathers had no easier time of it in medieval epic and romance than they probably did in real life; see Bouchard 77–78. Genelun seems to have appeared in an ambivalent position vis-à-vis Roland at the outset.

[50] In 2 Samuel 4 Saul's son, Ishbosheth, who is innocent of any wrongdoing against David, is killed in his bed by his captains Baanah and Rechab. Expecting a reward from David, they meet their death at his hands because they have slain a righteous man. If this passage is the one to which Stricker refers, it has several connections to the theme of treachery, since Ishbosheth was betrayed by his men and was avenged by the future king, David.

Medieval rulers frequently saw themselves as David figures: see Hugo Steger, *David Rex et Propheta* (Nuremberg: Carl, 1961), 128.

[51] "dem du den tôt hâst gegeben" [whom you have killed] (7146).

[52] Planck, *Gerichtsverfahren* I, 357.

[53] Genelun's *mortlîcher rât* [murderous counsel] (7157). For a discussion of the legal aspects of the accusation, see Planck, *Gerichtsverfahren* I, 359–60, esp. 360. Hirsch says that the accusation begins the penal procedure and forces the judge to apprehend the accused or, if he flees, to order his capture (Hans Hirsch, *Die hohe Gerichtsbarkeit im deutschen Mittelalter,* 2nd ed. [Darmstadt: Wissenschaftliche Buchgesellschaft, 1958], 36–37). G. Buchda, "Anklage," *HWBDR*, vol. 1, cols. 171–75 (col. 172) says that in the Middle Ages the legal process usually began with a private accusation. In "Gebärdensprache im mittelalterlichen Recht," *FMS* 16 (1981): 363–79 Ruth Schmidt-Wiegand notes that the accuser, with the accusation,

puts the matter in court and gives up the private justice of the feud or blood revenge (369).

[54] Stricker spells the name with an "i" rather than an "e".

[55] The passages in question are *RL* 6101–13 and *KG* 7155–68. See Canisius-Loppnow 217 and no. 22; Brunner, *Land und Herrschaft* 78; Bouchard 22–23.

[56] Reuter 318: "Das Einleiten eines 'Gerichtsverfahrens' bedeutete durchgehend die Absicht einer härteren Vorgehensweise. Der Herrscher konnte durch seine Kontrolle über das sogenannte Hofgericht im Extremfall eine Art konsensuales Ausschließen eines Magnaten aus der politischen Gemeinschaft so gut wie erzwingen und gleichzeitig die anderen Mitglieder der politischen Gemeinschaft als Träger seines Konflikts miteinbeziehen" [The introduction of a "court proceeding" generally indicated the intent to proceed with a more severe course of action. The ruler could, through his control of the so-called *Hofgericht,* force in an extreme case a kind of consensual expulsion of a magnate from the political community and, at the same time, involve the other members of that community as the supporters of his conflict].

[57] "du solt in leben lân, / im wirt ein tôt an getân, / daz sîniu kint und ir kint/ gesmâhet und geschendet sint" [You should let him live, he will have a death inflicted on him that will disgrace and dishonor his children and theirs] (*KG* 7165–68). See Hirsch, *Gerichtsbarkeit* 37.

[58] An earlier passage in the work, however, shows to the extent to which Karl could be bound by the decision of his council. In the scene in which Genelun convinces the council that Roland is the best person to leave in charge of the forces remaining in Moorish territory (3501–24) Karl is full of concern and anguish but does not dare counter their decision [ers in niht triwete versagen] (3504). This passage is similar to its counterpart in the *RL* (2965–84), but the *KM* version (A451b, 41–52, 693–94), which is often close to the *RL* text, diminishes greatly the influence of the council. Klein, "Strickers 'Karl'" 301–2 does not include either this passage or the trial scene in her discussion of Stricker's apparent reduction of conflicts of interests between the nobles and Karl.

Gerd Althoff addresses the effect of various types of affiliations in his "Konfliktverhalten," where he notes (335): "Bei der Austragung von Konflikten, . . . wurden im Mittelalter eben nicht nur die herrschaftlichen Bindungen aktiviert und genutzt, sondern gleichermaßen die verwandtschaftlichen und die freundschaftlich/ genossenschaftlichen" [In the settlement of conflicts in the Middle Ages, . . . not only the political ties were activated and used, but also those arising out of friendship or collectives]. Stricker gives an example of the fluidity of alliances in conflict situations earlier in this work: when Genelun returns from his traitorous mission, he secretly enlists the support of the unsuspecting Bavarian Naymis, who has Karl's ear. Playing on the strength of Naymis's influence with the emperor, he asks Naymis to urge Karl to accept the commitments Genelun has made (3266–352).

[59] "des nam sîn êre ein ende" [his high standing came to an end because of that] (7171).

[60] See Canisius-Loppnow 218–20 for a discussion of the significance of the donkey ride, which is common to both versions (*RL* 6123–26).

⁶¹ See *RL* 8339–570; *KG* (10100–300); *KM* A485, 8–A487b, 57. Common to all three accounts are the phrases used to describe Karl: *gotes chemphe* (*RL* 8453), *gotes kempfe* (*KG* 10160), and *godes kempe* (*KM* A485, 24) All three works speak of God's judgment (*urtaile, RL* 8546; *urteil, KG* 10279; *ordel, KM* A487. 15) at the end of the battle, given directly in a voice from Heaven. While the outcome of the judicial duel was supposed to be God's will, the fact that God himself renders the verdict, instead of making it apparent by the choice of the victor, indicates the importance of the battle of the Christians against the heathens, as well as the preeminence of Karl, either as a saint or as an emperor or both. Only Stricker, however, adds another detail that comes directly from the procedural rules in trial by battle: "In was alsô gerumet, / daz si dehein griezwarte schiet" (10152–53). "An open space was made for them so that no warden had to separate them."

⁶² In the *RL* this scene comes immediately before the climactic battle with the heathen (7534–80); in Stricker it appears immediately prior to the apprehension and trial of Genelun (10505–719).

⁶³ (10510, 10521); *neve* also noted in 10531, 10555, 10574, 10630, 10639, and 10656. The *RL* only refers to it once more (7511). See Canisius-Loppnow 133–34 for a discussion of the meaning of *neve*. As in the *RL, neve* is used in the specific meaning of Karl's sister's son. Konrad's work mentions the relationship only (7511), not the *triuwe*, in this context.

Stricker's mention of Karl's great *triuwe* toward Roland leaves open the possibility that this bond might presuppose legal actions on his nephew's behalf. It is particularly striking, coming as it does at the beginning of this section and before the repeated references to their blood relationship. See Karl Kroeschell, "Die Treue in der deutschen Rechtsgeschichte," *Studi Medievali* 10 (1969): 465–89 for an analysis of the meanings of *fides, fidelitas, infidelitas*, and *fides facta* in the Middle Ages (476–87). Kroeschell sees no evidence for Germanic or German *Treue*; he does find legal evidence for a strictly formal relationship in the sense of a contract; where there is an emotional element in the relationship, the source is Christian virtue, not the Germanic world. (487). See also Frantisek Graus, "Herrschaft und Treue: Betrachtungen zur Lehre von der germanischen Kontinuität," *Historica* 12 (1966): 5–44, who notes that a *Treuepflicht* in a legally binding sense did not exist before the Carolingian period and was only fully developed in the Middle Ages (8).

⁶⁴ Sigrid Widmaier, *Das Recht im "Reinhart Fuchs"* (Berlin: De Gruyter, 1993), 26. Hirsch, *Gerichtsbarkeit* 35 says that in cases of wrongful death, the death is an insult to those remaining behind, as well as a damage that must be made good. Therefore, the relatives are called upon to avenge it with and without the help of the courts. See also Bouchard, who notes the thoroughly positive connotations of the maternal uncle / nephew relationship in literature — though she mentions that there was a great deal of ambivalence about stepfathers, with Ganelon as a prime example (77–78).

⁶⁵ Widmaier indicates that relatives were responsible (25). For a definition of *mage* see *DRW*, vol. 8 (Weimar: H. Böhlaus Nachfolger, 1984–1991), cols. 1574–77; for *künne*, see *DRW*, vol. 8 (Weimar: H. Böhlaus Nachfolger, 1984–1991), cols. 113–115.

⁶⁶ Konrad hints at this relationship ("an wem mach ich mich nu verâze? / getruobet ist al mîn kunne" [On whom can I now depend? My whole family is saddened]

[7536–37]) but does not delineate it in the clear and forceful manner in which Stricker does.

[67] The importance of the family in giving military as well as other kinds of support is apparent in the behavior of Genelun's relatives as well as Otto's. Kroeschell, *Deutsche Rechtsgeschichte* 140 discusses the tendency of the later imperial Carolingian nobility to align themselves with the old tribal divisions — Swabian, Saxon, Franconian, etc. He notes that the German kings never succeeded in forging a strong link between these entities and the monarchy.

The primacy and strength of the Holy Roman Empire was, of course, an important topic during Barbarossa's reign and at the time Stricker was writing *Karl der Große*. Edmund Stengel, "Der Machtgedanke und das Kaisertum Karls des Grossen," *Abhandlungen und Untersuchungen zur Geschichte des Kaisergedankens im Mittelalter* (Graz: Böhlau, 1965), 31–55 (34–46) discusses Stricker's work in the light of the ideas of Otto von Freising and the *Kaiserchronik* about Karl and the founding of the empire. Salient points of the imperial party's position were the idea that the empire, dealing from a position of military superiority, was founded independently of the pope. In Stricker's work an angel tells Karl to conquer the empire in Rome and subdue it in the surrounding countries by force, as well (331–58). The necessity for military supremacy, which comes to the fore in the Genelun section, lies at the center of the imperial party's justification for its position. Since this group, as Stricker's introduction reflects, see their authority coming directly from God, who commands them to maintain the empire by force of arms, any entity that weakened that strength had to be extinguished. Therefore, Karl's repeated laments about the loss of Roland's strength take on added significance.

[68] Anton Schwob, "*fride unde reht sint sêre wunt:* Historiographen und Dichter der Stauferzeit über die Wahrung von Frieden und Recht," *Sprache und Recht: Beiträge zur Kulturgeschichte des Mittelalters,* vol. 2 (Berlin & New York: De Gruyter, 1986), 846–68 (868) notes that the reputation of the empire depended on the maintenance of peace and the rule of law.

[69] Much shorter in length, the corresponding passage in the *RL* to *KG* 10612–33 contains the central themes of Stricker's version but without the references to fortresses, vassals, and the emperor's plight:

> An wem macht ich mich nu verlaze?
> getrübet ist al min kunne.
> diu lant du mir elliu dwunge:
> du ervachte di stainherten Sachsen
> und die swertwachsen
> Swabe unt Francken.
> di habet mich nu ze undancken.
> ich wird* in uil smaehe. (7536–43)

[On whom should I now depend; my whole family is saddened. You conquered the lands completely for me. You subdued the rock-hard Saxons and the skilled Franconian and Swabian swordsmen. They will now resist my authority. I will be scorned by them.]

[70] Karl alludes briefly to Roland's importance for the empire shortly after his death and before his own battle with the Moors: "er [Roland] hât mich sorgen dicke erlôst, /

er was vil gar des rîches trôst" [He had often freed me from cares, he was very much the protector of the empire] (9119–20). This passage anticipates and underscores the importance of this theme in the accusation and trial of Genelun.

[71] Hirsch, *Gerichtsbarkeit* 37, 39. Dieter Werkmüller, "Handhafte Tat," *HWBDR*, vol. 1, cols. 1965–73 (col. 1970) notes that in Germanic times the entire focus rested on the victim, not the damage to the state.

[72] Klein, "Strickers 'Karl'" 321, note 59 says that this episode came from a younger version of the Old French *Chanson,* as does Geith, *Carolus Magnus* 182–83; see also Karl Stackmann, "Karl und Genelun: Das Thema des Verrats im Rolandslied des Pfaffen Konrad und seine Bearbeitungen," *Poetica* 8 (1976): 258–80, esp. 270–74; Canisius-Loppnow 230–31. Von der Burg, *Strickers Karl* discusses the possible relationship of this incident to various branches of the French material (243–49, 251–52).

[73] Klein, "Strickers 'Karl'" 321 n.59, notes that Otto's exemplary fidelity stands in sharp contrast to Genelun's lack of it.

[74] "ine wirde dir niemer mêre holt. do du mir nicht dienen woltest, als du von rehte soltest" [I will no longer be favorably disposed toward you. When you did not intend to serve me as you were legally bound to do] (11406–8). See *DRW,* vol. 6 (1961) cols. 34–38, esp. 34–35. See B. Distelkamp, "Hulde," *HWBDR*, vol. 2, col. 256 for the obligations of a lord to a faithful vassal (*Gnade*); Distelkamp, "Huldeverlust," *HWBDR,* vol. 2, cols. 259–62 (cols. 260–61) notes that the loss of property received from the ruler and of a place at court were common punishments for bad behavior on the part of vassals in the early Middle Ages, while in later centuries fines were used to bring the miscreant back into the ruler's good graces. Gerd Althoff, "Huld: Überlegungen zu einem Zentralbegriff der mittelalterlichen Herrschaftsordnung," *Spielregeln der Politik im Mittelalter: Kommunikation in Frieden und Fehde* (Darmstadt: Primus, 1997), 199–229 provides a thorough discussion and history of research on this topic. The person threatened with the loss of *hulde* saw that as a powerful incentive to change his behavior through a significant attempt to gain his lord's favor (205). See also H. Krause, "Gnade," *HWBDR,* vol. 1, cols. 1714–19 (cols. 1715–16); Konrad Beyerle, "Von der Gnade im Deutschen Recht" (Göttingen: Vandenhoeck & Ruprecht, 1910), 10–11. Karl's punishment of Otto could have two sources: that of the emperor toward one of his retainers, who failed in his obligation, and that of the judge. The *Sachsenspiegel* notes that someone who promises to bring a man to court and is unable to do so has to compensate the court according to the seriousness of the charged offenses if they can be proved to have occurred (*The Saxon Mirror* 118). Genelun's flight has put him in the legal position of being guilty as charged.

[75] Stackmann, "Karl" 273 notes that Otto is not a traitor in the same way that Genelun is, since he does not misuse his position as counselor to practice deceit. In Stackmann's view, *verrataere* here means simply someone guilty of an *untriuwe*.

[76] The text reference in *Karl der Grosse* is line 11419. For "lehen" see *DRW,* vol. 8, cols. 880–95, esp. 881; for "eigen," *DRW,* vol. 2, cols. 1321–27; Matthias von Lexer, *MHDHWB,* vol. 1, col. 518: "eigentum, namentl. ererbtes grundeigentum im gegens. zum *lêhen*"; see also "Eigen," *HWBDR,* vol. 1, cols. 877–78; *DRW,* vol. 2,

col. 1321. Brandt notes that Karl has the authority to grant "lehen unde eigen" (100).

[77] Diestelkamp, "Huldeverlust" cols. 260–61; Beyerle 10–11.

[78] Karl-Heinz Spieß, "Lehn(s)recht, Lehnswesen," *HWBDR,* vol. 2, cols. 1725–41 (cols. 1728, 1735); G. Theuerkauf, "Felonie," *HWBDR,* vol. 1, cols. 1098–99.

[79] Widmaier 53–54, note 154; His 114–17.

[80] "wan daz ez laster waere, ich raeche ez iezuo an dir" [If it would not be a disgrace, I would avenge myself immediately on you] (11428–29).

[81] See Stackmann, "Karl" 272, who concurs that the intended meaning is that Otto would otherwise be killed for his deed, except that it would be *laster. DRW,* vol. 8, cols. 736–39 lists five meanings, including an injury through word or deed to one's reputation, the condition of being so injured, an offense against divine and human law, and a mistake or character weakness.

[82] See *DRW,* vol. 8, cols. 737, 738.

Hirsch, *Gerichtsbarkeit* 14, notes that the term *Verbrechen* was not current in Middle High German legal sources. The words used were *ungetat, laster,* and *missetat* (see vol. 9, cols. 676–79, esp. 676). See also Horst Haider Munske, *Der germanische Rechtswortschaft im Bereich der Missetaten: Philologische und sprachgeographische Untersuchungen,* I: *Die Terminologie der älteren westgermanischen Rechtsquellen* (Berlin: De Gruyter, 1973), 226.

[83] 11406: "ine wirde dir niemer mêre holt" [I will no longer be favorably disposed or faithful to you]. See Distelkamp, "Huldeverlust" cols. 259, 260. *KG* 11420–21 confirms this state of affairs: "dune wirst niemer mannes wert / ze hove noch ze teidinge" [You will not have the rights of a vassal, either at the court (gatherings of the emperor and his vassals) or in court (in the legal sense)].

[84] Widmaier 79; Brunner, *Land und Herrschaft* 38; Gerd Althoff, *Verwandte, Freunde und Getreue: Zum politischen Stellenwert der Gruppenbindungen im früheren Mittelalter* (Darmstadt: Wissenschaftliche Buchgesellschaft, 1990), 77.

[85] Stackmann, "Karl" notes (274) that precisely because Genelun flees with the help of his relatives, who do not hesitate to act against the interests of the empire for their kinsman, no one doubts that a capital offense has occurred.

[86] Stackmann, "Karl" notes (273) Otto's restraint in this matter. Geith, *Carolus Magnus* 183, 315 n. 95 finds both the length of the Otto passage and the new elements, such as the rebellion of the nobles, unusual. Had Geith analyzed the trial scene, he probably would have seen why Stricker puts his own stamp on this section: the Otto incident helps Stricker to advance his own narrative emphases. See also Sabine Böhm, *Der Stricker — ein Dichterprofil anhand seines Gesamtwerkes* (Frankfurt am Main & New York: P. Lang, 1995), 164.

[87] The strength of the narrator's objection to this self-help justice is apparent in the choice of adjective used to describe the relatives and their decision: they are the *tumben* [rash, foolish] who advise *tumplîche* (11461, 11464). By implication, this adjective applies to Genelun himself, who has taken just that course.

[88] "Und mîn gerihte drumbe neme" [And listen to my justification about it] (11479). "geriht nemen" = "Rechtfertigung anhoeren," Matthias Lexer *Mittelhochdeutsches*

Taschenwörterbuch (Stuttgart: S. Hirzel, 1992), 63. For a survey of meanings of *Gericht* in medieval sources see *DRW*, vol. 4, cols. 299–315.

[89] When Genelun is definitively vanquished, Stricker uses the word *ungetriwe* [unfaithful] to refer to him (11581, 11603).

[90] Lexer, *MHDHWB*, II, cols. 377–78. For information on the role of a medieval judge, see Planck, *Gerichtsverfahren* I, 87–91. Planck notes that in individual cases, where the legal issue in question was not a matter of contention, a judge could act without the advice of those individuals whose legal responsibility it was to ascertain guilt or innocence (in Karl's case, the nobles). Where there was disagreement, as in the case of Genelun, the court had to be assembled. Other reasons to involve the court were to intensify the significance of the verdict and for security reasons. The judge then conducted the trial and carried out the decision of the court. See also Gernot Kocher, "Richter," *HWBDR*, 5 vols., ed. Adalbert Erler, U. Kornblum, and G. Dilcher (Berlin: E. Schmidt, 1964–1998), IV: pt. 2, cols. 1033–40, esp. cols. 1036–37.

[91] "daz du mich hâst gescholten, / daz wirt dir wol vergolten" [As you have insulted me, so you shall be paid back] (11543–44). See "Ehre," *HWBDR*, vol. 1, col. 848. *Gescholten* implies more than just negative comments. Horst Haider Munske notes that *schelten* has been the usual word for "insult" since Old High German times (*Der germanische Rechtswortschatz im Bereich der Missetaten* 256).

[92] Planck, *Gerichtsverfahren* I, 767. See also Werkmüller cols. 1765–68: an accused caught in the act, which included flight, had put himself outside of the order of law in the community and, therefore, had no rights, because his deed condemned him to death. Langobardic law mentions specifically the right to kill a suspect caught in flight. While there were no restrictions on the right of a private individual to kill a person caught in the act in Germanic times, these rights became more and more limited in the course of the Middle Ages.

[93] See Schmidt-Wiegand, "Gebärdensprache" 373. See also Althoff, "Konfliktverhalten" 342.

[94] "daz im des keisers hulde / versagt was âne schulde" [that the emperor's favor was denied him without reason] (11603–4). See Widmaier, *Recht* 89, no. 160; Lexer, *MHDHWB*, III, cols. 209–10.

[95] Lexer, *MHDHWB*, II, col. 2006 lists one meaning as "Beweis" [proof]. See Ruth Schmidt-Wiegand, "Urkunde," *HWBDR*, 5 vols., ed. Adalbert Erler, U. Kornblum, and G. Dilcher (Berlin: E. Schmidt, 1964–1998), 35. Lieferung, cols. 576–77 for an explanation of the range of meanings this word had in the medieval legal context.

[96] Widmaier 175, no. 347.

[97] *DRW* 2, col. 655. See also Kaufmann, "Buße," *HWBDR*, 5 vols., ed. Adalbert Erler, Ekkehard Kaufmann, and Wolfgang Stammler (Berlin: E. Schmidt, 1964–1998), I: cols. 575–77 (col. 575): Kaufmann notes that the willingness of the injured party to accept material remuneration for the wrong inflicted on him, instead of declaring a feud, as Otto does here when he refuses to start a feud against Karl, was an important step in building a rule of law. See also Widmaier 88, no. 153 and *Saxon Mirror* 183–84.

[98] "daz disiu werlt nie gewan / deheinen getriwern man, / danne dû bist unde ie waere" [that this world never had a more faithful man than you are and always were] (11637–39).

[99] E. Kaufmann, "Rache," *HWBDR,* vol. 4, pt. 1, cols. 126–27 (col. 126). See also W. Preiser, "Blutrache," *HWBDR,* vol. 1, cols. 459–61. Schmidt-Wiegand, "Prozeß Ganelons (Geneluns)" *HWBDR,* 5 vols., ed. Adalbert Erler, U. Kornblum, and G. Dilcher (Berlin: E. Schmidt, 1964–1998), IV: pt. 1, col. 20 notes that Karl's rejection of revenge is new. See Brunner, *Land und Herrschaft* 17: recourse to the courts was one of the ways a ruler could limit the feud.

[100] Kaufmann, "Fehde" col. 1090. Ruth Schmidt-Wiegand, "Mord und Totschlag in der älteren deutschen Rechtssprache," *Forschungen zur Rechtsarchäologie und Rechtlichen Volkskunde* 10 (Zurich: Schulthess, Polygraphischer Verlag, 1989), 47–84 (56–59, 63–64, 66) discusses the continuing prevalence of the feud in the high Middle Ages.

[101] Althoff, "Konfliktverfahren" 351–52.

[102] Lexer, *MHDHWB,* II, col. 2014; Widmaier, *Recht* 166. See also Gerald Buchda, "Gerichtsverfahren," *HWBDR,* vol. 1, col. 1553.

[103] E. Kaufmann, "Urteil[rechtlich]," *HWBDR,* 35. Lieferung, cols. 604–9 (col. 607). See also Buchda, "Gerichtsverfahren" col. 1553; Planck, *Gerichtsverfahren* I, 248–53. Kocher, "Richter" cols. 1036–37 discusses Charlemagne's changes in making the position of the judge more clear (col. 1036). Karl is both the affected relative and the judge, a position he held in the *Chanson de Roland* (*CR*), as well; medieval French legal practice in the thirteenth century saw nothing abnormal about this situation. See Rossi 947; see Schulz 67–71 for a discussion of Karl's role as judge in the *RL*. Schulz sees the role of the *phachte* [written law] in the *RL* as a decisive difference between the trial scenes in the *RL* and the *KG* (71–72, no. 88).

[104] Kaufmann, "Urteil[rechtlich]" col. 607 says that medieval verdict-finders did not distinguish between legal principles with universal applicability and the concrete verdict in a given case. See also Buchda, "Gerichtsverfahren" 1553; Julius Wilhelm Planck, *Die Lehre von dem Beweisurtheil* (Göttingen: Dieterich, 1848), 3–10.

[105] Planck, *Gerichtsverfahren,* I, 98–100. In the false privilege of Charlemagne, which appeared on January 8, 1166, shortly after the December 29, 1165 canonization of Charlemagne, Charlemagne appears as the steward of the Law, a power that he exercised in conjunction with the princes of the realm. Folz notes that this description was a mirror of the aristocratic conception of government during Barbarossa's time and was a procedure that he himself made frequent use of. In the *RL* Karl seems limited by the presence of the peers, reflecting the strong bonds in the pyramidal feudal structure (Robert Folz, *Le Souvenir et la légende de Charlemagne dans l'Empire germanique médiéval* [Geneva: Slatkine Reprints, 1973] 243, 249). Other documents that cite Karl in a legal context are listed in Karl Kroeschell, "Recht und Rechtsbegriff im 12. Jahrhundert," *Probleme des 12. Jahrhunderts: Reichenau Vorträge, 1965–67, VuF,* vol. 12 (Konstanz: Thorbecke, 1968), 309–35 (333–34).

[106] See Planck, *Gerichtsverfahren* I, 169–71.

[107] ". . . hoeren unde sehen /, den mort, der von im ist geschehen" (11651–52). His notes (25) that in the German Middle Ages murder was often grouped together with

treason. Schmidt-Wiegand says that the charge against Genelun in Stricker's work concentrated on murder ("Prozeß Ganelons (Geneluns), " IV: pt. 1, cols. 18–21).

[108] See Planck, *Gerichtsverfahren*, I, 249–50 on the opponents' right to be heard.

[109] Althoff, "Konfliktverfahren" 336. See also Althoff, "Colloquium familiare-Colloquium secretum-Colloquium publicum: Beratung im politischen Leben des früheren Mittelalters," *FMS* 24 (1990): 145–67 (163–64).

[110] Canisius-Loppnow notes this in regard to the *RL* (240).

[111] Althoff, "Konfliktverfahren" 337; Althoff, "Hulde" 205. See also White, esp. 91–92, where he provides a general discussion of the potential at various stages of the ordeal process for conflict resolution, and 104–5, where he analyzes in a general manner the effects of an upcoming ordeal on conflict negotiation in the judicial proceedings.

[112] Interestingly enough, in the section in which Karl believes that Otto has behaved treacherously toward him, Karl describes his transgression in part in terms of service: "do du mir nicht dienen woltest, als du von rehte soltest" [When you did not render service to me as you were obligated to do] (11407–8:). Fidelity to the emperor, made manifest in assistance, seems to be central in determining whether or not treachery took place (see Otto scene) as well as in making amends for it later. Rossi notes that since treason is always the occasion for judicial combat, the loyalty of the accused in regard to the king is always a paramount consideration (946–47).

Willoweit discusses service as compensation for the killing of Bishop Konrad of Würzburg in the early thirteenth century; in this case the service was set by Innocent the III and consisted in large part of penitential acts (214–18).

[113] "ze buoze stân" (11684). See Schmidt-Wiegand, "Gebärdensprache" 366, 375.

[114] Stricker has changed the position of Karl's vow that he would not take all the gold of Arabia for this traitor, placing it before Genelun's attempt to clear himself instead of after it, where it occurs in the *RL* (8773–78). Karl's resistance to the temptation of wealth that would adversely impact his perceived mission is already apparent in Stricker's description of his campaign against the heathens (882–92). Another passage in which Marsilie's offer of riches is expressly linked with anti-Christian behavior comes in Bishop Turpin's speech warning Karl not to accept Marsilie's gold but to seek the reward of God, eternal life (1664–70). This section foreshadows the scenes in which Genelun is happy to accept the heathens' money.

[115] Genelun and his family see the offer in this light: in his conversation with Blanschandiz, during which he arranges for the betrayal of Roland, Genelun expects that he and his family will be able to come to an arrangement regarding reparations with Karl. Genelun refers to this as *suone* (2448).

Schmidt says: "Die festen Bußsätze sind mit den Volksrechten . . . verschwunden" (56). They existed in connection with feud and blood revenge; see also Hirsch, who notes that, as the concept became more widespread that murder was the most serious crime, the effectiveness of *Totschlagssühne* as a means of redress became weaker and weaker (39). See Schmidt-Wiegand, "Mord und Totschlag" 69, 82; *Saxon Mirror* 21. For a discussion of *Sühne* in cases of wrongful death, see Brunner, *Land und Herrschaft* 63–64.

[116] Werkmüller cols. 1965–66.

[117] Canisius-Loppnow has a lengthy discussion on the legal implications of this means of physical restraint (228–32). See also Planck, *Gerichtsverfahren*, I, 765–67, 771–76, where procedures involving defendants caught in the act are described. Werkmüller cols. 1968–69 notes that a person caught in the act was brought bound before the court; Ruth Schmidt-Wiegand, "Prozeß Ganelons (Geneluns)" believes that Stricker simply left this detail out to simplify things.

[118] See *RL* 8739–45. See Erich Klibansky, *Gerichtsszene und Prozeßform in erzählenden deutschen Dichtungen des 12.–14. Jahrhunderts* (Berlin: Ebering, 1925), 60–61; Canisius-Loppnow 231; *DRW*, vol. 2, col. 339; Kaufmann, "Binden" *HWBDR*, vol. 1, cols. 437–39 (cols. 437–38). Schmidt-Wiegand, "Prozeß Ganelons (Geneluns)" sees the absence of protest by Genelun's relatives as a parallel to Stricker's leaving out Konrad's characterization of Genelun as *der besten genôz*, that is, of a rank equal to that of prince. Schulz discusses this problem briefly.

[119] See Brandt 149 for a comparison. William Ian Miller, *Humiliation and Other Essays on Honor, Social Discomfort, and Violence* (Ithaca NY: Cornell UP, 1993), in a passage that certainly would have appealed to Genelun, writes: "In a regime in which one is a juridical equal among other equals and does not expect to be oppressed by authority, one's antennae are finely attuned to insult, grievance, and injury from one's peers. Equality in this setting means the publicly recognized right of the wronged person to redress. Should redress be denied, more is at stake than the narrow legal matter of the denial of a cause of action; what is at stake is one's continued status as an equal" (77).

[120] Stricker's work refers to Genelun's crime as *mort* on several previous occasions: As they hear Roland's horn, Karl and Naymis, realizing what has happened, have Genelun bound. Naymis refers to Genelun's crime as follows: "im ist der tôt vil gewis, / sît uns sîn mortlîcher rât / diz herzeleit gebrûwen hât" [Certain death awaits him, since his murderous counsel has caused this misery] (7156–58). When they hear the horn again, Karl's people are distraught; Roland's death is referred to again as murder (7900–904).

[121] Hirsch 37, 39; Schmidt 57. Schmidt-Wiegand, "Mord und Totschlag" notes that the *Sachsenspiegel* does not allow for *Totschlag* in the course of a feud, paralleling the general development (82). According to *Reichsrecht*, *Totschlag* had been a capital crime since the twelfth century.

Hand in hand with this development was a growing tendency toward corporal punishment. See His 3, 70–71; Richard Schröder and Eberhard von Künßberg, *Lehrbuch der deutschen Rechtsgeschichte* (Berlin: De Gruyter, 1932), 838; Hermann Conrad, *Deutsche Rechtsgeschichte*, vol. 1 (Karlsruhe: Müller, 1962), 438; and Gunter Gudian, "Geldstrafrecht und peinliches Strafrecht im späten Mittelalter," *Rechtsgeschichte als Kulturgeschichte: Festschrift für Adalbert Erler zum 70. Geburtstag*, ed. A. Fink et al. (Aalen: Scientia-Verlag, 1976), 273–88 (273–74). See also Pieter Spierenburg, *The Spectacle of Suffering: Executions and the Evolution of Repression* (Cambridge & New York: Cambridge UP, 1984), 5.

[122] See D. Meurer, "Tötungsdelikte," *HWBDR*, 34. Lieferung (Berlin: E. Schmidt, 1992) cols. 286, 288; Widmaier 77. 210. (Karl seems to use *tôtslac* in a metaphorical sense in l. 11441.) See also R. Schmidt-Wiegand, "Mord (sprachlich)," *HWBDR*, vol. 3, cols. 473–75; *DRW*, vol. 9, cols. 861–68 notes that *mord* originally was a

general term for death but then became distinguished from manslaughter through the element of secrecy (col. 861); it also could be used for public killing in a duel (col. 866); Hirsch discusses the terminology problems (41–42). See also His 123, 125 where he discusses the element of secrecy as a major consideration in murder charges. Hirsch 24–25, 39–40 discusses the existence of secrecy and deception as the characteristics linking theft, treachery, and murder. Other circumstances that led to a murder charge in the medieval German area were killing for the sake of gain or breach of a relationship of trust (His 125). His also notes that while every killing could be and often was referred to as murder, homicide and murder were almost always treated differently (123). See also Canisius-Loppnow 211–13. Schmidt-Wiegand, "Mord und Totschlag" 58–59 notes that manslaughter of relatives in the course of a feud constituted murder. Hirsch says that consideration of intent is a modern idea and that, until into the thirteenth century, the deciding factor as to whether a homicide was murder lay in the presence or absence of stealth or secrecy (39).

[123] Hirsch notes that the attitude of the perpetrator had a great deal to do with deciding whether a death was murder or manslaughter. Manslaughter is an "erbar sach" in the Austrian sources he cites (80).

[124] "publicly, before the Empire" (i.e, the council of nobles). See *RL* 8742–45.

[125] Brunner, *Land und Herrschaft* 73–75. *Absage* has the meaning of declaring a feud: *DRW*, vol. 1, cols. 221–27 (col. 222).

[126] See Canisius-Loppnow 232–38; see also E. Kaufmann, "Fehde" cols. 1086, 1090–92; Herbert Asmus, *Rechtsprobleme des mittelalterlichen Fehdewesens* (Göttingen: Thèse Droit, 1951), 8.

[127] See Brandt 149. Schmidt-Wiegand, "Prozeß Ganelons (Genelüns) says that Stricker relates the accusation, the defense, and the accompanying argumentation much more closely to each other than does Konrad; in addition, he treats the announcement of a state of feud in much more detail than does his predecessor.

[128] Schmidt-Wiegand, "Prozeßform" 6. For *Leid, DRW*, vol. 8, cols. 1140–43 (col. 1140) lists "Unrecht, Ehrverletzung, Beleidigung, Schande," as well as physical injury. For *klagen, DRW*, vol. 7, cols. 1045–50 (col. 1045) says: "bei Gericht in förmlicher Weise Recht suchen." For *widersagen,* Lexer lists "fehde und krieg ankündigen" (*MHDHWB*, III, col. 851). His lists it as one of the formal legal terms for the announcement of a feud (61).

[129] Although comparable lines do not appear in the *RL,* the corresponding sections for the first and third quotations are 1382–1403 and 1465–67. Genelun has, perhaps, brought this nomination on himself by being the only one among the council of nobles to recommend accepting Marsilie's offer and going home to their families. Roland's nomination of him could thus be seen as choosing the Frank with the most sympathy for the Muslims, the one best able to make an agreement (1678–1701; 1760–90). The first of these passages is critical of his stepson. Bishop Turpin attacks Genelun's suggestion, which indicates that it does not have the sanction of the Church, whereupon Genelun becomes extremely angry at the bishop (1812–13). These passages foreshadow his later apostasy.

[130] Karl had reason to make such a demand: Marsilie had beheaded two earlier emissaries (*KG* 1417–21). The text makes it clear that the messenger will not only have

Karl's protection but also will be fulfilling God's will: the saintly Bishop Johannes recommends the sending of a messenger (1879–96). Genelun's anger at being nominated shows how little he trusts in God.

[131] Brault l. 329.

[132] Brunner, *Land und Herrschaft* 19; Asmus 8–10. Asmus distinguishes between blood revenge and the feud on the basis of class differences and the nature of the crime. Blood revenge in the Middle Ages was open to all only in the case of serious crimes such as murder, fatal insult, and serious injury, while the feud was open only to the nobility but could be used in all kinds of legal situations. See also Althoff, "Konfliktverhalten" 336, where he notes that incidents that to us seem petty could serve as the rationale for armed conflict.

A further reason for the feud, though it does not come up in the trial scene, might lie in the inheritance question, which is given a lot of space in both MHG works. Genelun is afraid that his death will cause Roland to take his stepbrother Baldewin's inheritance. *RL:* 1445–51, 1690–1709; *KG* 1989–2008, 2057–60, 2227–50. In both works Roland assures Genelun that he would never do such a thing, citing his relationship with Karl as surety. *RL* 1476–85; *KG* 2079–86. Canisius-Loppnow 151–71 gives a helpful detailed discussion of the legal realities behind Genelun's fears. While her thesis that Genelun represents the heathen attitude toward inheritance and Roland represents the Christian attitude seems a bit forced, her point that Roland's reply to Genelun is certainly infused with the Christian ethos is well taken. For remarks on trial by battle and the feud, see Brunner, *Land und Herrschaft* 32–33 and Mitteis 264.

[133] Genelun's argument that Roland was sending him to his death overlooks the fact that Roland volunteered to go on the mission himself (1897–1904). Moreover, in all three versions Karl expressly says that it is he, not Roland, who is sending Genelun/Wellis on the mission. (*RL* 1427, *KG* 2036, *KM* A440b, 69) Neither the *RL* nor *KG* mention one legal component of the declaration of feud: the waiting period. Brunner, *Land und Herrschaft* 76 says that a there was a waiting period between the declaration of a feud and the beginning of hostile action. Customary law and *Landfrieden* recommended at least three days, but compacts frequently stipulated as much as a month. Genelun swears that if he returns, the twelve (*RL* 1640–47) or Roland (*KG* 2178–82) will regret sending him on this trip. But he begins the secret negotiations that will end in their deaths shortly after he leaves Karl's encampment.

[134] *Vient,* Lexer *MHDHWB,* III, col. 333; *RL* 1640, *KG* 2177. The implied perpetrators of the *leit* differ in the two works. Stricker's Genelun gives Roland the entire blame for his mission to the Muslims, while the *RL* Genelun blames the twelve peers (*KG* 2178–82; *RL* 1641).

[135] Brandt notes the connection of part of this section to Genelun's defense (149).

[136] Althoff, *Verwandte* notes that the generally accepted hierarchy of social bonds in the Middle Ages placed those of family and friends before those of the state, such as feudal obligations (2). Moreover, in a group of blood relatives, all had an obligation (5). Though these ties did weaken in the course of the Middle Ages, there are still references in the later medieval period to family help with feuds (32). Genelun, sure of his relatives' support and his close ties with the emperor, counts on his position to determine the treatment received from the court. The growth in the application

of the penal code as the *Landfrieden* became more established, however, slowly eroded the notion that certain classes should be treated differently. See Schmidt 59–60.

[137] See Stackmann, "Karl" 266–67, 270 for a discussion of Genelun's moral depravity; see also Von der Burg, *Strickers Karl* 335. Spierenburg discusses the transition from the Germanic compensation system of *wergeld* to a penal approach, noting that "As long as the law merely attempts to encourage reconciliation, it is likewise indifferent to a moral appreciation of the acts which started the conflict" (5).

[138] Friedrich Ohly, "Beiträge zum Rolandslied," *Philologie als Kulturwissenschaft: Studien zur Literatur und Geschichte des Mittelalters. Festschrift für Karl Stackmann zum 65. Geburtstag,* ed. Ludger Grenzmann, Herbert Herkommer, and Dieter Wuttke (Göttingen: Vandenhoeck & Ruprecht, 1987), 90–135 mentions (98) a Germanic/secular concept of honor that dominates the Genelun sections. E. Kaufmann, "Fehde" col. 1085 notes that the *Sühne* differed from the court's verdict in that it was a mutually agreeable decision, not one forced on either party by the court.

[139] Brunner, *Land und Herrschaft* 50–51 discusses those who had the right to feud and those who did not. Even in the case of individuals regarded as outlaws, the feuders believed firmly that they were legally justified in defending their cause, which they believed to be legitimate. How much more, then, would Genelun, as a brother-in-law of the king, believe that he had a legal right to a feud.

[140] Canisius-Loppnow 235–36 cites the case of the murder in 1225 of the archbishop of Cologne, who was killed by his nephew, Count Friedrich of Altena, in a private feud — a case, however, that had serious political consequences. Like Genelun, he was accused of *mort,* and a judicial duel was offered. This incident shows that the struggle between the aristocratic custom of legal self-help and procedural justice that *KG* reflects was still going on at the probable time of composition of Stricker's work.

[141] See Stackmann, "Karl" 266–67: citing 3772–76, Stackmann says that Genelun's decadence in his personal life clouds his ability to see the essential law, insight that would prevent him from treason.

[142] The connection with the Devil begins early in the work: when Genelun begins the negotiations with Blanschandiez, he gives his soul as surety for his treacherous oath (2396–97); shortly thereafter, as the two sit under the olive tree (2480–85), he is compared to Judas. The narrator then notes that the Devil had taken command of Genelun (2514). Immediately before Genelun's report to Karl, the narrator says that Genelun had installed the Devil in the depths of his heart. At the close of his negotations with Marsilie, those involved, including Genelun, swear on idols (2870–82). Klein, "Strickers 'Karl'" 305–6, discusses Stricker's rejection of reward for fighting the heathen as a definite change from Konrad's work. For a detailed analysis of Genelun as Devil figure in the *RL* see Ohly, "Beiträge" 91–98.

[143] Brunner, *Land und Herrschaft* 41 comments on the status of wars on behalf of the Church; see also Reuter 302, and Althoff, "Königsherrschaft" 288–90, who discuss conflict resolution among king and nobles in eleventh-century German lands.

[144] Already in the late eleventh century distinctions were made between justifiable and unjustifiable grounds to declare a feud. Fidelity to the king, concern for the general welfare, or revenge for a private wrong were considered suitable reasons. See Reuter 304.

¹⁴⁵ Brunner, *Land und Herrschaft* 84 says that in the case of plunder and burning, which were the usual methods of waging a feud, and therefore not criminal in that context, to describe them as criminal acts was to claim that the feud had no legal justification. In a parallel way, Karl's description of Roland's death as murder instead of a legally sanctioned vengeance is a rejection of Genelun's defense. See also Schmidt 59.

¹⁴⁶ See Brunner, *Land und Herrschaft* 76. Reuter lists (318) several instances of court cases involving the monarch and important nobles in the Salian period in which the nobles balked at giving the king the verdict he wanted. These cases include Heinrich II against Markgraf Gunzelin von Meißen and Konrad II against Adalbero.

¹⁴⁷ "swer im verteilte sîn leben, / der vorhte er würde drumbe erslagen" [Whoever among them condemned Genelun feared that he would for that reason be killed] (11752–53). Brandt notes (144) that Stricker inserts the two sections beginning with 11748 and 11755. They expressly give fear as the motivation for the nobles' silence and make it clear that Karl understands the reason. Brandt notes that while the situation is the same in both works — the threat to the legal and political system that another strong power causes — the lines are more clearly drawn in Stricker.

Two prominent rulers had fallen victim to private revenge killings within living memory at the time Stricker wrote *KG:* Philipp von Schwaben in 1208 in Bamberg and Archbishop Engelbert of Cologne, killed by his nephew in a quarrel over an inheritance, in 1225. The king's verdict of death on the wheel was disputed, and a judicial duel was demanded, which shows that the concept of feud rights was alive and well about the time that Stricker was writing his work. See Schmidt-Wiegand, "Mord und Totschlag" 63–64; Willoweit, "Gewalt und Verbrechen" 215–20, for the revenge killing of Bishop Konrad von Querfurt of Würzburg by his own relatives in 1202.

¹⁴⁸ "küniges namen" [rank of king] (11771); Brandt 145. Moreover, in the *RL* Karl says only that he will no longer wear the crown (8820), while in the *KG* he mentions giving up "küneges namen" as well as the crown (11771). According to Brandt, this addition is a significant one, since it refers to his function in the internal political system, a function that would become impossible if Genelun's family possessed enough power to free him.

¹⁴⁹ See Schmidt 51–52. Althoff, *Verwandte* notes (188) that there were many anecdotes about the ability of Karl to maintain the upper hand when he took counsel with his nobles; Althoff mentions one written down in the twelfth century.

¹⁵⁰ Rossi discusses the weak position of Charlemagne in the CR and notes that in twelfth-century France, royal justice was defenseless against barons more powerful than the king and only grew in strength over against the nobles in the course of the thirteenth century (950); see also Jacques Heers, *Family Clans in the Middle Ages,* trans. Barry Herbert (Amsterdam & New York: North-Holland, 1977), who notes that stable royal control limited the power of family clans (6).

¹⁵¹ See Brandt, who notes that their depressed reaction can arise for no other reason, since Karl did not criticize Genelun directly in this speech (145).

¹⁵² There are two speeches in Stricker, one in the *RL* (*KG* 11708–20, 11737–47; *RL* 8773–84).

See Holzhauer, "Zweikampf," who notes (280) that Konrad's *RL* limits the right to feud because of the damage done to the Church. See also Brunner, *Land und Herrschaft* 101; Rainer Zacharias, "Die Blutrache im deutschen Mittelalter," ZfdA 91 (1962): 167–201 (169).

[153] This section begins in both works with the challenge of Pinabel (*KG* 11775, *RL* 8785; 430 lines in Stricker vs. 231 in Konrad).

[154] Konrad: "er widersagt in offenliche" [he openly declared a feud] (8796). Stricker begins his speech with the charge "ern hât deheinen mort getân" [He has not committed a murder] (11798).

[155] E. Kaufmann, "Urteilsfindung/Urteilsschelte," *HWBDR*, 35. Lieferung, cols. 619–22 (col. 620). See also Holzhauer, "Zweikampf," who notes that Konrad emphasizes the legal question more than the Old French work does (279). Canisius-Loppnow discusses the *Urteilsschelte* in the *RL* (242–44, 247–48); Böhm notes that this scene with Pinabel ties the parts of the trial together more closely than in the *RL* (166).

Pinabel's role as Genelun's champion corresponds to contemporary legal realities. With the possible exception of Bavarian law, there were conditions about the use of champions. See Holzhauer, "Zweikampf" 281–82.

[156] Hirsch, *Gerichtsbarkeit* 36–37, esp. 37; see also Schmidt 58–59.

[157] *RL* 8823–58; *KG* 11815–44. Canisius-Loppnow discusses the use of the David/Tirrich-Goliath/Binabel parallel, which does not exist in the Oxford MS of the *Chanson de Roland*. She believes that it adds a legendary quality to the work, since in any context but that of a legend, it would have contradicted the attitude of church legal scholars, who believed that calling on the example of David and Goliath in judicial duels was a temptation of God. Dietrich, the David figure, represents Karl, who was frequently referred to as a new David in the Latin literature of the Carolingian era (250). See Wolfram von den Steinen, "Karl und die Dichter," in *Karl der Große: Lebenswerk und Nachleben,* ed. Wolfgang Braunfels, vol. 2, ed. Bernard Bischoff (Düsseldorf: Schwann, 1967), 63–94 (64, 76–77, 79–80, 83–84). According to Von Steinen, the titling of Karl as David shows the nearness of Karl to the Old Testament figure, himself the prototype of the only true King, Christ. The mere comparison with David had been in use since the time of Emperor Konstantin (77). Einhard and Alciun cited parallels of Karl with David: Saurma-Jeltsch, "Karl" 12. If the David/Goliath parallel is present to reinforce the legendlike significance of the battle, as the presence of Durndart does, then the implied reference back to Karl, the David-like emperor, adds to the weight of right on the emperor's side. Konrad himself makes the association between Henry and David at the end of his work (9039–44, 9066–68); for a discussion of these ties and other links of Henry the Lion with King David, see Geith, "Das deutsche und das französische Rolandslied" 79–82.

[158] "dâ eret er daz reht mite" [He thereby honors the law] (11836).

[159] "God Himself must see the battle and let justice happen to both of us." Hüpper-Droge concludes that *kampf* and etymologically related words were loan words from Latin that began to be used in the meaning of judicial duel in the tribal law codes and then entered into Old High German with this meaning (630–34, 641–42, 644, 646–47, 649, 650–55). She cites the use of this word-family in the *RL* (655) in this

context. Both Konrad and Stricker make frequent use of these words in the challenge scenes (*RL* 8804, 8856, 8878, 8900; *KG* 11797, 11810, 11818, 11819, 11837, 11841, 11843, 11846, 11851, 11870, 11885, 11933). The legal nature of these scenes in both works is deepened for the modern reader when this meaning is kept in mind, as in the following example. When Stricker's Pinabel challenges Genelun's accusers, he says, "der Genelûnen schuldec saget / ern müeze mit kampfe mich bestân" [Whoever accuses Genelun must challenge me in battle (a judicial duel)] (*KG* 11796–97). See also *DRW*, volume 6 (Weimar: H. Böhlaus Nachfolger, 1967) col. 1036.

[160] See *KG* 11826, 11830, 11834, 11843; pronoun *er*, 11836.

[161] *RL* 8833, 8834, 8839, 8840, 8843, 8848, 8851, 8852; reference to St. Dionisii, 8858.

[162] Canisius-Loppnow translates 8833 as *Landesverrat*, since she maintains that Karl's empire is identical with Christianity (248–49). In her opinion, exclusion from *cristinlichem rechte* (8838–39) also banishes Genelun from Karl's empire.

[163] Canisius-Loppnow says that the quality of excessive pride (*RL* 8844), which Konrad otherwise ascribes to the Moors and Genelun, show that Binabel, too, is a heathen (249–50).

[164] Pinabel functions as Genelun's champion, just as he did in the *CR* and in the *RL*. The practice of using champions appeared already in the Germanic legal codes; see Hüpper-Droge 631–33, 641, 645. Canisius-Loppnow notes that Genelun's changed status as a bound and tortured defendant accused of murder and treason made it impossible for him to fight himself. Genelun's flight in Stricker's work is evidence of his guilt and adds to the reasons why he cannot defend himself (243–45).

[165] *RL* 8859–72; *KG* 11845–84.

[166] W. Ogris, "Geisel," *HWBDR*, 5 vols., ed. Adalbert Erler, U. Kornblum, and G. Dilcher (Berlin: E. Schmidt, 1964–1998), I: cols. 1445–51 (cols. 1447–48) notes that one of the obligations of medieval vassals was to serve as hostages for their liege lord. Althoff, *Verwandte* notes (21) that hostage-taking and oaths were both categories that obligated the entire group. See also Holzhauer, "Zweikampf" 278; Baist 448.

[167] See Holzhauer, "Zweikampf" 275–76, where he discusses the early medieval practice of replacing the oath with the trial by battle. Hüpper-Dröge notes varying attitudes in Germanic legal codes toward the oath and the trial by battle (627–28, 636–38, 640). Oaths were not sufficient to clear a defendant of a capital crime among the Langobards and the Bavarians (640).

[168] Canisius-Loppnow discusses the aspects of liturgical practice that appear in the *CR* and in the *RL*. Konrad leaves out the extensive liturgical practices that appear in the French work, reflecting, she believes, the increasing discomfiture of the Church with the judicial duel. Konrad mentions only the ceremonies held for Tirrich, since Binabel is on the side of evil. She suggests that the absence of the oath in Konrad may be due to the fact that one of the two must commit perjury, which was a grave sin (253–56).

[169] Rüdiger Schnell, "Rechtsgeschichte, Mentalitäten und Gattungsgeschichte," *Literarische Interessenbildung im Mittelalter*, ed. Joachim Heinzle (Stuttgart &

Weimar: Metzler, 1993), 401–30 (420–21) notes that in literature the weaker individuals, who are always on the side of the right, win. This state of affairs is well suited to show God's powerful intervention. See also Schmidt-Wiegand, "Prozeßform" 9.

[170] See Hirsch, *Gerichtsbarkeit* 179–81, who discusses the changes in the content of the *Königsbann* in the context of the transition to a penal from a compensatory legal tradition.

[171] Stricker's meticulous attention to legal detail shows up in his comments about the ordeal site. Fields and meadows were naturally the best places for battles as well as for duels (Hüpper-Droge 630); Stricker notes that the trial was to take place "ze velde" (*KG* 11894). A circle, which was a frequently used demarcation in legal matters in the Germanic world (Hüpper-Droge 636) is drawn (*KG* 11895). See *DRW*, vol. 7, col. 1417; Gernot Kocher, "Friede und Recht," *Sprache und Recht: Beiträge zur Kulturgeschichte des Mittelalters. Festschrift für Ruth Schmidt-Wiegand* (Berlin & New York: De Gruyter, 1986), 405–16 (407). Stricker, unlike Konrad, specifically mentions that the circle was not violated (*KG* 11945). The court officials present who saw to that were the *griezwarten* (11935); see *DRW*, vol. 4, col. 1109.

[172] For the significance of the weapon as a quasi-independent agent with a mystical life of its own, see Nottarp 19; Holzhauer, "Zweikampf" 277. In a discussion of weapons used in such ordeals, Hüpper-Dröge mentions the sword in this context (637). Durndart's presence is, therefore, significant for two reasons: its legendary power and its function as a symbol of the law. Dieter Pötschke, "Rolande als Problem der Stadtgeschichtsforschung," *Jahrbuch für die Geschichte Mittel- und Ostdeutschlands* 37 (1988): 4–45 notes (10) that in Konrad's *RL* Durndart is mentioned once as an instrument of law, as a protection for widows and orphans (6868); Von der Burg, *Strickers Karl* notes (255) that Stricker's use of the legendary sword, which goes beyond literary tradition, is a sign from God about who will prevail and needs to be seen in conjunction with the scene at the beginning of the work, when an angel gives Karl Durndart, the horn, and a glove (364–85). Schnell, "Strickers 'Karl'" notes (62) that the *RL* does not contain the account of the angel giving Karl Durndart the horn and the glove. (Relevant passages: *RL* 55–64; *KG* 325–446, esp. 365–76.) Stricker also uses the swords as a motif in the betrayal and its avenging. As Genelun departs on his mission, Karl gives him a special sword, second only to Durndart (*KG* 2149–54). Later, as Genelun discusses the upcoming battle with the Franks, he boasts about the superiority of Frankish steel and cuts through the best Saracen helmet like butter with Karl's sword to prove his point. He gives Marsilie this sword with the expectation that Marsilie will use it to kill Roland (2846–69).

[173] Canisius-Loppnow notes the legendlike quality of Tirrich's victory, the struggle between representatives of God and the Devil in Konrad's work (261).

[174] *KG* 11959, 11963, 11969, 11998, 12070. Konrad frames the encounter in the prayers of the nuns, people, and the emperor and the Te Deum at the end, in contrast to Stricker's emphasis on Dietrich (*RL* 8881–95, 8988–92).

[175] "ich waene uns got bescheiden habe, sprach Dietrich wider in, daz ich mit rehte hie bin" ["I believe that God has judged the matter between us," said Dietrich to him, "and that I am here with the force of the law"] (12070–72). (Note: Lexer, *MHDHWB*, II, col. 379 lists many phrases containing the words "mit reht," which all have to do with legal meanings connected with courts, law, and/or verdicts.)

[176] Schnell, "Strickers 'Karl'" 61, no. 64, in his discussion of Karl as a saintly figure, notes that the protection of widows and orphans belonged to the portrayal of a saint. The text here does speak of revenge, so perhaps the Germanic tradition would be more operative in this passage. Certainly there are many sections of Stricker's work, as Schnell points out (61), that emphasize Karl's saintliness.

[177] See Distelkamp, "Hulde" col. 256.

[178] Wolfgang Schild, *Die Geschichte der Gerichtsbarkeit vom Gottesurteil bis zum Beginn der modernen Rechtssprechung* (Hamburg: Nikol-Verlag Gesellschaft, 1997) notes that this punishment was reserved in many times and places for serious political crimes (208).

[179] Brunner, *Land und Herrschaft*, in discussing the punishments that awaited those who killed with stealth, as opposed to those who killed in the course of a feud, says that the shameful forms of execution, such as hanging or the wheel, awaited the thieves and those who killed in secret. The more honorable form of execution, beheading, which Genelun's relatives received, was not available to them. Genelun's death reflects the utter contempt in which he was held, dishonor, and a rejection of his claim that he had a legal right to feud (74–75). See also His 82 and Schmidt 62.

[180] See *RL* 9012–14; *KM* A532b, 67–A533, 2.

[181] 12155–82. The *RL* contains a shorter version of the punishment of Genelun's supporters (8997–99; 9005–7), which seems to be limited to the hostages and does not extend to the other family members. The text says that his family should not grow in the world but adds that it is the hostages who are killed. Since the hostages were relatives, it is possible that the punishment was limited to them; while in the *KM* it is clear that the loss of property and other penalties extends to the entire family — punishment that does not kill them but will disadvantage them throughout their lives.

[182] Schnell, "Strickers 'Karl'" 55–58 discusses Stricker's portrayal of Karl as a saintly figure.

[183] Folz, "Charlemagne" 87, 89–90; Farrier 143; Adalbert von Keller, *Karl Meinet* (Stuttgart: Litterarischer Verein, 1858; rpt. Amsterdam: Rodopi, 1971) will be the edition cited in this book.

[184] Von der Burg, *Strickers Karl* 198, 209–21 notes that Stricker (*KG* 450 ff., 465) mentions Aachen as the coronation city and Karl's dedication of a church complex to Mary. Ohly, "Legende" 304–5 gives information on the veneration of Karl in Aachen from the late twelfth century, including the liturgical use of the Latin Pseudo-Turpin Karl-Roland legend from 1215 at the latest. One of the early articles on the *Karlmeinet*, P. Kanzeler's "Ueber *Karlmeinet*: Ein Versuch, dieses vor ein Paar Jahren aufgefundene Gedicht einem aachener Verfasser zuzuschreiben," *Annalen des Historischen Vereins für den Niederrhein, insbesondere das Alte Erzbistum Köln*, 11–12 (1862): 86–96, already suggested that the compilation came from an Aachen cleric in the first half of the fourteenth century, proposing that a head of the Franciscan cloister in Aachen, Hermann van Lemburch, active in the 1330s, fits the initials at the beginning of the work that are supposed to indicate the author (86–96, esp. 92–93). See Hartmut Beckers, "Die *Karlmeinet*-Kompilation: Eine deutsche *vita poetica Karoli Magni* aus dem frühen 14. Jahrhundert," *Cyclification: The Develop-*

ment of Narrative Cycles in the Chansons de Geste and the Arthurian Romances, ed. Bart Besemusca, Willem P. Gerritsen, Corry Hogetoorn, and Orlanda S. H. Lie (Amsterdam: North-Holland, 1994), 113–17 (113, 115); Gertrud J. Zandt, "Zur *Karlmeinet*-Kompilation," in *Cyclification: The Development of Narrative Cycles in the Chansons de Geste and the Arthurian Romances,* ed. Bart Besemusca, Willem P. Gerritsen, Corry Hogetoorn, and Orlanda S. H. Lie. (Amsterdam: North Holland, 1994), 198–99 (198) also believes that the work was written in Aachen and suggests that not only the *RL* but also a lost lower Rhine dialect version of the *RL* were the sources for the fifth section, which contains the Roland material.

[185] Farrier 344 lists Stricker's *Karl* as one of his sources. See also Folz, "Charlemagne" 87–89; Beckers, "Die *Karlmeinet*-Kompilation" 115 lists the *RL* but takes no position on any other specific source. Keller, *Karl Meinet* 853–54 says that the writer lists a French, a *welsche* (Romance language), and a Latin source.

[186] For comments about the judicial system and urbanization, see Spierenburg 6–7. For discussion of changes in attitudes towards the feud, see E. Kaufmann, "Fehde" cols. 1083–91; Joachim Gernhuber, *Die Landfriedensbewegung in Deutschland bis zum Mainzer Reichslandfrieden von 1235* (Bonn: Röhrscheid, 1952), 13–14, 49; Brunner, *Land und Herrschaft* 35; Mitteis 264; Althoff, "Konfliktverhalten" 332; Spierenburg 4.

[187] See Brandt, *'erniuwet,'* 149; Canisius-Loppnow, *Recht* 232–38.

[188] Althoff, "Konfliktverfahren" 336. See also Althoff, "Colloquium familiare" 163–64.

[189] Esther Cohen, *The Crossroads of Justice: Law and Culture in Late Medieval France* (Leiden & New York: Brill, 1993) notes that "the authority of government explicitly doing justice was the central motif of executions" (162). See also Spierenburg 55.

[190] See comparable passages in the *RL:* 1384–1403, 1420–23, 1459–67; in *KG:* 1989–2008, 2027–32; 2053–68. Von der Burg, "Konrads *Rolandslied*" 329, in listing a series of omissions due to manuscript transmission problems, notes the *KM* writer's omission of ll. 1400–403. While Von der Burg sees no reason from the point of view of content for any of these omissions, the consistent tendency of the *KM* writer to deemphasize the issue of the feud may have contributed to his tendency to shorten this passage.

The text of the *Karlmeinet* (*KM*) used in this study is the 1971 reprint of Adalbert von Keller's edition of 1858. Future citations will appear in the text.

[191] A441, 9. See *RL* 1417, 1435–41; *KG* 2024, 2041–48. The glove, as a part of the official garb of popes, bishops, kings, and warriors, had great force as a legal symbol, often representing the hand of the official. It could represent the protective, as well as the powerful, hand. Frequently it was given to the messenger to take to the person to whom the message was sent. A. Erler, "Handschuh," *HWBDR,* 5 vols., ed. Adalbert Erler, Ekkehard Kaufmann, and Wolfgang Stammler (Berlin: E. Schmidt, 1964–1998), I: cols. 1975–76 (col. 1975); M. Köbler, "Hand," *HWBDR,* vol. 1, cols. 1927–28 (col. 1927). See also Richter 241–42, who notes that the stab was the original symbol of royal power; L. Carlen, "Stab," *HWBDR,* vol. 4, pt. 2, cols. 1838–44 (cols. 1838–39). Berent Schwinekörper, *Der Handschuh im Recht, Ämterwesen, Brauch, und Volksglaube* (Sigmaringen: Thorbecke, 1981), 40–63.

Vreden, A441, 8–9. Lübben lists meanings of "truce," "armistice," and "protection" for this word (539).

[192] See *RL* 1427–28; *KG* 2035–37. The *KM* author follows the *RL* in his inclusion of the names of two Franks whom the Muslims beheaded (*RL* 1454–57; *KM* A441, 31–441b, 1). Stricker deletes them, but his Karl makes heathen representatives swear that Genelun will have safe conduct (*KG* 2194–2202).

[193] *RL* 1468–85; *KG* 2069–86.There are some differences in this version regarding the gifts of Karl to Wellis. Stricker's Karl gives Genelun a special sword, inferior only to the legendary Durndart (2149–54), a weapon whose role is greatly reduced in *KM*. (In both the *RL* and the *KG* the excellent sword has a Bavarian connection (Naymis), but the *RL* expends more detail on it (*RL* 1583–1605; *KG* 2150–54). While other presents are mentioned, no sword is given to Wellis, though the presentation of insignia, engraved in gold, to present to Marselie (A442, 25–31) and a splendid horse (A443b, 35–44) are maintained from the earlier versions. The horse is given expressly out of "minne ind vriuntschaff" (A443b, 37). *Vriunt* could mean either relative, lover, or friend; Lexer, *MHDHWB,* III, col. 527 lists related meanings for *vriuntschaft* (col. 527).

[194] "Vele leue swager myn" [My beloved brother-in-law] (A442b, 65). Von der Burg, "Konrads *Rolandslied*" 331 cites l. 1535f, "der helige engel mûze dîn geverte sîn / und beleite dich her widere gesunt" [The holy angel must be your companion and lead you safely back again], as a Tobias reference; Stricker's Karl asks God to accompany Genelun (*KG* 2128–29).

[195] See the Apocrypha, Tobit 4–12.

[196] See Ohly, "Legende" 299. Ohly notes that in the *RL* Karl, according to the model of Christ, chooses the twelve peers to battle the heathen directly after his dream in which the angel appears. While a strictly postfigurative comparison in which Karl represents Christ and Genelun represents Judas is not possible, since Roland, not Karl, dies, the strong identification of Karl with his beloved nephew adds more weight to the opprobrium heaped on the Genelun figure. Zagolla discusses a pretrial postfigurative reference to Genelun/Wellis as Judas (258–59). Both versions describe Judas's treachery, then that of Genelun/Wellis (*RL* 1926–33, 1936–43; *KM* A447, 30–38; A447b, 46–52).

[197] Stricker's version (*KG* 2480–87) is much shorter, omitting reference to Judas's violent end and to the preordained nature of his treachery, which the other two works include. In the *RL* and the *KM* Genelun/Wellis's victims are Christians (*RL* 1939, *KM* A447b, 48), while in Stricker's they are warriors (*KG* 2485–87), a further example of Stricker's concern with the affairs of the empire. See Richter 272–73; he notes that Genelun's betrayal repeats Judas's betrayal of Christ (273). See also Ott-Meimberg, *Kreuzzugsepos* 205–10 and Canisius-Loppnow 216, 218. Klein, "Strickers 'Karl'" 306 says that Genelun's love of riches made him such an extraordinary ally of the Devil that he was comparable only to Judas. Von der Burg, *Strickers Karl* 335–36 notes that in the scene with the heathens Stricker makes an addition indicating the amount of money (one hundred thousand marks, l. 2491); Von der Burg believes that in the context of the other passages in which Stricker comments negatively on the money motif, Stricker shows that Genelun's major character flaw was his love of money, which certainly connected him closely with Judas.

[198] Both the *RL* (2375–2414) and *KG* (2883–2940) have this passage, which asserts that Genelun betrayed two great empires — obviously, the kingdom of God and the Holy Roman Empire. Both works specifically mention the *stab* (*RL* 2404, *KG* 2934), the sign of imperial authority that Genelun took with him on the journey to the heathen camp.

[199] Binding was a way of securing the means of proof: see E. Kaufmann, "Binden" col. 438; His 138.

[200] See A489, 3–22; A489b, 44–58.

[201] The *KM* author frequently adapts his portrait of Karl to keep him above political calculations. An example from much earlier in the text, in which he makes an obvious change from what appears in both the *RL* and the *KG,* comes during the scene in which Wellis, like Genelun in the other two works, recommends that Roland stay behind to lead the guard. In both the *RL* (2965–84) and the *KG* (3501–24), forced by the assembly to agree to Genelun's proposal, Karl says that Genelun's suggestion was not made from good motives (*RL* 2988, *KG* 3518). When Wellis tells Karl that Roland is the best man to leave behind, Karl welcomes the decision, because, as the narrator adds, he knew nothing of Wellis's evil deed. (A451–11, 20). Only later in the day does Karl, in his characteristic highly emotional way, have some unfocused anxiety about their fate, but Wellis is not mentioned (A451b, 41–52).

[202] Unless the fallen Franks are given a proper burial, unclean animals will devour their corpses. This comment could function as a foreshadowing of and a contrast to Wellis's fate (A491b, 53–A492, 4).

[203] The inclusion of this section forms another parallel to Stricker, since the scene is absent in the *RL*. The apparent manner of referencing Stricker resembles that in the scene dealing with Karl's grief: a highly condensed version of the source.

In Stricker's version Genelun escapes during the confusion surrounding Alita's sudden death. Since the *KM* author includes a dream interpolation and places her death later, he may have reason to suppress the reasons for Wellis's escape and pick up the action immediately prior to the capture.

The careful manner in which the *KM* writer adapts is apparent not only in his consistency in virtually eliminating references to the feud but also in small details. Stricker's account says only that Otto's companions came to his rescue when Genelun threatened to overcome him (*KG* 11577–79), while the *KM* author gives them names, Sampson and Jorius (A494, 20–21).

Other changes by the *KM* writer include the omission of the fiery scene between Karl and Otto in Stricker's version, in which Otto is condemned as a traitor and threatened with the loss of position and power; the considerable shortening of the detailed legal and theological attack Otto makes on Genelun in Stricker's work to a brief accusation of murder (A493, 30). For the *KM* writer it suffices to say that a traitor who has caused Otto's standing serious damage is now within his grasp; he hopes that capture will restore him in Karl's eyes (A493b, 36–38).

[204] See Otto's prayer for assistance in Genelun's capture (*KG* 11483–90).

[205] (A496, 15–A496b, 41); Werkmüller says that any person accused of a crime who tried to resist capture or flee could be killed on the spot (col. 1968). See previous discussion of binding in this chapter.

[206] "Und dede eme bereyden / Martele ind vngemach" [And ordered him to be tortured and made miserable] (A495, 11–12); Lübben, *"Martele"* 220. It is unclear whether this treatment was inflicted to punish Wellis or to make him confess to a crime those present knew he had committed. "Marter" (torture) existed in Roman law, died out during the early Middle Ages, and slowly reappeared in the course of the thirteenth century, becoming prominent then and in the later Middle Ages as a means of extracting confessions and providing legal proof. See Peters, *Torture* 54–58. If intended to produce a confession, its appearance in this work could be a reflection of contemporary legal practice. Thomas Bestul, *Texts of the Passion: Latin Devotional Literature and Medieval Society* (Philadelphia: U of Pennsylvania P, 1996), 153–55; R. Lieberwirth, "Folter," *HWBDR*, vol. 1, cols. 1149–52 (cols. 1149–51); Goodich 49–50, 55.

[207] A495, 19–32 includes words that reflect the seriousness of Karl's charges against Otto, as does the extent of the compensation that Karl promises Otto and his family. "Begroessen" (A495, 22), MHG *begrüezen*, has legal meanings, including to speak to in court, or to accuse. (Lexer, *MHGHWB*, I, col. 148). Like Stricker, the *KM* writer uses *boessen* (A495, 23) in regard both to reputation or standing ("dynen eren," A495, 24) and to power and wealth (A495, 26). MHG *Buoze* can mean either penance in a religious sense or damages in a legal one (Lexer, *MHDHWB*, I, col. 389). In sharp contrast to Stricker, where Otto's relatives threaten violence against Karl, the passage involving compensation to them in A495, 23–32 is the only one in which Otto's relatives are mentioned.

[208] *KG* 11621–28: Stricker's Otto says only that he is happy that Karl sees his innocence and has restored him to favor; compensation is up to the emperor. The *KM* Otto's speech is much longer than in Stricker (A495b, 40–63; *KG* 11621–28). The only three lines that the two works have in common refer to leaving the matter of compensation up to Karl (*KG* 11626–28, *KM* 495b, 57–59); the passages are virtually identical. The *KM* Otto adds that Karl has already given him more than he is worth, which Stricker's Otto certainly does not.

[209] *RL* 8685–8729; *KG* 10980–11286 (11180–235 parallel the *RL* account); *KM* A495b, 41–A512, 14. The *KG* writer, however, places the scene after Otto's recapture of Wellis instead of where it is in Stricker. In the *KG* it is the occasion for Genelun's escape and Otto's chase.

[210] Stricker does include two short passages about Karl's outbursts of grief that were occasioned by the meeting with Alita/Alda (*KG*11230–36, 11265–78. Cf. *KM* A507, 21–23; A507b, 40–54; A508, 14–508b, 44; A511, 9–A511b, 40).

[211] Mitchell B. Merback, *The Thief, the Cross and the Wheel: Pain and the Spectacle of Punishment in Medieval and Renaissance Europe* (Chicago: U of Chicago P, 1999), 155–57; Bestul 146, 153–54.

[212] Perhaps the most singular passage in this section is Alda's prophetic dream and the conversation with her priest, which was not mentioned in the *RL* or in Stricker. En route to meet Karl, Alda has a series of dreams about Roland and Oliver and their deaths; the dreams involve a series of scenes with birds and animals, many of them violent. Three birds visit Alda: a white falcon lands on her head and takes her to a mountain and leaves her (A502, 6–20); an eagle attacks her with his claws and bites

her, bringing Karl to her rescue (A502b, 60–A503, 6); and a sparrow hawk flies out of her mouth and sits between Roland and Oliver (A504b, 37–45). Lions and bears fall on Roland and Oliver in the woods; Roland attacks one lion with Durndart (A502, 23–56). Roland, Oliver, and the twelve peers are swallowed up in the earth after being betrayed by Wellis (A503, 9–28). Near the end of the dream Alda sits in a dark wood in her shift; an old man with a gray beard seizes her and takes her to a cathedral on a mountain, where she sees Roland and Oliver lying, apparently dead. Then Karl hunts a stag in the woods with the dogs; see Beryl Rowland, *Animals with Human Faces: A Guide to Animal Symbolism* (Knoxville: U of Tennessee P, 1973), 64, who notes that the dog pursuing in the figurative stag hunt, where the stag is Christ, represents virtue. When Roland and Oliver come, she calls to them, but they do not recognize her and disappear into the earth. She sees them in a church, but they turn away from her as if they do not know her (A503b, 40–A504b, 34).

The list of dream scenes in which Roland and Oliver meet their deaths in various situations has some parallels to the narrative at the end of Genelun's trial, in which various forms of capital punishment are discussed. Here, as in other sections of the *KM*, the writer shows a marked predilection for repetition to make his point. The burden of guilt already laid on Wellis is added to in Alda's dream, because the dream reveals that Roland is dead at Wellis's hand. The negative imagery, including the lion and bear and dark forest, contains allusions to evil and/or the devil, in the case of the lion, which could represent either the heathens or Wellis (Rowland 33, 120). Wellis's appearance in Alda's dream and in the stars as the perpetrator represent extrajudicial means of condemning him, fulfilling a narrative function similar to Karl's frequent transports of grief.

Not only dreams but also the heavens confirm the truth of Alda's dream: Magnus, the wise man accompanying them, has analyzed the configuration of the stars and knows that Roland and Oliver are dead and that Wellis is the traitor (A504b, 59–A505, 3). If God's creation recognizes Wellis as the guilty party, his chances of winning a trial by battle would be nil.

[213] See Merback 150–51 and Bestul 56–60 for comments on the imitation of Christ through the contemplation of suffering.

[214] After Otto's recapture of Genelun, Karl orders him brought to Aachen for trial before the princes (*KG* 11640–52). The position of Wellis's escape in the *KM* narrative would account for the changes.

[215] References to legal meanings of certain words in this passage can be found in the following sources: *verteilen*, Lexer, *MHDHWB*, III, col. 267; *The Saxon Mirror* 186 explains that *Lên* refers to the contract; *lant*, 190, could mean land under cultivation. (See also *DRW*, vol. 8, col. 317.) The passage here thus covers both the contract and, in the following line, the property itself. (The *leyn* form was a Middle Franconian variation; see Hermann Paul, Peter Wiehl, and Siegfried Grosse, *Mittelhochdeutsche Grammatik* (Tübingen: Niemeyer, 1989). *Y* in Middle Franconian frequently functioned as a sign of lengthening; see 166. Dobozy notes that *wîp*, the more common form of the word, means a married adult woman or wife, as opposed to *maget*, a single woman (*The Saxon Mirror* 200). A. Laufs and K.-P. Schroeder, "Landrecht," *HWBDR*, 5 vols., ed. Adalbert Erler, U. Kornblum, and G. Dilcher (Berlin: E. Schmidt, 1964–1998), II: cols. 1527–35 (col. 1527) notes that this term came about

with the development of new legal groupings during the Middle Ages. By the first half of the thirteenth century the concept was well established. See also *"Land(es)recht," DRW*, vol. 8, cols. 547–55 (col. 547) for a citation from around 1120 for the term used in the sense of law valid for a given region *The Sachsenspiegel* has almost thirty occurrences of the word, which differentiates the *landes recht* in Saxony from the *mannes recht* of the Bavarians, Swabians, and Franks. Since the probable area of composition of the *KM* was closest geographically to Saxony, it is not surprising to find our author referring to the concept.

[216] The cloister of St. Denis was dedicated to St. Dionysius and contained the banner that Karl supposedly received from the pope, a banner that became a symbol of French national unity (Spiewok, "Karl der Große" 2).

[217] E. Kaufmann, "Rädern," *HWBDR*, vol. 4, pt. 1, cols. 135–38 (col. 135) lists it as the third most common form of capital punishment in the Middle Ages, coming after hanging and beheading; Merback 158–97. It foreshadows the extensive list of degrading physical punishments suggested for Wellis.

[218] "dat hey mich ind myn man verreit" [That he betrayed me and my men] (A516b, 38).

[219] The *KM* writer's predilection for doubling to increase narrative tension comes to the fore at this point in the trial scene, as well, where he doubles the judicial duel. This incident involving Gundeluff, king of Frisia, a well-known and respected monarch, does not appear in Stricker's or Konrad's versions. The fact that the *KM* compiler includes two judicial duels at this time in the fourteenth century could indicate their abiding popularity.

[220] This quotation comes at the end of Gundeluff's speech (A516b, 47–A517, 20); *clagen*, the technical word for a legal accusation, appears in A516b, 54. The verb *vechten* (517, 15) frequently refers to the fighting in a judicial duel (Lübben 471).

[221] *The Saxon Mirror* 87–88.

[222] Schwineköper, *Handschuh* 95–96.

[223] *The Saxon Mirror* 88: "If he (the defendant) does not come at the third summons, the plaintiff stands up and offers to fight. He swings two blows and makes one thrust into the wind. With that act, he convicts the defendant for the charges as he had spoken them. The judge shall then sentence him as if he had been convicted by the combat."

[224] E. Kaufmann, "Binden" col. 438; Planck, *Gerichtsverfahren*, I, 773–74. Planck notes that a defendant who appears before the court on his own free will and unbound has a far greater chance to use an oath to clear himself (771). There were protections for the defendant who was apprehended and restrained. Planck says that the bound defendant must be brought to court immediately or the accuser loses the right to deliver him and will himself be accused of unlawful behavior (769).

[225] Those called to judgment seem to include both the higher and lower nobility. The *KM* author refers to "Here (lords) ind knechte" (A520b, 36), "guden knechte" (A520b, 41), "arme ind riche" [poor and rich] (A520b, 44), and "vursten" [princes] (A521b, 64). *Gude knechte*, according to Lübben 179, means knightly birth. *The Saxon Mirror* 198 says: "A boy or man in general; . . . certainly someone in a subordinate service relationship since the terms *herr* and *knecht* form an opposition." Planck, *Gerichtsverfahren* I, 99–100.

The word *ordel* appears in A520, 22, A520b, 35. Lübben 256 translates *ordel* as "Urteil" (verdict) or "Gericht" (judgment). The *KM* author also uses the word in a passage in which a voice from Heaven speaks to Karl during a battle with Baligain, in which the voice says "Dat ordel is ouer en gedaen" [The verdict regarding him has been made] (A487, 15). Here it refers to the heathen king.

[226] "Dat hey syne truwe hedde zo brochen / Ind vmb den mort were an gesprochen" [He broke his word and was accused of murder] (A520, 26–27).

[227] This passage, which is first addressed to a powerful lord, Gerard (A520, 19–20), has no exact parallels in the *RL* or *KG;* it occurs shortly before Pinabel's arrival with his small army.

"Eynen kamp vechten soulde" [Should fight a battle] (A520, 30). Lübben 167 indicates that *kamp* was frequently used to mean judicial duel, as is *vechten* (471).

[228] This text fuses the relatives' action into the implied threat of force on the part of Wellis's family and gives them to Pinabel as a retinue of 500 armed men plus another powerful family member, Herffen van Leun (A520b, 51–67).

[229] *RL* 8785–88, *KG* 11807–10; in this case the *KM* author is closer to the *RL* text (*dat boich*, A521, 6).

[230] See previous *RL* and *KG* discussion of Pinabel's defense of Genelun, which rests on Genelun's supposed declaration of feud.

[231] See previous discussion of compurgation.

[232] *Ouvel* (Lübben, "übel" 259); *Ungenade* has a wide range of meanings, including "Plage, feindliches (widerrechtliches) Benehmen; Ungunst," Lübben 438; *"quadem rade"*: *quat* can mean "böse, schlecht, . . . falsch, verräterisch, . . . zornig" (Lübben 288); *rade,* "Befehl . . . Beratung . . . Entschluß . . . Vorhaben" (Lübben 293); *laster,* "Verachtung, Lästerung" (Lübben 198).

[233] After Wellis concludes the discussion under the olive tree with Blantschandiz, the narrator indicates yet again the great reputation that Wellis enjoys: noting that all that glitters is not gold or even silver, he praises Wellis's noble appearance (A447b, 69–448, 4). Later, in the fight scene with Otto, the narrator pays tribute, in a somewhat backhanded way, to Wellis's skill and great reputation as a knight (A493b, 44–46).

[234] Although *vechten* is frequently used as the term for fighting a judicial duel, it can also mean "kämpfen, erstreiten" (Lübben 471); Gerhard Köbler, "Land und Landrecht im Frühmittelalter," *ZSSRGGA* 86 (1969): 1–40 notes (2) the significant change toward *Landrecht* from *Stammesrecht* that characterized legal life in the German lands in the thirteenth century.

[235] See Lübben 103, Lexer, *MHDHWB*, III, col. 267.

[236] *Kint* can have the meaning of noble minor; see Lexer, *MHDHWB*, I, col. 1575.

[237] *RL* 8823–25; *KG,* 11820. This change is typical for the *KM* writer, who leaves out most sections of Stricker's work dealing with family ties. Another component of the Dietrich description in both earlier works was the David-Goliath comparison, which is missing here. The discussion of this point in the Stricker section emphasized the imperial connotations of this comparison. Since Dederich in this version is not a blood relative of Roland and, therefore, has no connection with the monarchy, the

KM author may not have thought the comparison was appropriate. Certainly the religious aspects of it would not have put him off, since he adds a number of those himself.

[238] *The Saxon Mirror* 87–88.

[239] *Ordel* means "verdict" or "court"; obviously "verdict" in this context (Lübben 256). *Verteilen* has the legal meaning of depriving through a verdict (Lexer, *MHDHWB*, III, col. 267).

[240] "Doer," A524, 12; words with this root occur in A524, 16 and 21.

[241] "Ind myn truwe ind myn recht" [in my fidelity and in my just cause] (A524, 30). *Recht* (Lübben 294) has several legal meanings, including means of proof and legal decision, which would seem to be the most suitable here.

[242] *Borgen* (Lübben 62) relates to legal guarantees; for discussion of use of gloves see A524b, 41–42. *Starcks gerihte*, A524b, 52: Lübben 118 gives "means of court," "verdict" and "punishment" for *gerihte*; *verrederen* [traitors] (A524b, 56) and *mortz* [murder] (A524b, 59) have legal meanings as well.

[243] *KG* 11855–59; *KM* A524b, 44–59.

[244] In Stricker's work they were already at Aachen for the trial. (*KG* 11665–71), as was the case in the *RL* (8681). In *KM* the trial is held in the palace in Louwen (A515b, 54).

[245] *RL* 8905–9; *KG* 11926–32, 11944–48.

[246] Naymes and Oyger initiate these defensive efforts (A527, 3–21). There are no similar passages in the two earlier versions.

[247] See A526b, 50–59, where Oyger gives his horse to Dederich. Immediately prior to the judicial duel, Karl's nobles assemble a force of armed knights to put down violence should it occur (A527, 1–21). Another example of featuring the nobility occurs in regard to Oyger's sword, Kurtan, given to Dederich, which figures prominently in the battle scene; Dederich gives it credit for saving his life, and the gravely wounded Pinabel calls it the Devil's sword (A528, 10–A528b, 44). The sword is mentioned by name again when Pinabel is given a mortal wound (A529, 14–16). Moisan notes that the historical Ogier was an important figure at Pepin's court and was at one point not well disposed towards Charles (374–75).

[248] In an early-fourteenth-century work, *Karl der Große und die schottischen Heiligen*, which is a mixture of legend, chanson de geste, and founding legends of monasteries, there is a section on Karl's establishment of Aachen and the role of Irish clergy in its formative years. This section also contains an account of St. Patrick's work in Ireland and that of his successors in Christianizing England and northwestern Europe. This text, which was probably written down in Regensburg between 1300 and 1350, is based on an earlier Latin source, the *Libellus de fondacione ecclesie consecrati Petri Ratispone*, which can only be dated approximately toward the mid-thirteenth century. See Frank Shaw, ed., *Karl der Große und die schottischen Heiligen* (Berlin: Akademie-Verlag, 1981), xxi, xxv, xxxiii–v, xxxix; Shaw, "Karl der Große und die schottischen Heiligen," *VF*, vol. 4 (Berlin & New York: De Gruyter, 1983) cols. 1004–6. The existence of this legend about the founding of Aachen and its connection with the Irish mission and St. Patrick could explain the choice of St. Patrick's relics and the seriousness with which this judicial ordeal was imbued (2060–40; the first Irish missionaries

are commissioned directly by St. Patrick himself, 2179–80). In addition, this reference offers further support for Aachen as the home of the *KM;* an added attraction for the *KM* compiler could have been this legend's reference to Karl's struggles against the heathen (2925–54). Goodich 2–4, 150–52. See Barbara Abou-El-Haj, *The Medieval Cult of Saints: Formations and Transformations* (Cambridge: Cambridge UP, 1997), 147, where a map of major sites where the cult of the saints was popular shows a heavy concentration in the area near Aachen.

[249] Hattenhauer, *Recht der Heiligen* 70–71. *Auctoritas* in the sense of guaranty is a concrete legal procedure that played a role in Roman law. See also Anton Legner, *Reliquien in Kunst und Kult zwischen Antike und Aufklärung* (Darmstadt: Wissenschaftliche Buchgesellschaft, 1995), 39–41, for references to legal matters where relics were involved.

[250] Hattenhauer, *Recht der Heiligen* 66–67, 74.

[251] *KM* A526, 30; see also A526, 24–34; *ungezemelich,* A526b, 38; see A526, 35–A526b, 38.

[252] See *DRW,* vol. 7, cols. 1468–69. The two earlier versions do not list the individuals who serve as wardens (*RL* 8913; *KG* 11935). The *KM* author names the five nobles, showing once again his tendency to give high-ranking aristocrats a great deal of attention.

[253] See *RL* 8937–45 and *KG* 12007–44.

[254] The question of rank and the appropriateness of vassalage are addressed in the comparable passage in the *RL,* where Tirrich tells Pinabel that Pinabel is, like Tirrich, a prince, and that he should be acknowledging his fealty to the emperor (8946–48).

[255] *Meyne eyde* (A529b 44–46).

[256] The verb used, *verdeylen* (A529b, 51), does not appear in Lübben. Lexer, *MHDHWB,* III, col. 267 lists both "to cut into pieces" and "to condemn" for *verteilen.* Since Pinabel was hanged on the gallows, the latter seems to be the appropriate meaning. D. Marschall, "Hängen," *HWBDR,* vol. 1, cols. 1988–90 (col. 1989) says that hanging was considered an ignominious death. Marschall indicates that it was already the preferred form of execution for treason in Germanic times, and that this tradition survived into more recent periods.

[257] The *KM* author substitutes hanging on the gallows for the earlier versions' public display of Pinabel's head on a spear (*RL* 8983–87; *KG* 12073–77).

[258] This statement comes immediately before the catalog of possible punishments, which was also not present in the previous German *Karlsepik.* Merback notes that sentencing had become more public in the later Middle Ages, with a list of crimes and a public confession (132).

[259] For *missedât,* Lübben lists the meanings of misdeed or sin; for *mis-dôn,* he lists "to make a mistake, commit an injustice or wrong" (230). Even the milder translations of these words express a degree of insight into the wrongful nature of his behavior that is lacking in the earlier Genelun figures, while the stronger meanings indicate some repentance.

[260] See E. Kaufmann, "Rache," *HWBDR,* vol. 4, pt.1, cols. 126–27. He notes that the status of *Rache* as a legal word is somewhat unclear, but that when the concept

was used in earlier times, it was in connection with the feud. It was the private act of revenge by the injured party for a real or assumed illegal act of revenge.

[261] Richard Kieckhefer, *Unquiet Souls: Fourteenth-Century Saints and Their Religious Milieu* (Chicago: U of Chicago P, 1984), 138.

[262] Merback traces a concern with making a good end — dying repentant, with hope of eventual salvation — back to the evolving of the doctrine of purgatory and the accompanying penitential system. The spectacle of a heinous criminal throwing himself on God's mercy could give the spectators, concerned about the state of their own souls, hope that they too might be spared damnation (143-46).

[263] Kieckhefer 122-37. He also notes that lay spirituality at this time was essentially monastic (14-15).

[264] Merback says that the "good death" of the penitent criminal cancels out the "bad death" of his victim(s), who died without the last rites and with no chance to repent (146).

[265] Merback notes that in late medieval art, Judas often appears in depictions of the Crucifixion (30). To drive home the similarity of Wellis with Judas, the *KM* author even cites the evangelists: Matt. 26:24 and Mark 14:21 (A531, 23). Schulz notes that the typological analogy with Judas precludes any possibility of concession or mercy toward the Genelun figure (54).

[266] Cohen, *Crossroads* discusses nudity in an execution ceremony as a means of conveying infamy and degradation, practices that obtained in late medieval European society (169-70). Nakedness deprived the accused not only of the status formerly granted to him but also even of his humanity, since it was associated with savagery.

[267] Merback 128-29, 135.

[268] Esther Cohen, "Symbols of Culpability and the Universal Language of Justice: The Ritual of Public Executions in Late Medieval Europe," *History of European Ideas* 11 (1989): 407-16 (408-9); Merback 19-20. Goodich notes that the martyrdom of saints such as the Holy Innocents and St. Sebastian accustomed the public to displays of extreme cruelty (49). Kieckhefer 2-3, 89-121.

[269] Merback 19-20, 44-45, 62-63, 102-3; Kieckhefer 98-113. Kieckhefer notes that Germany produced an especially high number of writings about the Passion (100). For further comments on the internalization of Christ's crucifixion in medieval religious life, see Caroline Walker Bynum, *Holy Feast and Holy Fast: The Religious Significance of Food to Medieval Women* (Berkeley: U of California P, 1987), 246-59.

[270] See Merback 136-38, 210-15. Merback mentions Ulrich Tenngler's *Layenspiegel*, the first printed law code in the vernacular, whose first edition was printed in Straßburg and Augsburg in 1509 and whose punishments "conclude with the total dissolution of the body" (136). A printed version of this codex was not available; Wolfgang Schmitz, *Der Teufelsprozeß vor dem Weltgericht nach Ulrich Tenngler's Neuer Layenspiegel von 1511 (Ausgabe von 1512)* (Cologne: Wienand, 1980) includes a section of it. In his commentary Schmitz notes that the third book of the *Layenspiegel* deals with corporal punishment (44).

[271] Schmitz 213; see also Schmidt-Wiegand, "Gebärdensprache" 373.

[272] In both the *RL* and the *KG* the hostages are beheaded. For hanging, see His 82.

[273] Merback 141; E. Kaufmann, "Feuerstrafe," *HWBDR,* vol. 1, cols. 1125–28; W. Schild, "Verbrennen," *HWBDR,* 35. Überlieferung, cols. 673–80; Cohen, *Crossroads* 191.

[274] Merback 188, 214–15. Tearing apart the body with horses also has a history in connection with Judas, both in the Bible (Acts 1:18) and in legend; see Ohly, "Beiträge" 91–92; Caroline Walker Bynum, *The Resurrection of the Body in Western Christianity, 200–1336* (New York: Columbia UP, 1995) says that chronicle accounts indicate that dismemberment was the most extreme form of execution, kept for the most heinous crimes. The manner in which dismemberment was carried out reflected the crime of which the unfortunate criminal was convicted, so that onlookers were able to determine what that crime was through the manner of dismemberment and display (323–24). For the connection between animalization and criminal cases, see Cohen, *Crossroads* 180.

[275] Several recent studies open new lines of approach to the question. Bestul analyzes passion narratives in the high and late medieval Rhineland, among other places, looking at the cultural context in which they occur. Merback, building on the work of Esther Cohen, Pieter Spierenburg, and others, explores the growth of representations of Calvary scenes in late medieval European art and their interconnections with medieval devotional life and with the criminal justice system concerning the Passion of Christ. His book focuses extensively on the different artistic treatment given the two thieves on the crosses, whose wounds and suffering are shown in much more gruesome detail than that of Christ.

[276] Bestul 7–10.

[277] Robert Priebsch, ed., *Christi Leiden in einer Vision Geschaut* (Heidelberg: Winter, 1936). Bestul notes that this work came out of a long tradition in both Latin and vernacular writings on the Passion (64, 146–64). Kieckhefer notes that these nearly clinical descriptions were intended to inspire compassion and penitence in the onlookers (103–6).

[278] Bestul 153–55, 157.

[279] See Bestul 160–61; he believes that the representations of torture in the Passion helped to show that the human body could be treated in this way, making acceptance of torture as part of the order of things easier.

[280] Cohen, "Symbols" 408; Spierenburg notes that the increase in corporal and capital punishment that took place from the twelfth through the sixteenth centuries did not reflect a morbid increase in interest in the spectacle of violence and misery. He sees it as a reflection of the growing entrenchment of the criminal justice system (12).

[281] Merback 132.

2: The Ordeals of Tristan and Isolde

WHILE THE CHARLEMAGNE EPICS provided us with dramatic contexts of murder, treason, and power struggles for trial by battle, trial by fire — the ordeal of choice in cases involving adultery — is more at home in the romance. This ordeal makes its most famous literary appearance in one of the great narrative traditions of medieval literature, the tragic love story of Tristan and Isolde. In the case of the Tristan material as Gottfried von Straßburg shaped it, including his famous commentary on the ordeal by fire, we are in the fortunate position of being able to compare contemporary attitudes toward both ordeals portrayed in the same work, ordeals that, as we have seen in the introduction, suffered widely different fates historically. Although we know little about Gottfried von Straßburg, except that he probably received a master's degree from the new university in Paris and served in the office of the bishop of Strasbourg,[1] he does tell us something about his sources, the principal one being Thomas of Britain. It is clear from the prologue that he knew other versions of the Tristan story, but Thomas's is the only one of which he approved.[2] Such explicit statements about sources are rare in medieval literature, but an even more interesting aspect is why Gottfried believed that Thomas's version of the story was best. Perhaps his choice had to do with Isolde; in Thomas, Tristan's love for Isolde means more to him than his honor.[3]

The origins of the Tristan material probably lie, like much of medieval romance, in the vast repository of Celtic tales.[4] The Celtic story involves events in the narrative cycle about King Finn, in which Grainne falls in love with her husband's vassal Diarmaid and uses magic to have her way with him; Diarmaid is a most reluctant lover but cannot free himself from the curse put on him. When and in what stages the transformation that resulted in the story as we have it in Thomas and Gottfried took place cannot be established with certainty. What is known is that between approximately 1150 and 1190 three versions of the Tristan story appeared: Thomas of Britain's, Eilhart von Oberg's, and Béroul's. The latter two are often referred to as part of the jongleur literary tradition, while Thomas, whose retelling of the story emphasizes both elegant manners and psychological depth, falls into the courtly category.

This classification is not entirely fair, since both Eilhart and Béroul contain courtly elements. Thomas's reworking of the story, however, marked a real departure from the emphasis on adventure and trickery in the other two works. The situation that Thomas addresses — what role does love between the sexes play in a society in which the purpose of marriage among the nobility is to cement alliances and increase wealth? — seemed to interest Gottfried, as well (12279–357). Fidelity in marriage, at least on the wife's part, was expected both for succession and for religious reasons. Thomas sought to show that in such a situation individuals who fell deeply in love deserved more sympathy than the censure that was apparent in other versions. With this approach Thomas changed the emphasis of the work and imbued the major events of the story with psychological connections and an internalizing of the love relationship.[5]

Certain narrative elements were always present in the Tristan tradition, among them the duel with Morold and the poisoned sword.[6] However much the presentation of this incident varies, the battle puts Mark and the nobles in Tristan's debt, because he risks his life to save Cornwall. In addition, the infection caused by the poisoned sword takes Tristan to Ireland, where he meets Isolde. Brother Robert's translation of Thomas's version of the duel shows many parallels with Gottfried's account: both narratives emphasize legal maneuvers and issues, with much the same emphases, though there are no allegorical figures to aid Tristan, as in Gottfried's account, nor does God's role and presence seem as pervasive as in the German work.[7]

While the Morold scene is ubiquitous, the situation is different with regard to Isolde's ordeal by fire. Eilhart does not know it at all. The ordeal is faked with Tristan's complicity in Béroul, where it differs greatly in tone and psychology from Gottfried's version. Iseut sends a message to Tristran beforehand, telling him to disguise himself as a leper. In the period leading up to the ordeal Tristran amuses himself by begging leggings from King Arthur and other articles of clothing from assembled nobles and sinking Iseut's accusers in the mud of the ford. Iseut asks Tristran to be her pack horse to carry her across; Béroul notes that she rides him like a horse. After Tristran performs this service, the queen urges Arthur not to give this well-fed leper any more alms. She swears an oath that no man except Mark and the leper have ever been between her thighs.[8] While Gottfried preserves the complicity between Tristan and Isolde to fake the ordeal, the comic elements in Béroul's version, which were probably influenced by the fabliau tradition,[9] are replaced in Gottfried by strong and conflicting emotions of fear and desperation. Brother Robert's translation of Thomas contains an account similar in many respects to Gottfried's: Tristan is disguised as a pilgrim, not a leper, and, except for a reference Isolde makes to her white thighs, the sexual innuendo that pervades the scene in Béroul is absent.[10] The ordeal scenes in both Thomas and Gottfried reflect their penchant for reshaping the traditional narrative material to achieve thematic and character development.

The wealth of legal detail in Gottfried's account surpasses that even of Thomas's work as we have it through Brother Robert. It should, therefore, come as no surprise that no ordeal in medieval German literature has received more critical analysis than Isolde's famous ordeal by fire.[11] Not only the heat of Isolde's passion but also Gottfried's biting commentary have drawn critics eager to use both the high drama and Gottfried's remarks on the procedure as support for their interpretations of the entire work. While the other ordeal — the trial by battle with Morolt, the brother of Queen Isolde of Ireland — has received less attention, the amount of legal learning Gottfried displays there is just as extensive as in Isolde's hearing and trial.[12] Previous studies dealt either with one ordeal or the other or used the two ordeal scenes as part of a larger interpretative structure. In contrast, the present study will place these events in the legal and literary context of ordeals in the early thirteenth century to see how Gottfried's version might reflect influences and attitudes of the period. While this analysis does not use the ordeals as cornerstones for a thesis about the entire work, it does have implications for current research on *Tristan*.[13]

Gottfried's approaches to the two ordeals could not be more different; an overview of the scenes dealing with the judicial duel is instructive in this regard. Missing are sardonically ironic commentaries; missing are attempts to pervert the process of justice through oaths that are literally true but at the heart false. Instead, the language of legend and the chanson de geste, as well as allegorical elements that Gottfried uses at significant and serious parts of the work such as Tristan's knighting and the love grotto, clothe the judicial duel with narrative approbation. Not only do the type of ordeal and the presentation differ; the legal matters in question also contrast sharply. The judicial issue in the Morolt narrative concerns the terms of a political and financial contract that has involved the people of Cornwall in the payment of tribute. While that ordeal centers on interpretation of the facts, the emphasis in Isolde's is on true or false oaths in a case of adultery. The theological questions that hang in the charged air around Isolde during her ordeal are not at issue in the Morolt section.

The battle with Morolt is, of course, necessary to motivate Tristan's journey to Ireland and the introduction of Isolde into the narrative. But the extensive detail with which Gottfried portrays the event, as well as the borrowing from various literary genres, the allegorical allusions, and the obvious moral approbation apparent in the course of the action, indicate that this fight has more significance than simply to advance the plot.[14] A particular interpretative point at issue is the character of Tristan and its relation to Gottfried's opinion of chivalry. Scholars such as W. T. H. Jackson, Dennis Green, and Peter K. Stein belong to what might be called the "Tristan the Trickster" school. In their view, his perceived manipulative and deceptive behavior constitutes an attack on chivalry and they claim to find support for their interpretation in the judicial duel with Morolt. As in the case of the ordeal by fire, these critics use the battle with Morolt as evidence for a larger interpretative question. Indifference to legal history leads them to conflate unilateral and bilateral ordeals; they also do not address medieval legal realities and courtroom procedure. This lack of knowledge leads both to mis- and overinterpretation. Rüdiger Schnell has affinities with this group, since he believes that Tristan tries to manipulate God in this incident. Although he is more interested in legal matters than most critics, he sees this fight as supporting evidence for attempts in the work to exploit God.[15]

A vital link in the chain of events that bring Tristan to Ireland, the duel with Morolt is the only judicial duel in the work that actually comes about. Tristan dispatches Morgan in a fight, while the proposed duels in the Truchseß and Gandin episodes never happen.[16] The legal issue provoking the battle involves the tribute that Cornwall had to pay Gurmun of Ireland. This tribute, described as "zins" in the original text, was a result of Cornwall's subjection by Gurmun. The word *zins*, Lat. *census*, was a well-established legal term in the Middle Ages and was used in commercial, as well as in governmental, affairs.[17]

The payment of the tribute had been established in a treaty. Tristan and Morolt use four words with legal meanings to describe the guarantees and terms of this relationship: *sicherheit, eit, gelübede,* and *triuwe*. All four can mean a promise or an agreement; yet, there are different shades of meaning.[18] *Sicherheit* could mean the treaty itself, while the oath [*eit*], in addition to denoting a promise, was also the means through which an agreement received legal standing. The oath owed its force and standing to its function as a kind of self-curse that called down penalties on violators. The Christianization of the oath only increased its gravity for the individual. The oath in question is not a purgative oath, such as Kunigunde swore, but a promissory one. These types of oaths, common in the Middle Ages, took a variety of forms; some of them, such as the subject's oath, were probably modeled on Roman law.[19]

From the thirteenth century onward *gelübede* is well documented as a legal term for obligation; renunciation incurred loss of reputation as well as legal rights and was equated with perjury. Morolt's line of defense is, therefore, a potent one: choosing those parts of the agreement that corroborate his legal position, he accuses Tristan and thereby the rest of the nobles of oath-breaking, which was a kind of perjury, as well as of breaking their *triuwe* [fidelity] and *sicherheit*. In the Middle Ages the breach of any kind of formalized promise was considered a breach of fidelity.[20] These charges were laden with most serious legal implications, which is why Tristan immediately goes on the counterattack.

Tristan quickly punctures Morolt's legal strategy, which, like most such strategies, is long in the tooth: you do not have a case. The hope is always that an uninformed or dull-witted opponent will accept the other's statement at face value and give up. Tristan, however, knows the terms of the treaty and in a cogent and precise response seizes the legal initiative from Morolt. Refusal to pay tribute does not break *triuwe unde eit:* Tristan points out that the terms of the agreement provided for either the tribute or a duel or a battle between two armies as fulfillment of Cornwall's legal obligations (6359–76). Not only does Tristan have the specific treaty on his side; he could also have called on tradition: the right to dissolve an oath to an unjust lord had existed since Germanic times.[21]

Faced with the facts, Morolt still tries to place his opponent at a moral disadvantage. The choice of a battle or a duel is no choice, since he came alone, expecting no hostility. He intended to leave Cornwall as he had always done, with "rehte und ouch mit minnen" (6404), legal obligations fulfilled in a peaceful atmosphere. This phrase, a legal term extant in Latin that made its first appearance in a German legal code in the *Sachsenspiegel,* reveals that for Morolt *reht,* or law, still means the tribute, with no other options. Tristan seems to be basing part of his position on *lantrecht* and legal sovereignty.[22]

Morolt's interpretation of the treaty differs irreconcilably from that of Tristan and the nobles; the fact that a duel takes place at all indicates that Morolt's position rests on interpretation and not on incontrovertible fact. Since no compromise is possible between the two positions on the legality of the tribute, the issue must be settled, according to contemporaneous judicial practice, through a judicial duel. Like the ordeals of fire and water, the judicial ordeal was used in cases where the truth could not be established in other ways. This fact of medieval legal life has not been included in analyses by scholars who see the judicial duel as a tactical ploy that Tristan originates and as evidence of his lack of principle.[23] In fact, definite procedural rules laid out the sufficient reasons for judicial duels; moreover, as the only detailed analysis of law in *Tristan* points out, the fact that something needs to be proved places the duel in the category of a *judicium Dei,* since God intervenes on behalf of the right.[24]

God's active involvement appears from the beginning of Tristan's conversations with the nobles (6085–13, 6138–92).[25] He expressly states that if the battle turns out in his favor, it will be because God wills it so (6171–72). These passages deserve close attention, because in them Tristan lays out the issues involved and the outlines of the personification that Gottfried later expands prior to the battle. When Tristan returns to Mark's court, which is full of cringing barons preparing to sell their children into slavery to save their own lives, he bases his amazement on religious grounds: he says that it is completely against God's commandments to behave in this way (6105–10). Only one man and a duel are needed to change this situation; the man is assured of divine rewards immediately if he loses and later if he wins. God's commandments and their own reputations should impel them to find a champion who will put his fate in God's hands and not fear Morolt's strength. Tristan's references to divine intervention become much more frequent as it becomes apparent that he is the only noble ready to take on this task. If they leave matters to God and himself, he entreats God to let matters fall out well and restore them to their rights. If the battle has a positive outcome, it will be because of the power of God, who alone will deserve thanks if Tristan succeeds. He names God, justice, and his own strength of feeling as his three helpers who go with him into battle and compensate for his lack of experience (6138–92). This reference sets the stage for the personification that Gottfried introduces during the battle.

The role of God as the guarantor of justice (6170–72) and Tristan's protector (6155, 6158, 6184) appears frequently in Tristan's speeches throughout the Morolt section. Similar statements figure prominently in the speeches of saintly characters about to undergo ordeals — Kunigunde and Richardis come to mind.[26] In this regard Tristan's statements, reminiscent as they are of legend material, serve several functions. Like the courageous and holy figures of legend and Karl's champions, Tristan stands unequivocally in the right. In other ordeal material in literature, only the figures who are right in a religious sense and who will emerge victorious speak so calmly about losing. Similar speeches are missing from the section involving Isolde's trial by fire; indeed, the comparison of Gottfried's two ordeals with the legend accounts will offer striking contrasts in many instances. Throughout the quarrel with Morolt, God's role in the rule of law appears in a much different light than in the later court scene. Tristan describes God here as the supreme arbiter who ensures that right triumphs. The contrast with Gottfried's famous commentary on the pliant Christ could not be more marked.[27]

One of the major functions of the ordeal by battle was to combat perjury; for this reason we find it often in cases connected to oaths or treaties, since the breaking of a promise was equated with perjury. Such is the case in the situation with Morolt. Because the issues surrounding a trial by battle were often major ones, the stakes were high, involving such considerations as the loss of property, a hand, legal protection, or one's own life. Consequently, these fights were often bestially ferocious, as is the case with Tristan's struggle.[28] A vicious fight, in which each side took whatever advantage possible, should not be taken as a mark of a calculating and devious character, as critics of Tristan and chivalry have frequently assumed. Indeed, recent research has shown that German literature of Gottfried's day contained such ruthless battles by aristocratic heroes whose conduct was never questioned.[29]

As the introduction indicated, many factors apart from divine intervention could determine the course of a fight; for this reason, there was much concern with deception. Morolt gives us a good example, since he comes equipped with poison on his sword. In contrast to the ordeal by fire, which involved the accused and the elements, the trial by battle demanded neither a direct response from the natural world nor an immediate sign of divine intervention.[30] Consequently, critics who fault Tristan for deviousness in this encounter cannot credibly maintain that his prayers for assistance were an attempt to manipulate God similar to Isolde's.[31] There are two distinctive differences: first, in a battle God is not asked to reply through the natural order of inanimate things; second, in a battle there were no literally true but inherently false oaths, which are an attempt to manipulate God.

Since a judicial duel was the legal remedy of last resort, it was preceded by lengthy statements about the case. These statements took place in a courtroom before the peers of the realm and the ruler; the latter usually functioned as judge, as Charlemagne did in Genelun's trial. The paradigmatic literary judicial duel, appearing in Priest Konrad's late twelfth-century work, with which Gottfried certainly could have been familiar, was the one relating to Genelun's guilt in the German versions of the Song of Roland. Medieval judges did not have to be neutral, as Charlemagne certainly was not. While Mark functions nominally in this regard in the Morolt episode, he behaves in a much less active way than the bishop of Thames, the presiding official, in the hot-iron ordeal. Mark appears only on the sidelines to wring his hands at the risk to his beloved nephew and to help arm him. While both of these activities were based on the traditional responsibility of a brother for the safety of his sister's son, the manner in which Mark carries them out causes Gottfried to note that the most timid of women could not have been more distraught (6524–25).[32] Tristan does take center stage in the negotiations, causing Morolt to refer sarcastically to the newly knighted youth as the *voget* for Cornwall.[33]

In his formal challenge to Morolt, Gottfried's Tristan shows an intimate knowledge of legal procedures surrounding a judicial duel. He first makes all parties aware of what is at issue: whose interpretation of the law is correct (6450–53). As a gage of battle, he offers his glove. The rationale behind this gesture is to offer surety that the duel will take place. Gloves, used since Franconian times as guarantees in cases of debt, signified in a duel that the participants owed each other a battle[34] (6454, 6486–87). Further indication of Gottfried's extensive understanding of courtroom procedure is Tristan's awareness that he can spoil his case by misspeaking: he asks the king and all others present to listen to his presentation of the case for a judicial duel and make sure that he does not break any rules (6458–60).[35] The clear and precise statement that follows of what he intends to prove with the ordeal could only have been produced by a writer with legal knowledge or experience: that neither Morolt, his lord, nor any other man has a right to exact tribute from Cornwall and England by force. The duel is to cover all eventualities, leaving no opportunity for anyone to find a loophole later. Tristan's case will be proved before God and the world on the person of Morolt, who is responsible for the shame and misery that has befallen these two lands (6461–72).

Not only the larger legal issues but also the details of legal procedure appear in Gottfried's account. Judicial duels generally took place at a subsequent date; Tristan and Morolt's is set for three days later (6494–95).[36] Negotiations also decided the site for the battle; in this case an island so close to the mainland that everyone can see the battle is chosen (6721–26). Though otherwise unknown in other Middle High German literary descriptions of judicial ordeals, such a site was frequent in Old Norse saga accounts.[37] Because of the proximity of the island to the mainland, no one other than the combatants was allowed on the island (6727–30). Such firm rules, usually threatening the death penalty to interlopers, were common in order to avoid interference with justice.[38]

As the battle draws near, Gottfried paints a revealing picture in the approach of the two combatants — a picture that sums up their attitudes toward the encounter. Morolt, as we have seen in the court assembly, trusts in his strength and experience. Confidence in one's own ability instead of God's help is also characteristic of Pinabel in the Roland material, which has much of the hagiographic legend in it. Morolt puts on an imposing display for the benefit of the spectators on the mainland: he gallops his horse at full tilt, thrusting with his lance, as if he were engaged in courtly games. Tristan, meanwhile, stands before his boat and bids an earnest farewell to Mark and Mark's subjects. He asks God to restore justice and go with him in the battle (6745–84).

Before the blows begin, both combatants go on the offensive in other ways: Tristan sets his boat adrift, because only one of them will survive the encounter. Morolt addresses him with the familiar form of the personal pronoun, either as a sign of lack of respect or as a signal that all social conventions are laid aside now that the battle is imminent.[39] The typical epic convention of the defendant's offer of a bribe appears here, as it does in Stricker's *Karl der Grosse* during the duel to prove Genelun's guilt. In both of these cases the defendants are much bigger and more experienced gladiators. Consequently, in each case the refusal of the offer enhances the stature of the plaintiff.[40]

Emphasis on the uneven physical odds calls the David/Goliath comparison to mind and lends further support to the argument that God is on Tristan's side. Indeed, the parallels between David/Tristan, Saul/Mark, and Goliath/Morolt appear throughout the Morolt incident. The Hebrews, like the Britons, have the choice of duel or battle; none of them are prepared to fight Goliath individually. Both Tristan and David come from outside the country, and both are accused of arrogance. Although both are inexperienced in such battles, both trust in God, knowing that the attack from the opponent is an attack on God, as well. Saul and Mark both advise against the battle, but both arm their defenders. David and Tristan both leave permanent reminders of their victory in their victims' foreheads, and both behead their opponents.[41] These striking parallels reinforce the other indications in the narrative that God is on Tristan's side.

As the fight commences, Tristan, despite an energetic offensive, soon begins to get the worst of it at the hands of the experienced Morolt, who is described as one led by the devil (6852) and then as the devil's condemned vassal (6906).[42] Such descriptions are a staple of these encounters, particularly in the language of legend and the Charlemagne material; we find them almost word for word for Pinabel in the various versions of Genelun's trial. Like Pinabel, Morolt trusts in his own strength and is on the wrong side. Such a description only enhances the character of the protagonist, as do many other elements of Gottfried's characterization, and point up sharply the difference in Gottfried's portrayals of the two ordeals.

The detailed account of the fierce battle sets the stage for divine intervention and the allegorical elements that characterize the decisive part of the fight. Against Morolt's strength, equivalent to that of four men, Gottfried sets God, Right, and Willing Heart as Tristan's companions in arms.[43] As God and Right ride in to help, Tristan senses their presence and spurs his horse on to one last charge so that Morolt is overturned. Slicing off Morolt's sword hand before he remounts, Tristan then beheads him.[44]

To understand fully the significance of the presence of allegorical figures during this ordeal, it is necessary to examine briefly Gottfried's use of allegory and personification in other parts of the work. It appears most significantly in the knighting of Tristan and in the love grotto scene, crucial sections of the work that use allegorical devices to present a favorable portrayal or positive aspects of the event in question.[45] Of these two passages, the knighting ceremony has the most relevance, since it, like the duel with Morolt, relies on the use of personification rather than on the extended allegorical composition of the love grotto scene.[46] Moreover, the duel with Morolt occurs not long after Tristan's knighting and shows other parallels, such as the equipping of Tristan. In the knighting ceremony Vulcan makes his armor; in the Morolt scene Mark equips his nephew. In the knighting scene four figures — Mettle, Means, Discretion, and Courtesy — prepare Tristan to be a knight (4565–88; 4965–74). In the Morolt scene Right and Willing Heart are his companions in arms.[47] Their presence sets this battle apart from others used to settle disputes, such as the one with Morgan that immediately precedes the judicial duel. Another connection between the investiture and the judicial duel appears in the descriptions of Tristan's armor. In both sections images of the Dart and the Boar, symbols of courage and love's torture, appear on his armor (4942–49; 6594–98; 6614–16).[48] Morgan has made slanderous remarks about Tristan's birth, which leads to his immediate dispatch by the alleged bastard. There are no elaborate descriptions of armor, of inner strengths, or of allegorical figures. The similarity with the knighting ceremony and the absence of such descriptions in the fight with Morgan, which stands between the two, show that for Gottfried the ordeal by battle was a significant event that he treated with seriousness and a certain amount of approbation. The personification of justice, making it a semidivine being, provides Gottfried with another rhetorical technique to emphasize the rightness of Tristan's cause in this judicial duel.

Further evidence that Tristan stands on God's side lies in Morolt's — the devil figure's — use of poison. Both ordeals involve poison: in the judicial duel Morolt fights with a poisoned sword; in the trial by fire Isolde delivers what Gottfried describes as a poisoned oath. In both cases he uses the relatively rare Middle High German word *gelueppet*.[49] The nominative form, *gelueppe,* can mean either poison or magic salve. Magic fell more and more into disrepute at this time for two reasons: the rationality of Roman law, which was undergoing its great revival in the twelfth and thirteenth centuries had no place for it; nor did Christianity. Its influence was seen particularly on the oath, which was no longer true or false according to a blind adherence to formulaic rules but only insofar as it reflected actual fact, as well as the soul of the giver of the oath.[50] While Morolt's poisoned sword is essential for the plot to unfold, both contexts in which Gottfried uses this word are clearly negative. Morolt represents an unjust cause and is, as we have seen, a representative of the devil; he, therefore, does not hesitate to use a poisoned sword whose wound can be healed by only one person.[51] That it can be healed by only one person implies that the healer has quasi-magical powers. While Gottfried does not describe Isolde as a she-devil, the use of the same unusual word for her oath could give us an important clue about his attitude toward the trial by fire.

Gottfried's artistic goals in his presentation of the judicial ordeal in *Tristan* and its place in an interpretation of the entire work are tasks that lie outside the purview of this study. Attention to the legal realities that constitute his version of the story, however, reveals that Tristan seems to be behaving in a straightforward and honorable, even highly brave, manner that was not inconsonant with the customs surrounding the judicial duel. Gottfried's positive treatment of trial by battle, with invocation of allegory and biblical image, forms a striking contrast to his well-known sardonic commentary on trial by fire. What implications these differences might have in understanding his views on the character of the protagonists and on the nature of God must be left to those who look at the work as a whole.

Like the two ordeals in the *Kaiserchronik* and *Heinrich und Kunegunde,* Isolde's is part of a trial convened to settle a controversy that weakens the monarchy. But whereas the ordeal in the previous works served primarily to confirm the high moral virtue of two women unjustly attacked, Isolde's ordeal serves to acquit a woman who is most assuredly guilty as charged. The question of Isolde's adultery was not simply a marital problem; since she was a queen, the possibility of an accusation of treason was present; political considerations were also a factor in the preceding legendary accounts.[52]

The degree of legal detail Gottfried presents, as the accusations against Isolde reach such a point that Mark must act, parallels the attention to legal matters apparent in the judicial duel with Morolt and is far more extensive than in the corresponding scenes in the legends. As in the legends, the presence of rumors that will not rest and the king's own doubts force a public resolution of the issue. Unlike the German emperors who have no plan of action other than to wait for the ordeal's results, however, Mark wants to stop the gossip and convince the nobles of that which he wants to believe himself, that is, that his wife and nephew are innocent (15275–79). In these preliminary procedures Mark, like his historical counterparts, is much concerned with his reputation and the effect of the rumors about Isolde on it (15286, 15298, 15322–24, 15325–30).

In the Richardis and Kunigunde legends the course of events surrounding the ordeal involves the advice of the queen at the point at which the king becomes aware of the rumors. Their unswerving marital fidelity gives them a standing in the matter that Isolde cannot have, since she has never been faithful to her husband. Indicative of the gulf between them, Mark, unlike the emperors, does not confront his wife directly with her infidelity. Unsure of her, he turns instead to an inner circle of princes he believes he can trust[53] (15280–82) and tells them that he will have no more contact with Isolde until the matter is settled (15291–94). They advise him to call a *concilje* in London and to turn to the leaders of the church versed in *gotes reht* (canon law, 15300–305).[54] Mark makes the arrangements, setting the date after Pentecost and inviting both clergy and laity (15308–15).[55]

When Mark opens the council, he addresses the princes of the realm, from whom he asks advice; but the bishop of Thames, described as having the intelligence of the experienced older person (15342–48), is the only speaker whose remarks are quoted.[56] He emphasizes first the legal parity of the bishop's class with that of the other princes of the realm. Using the terms *überkomen* and *überseit*, he presents a precise legal evaluation that reminds the king that Isolde and Tristan have not been caught in adultery.[57] Since that is the case, the most likely punishment Isolde could expect would be separation from Mark and public disgrace. Loss of her reputation is a real worry to the queen and is undoubtedly a major motivation for her subsequent conduct (15319–20). Two sources of jurisdiction for a wayward wife were that of the Church, which could demand penance and allowed separation, and that of the husband. Generally the punishment for a wife caught in the act of adultery was more severe. The distinction between eyewitness evidence and other kinds was not always made, however, and the husband could choose to be quite stern. In most instances the Church had a mitigating influence in this area, as did the general realization among the nobility that brutality toward women was uncourtly.[58]

Without proof of any kind being brought forward to substantiate the accusation, the bishop asks rhetorically how any judgment can be brought against the two (15374–79). The unsubstantiated accusation [*inziht*] refers to a special type of procedure regarding reputation that was common in medieval legal life. Proceedings of this kind might be opened by anything that caused suspicion and could not be conclusively proved, including pieces of circumstantial evidence and rumors, but it was not necessary to describe the evidence to begin the hearing. The defendant could clear the charges with an oath. Closely connected with *inziht* was *liument,* which could mean malicious gossip; the bishop of Thames uses the word twice, in connection with *inziht*. The legal procedures involved with these two categories were similar, since both could begin on the basis of a rumor.[59] In establishing the reasons for the proceedings the bishop mentions the injury done to Mark by these suspicions (15404–9) and indicates that since Isolde is accused of such misdeeds, she should be brought before the assembly so that all can hear Mark's accusation and her reply.[60]

While rumors lead to the ordeal in the legends, they do not contain the explicit legal procedure that Gottfried includes and that characterizes the entire episode. The careful legal nature of Gottfried's trial scene for the ordeal by fire contrasts sharply with the legends, where innocent queens offer extravagant, emotional, all-encompassing oaths. Gottfried's skilled use of legalities is an implicit comment on Isolde's guilt, because the *inziht* procedure, with its inherent uncertainty and lack of eyewitness evidence, parallels the ambiguity of the entire scene — an ambiguity that implies Isolde's guilt just as the unrestrained oaths of the unjustly accused queens indicate their innocence.

The careful, deliberate wording of the bishop's recommendation — which continues in his charge to Isolde (15428–68), in which he repeats the charges with legal terminology — diverges sharply from the corresponding scene in Kunigunde's trial.[61] Beyond the fact that Gottfried shows here, as in the scene with Tristan and Morolt, that he is well versed in legal matters, the extensive attention to detail by Mark and the bishop could be an attempt to establish the validity of the results so as to calm the nobles. Unlike Heinrich II's peers in the legend of Queen Kunegunde, Mark's court despises Tristan and would be only too happy to see his ruin. The precise but fair courtroom procedures, with the bishop making a gracious and generous presentation to Isolde, contrasts strikingly with her determination to deceive everyone. Gottfried's use of careful legal detail to assure fairness in the case heightens the tension in the reader, who knows that Isolde must undermine the system.

After the bishop of Thames finishes his speech, Isolde comes before the court and the actual trial begins. As she steps to the center of the stage, the word used to characterize her is *gesinne* [clever],[62] which typifies her approach throughout. Unlike Kunigunde, whose only concern is to clear her name, Isolde, confronted with charges that will not go away, attacks the motivation of the rumormongers — an age-old strategy in disputes. Even the bishop has noted in his speech to the council that part of the human condition is an unfortunate weakness for others' scandals (15396–403), and he tells Isolde that the rumors may arise from reprisal against her (15445–46). Building on his comment, she says that distinction always arouses resentment, just as Mark indicated at an earlier point (8387–414) regarding the barons' jealousy of Tristan (15476–88).[63] The kindly bishop's intent to be fair and generous gives Isolde a chance for an explanation that does contain truth: the barons are envious. But this partial truth hides a lie, just as Isolde's oath does.

Isolde's rationalization for the accusation and her vulnerability to such rumors is that she is a foreigner, bereft of the protection of family (15492–98).[64] While designed to arouse pity on the part of Mark and the bishop of Thames, Isolde's explanation describes a state of affairs that does have a bearing on her legal situation. Since she has no relatives of standing present, she cannot avail herself of oathhelpers. Consequently, she cannot offer to clear herself of the charge through the character witness of her relatives; in such cases an ordeal could be mandatory, since it was the only means available of establishing truth.[65]

Isolde — who may well have been aware that she had no real choice in the matter, given both the enmity of the barons and her status as a foreigner, as well as the seriousness of the charge — offers to do whatever the court asks of her to clear her name. Isolde never intimates what she wants but leaves the decision to Mark (15503–10).[66] Such behavior was common among the accused; agreeing to undergo an ordeal was a maneuver that an individual on the defensive might use to imply innocence. If the accused person is so willing to submit to any ordeal, then that person may be wrongly accused and confident of acquittal. The literary effect of Isolde's willingness to do whatever is asked presents her in a suppliant, agreeable posture to the judges as she, maintaining her innocence, makes an effort to elicit their sympathy. Her behavior stands in sharp contrast to that of the queens in the legends, as well as to that of Isönd in the *Tristramssaga*, who demand the form of proof with the highest potential danger to clear their names. Isönd even adds that, should she fail, the king should burn her at the stake or have her torn apart by horses.[67] If Brother Robert, the translator of Thomas's work into Old Norse, has remained faithful to his source in this section, then apparently Thomas's version of this scene is much closer to the queens of legend than Gottfried's. Here, as at other points, Gottfried seems to have made changes, whether by omission or addition, that underscore the difference between Isolde and the saintly consorts of legend. Rather than extravagant denials of innocence and insistence on ordeals far more terrifying than the hot iron, Isolde plays for sympathy both as a foreigner and as the object of envy.[68]

Mark's reply is terse and legalistic in tone but advantageous for Isolde in that instead of stating the charge against the queen he asks Isolde to do what she has offered to do and chooses for her the ordeal of the hot iron (15520–27).[69] The bishop's presentation of the accusation against Isolde is highly general, implying adultery on the queen's part with Tristan (15446–48). A discreet and circumspect accusation makes the situation much easier when the time to swear the oath comes, because a defendant who is both guilty and clever can avoid making a false statement. In Isolde's case, the charge did not demand such a detailed oath.

Gottfried's portrayal of the ordeal is short in comparison with the contemporary accounts of church rituals connected with the judgment of God. (15634–730). What did Gottfried leave out, what did he include, and what might it have meant? He omits several steps, such as the procession from the church to the place where the ordeal would take place; the *aspersio,* the removal of the iron from the fire and the prayer over the hot iron; as well as the exorcism of evil spirits and the banning of deception from the proceedings. Generally the person about to undergo an ordeal spent the previous three days in fasting and prayer and the night before in the church.[70] Other sections of the process receive only cursory attention. The long liturgy that Isolde had to sit through and that would put a guilty person into a nervous state is described in two lines (15651–52). The blessing of the iron and the *adjuratio,* both of which were parts of the ordeal, are covered in only six lines (15637–42).[71] If we compare the legal sections of the trial by battle, the battle itself, and the detailed and lengthy description of the two meetings prior to the ordeal by fire (the first with Mark's trusted advisers, the next with the bishop of Thames), the cursory manner in which Gottfried passes over much of the procedure for the ordeal itself is striking.

What conclusions can one draw from Gottfried's account? The first and most obvious is that he, like the two writers of legends, is not interested in reporting all of the events of the ordeal. Since his interest focuses on the queen — her appearance, her behavior, her fear, and her deception — he does not stress the preparatory steps for the ordeal because Isolde is not in center stage during them.[72] Another possible reason for the rather perfunctory account of this part of the trial could be that, as a cleric himself, he was reluctant to give the liturgy a prominent role in a procedure of which he himself seemed to be critical.[73] Only with the mention of the iron's being laid in the fire, making Isolde, the problematic penitent, the center of attention, does Gottfried give more detail. He describes her short skirt and hair shirt with sleeves rolled back almost to the elbows (15656–63). Her attire seems to reflect usages connected with preparation of the defendants. In earlier times the accused had to be undressed before he could undergo the ordeal, a custom that was rooted in the pre-Christian era. In the Middle Ages there was a partial undressing, including the removal of shoes and shaving of all hair to preclude the possibility of concealment of devices intended to change the outcome of the ordeal.[74] The special clothing not only reflected the humble, penitential attitude that the defendant was supposed to have but also was yet another precaution against rigging the ordeal — not, as some critics have suggested, a decision that Isolde made to display her slender ankles in an age that saw few of them in public and thereby win sympathy.[75] Isolde orchestrates her behavior prior to the ordeal with the same care that shaped her presentation before the council and her plans with Tristan. Consistent with her public appearance is the gentle, forgiving manner with which she reacts to the clumsy pilgrim's attempt to assist her, a manner that finds favor with those present (15603–11).

While there is much in the ordeal procedure that she cannot control, Isolde's influence on the course of events is nowhere more apparent than in the manner of her oath. The nature of the judicial oath at this time was still in flux. While the clergy were keenly aware of the Christian understanding of the oath — that it must be true in all senses of the word, internally as well as externally — the nonclerical population still saw the oath largely as a matter of form: if performed correctly, it constituted truth. Truth resided not outside the oath but in the oath itself.

The narrative confirms at two different points that this magical, pre-Christian understanding of the oath is still operative in the ordeal scene in *Tristan*. During the interval of six weeks before the ordeal, as Isolde is alone with her quandary, she prepares a ruse that, as Gottfried puts it, presumes heavily on God's courtliness (15550–52).[76] The ruse is necessary only if the belief in the magical power of the oath is still operative. An even more explicit reference to the persistence of older ideas appears as Isolde stands before the relics, ready to swear her innocence. Many of those present want to prescribe the queen's oath and not leave it to her own formulation (15681–96). They are afraid that Isolde will do exactly what she does, which is to seize the initiative and formulate her own oath (15697–723). Central also to this pre-Christian understanding of the oath was the absence of transcendental meaning: the oath and that to which it attested corresponded to one another. Isolde does not commit perjury; she does not say that she did not do something that she did do. As long as there is a formal correspondence, the oath is in order. How Mark and the rest of the court interpret it is not relevant.[77]

These considerations and background help greatly in understanding Isolde's oath, her ordeal, and Gottfried's famous commentary on trial by fire. Isolde's trial and acquittal presented Gottfried, as a well-educated cleric of the early thirteenth century, with an archaic interpretation of law and God's role in human affairs that was at odds with prevailing intellectual currents among Peter the Chanter and his students in late twelfth-century Paris, where Gottfried had received his education at the new university.[78] Gottfried's own attitude toward the *Tristan* material seems to be expressed not only in the content of his famous critique but also in his use of the infrequent medieval German word *gelüppeter* (15748), which had both literal and figurative meanings[79] — "poison" and "deception," respectively — to describe Isolde's oath. Gottfried used the word earlier in *Tristan* to describe Morolt's poisoned sword in the judicial duel with Tristan (l. 6943). This word has no positive qualities. In both cases, that of Morolt's poisoned sword and Isolde's poisoned oath, the toxin is invisible to those affected.[80] Gottfried's stinging epithet and his eloquently sardonic commentary reflect distaste for the ordeal common among the French intelligentsia of his day. As the introduction to this study has indicated, intellectual opposition to the ordeal, especially strong in late twelfth-century Paris, centered on its roots in superstition and the attempt to manipulate or tempt God, proving the fundamentally unorthodox character of the ordeal process. The picture of Christ Gottfried presents in his commentary forms a seamless web when seen in the light of Isolde's oath and ordeal:[81]

> da wart wol goffenbaeret
> und al der werlt bewaeret,
> daz der vil tugenthafte Crist
> wintschaffen alse ein ermel ist:
> er vüeget unde suochet an,
> da manz an in gesuochen kan,
> alse gevuoge und alse wol.
> als er von allem rehte sol.
> erst allen herzen bereit,
> ze durnehte und ze trügeheit.
> ist ez ernest, ist ez spil
> er ist ie, swie so man wil.
> daz wart wol offenbare schin
> an der gevüegen künigin:
> die generte ir trügeheit
> und ir gelüppeter eit,
> der hin ze gote gelazen was,
> dasz an ir eren genaz. (15733–49)[82]

[Then it was revealed and affirmed before all the world that the very virtuous Christ is as supple as a windblown sleeve. He adapts to whatever shape one demands of him, as smoothly and as well as he should do. He is open to all hearts, for fidelity or for deception, whether it is serious, whether it is a game, he is just as one wants him. That became apparent with the clever queen. She survived her deceit and her poisoned oath sworn to God.]

Her oath, literally true but still poisoned or perverted, corresponds to the innate corruption of the picture of Christ given above, a Christ who lets humans mold him rather than the opposite. One is reminded of the comment of church historians that the Pelagian Christian needs a Nestorian Christ.[83] Trying to force God to do our will presupposes a conception of God that fits our own designs. The ordeal by fire and the subsequent commentary lead one to the conclusion that since the concept lying behind this ordeal was in reality anti-Christian, in that it forced God to react when people wanted him to, giving him less than absolute freedom, then God must, indeed, be "as supple as a wind-blown sleeve," ready to do our bidding and not minding too much if the intent is false or true. In other words, the perversion of the New Testament picture of Christ, which Gottfried presents in an ironic way, parallels the fundamental perversion of the unilateral ordeal and Isolde's attempt not only to deceive those present but also to control God by forcing him to acquit her.[84]

The moral indifference of the pagan concept of the oath parallels the Christ who is open to all, whatever their plans for good or for evil. Indeed, as Gottfried says, in such circumstances it does not matter whether it is true or whether it is a game. Control of God was, however, an essential part of the unilateral ordeals: they could not have performed the judicial function that justified their existence if there were not a reaction from the natural order that was judged to be divine. The bilateral judicial duel was different: no direct and immediate reaction from nature was needed. As the introduction indicated, for this reason and because a priest was not necessary for ratification of the ordeal, trial by battle persisted as a valid judicial proceeding for a much longer time than the unilateral ideals that the Fourth Lateran Council, for all intents and purposes, destroyed.[85] It is, perhaps, easier for us to understand why ordeal by battle survived for so long if we look at the belief at the core of trial by battle, which is that God supports the side that is in the right — or at least, more in the right; this belief was and is prevalent in the three monotheistic religions. There is an important theological distinction between asking for God's support in a situation in life, whether in court or on the battlefield, and asking God to render an independent and verifiable verdict on demand through the natural order. The latter is more clearly an attempt to manipulate God. While there was clerical opposition to trial by battle, much of this opposition had to do with the loss of life that attended it and the understandable wish of the clergy to be exempted.[86] The secular world, less concerned about the death of one's fellow man, reacted differently: trial by battle remained a constant in medieval legal life until well into the fifteenth century.

Gottfried's text seems to reflect these attitudes. It is difficult otherwise to explain the vastly different approaches to the two ordeals in the same work — ordeals that were in Gottfried's source and with which he had to deal. The trial by battle uses the language of legend and chanson de geste in its description of Morolt and Tristan; their encounter shows some similarities to the judicial duel in two surviving German versions of the *Song of Roland*, analyzed here, as well as to the battle of David and Goliath. These similarities are most striking in the descriptions of the protagonists: both in the *Karlsepik* and in *Tristan* the older, larger, more experienced combatants, Pinabel and Morolt, stand unequivocally on the side of the devil, while Dietrich and Tristan, their younger, inexperienced opponents, must rely on God's help and intervention. In Tristan's case, God, the supreme arbiter in this encounter, appears with allegorical personification to aid the young man. The portrayals of the judicial duel in the Karlsepik and in Tristan show the influence of hagiographic legend in their depictions on the protagonists. Such allegorical material is absent in the ordeal by fire; instead, we have a biting commentary on the perverted concept of God necessary for the ordeal by fire to function as Isolde wishes. A further clue to Gottfried's attitude toward Isolde's manipulation of ordeal procedure lies in his use of the Middle High German *gelüppet* [poisoned] for her oath, the same word he used for Morolt's sword. In both cases deception and manipulation seem to draw his sharpest verbal fire.

Evidence in the text and parallels drawn from contemporary legal practice, as well as chanson de geste material, indicate that the ordeal by battle appears in a favorable light in this work, reflecting the general acceptance that it still enjoyed in the upper strata of society, while the ordeal by fire, one of the unilateral ordeals, was falling into intellectual disrepute. For the modern reader 800 years later an ordeal is an ordeal — an irrational means of proof that has no place in the legal system. Legal historical research shows that medieval people made distinctions between types of ordeals; to assume otherwise, conflating bilateral and unilateral ordeals and demanding that Gottfried have the same attitude toward both, seems to disregard both textual evidence in *Tristan* and historical realities.[87]

Not only the legal context of the time but also the literary milieu seem to have shaped Gottfried's presentation of these two ordeals, as we have seen for the judicial combat and the *Karlsepik*. In the case of Isolde, the legends about the saintly queens Richardis and Kunegunde appear to function as a foil against which Gottfried limns his own portrait of a queen more enigmatic than virtuous. Instead of the emotional, intense denial of infidelity to their consorts in the royal quarters, we find the firm but kindly bishop of Thames in court with Isolde; the detailed legal proceedings substitutes for the intimate scene of the loving queen protesting her innocence. Instead of an extravagant oath with no qualifications, we have a carefully planned ruse with an oath to match. And instead of a triumphant acquittal, we have a sardonic commentary on the whole process at the point in the legends in which clergy and laity alike rejoiced at the revelation of sanctity in their midst. If the portraits of Kunigunde in Latin and in Middle High German were meant in part to portray an anti-Queen Isolde, we can see Gottfried at work in his version to present an anti-Kunigunde. No other Middle High German author has given more direct evidence of familiarity with the literature of his day than Gottfried, with his famous literary excursus (4589–820); his skillful use of material from the legend and from the *Karlsepik*, as well as his intimate knowledge of legal procedures, presents us with carefully nuanced, differing presentations of two kinds of ordeals, a presentation that reflects in large part both intellectual currents and legal realities of the day.

Notes

[1] W. T. H. Jackson, *The Anatomy of Love: The Tristan of Gottfried von Strassburg* (New York: Columbia UP, 1971), 31; Gottfried Weber and Werner Hoffmann, *Gottfried von Straßburg* (Stuttgart: Metzler, 1981) note that early Tristan manuscripts seem to come from Alsace (13–16).

[2] Friedrich Ranke, ed., *Tristan und Isold* (Bern: Francke, 1946), ll. 131–59. Thomas's version in Old French no longer exists, except for a few fragments; the closest we can get to it is an Old Norse translation by Brother Robert in 1226. See Christoph Huber, *Gottfried von Straßburg: Tristan* (Berlin: E. Schmidt, 2000), who also discusses in some detail areas in which the surviving fragments of Thomas's version can be compared with Gottfried, as well as the discovery in 1995 of important leaves of a Thomas manuscript (20–21).

[3] Jackson 33; he also notes that the only other version about which this observation can be made is in regard to Béroul's work, which could be either later or contemporaneous with Thomas (35); see also Huber, *Gottfried: Tristan* 20.

[4] Readers interested in the origins and growth of the Tristan legend can consult the following works: Gertrude Schoepperle, *Tristan and Isolt: A Study of the Sources of the Romance*, 2 vols. (New York: B. Franklin, 1960); Roger Sherman Loomis, *The Development of Arthurian Romance* (Mineola, NY: Dover, 2000), 74–91; Norris Lacy and Geoffrey Ashe, eds., *The Arthurian Handbook* (New York: Garland, 1988), 92–94, 108, 224, 399–401; Norris Lacy and Geoffrey Ashe, eds., *The New Arthurian Encyclopedia* (New York: Garland, 1996), 35–37, 127–28, 206–21, 450–51, 462–65; W. J. McCann, "Tristan: The Celtic and Oriental Material Re-examined," *Tristan and Isolde: A Casebook,* ed. Joan Tasker Grimbert (New York & London: Garland, 1995), pp. 3–35; for a discussion of the various versions of the Tristan story in European literature, see Weber and Hoffmann, *Gottfried* 31–57; Peter K. Stein, "Tristan," *Epische Stoffe des Mittelalters,* ed. Volker Mertens and Ulrich Müller (Stuttgart: Kröner, 1984), 365–94. The most recent critical edition of Béroul is that by Stewart Gregory: *The Romance of Tristan by Béroul* (Amsterdam: Rodopi, 1992); for Thomas, *Les Fragments du roman de Tristan, poème du XII siècle: Edités avec un commentaire,* ed. Bartina H. Wind (Geneva: Droz / Paris: Minard, 1960). French translations include Jean-Charles Payen, trans., *Tristan et Yseut* (Paris: Garnier, 1974); Daniel LaCroix and Philippe Walter, trans., *Tristan et Iseut: Les poèmes français, la saga norroise* (Paris: Librairie générale française, 1989); Christiane Marchello-

Nizia et al., trans., *Tristan et Yseut: Les premières versions européenes* (Paris: Gallimard, 1995); Michael Benskin, Tony Hunt, and Ian Short, trans., "Un nouveau fragment du *Tristan* de Thomas," *Romania* 113 (1992–95): 289–319.

[5] See Huber, *Gottfried: Tristan* 19–20; Jackson 36–37; Weber and Hoffmann 39–49; Norris J. Lacy, *Béroul* in *Early French Tristan Poems*, ed. Lacy, vol. 1 (Cambridge: D. S. Brewer, 1998), ix–xi.

[6] The missing part of Béroul's work includes the battle with Morold; see Lacy, *Béroul*.

[7] See Paul Schach, trans., *The Saga of Tristram and Isönd* (Lincoln: U of Nebraska P, 1973), 37–44; Vickie L. Ziegler, "Points of Law at the Point of a Sword: Tristan's Duel with Morolt in the North Sea World," *The North Sea World in the Middle Ages*, ed. Thomas R. Liszka and Lorna E. M. Walker (Dublin: Four Courts P, 2001), 33–51.

[8] Lacy, *Béroul* 215, comments on the ongoing sexual innuendo in this passage. See *Béroul* ll. 3288–4231.

[9] Lacy, *Early French Tristan Poems*, vol. 1, 6.

[10] Schach 89–94.

[11] Virtually every critic who has made an extended treatment of Gottfried's work has commented on the ordeal scene, while many individual analyses of it have appeared. Rüdiger Schnell, *Suche nach Wahrheit: Gottfrieds "Tristan und Isold" als erkenntnisreicher Roman* (Tübingen: Niemeyer, 1992) gives a useful summary of the literature (62–65), dividing the critics into two main camps: those who take Gottfried's famous commentary on the ordeal by fire seriously, whether as blasphemy or in terms of God's mercy, and those who understand it as ironic criticism, whether of a courtly concept of God or of the institution of the ordeal. The following articles and books, listed chronologically, are representative; those marked with an asterisk interpret Gottfried's commentary as a criticism of the ordeal: *F. Piquet, *L'Originalité de Gottfried de Strasbourg dans son poème de Tristan et Isolde* (Lille: Au siege de l'Université, 1905), 260–69; Helmut de Boor, "Die Grundauffassung von Gottfrieds Tristan," *Deutsche Vierteljahrsschrift für Literaturwissenschaft und Geistesgeschichte* 18 (1940): 262–306, rpt. in *Gottfried von Straßburg*, ed. Alois Wolf (Darmstadt: Wissenschaftliche Buchgesellschaft, 1973), 25–73 (48); Max Wehrli, "Der Tristan Gottfrieds von Straßburg," *Trivium* 4 (1946): 81–117, rpt. in *Gottfried von Straßburg*, ed. Alois Wolf (Darmstadt: Wissenschaftliche Buchgesellschaft, 1973), 97–134 (106–7); Bodo Mergell, *Tristan und Isolde: Ursprung und Entwicklung der Tristansage des Mittelalters* (Mainz: Kirchheim, 1949), 177–79; *Friedrich Maurer, *Leid: Studien zur Bedeutungs- und Problemgeschichte* (Munich: Francke, 1951), 225–26; Gottfried Weber, *Gottfrieds von Straßburg: Tristan und die Krise des hochmittelalterlichen Weltbildes um 1200*, 2 vols. (Stuttgart: Metzler, 1953), I: 119–27; *M. Bindschedler, "Gottfried von Straßburg und die höfische Ethik," *Beiträge* 76 (1954), 1–38 (31–33); *W. Schwarz, *Gottfrieds von Strassburg Tristan und Isolde* (Groningen: Wolters, 1955), 9–11; Petrus Tax, *Wort, Sinnbild, Zahl im Tristanroman* (Berlin: E. Schmidt, 1961), 104–9; *Theodor C. Van Stockum, "Die Problematik des Gottesbegriffs im 'Tristan' des Gottfried von Strassburg," *Koninklijke Nederlandse Akademie von Wetenschappen. Afd. Letterkunde. Verslagen en mededeelingen, nieuwe reeks* (deel 26, no. 9, 1963): 3–27; *Rosemary N. Combridge, *Das Recht im*

"*Tristan*" *Gottfrieds von Straßburg* (Berlin: E. Schmidt, 1964), 85–96, 104–6; *Werner Betz, "Gottfried von Straßburg als Kritiker höfischer Kultur und Advokat religiöser Emanzipation," *Festschrift für Konstantin Reichardt*, ed. Herwig Zauchenberger and Christian Gellinek (Bern & Munich: Francke, 1969), 168–73 (169–70); H. Newstead, "The Equivocal Oath in the Tristan Legend," *Mélanges Rita LeJeune*, vol. 2 (Gembloux: J. Duculot, 1969); 1077–85; Jackson 116; E. C. York, "Isolt's Ordeal: English Legal Customs in the Medieval Tristan Legend," *Studies in Philology* 68 (1971): 1–9; Wiebke Freytag, *Das Oxymoron bei Wolfram, Gottfried und anderen Dichtern des Mittelalters* (Munich: Fink, 1972), 176–85; *Ruth Goldschmidt-Kunzer, *The Tristan of Gottfried von Strassburg: An Ironic Perspective* (Berkeley: U of California P, 1973), 134–40; *T. A. Kerth, "With God on Her Side," *Colloquia Germanica* 2 (1978): 1–18, esp. 8–12; Werner Schröder, *Text and Interpretation: Das Gottesurteil im Tristan Gottfrieds von Straßburg. Sitzungsberichte der wissenschaftlichen Gesellschaft an der Johann Wolfgang Goethe Universität Frankfurt/Main* (Wiesbaden: Steiner, 1979); *Rüdiger Schnell, "Rechtsgeschichte und Literaturgeschichte: Isoldes Gottesurteil," *Akten des VI. Internationalen Germanisten-Kongresses Basel 1980*, ed. Heinz Rupp and Hans-Gert Roloff, part 4, *Jahrbuch für Internationale Germanistik* 8 (Bern, Frankfurt am Main & Las Vegas: P. Lang, 1980), 307–19, esp. 312; Jean Fourquet, "Der wintschaffene Christ," *La Legende du Tristan au moyen âge*, ed. Danielle Buschinger (Göppingen: Kümmerle, 1982), 109–11; *Tomas Tomasek, *Die Utopie im "Tristan" Gotfrids von Straßburg* (Tübingen: Niemeyer, 1985), 76–78; *Christoph Huber, *Gottfried von Straßburg: Tristan und Isolde* (Munich: Artemis, 1986), 86–90; Klaus Grübmüller, "'*ir unwarheit warbaeren*': Über den Beitrag des Gottesurteils zur Sinnkonstitution in Gotfrids Tristan," *Philologie als Kulturwissenschaft: Studien zur Literatur und Geschichte des Mittelalters. Festschrift für Karl Stackmann* (Göttingen: Vandenhoeck & Ruprecht, 1987), 149–63, esp. 155–58; *Herbert Kolb, "Isoldes Eid: Zu Gottfried von Straßburg, Tristan 15267–15764," *ZfdPH* 107 (1988): 321–35; A. Wolf, *Gottfried von Straßburg und die Mythe von Tristan und Isolde* (Darmstadt: Wissenschaftliche Buchgesellschaft, 1989), 198; Marion Mälzer, *Die Isolde-Gestalten in den mittelalterlichen deutschen Tristandichtungen: Ein Beitrag zum diachronischen Wandel* (Heidelberg: Winter, 1991), 184–89; Schnell, *Suche* 59–80; Kelly Kucaba, "Höfisch inszenierte Wahrheiten. Zu Isolds Gottesurteil bei Gottfried von Straßburg," *Fremdes wahrnehmen — fremdes Wahrnehmen*, ed. Wolfgang Harms and C. Stephen Jaeger (Stuttgart & Leipzig: Hirzel, 1997), 73–93; Schild, "Gottesurteil." Schnell, "Rechtsgeschichte, Mentalitäten" notes that Gottfried's literary criticism of the ordeal parallels the criticisms of it in the writings of theologians (423).

[12] Critics have generally taken two main approaches to the analysis of this ordeal: some claim that the ordeal is portrayed in a serious manner, in which Tristan fights for God and law; others hold that the ordeal furnishes material for a critique of Tristan and/or the judicial duel. See Schnell, *Suche* 89. The "critique" group includes Goldschmidt-Kunzer, *Tristan* 45, 58–68; Dennis Green, *Irony in the Medieval Romance* (Cambridge: Cambridge UP, 1979), 60–61, 88–89; Peter K. Stein, "Tristans Schwertleite: Zur Einschätzung ritterlich-höfischer Dichtung durch Gottfried von Straßburg," *Deutsche Vierteljahrsschrift für Literaturgeschichte und Geistesgeschichte* 51 (1977): 300–352 (340–43); Walther Haug, "Âventiure in Gottfried von Straßburgs Tristan," *Festschrift für Hans Eggers zum 65. Geburtstag*, ed. Hubert

Backes (Tübingen: Niemeyer, 1972), 88–125 (109–11); Jackson 148–50; Tax admits that Gottfried portrayed the battle as a judgment of God but neglects legal research (39–44); Tomasek mentions the trial by battle only in passing but believes that Gottfried is skeptical of both ordeals (76); Schnell, *Suche* 89–94.

Critics who do not believe that irony is the dominant factor here include, of course, Cambridge (see note 3), de Boor, "Grundauffassung" 48; Van Stockum 15; Blake Lee Spahr, "Tristan versus Morolt: Allegory against Reality?" *Helen Adolf Festschrift*, ed. Sheema Z. Buehne, James L. Hodge, and Lucille B. Pinto (New York: Ungar, 1968), 72–85; Ulrich Ernst, "Gottfried von Straßburg in komparatistischer Sicht: Form und Funktion der Allegorese im Tristanepos," *Euphorion* 70 (1976): 1–72 (14–18); Urban Küsters, "Liebe zum Hof: Vorstellungen und Erscheinungsformen einer 'höfischen' Lebensordnung in Gottfrieds *Tristan*," *Höfische Literatur, Hofgesellschaft, Höfische Lebensformen um 1200*, ed. Gert Kaiser and Dirk Müller (Düsseldorf: Droste, 1986), 141–76; Huber, *Gottfried: Tristan* 59–60; Maria Nussbaum-Kleager, "'Uzen' and 'Innen': Language and Meaning in Gottfried von Strassburg's *Tristan*," Diss. SUNY Binghamton, 1987 156–68 believes the judicial duel supports a just cause and notes the David parallels (165–66) but is critical of Tristan's sensuality (168–69). Other discussions of the Morolt episode include Piquet 139–62; Maurer 219–20; Irene Lanz-Hubmann, *"Nein unde Já": Mehrdeutigkeit im "Tristan" Gottfrieds von Straßburg: Ein Rezipientenproblem* (Bern: Lang, 1989), 117–21; Mark Chinca, *History, Fiction, Verisimilitude: Studies in the Poetics of Gottfried's Tristan* (London: Modern Humanities Research Association for the Institute of Germanic Studies, U of London, 1993), 104–9. Piquet notes (149) that Gottfried's presentation of the conflict between Morolt and Tristan as a judicial duel represents a modernizing of the subject matter; as the subsequent analysis will show, Gottfried is reflecting contemporary legal practice in this regard. See my comparison of Gottfried's version of the battle with Morolt and Brother Robert's Old Norse translation of Thomas in "Points of Law at the Point of a Sword."

[13] Though much has appeared on the ordeal and on conflict resolution since she wrote it, Cambridge's book on law in *Tristan, Das Recht im Tristan Gottfrieds von Straßburg*, is an extremely thorough study and is consistently helpful. The present study differs from hers in several ways, the first of which is that it takes advantage of approximately forty years of historical research. The other areas in which my analysis departs from Cambridge, as well as from Rüdiger Schnell, who has dealt seriously with legal issues in *Tristan* in his article "Rechtsgeschichte, Mentalitäten" and his book *Suche*, is in the more extended analysis of the battle with Morolt and in the way the two ordeals reference each other. My study also differs from Cambridge's and Schell's in that it places Gottfried's portrayal of both ordeals in the context of other literary ordeals, such as those of the legends and the *Karlsepik*.

Schild, "Gottesurteil" does not distinguish between unilateral and bilateral ordeals (74–75). Using Gottfried's criticism of the ordeal by fire as his basis, he briefly discusses the trial by battle with Morolt (72) and comes to the conclusion that since God helps Tristan in this ordeal, he is doing the same for Isolde.

[14] Cambridge notes the detail, the use of allegory, and the moral element in the Morolt battle (48); her analysis (48–54) is a summary of some of the legal issues in the duel, though it does not look at this judicial ordeal in detail, the allusions to other genres, nor the relationship between the two ordeals. She does not believe that

Gottfried's commentary applies to this ordeal (49–50). She does cite one passage, 6162–64, in which Tristan tells the nobles that if it turns out badly, their case will not be damaged, as proof that Gottfried is skeptical of the judicial duel as a means to establish truth (49). If, however, these lines are seen in their context, all Tristan is saying is that if he loses, their distress will not increase, while, if he wins, it is because God wills it (6165–71). While she mentions the use of allegory, she does not analyze it. She believes the Morolt battle receives the narrative emphasis it does in order to justify Tristan's claim to be Mark's heir (48). Spahr notes that the care Gottfried uses in building up the allegory in this scene indicates the degree of significance he intended it to have (72–73). He gives useful background information on and interpretation of the allegorical figures but does not focus on the legal issues.

[15] Schnell, *Suche* 89–93; see his note 2. Althoff, "Spielen die Dichter" says that before critics can discern irony or comic effects in medieval literary texts, they must be very much at home in the culture in which they claim to discern them (71).

[16] Franzjosef Pensel, *Rechtsgeschichtliches und Rechtssprachliches im epischen Werk Hartmanns von Aue und im "Tristan" Gottfrieds von Straßburg*. Diss., Humboldt-Universität Berlin, 1961, 112.

[17] Jacob and Wilhelm Grimm, eds., *Deutsches Wörterbuch*, vol. 15 (Leipzig, S. Hirzel, 1956) cols. 1476–78 (col. 1477): "als zeichen politischer abhängigkeit und botmäszigkeit, vom oberherrn unterworfenen Völkern auferlegt diese bedeutung überwiegt in der ahd. und mhd. literatur. . . ." The Grimms cite in col. 1478 line 5979 in the Morolt episode from Gottfried's *Tristan* as an example of this meaning. For references in Gottfried's text see 5930, 5942, 5979, 5999, 6012, 6078, 6266, 6370, 6375, 6388, 6821, and 6826.

[18] Line references to these terms are as follows: *sicherheit* (6356, 6364), *eit* (6355, 6363, 6374, 6444), *gelübede* (6364), *triuwe* (6355, 6361, 6363, 6374, 6444). Lexer, *MHDHWB*, I, *eit*, col. 534; *gelübede*, col. 828; *sicherheit*, II, cols. 902–3; *triuwe*, II, col. 1520. *DRW*, vol. 4, cols. 43–48, lists a range of meanings, including "feierliches Versprechen, privatrechtliches Schuldversprechen, Dienst-, Amtsgelöbnis, Treugelöbnis," cols. 43–44.

[19] See Hattenhauer, "Der gefälschte Eid" 659–64; Schmidt-Wiegand, "Eid" 55–56. Harold D. Dickerson Jr., "Language in 'Tristan' as a Key to Gottfried's Conception of God," *ABÄG* 3 (1972): 127–45 notes the overall importance of oaths in *Tristan* (128–29). Dilcher, "Versprechenseide," *HWBDR*, vol. 1, cols. 866–70 notes (col. 868) that promissory oaths in the Middle Ages were not merely the strengthening of a sworn promise but also included legal obligation. A purgatory oath, made in the absence of conclusive evidence, absolved the accused of guilt and ended the potential for scandal. (*Saxon Mirror* 20; Richard M. Fraher, "Preventing Crime in the High Middle Ages: The Medieval Lawyers' Search for Deterrence," *Popes, Teachers and Canon Law in the Middle Ages*, ed. James Ross Sweeney and Stanley Chodorow (Ithaca, NY: Cornell UP, 1989), 212–33 (224–25).

[20] See Ekkehard Kaufmann, "Treue," *HWBDR*, 34. Lieferung (Berlin: E. Schmidt, 1992) cols. 320–38 (col. 328); G. Buchda, "Gelöbnis," *HWBDR*, vol. 1, cols. 1490–94 (col. 1493); H. Holzhauer, "Meineid," *HWBDR*, vol. 3, ed. Adalbert Erler, Ekkehard Kaufmann, and Wolfgang Stammler (Berlin: E. Schmidt, 1984) cols. 447–58 (col. 452).

[21] Planck, *Gerichtsverfahren*, II, 147. See Dilcher, "Eid," *HWBDR*, vol. 1, col. 869.

[22] H. Krause, "Minne und Recht," *HWBDR*, vol. 3, cols. 582–88, esp. cols. 584–85, where he cites the passage from *Tristan*, noting that *minne* here has a legal sense. See also Hermann Krause, "Consilio et iudicio: Bedeutungsbreite und Sinngehalt einer mittelalterlichen Formel," *Speculum Historiale: Geschichte im Spiegel von Geschichtsschreibung und Geschichtsdeutung*, ed. Clemens Bauer, Laetitia Boehm, and Max Mueller (Freiburg & Munich: Alber, 1965), 416–38 (436); *DRW*, vol. 9, cols. 653–58 (cols. 653–54) notes that it refers to mutual agreement and can occur in an agreement about material considerations in a legal dispute. This entry also lists the formulaic usage with *Recht* (col. 654). Further evidence that Morolt holds fast to the position that Cornwall is obliged to pay the tribute comes in his reply to Tristan (6443–49). The importance of the term for Morolt is apparent in his usage of it in the dramatic scene just before the fighting begins: "sus kome wir nicht ze minnen./ der zins muoz mit mir hinnen" [If we do not come to friendly terms, the tribute comes with me when I go] (6825–26). Küsters notes (146–47) the negative reference to it in connection with the Romans (l. 5995) and in the formula *lant unde reht* (l. 6423), near the end of the argument; see also Karl Kroeschell, "Recht und Rechtsbegriff" 310–11, 328–29, where he discusses the development of the idea and its appearance in literary texts, including Gottfried (no. 187, 329). See also A. Laufs and K. P. Schroeder, "Landrecht," *HWBDR*, vol. 2, cols. 1527–35, esp. cols. 1527, 1529; Gerhard Köbler, "Land und Landrecht" 2.

[23] Planck, *Gerichtsverfahren*, II, discusses legal practice (147). Literary critics who do not include this fact include Haug (111): "wenn er von daher die Auseinandersetzung zum gerichtlichen Zweikampf stilisiert, so ist das Taktik." Green, citing Haug, says: "Tristan converts a single combat into one concerned with the justice of the case for his own shrewdly calculated purposes . . ." (88); Schnell, *Suche* cites Haug, not customary legal procedure (86).

[24] For the duel as a judgment of God, see Planck, *Gerichtsverfahren*, II, 147; Combridge 52; Carbasse 388, Cram 11. Cram distinguishes, as does Nottarp (269–71) between a duel as *Entscheidungsmittel* and as *Beweismittel* and says that it was already a means of proof in the Burgundian law. For discussion of this distinction among German legal scholars, see Bartlett 114. See also Lea 103 and Gal 238, where he discusses the connection between a false oath and the judicial duel.

[25] Piquet notes that Tristan's speech to the nobles has a religious context that was missing in the saga (144). There is only one reference to God's assistance in Brother Robert's version; see Schach 39.

[26] See Edward Schröder, ed., "Deutsche Kaiserchronik," in *Deutsche Chroniken und andere Geschichtsbücher des Mittelalters*, vol. 1 (Berlin & Zurich: Weidmann, 1964), 15463–509 and Ebernand von Erfurt, *Heinrich und Kunegunde*, ed. Reinhold Bechstein (Amsterdam: Rodopi, 1968), 1490–1616.

[27] Schnell (90), citing the following passage, maintains that Tristan puts into his calculations the fact that he and God may lose, thereby making God the plaything of man: "got selbe, der mit mir sol gan ze ringe und ouch ze vehte, der bringe reht ze rehte! Got muoz binamen mit mir gesigen oder mir mir sigelos beligen: der waltes unde müeze ez pflegen!" [God himself must go into the circle and the fight with me,

may he bring justice to law! God must in truth win or lose with me; may God rule and be in charge of the outcome!] (6778–83). The last line of this passage, which puts the matter in God's hands, would seem to be the operative one here.

As the introduction indicated, uncertainty about the outcome of such ordeals was a given in medieval life, whether because God's will could not be known or because of possible trickery.

[28] See Lea 166–71. A judicial duel involving treason in 1127 culminated in Herman the Iron seizing the genitalia of his opponent, Guy of Steenvoorde, and swinging the unfortunate traitor by them. See Pirenne 93–95.

[29] Haug criticizes Tristan for stooping to any means to win (111); see also Green 88. Martin H. Jones, "The Depiction of Military Combat in Gottfried's Tristan," *Gottfried von Strassburg and the Medieval Tristan Legend* (Cambridge, U.K.: Boydell & Brewer, 1990), 45–66 (57–59) cites passages from Hartmann von Aue, Geoffrey of Monmouth, and Wace that show that even in nonjudicial combat ruthlessness and fierceness were common and did not occasion criticism. Spahr believes that the evil powers, whose representative Morolt is, must be completely destroyed (81).

[30] Bartlett 121. Edwards, introduction to Lea 7. See also Bongert 239.

[31] See Green 88; Stein, "Tristans Schwertleite" 342.

[32] Lambertus Okken, *Kommentar zum Tristan Roman Gottfried von Strassburg*, vol. 1 (Amsterdam: Rodopi, 1984–88) 186–87, 320.

[33] As we hold this part of Gottfried's description of the courtroom scene up against contemporary legal practice, we might ask if Gottfried uses this apparent departure from normal procedure as a means to characterize the weakness and inferior ability of Mark as compared to Tristan. It would certainly fit with many other incidents in which Mark seems to appear as an indecisive and insecure character.

[34] Okken 324–25. See also Schwinekörper 95–96; A. Erler, "Handschuh," *HWBDR*, vol. 1, cols. 1975–76 (col. 1976).

[35] See Planck, *Gerichtsverfahren*, I, 795.

[36] Such combats did not generally take place on the spot but at a time in the future; a delay of four to six weeks was common in southern Germany. Here we have three days. The protagonists had time to practice and to put their affairs in order, should the worst come to pass. They had to put up security for their reappearance; if the defendant did not show up, he was judged guilty. As noted earlier, usually the battle stopped with the setting of the sun. See Lea 173, 178; see Bongert 243, 246 for comments on the French situation.

[37] See O. Holzapfel, "Holmgangr," *HWBDR*, vol. 2, col. 219; he notes that sagas frequently describe duels fought on small islands according to definite rules. These duels often figured in legal questions. Holzhauer, in describing the origins of the judicial duel in the various Germanic legal codes and systems, discusses it in Old Norse society, saying it was often used in property matters ("Zweikampf" 272–73). Planck mentions the site in its legal context (*Gerichtsverfahren*, I, 795, 796). The *holmgangr* had long since been condemned in Iceland; Brother Robert's translation of Thomas avoids both the term and the island location, placing the battle on a seashore. See E. Kölbing, *Die nordische Version der Tristram Sage* (Hildesheim: Olms, 1978), 34. The legal status of the *holmgangr* in medieval Norway would most

probably not have been generally known in central Europe. See also Bartlett 105. In addition, Bartlett discusses the problematic nature of the sagas as reliable legal sources for periods three centuries before their composition and speculates that if they do not reflect accurate legal practices of an earlier period, then the probable source would be thirteenth-century Icelandic society, where duels may have continued to exist, in spite of their absence in legal codes.

[38] See Planck, *Gerichtsverfahren*, I, 796.

[39] Okken, *Kommentar*, I, 74.

[40] In this particular case, Morolt offers a second bribe after he has fatally wounded Tristan.

[41] See Okken, *Kommentar*, I, 304–6; Huber, *Tristan* 60. Ernst notes other parallels between David and Tristan, including the difficulties the outside strongman causes the population, their lament, the duel as a substitute for a clash of armies, the young challenger's unfailing trust in God in contrast to the proud arrogance of the outsider (14–15). The David/Tristan comparison touches other parts of the work: Tristan, like David, was both a soldier and a musician; both were involved in adulterous affairs.

[42] Schnell interprets ll. 6980–89, in which Gottfried notes that some may wonder where God and Right are when Tristan needs them, as a criticism of the belief that man can expect God to help him when he begs for it. Aside from the fact that believers still pray for such assistance today and that Tristan's expectations are totally within the framework of orthodox Christianity, Gottfried follows this section with a triumphant description of the appearance of God and Right, who bring a just verdict in the battle (6996–7001). The positive characterization of their help would not seem to fit with an ironic interpretation of the lines in which Gottfried wonders where God is. Another, perhaps less forced interpretation is at hand if we remember that Gottfried, with his clerical background, was steeped in the liturgy of the Psalms and familiar with the Book of Job. These books of the Bible contain frequent almost petulant and sometimes sarcastic references to the apparent slowness of the Almighty to respond. See, for example, Psalm 77: "Has God forgotten to be gracious? . . . Has his right hand grown weak? Has the right hand of the Most High changed?" *Revised English Bible* 506.

[43] De Boor notes that God and Right are an eternal pair that associate themselves with the earthly pair of Tristan and Willing Heart ("Grundauffassung" 48). Huber briefly discusses God and Right in this battle, noting that they are used as leitmotifs throughout this section and then appear in a tetrad construction during the battle, which is really a contest between good and evil (*Gottfried: Tristan* 59–60); Ernst discusses Gottfried's use of the four persons in terms of typological interpretation of texts (17–18).

[44] See discussion of swords used by the Dietrich figure in the *Karlsepik*, where they played a decisive role. Prior to the battle with Morolt, Gottfried describes the sword, which he says was a key element in Tristan's victory (6578–86).

[45] Gottfried changed the negative exile in the woods of his sources into a positive allegory of love; for comments on this point, see Hugo Kuhn, "Allegorie und Er-

zaehlstruktur," *Formen und Funktion der Allegorie: Symposion Wolfenbuettel, 1978*, ed. Walter Haug (Stuttgart: Metzler, 1979), 206–18 (208–10).

[46] For a discussion of the relationship between these two terms see Jon Whitman, *Allegory: The Dynamics of an Ancient and Medieval Technique* (Oxford: Clarendon P, 1987), 4–8, 263–72.

[47] C. Stephen Jaeger, *Medieval Humanism in Gottfried von Straßburg's* Tristan und Isolde (Heidelberg: Winter, 1977) describes striking parallels between the Morolt section and the knighting ceremony, especially "the parallel between Gottfried's four-fold rise to inspiration and Tristan's four allies. Gottfried envisioned the arming and battle with Morolt as the 'fulfillment' of much that was prophesied in the knighting ceremony" (124; see also 49–55). See also Spahr 78–80 for a discussion of the significance of Right and Willing Heart.

[48] See Okken, *Kommentar*, I, 279–80. Dirk Glogau, *Untersuchungen zu einer konstruktivistischen Mediävistik: Tiere und Pflanzen im "Tristan" Gottfrieds von Straßburg und im "Nibelungenlied"* (Essen: Item, 1993) summarizes the different meanings of the boar in the Middle Ages and sees the boar on the shield as having a twofold message: positive in regard to the courage of the knight and negative, i.e, related to the Devil, on account of Tristan's brutality in the battle with Morolt (83–97). As we have seen, this particular criticism of Tristan is ahistorical, since such battles were inevitably brutal. In this scene the boar appears in a positive description of Tristan in armor, a description that contains a great deal of light symbolism. Jaeger interprets the animal as a symbol of sensuality (119). See also Manfred Zips, "Tristan und die Ebersymbolik," *Beiträge zur Geschichte der deutschen Sprache und Literatur* 94 (1972): 134–52, esp.146–50; Johannes Rathofer, "Der wunderbare Hirsch der Minnegrotte," *Zeitschrift für deutsche Altertum* 95 (1966): 27–40 (38). Margaret Schleissner, "Animal Images in Gottfried von Strassburg's Tristan: Structure and Meaning of Metaphor," *The Medieval World of Nature: A Book of Essays*, ed. Joyce E. Salisbury (New York & London: Garland, 1993), 77–90 (81–82) examines the positive and negative aspects of boar imagery. In her opinion the use of the boar as a symbol during Tristan's knighting and the preparation for his duel with Morolt correspond to the positive side of boar symbolism, where the boar stands for the invincible warrior.

[49] See Tristan, ll. 6943, 15748. Grimm, *Deutsches Wörterbuch*, vol. 6 (Leipzig, 1885), col. 1312, *luppen, lüppen*, "arnzeikunst treiben, theils mit zaubersaften, die ein geschosz vergifteten"; *gelüpt*, "vergiftet" vol. 4.I.2 (Leipzig, 1897) col. 3110. Lexer, *MHDWB*, I, col. 1988; *DRW*, vol. 8, cols. 1508–9: *lüppe* could mean both a poisonous plant material as well as a magical preparation, the use of which was already legally punishable in 800 (col. 1508); *lüppen, luppen* meant to spread with poison, to poison (col. 1509).

[50] See Hattenhauer, "Der gefälschte Eid" 666.

[51] Tax does not mention the repetition of *gelüppet* during the commentary and interprets the poisoned wound as a deserved result of Tristan's brutality (40).

[52] Combridge 86.

[53] The secular princes' complicity in the chain of events that have bought Isolde here is only touched on in this scene, as Isolde mentions those who wished her ill (15480–

98). Tristan, not Isolde, is really the object of their hatred. Shortly after his true identity as Mark's nephew became known, Tristan had awakened considerable resentment at Mark's court because of his cultural and intellectual superiority — jealousy that Mark exacerbated by making Tristan his heir. The nobles' insistence on the marriage to Isolde has not resolved the situation, because no offspring resulted. Against this backdrop, Isolde's adultery with Tristan becomes potentially sinister. One of the purposes of the ordeal in a situation similar to that in which Isolde finds herself was to maintain the king's authority (Boulet-Sautel 280); that intent may lie behind the ordeal here, as well as the situation in which the tormented Mark reached a breaking point where he simply could not endure such rumors about the two people closest to him.

[54] H. W. Strätz, "Konzil," *HWBDR,* vol. 2, cols. 1132–36 (col. 1132) defines it as a gathering of prominent church officials charged with deciding important questions in issues involving the Church. Combridge notes that such a council did not exclude the presence of the laity; she notes that since the legal question involves not only adultery, but also a breach of faith against the monarch, questions of canon as well as secular law were involved (86–87). Kolb disputes Combridge's opinion; he believes that it is a secular court, with Mark in charge and the bishop of Thames representing the other peers as *primus inter pares* ("Isoldes Eid" 322–26).

[55] "Besprochen," l. 15309, Lexer, *MHDHWB,* I, col. 223, "beschuldigen, anklagen"; *DRW,* vol. 1, cols. 1481–83 (col. 1482), "vor Gericht ziehen"; see also l. 6459, when Tristan uses the word in the dispute with Morolt; "boteschaft," Lexer, *MHDHWB,* I, col. 332, can refer to a special court session; *DRW,* vol. 2, cols. 435–36 lists *Gerichtsbote* (col. 436, probable meaning here) as well as *Obergericht* (col. 435) as legal meanings.

[56] Kolb, "Isoldes Eid" 323–24; the oldest and most experienced prince generally had the most influence on the monarch.

[57] 15370; Lexer, *MHDHWB,* II, cols.1632–33, *überkomen,* "überführen"; 1653, *überseit,* "durch zeugen überführen."

[58] To what extent Isolde had legitimate fears about the death penalty being imposed is hard to determine. Since a *Konzil* could refer to a canonical court with a presiding figure such as the bishop of Thames, the death penalty became more unlikely. Brundage says that at this time canon law absolutely forbade the slaying of adulterous wives (388–39). Canonically sanctioned punishments included shaving their heads, displaying them with ripped clothing, and whipping them in public. See also Combridge, who says that while the death penalty in secular law for adulterous women was unlikely at this time, it was not totally out of the question (87–92). See also John W. Baldwin, *The Language of Sex: Five Voices from Northern France around 1200* (Chicago: U of Chicago P, 1994), 69–70.

[59] For references to *inziht* see 15381, 15401, 15406, 15443. H. Schlosser, "Inzichtverfahren," *HWBDR,* vol. 2, cols. 413–15 (cols. 413–14); Reinhard Müller, *Studien zum Inzichtverfahren nach bayerischen Quellen* (Leipzig: Weicher, 1939), 1–15. See also Combridge 93, 159–60; *DRW,* vol. 6, cols. 313–14.

For *liument* see 15400, 15406, 15463; W. Sellert, "Leumund," *HWBDR,* vol. 2, cols. 1856–58 (cols. 1856–57). Combridge notes that the two words often appear together (158); see her commentary on *liument* (162–63). See also *DRW,* vol. 8, cols. 1257–62; in its negative sense, the word could mean anything from nasty gossip to concrete suspicion of having committed an offense. Repeat offenders could count on a speedy conviction without a chance to clear themselves through an *Inzichtverfahren* or an oath, options offered to those in good standing in the community (col. 1258).

[60] L. 15416: *ansprache* (accusation) and *antwürte* (defense) are both used in a legal sense here; see *DRW*, vol. 1, *Ansprache*, cols. 730–32, esp. col. 731; *DRW, antwort*, vol. 1, cols. 756–58, esp. col. 756; Lexer, *MHDHWB*, I, col. 78, *ansprache*, "anklage"; col. 83, *antwürte*, "verteidigung des beklagten."

[61] "offenliche inziht" (15443), "besprochen" (15446), "liument" (15463), "antwürte" (15467).

[62] L. 15469; Lexer, *MHDHWB*, I, col. 915.

[63] Gottfried expresses this thought at the very beginning of his work and emphasizes it again and again in the reaction of others to Tristan and Isolde. (See especially 33–36; 13600–604; 13637.) See also Combridge 94.

[64] "bezigen," from *bezîhen, DRW*, vol. 2, col. 299; Lexer, *MHDHWB*, I, col. 259.

[65] Adolph Franz, *Die kirchlichen Benediktionen im Mittelalter*, vol. 2 (Graz: Akademische Druck- und Verlagsanstalt, 1960) notes that in Germanic legal tradition, when enough oathhelpers were not at hand, an ordeal was prescribed (312–13). See also Boulet-Sautel 283–84; Gaudemet 105; Combridge 94; R. Scheyling, "Eideshelfer," *HWBDR*, vol. 1, cols. 870–72 (cols. 871–72) notes that the presence of oathhelpers in the case of an oath maintaining one's innocence could be an alternative to an ordeal; see also Planck, *Gerichtsverfahren*, II, 136–45. Schild, "Gottesurteil" 55. Mälzer notes that as a foreigner, Isolde has her husband as her guardian (185); Hyams and Morris 93; Kolb, "Isoldes Eid" 327.

[66] Consistent with the judicial nature of the assembly, Isolde uses legal terms in her offer to the council: *gerihtes*, 15511, *behabene*, 15516, *DRW*, vol. 1; *behaben*, cols. 1434–35, has several legal meanings, including "to preserve," the sense in which it could be used here. See York 6; Combridge 93; Lea 45–46. In the *Tristramssaga* Isolde offers to undergo the ordeal of the hot iron or any other proof of her innocence. See Eugen Kölbling, *Die nordische Version der Tristram Sage*, vol. 1 (Hildesheim: Olms, 1978), 162; Joan Ferrante, *The Conflict of Love and Honor: The Medieval Tristan Legend in France, Germany and Italy* (The Hague: Mouton, 1973), 52. Schnell makes the fact that Mark chooses a matter of interpretative significance, not allowing for the possibility of English legal influence ("Rechtsgeschichte" 309).

[67] Bartlett 15; both in Georg Waitz, ed., "Vitae Sancti Heinrici Additamentum," *Monumenta Germaniae historica inde ab anno Christi quingentesimo usque ad annum millesimum et quingentesimum. Legum*, 5 vols., ed. Georg Heinrich Pertz (Hannover: Hahn, 1835–1889), IV: 819–20 (820) and in Ebernand von Erfurt's *Heinrich und Kunegunde* 1485–86 the princes are certain of Kunigunde's innocence, since she suggests the ordeal herself.

[68] The *Tristramssaga* contains a speech by Isönd about her vulnerability as a foreigner to malicious rumor. Schach 90.

[69] "Give us your guarantees, come forward at once and promise to undergo the ordeal of the hot iron as we instruct you here" (15522–26), "gewisheit tuon"

(15522), *DRW, Gewißheit,* vol. 4, cols. 808–9; "gerihte" (15520) here means a legal procedure, in this case, the ordeal; see *DRW,* vol. 4, *Gericht,* cols. 299–315 (col. 303); "vertriuwet" (15524), Lexer, *MHDHWB,* III, col. 277; Combridge 177, "to promise in a legal sense"; "bewisen," 15526, *DRW,* vol. 2, *beweisen,* cols. 269–73 (col. 272), "anweisen."

[70] Hyams and Morris note that whatever variations occurred in the rituals, all of them separated the person on trial from his daily life through sequestration, and, three days prior to the ordeal, prayer, fasting, contact with an unfamiliar priest. At the mass immediately prior to the ordeal, the defendant was warned not to accept the Eucharist if he were guilty for fear of direct physical consequences (109–10).

[71] Combridge 97–99. Se also Franz 350–53 for a description of the parts of ordeal liturgy for the ordeal by fire; Hyams and Morris discuss the difficulty in ascertaining what actual practice was (109–10).

[72] Combridge 98.

[73] Kolb, "Isoldes Eid" suggests a similar reason for the absence of detailed descriptions of Mark and Isolde's marriage: since Tristan and Isolde have committed themselves to long-term deception, Gottfried did not want to subject his listeners to a lengthy account of the joys of the marriage feast (326).

[74] Tomasek notes that *ermel* [sleeve] appears only three times in *Tristan,* two of them in this scene (15661, 15736). He suggests that the ability of individuals to conceal material to fake the ordeal in their sleeves is the reason why this particular part of the clothing is used for the comparison to Christ, because it emphasized the manipulative element of the ordeal (77–78). See also Eckhardt Holger, "'Wintschaffen' oder 'tugenthaft'? Zu Lösungsmethoden werkimmanenter 'Widersprüche' am Beispiel von Gottfrieds Verdikt über Christus," *Neophilologus* 81 (1997): 577–81.

[75] See Franz 328–29, 351–52. Okken 542; Combridge 109, no. 178; A. Erler, "Gottesurteil," col. 1770. H. B. Willson, "The Old and the New Law in Gottfried's Tristan," *MLR* 60 (1965): 212–24, here 213, refers to Isolde's attire as "self-castigating." Isolde's clothing does not represent a voluntary act of self-mortification but reflects what was prescribed for such occasions. Combridge 109, no. 178; Schnell, "Rechtsgeschichte" 311; Mälzer notes that for the hair shirt to cause discomfort, it had to fit tightly (186, no. 182). Jackson attributes Isolde's dress to a desire to express contrition and arouse sympathy (115).

[76] Okken cites other usage of the phrase *gotes höfscheit* in Hartmann von Aue, as well as corresponding phrases in Dante and in French literature (538–39). During the six weeks prior to the ordeal Isolde concerns herself with the possible loss of honor and with the anxiety of how she could make a lie seem true: "so twanc sie daz verholne leit, dasz ir *unwarheit* solte *warbaeren*" [her secret worry as to how to make her *lie true* put her under pressure] (15539–41).

[77] See Hattenhauer, *Recht der Heiligen* 73–76; Hattenhauer, "Der gefälschte Eid" 667–74, 680–84. Hattenhauer distinguishes between *Meineid* and *der gelüpptete Eid:* The person guilty of *Meineid* simply lies in the hopes that he will not be found out ("Der gefälschte Eid" 668). See also H. Holzhauer, "Meineid," *HWBDR,* vol. 3, cols. 447–58, and H. H. Munske, "Meintat," *HWBDR,* vol. 3, cols. 458–61; *DRW,* vol. 10, cols. 445–50 indicates that lies in court, as well as breach of promise in

which a certain behavior was promised, constitute *Meineid* (cols. 445–46); R. J. Hexter, *Equivocal Oaths and Ordeals in Medieval Literature* (Cambridge, MA: Harvard UP, 1975), 1–2; Schnell, "Rechtsgeschichte" 312–13 discusses the oath in terms of eastern origins, without reference to Germanic custom, but notes in passing that all of those present at Isolde's ordeal believed in the magical aspect of the oath.

[78] Baldwin, "Intellectual Preparation" 626–29; Hattenhauer, "Der gefälschte Eid" notes that Gottfried's disgust about this material had a theological basis: the Christian God was subject to a pagan understanding of the oath (671–72). He says (680–81) that the Church could not tolerate this pre-Christian interpretation indefinitely; if one could harm one's neighbor through a false oath, that was a sin, and a sin could not be the foundation of valid legal proceedings. Bartlett notes that Innocent III scolded the bishop of Straßburg in 1212 for using the ordeal to try heretics; this letter proves that the unilateral ordeal was alive and well in Gottfried's city during the probable time of composition of *Tristan* (53). The *Tristramssaga* does not contain any commentary on the ordeal; it says only that God was merciful (Schach 94; see also Piquet 265). If Brother Robert reflects Thomas faithfully on this point, it could support the thesis of Baldwin and Bartlett that the demise of the ordeal was due to a crescendo of clerical opposition that combined with the bureaucratic mechanism to promulgate the ruling; Thomas's work seems to have been written between 1160 and 1176 (See Gesa Bonath, *Thomas: Tristan* [Munich: Fink, 1985] 16–18).

[79] Combridge discusses the meaning of *gelüppet* in other texts and in the context of Isolde's ordeal (106–10). She does not mention the duel with Morolt when she discusses its usage as a designation for poisoned weapons; such poisons were frequently seen to be magical. The poison in this case consists of Isolde's deception. *DRW*, vol. 8, *lüppen, luppen*, col. 1509 lists the legal formulation, "gelüppter Eid," as a false oath, citing sources in Old High German and in Gottfried. Jacob Grimm, *Deutsche Rechtsaltertümer*, vol. 2 (Darmstadt: Wissenschaftliche Buchgesellschaft, 1983), 558 refers to *giluppi* as an oath that was either false or not kept.

[80] Hattenhauer, "Der gefälschte Eid" 668.

[81] Combridge notes that Gottfried's commentary stands exactly in the place where the legends would have proclaimed the wrongly accused queen's innocence (104).

[82] See Schnell, "Rechtsgeschichte" 308 for references to ordeal benedictions in the first three lines.

[83] See Claude B. Moss, *The Christian Faith: An Introduction to Dogmatic Theology* (London: Society for Promoting Christian Knowledge; New York: Morehouse-Gorham Co., 1961), 69.

[84] The subject of Gottfried's concept of God has received a great deal of critical attention. See Schnell, *Suche nach Wahrheit*, "Der verkannte Gott" 59–80 (Schnell interprets both ordeals in such a manner as to support his thesis of an inscrutable God whose ways are hidden from men); Combridge 96; Dickerson, "Language" 134–43; Hans Liermann, *Die Gottheit im Recht: Ein historisch-dogmatischer Versuch* (Munich: Verlag der Bayerischen Akademie der Wissenschaft; Beck in Kommission, 1969), 8–10; Freytag, *Oxymoron* 176–85; Hans-Günther Nauen, Die Bedeutung von Religion und Theologie im Tristan Gottfrieds" (Diss. U of Marburg, 1967), 45–48, 50–52; F. Hans Rolf, *Der Tod in Mittelhochdeutschen Dichtungen* (Munich: Fink,

1974), 212–28; Esther Quinn, "Beyond Courtly Love: Religious Elements in *Tristan* and *La Queste del Saint Graal*," *In Pursuit of Perfection: Courtly Love in Medieval Literature,* ed. Joan Ferrante, George D. Economou, and Frederick Goldin (Port Washington, NY: Kennikat P, 1975), 179–219 (199–200); Van Stockum 18–23; Schild, "Gottesurteil" 72–73.

[85] Bartlett 116–22.

[86] See Bartlett 117–20, esp. 119.

[87] Baldwin, "Crisis" notes the frequent congruence between the portrayal of ordeals in literature and in historical documentation (329).

3: Saintly Queens under Fire in the *Kaiserchronik* and in *Heinrich und Kunegunde*

WHILE ISOLDE'S ORDEAL certainly represents the most dramatic of the ordeals by fire in secular German literature, it needs to be seen in the context of the legends of saintly queens who underwent similar ordeals, since there seems to have been cross-referencing and implicit comparison between legend and secular literature.[1] Though Isolde was sexually active in both marital and extramarital contexts, the Richardis of the *Kaiserchronik* maintains that she has been faithful to her husband; the marriage of Heinrich and Kunegunde is portrayed in the legend as a spiritual or chaste one, though there is no historical evidence that such was the case.

Both of these accounts are relatively obscure, especially the Middle High German version of Kunigunde's life; but they contain much material of interest not only about ordeals but also about female spirituality in the medieval German lands.[2] Since these legends involve sexual fidelity or continence in marriage, a brief introduction to the significance of this theme will help to explain the context in which the demands for the ordeal arose, since both involved accusations of adultery. While there is no such creature as a medieval attitude toward sexual relations, there are recurrent and often diverging patterns regarding doctrines in regard to sexuality in the medieval church: sex for reproduction, sex as sinful and shameful behavior, and sexual relations in marriage as a symbol expressing the partners' love for each other.[3] The second current concerns us here: chastity, whether defined as total abstinence from sexual relations or as confining them to marriage, was seen as a virtue; abstinence from sexual relations within marriage was seen as an ideal, an exceptional situation. It is this exceptionality that causes the motif of chastity in marriage or the spiritual marriage to appear frequently in saints' lives, since hagiography deals with the extraordinary. When these motifs were coupled with royalty, they had a special impact, leading to the topos of the virgin monarch.[4]

The fictional accounts of the ordeals of the two historical queens are preserved in legends, which, as John W. Baldwin has noted, testify to an abiding faith in the ordeal; these two Middle High German narratives, from the mid-twelfth and early thirteenth centuries, give us an established framework in which to view the thirteenth-century ordeals of secular literature.[5]

Richardis and Kunigunde were both historical figures; but Richardis actually offered to undergo an ordeal, while Kunigunde's ordeal was a posthumous addition to her biography, probably influenced by the account of Richardis's experience.

To understand fully the significance of the story of the falsely accused queen in the *Kaiserchronik* we must look at her in the context of the work's scope and purpose. This massive text, the first chronicle in German and the first vernacular chronicle of the Roman Empire, portraying the succession of power from Julius Caesar through Konrad III, was written in Regensburg in the late 1140s or early 1150s. Unlike secular literary ordeals, the *Kaiserchronik* was not meant to be a fictional account written primarily for diversion. The author (or authors; whether there were one or multiple authors is not clear), like other twelfth-century writers, considered his work a history, intended for the edification of his readers; but his conception of what constitutes history was rather elastic. He made use not only of factual information but also of other nonhistorical sources, including legends, sagas, and material from antiquity that had been popular with early writers. He also left out thirty-two of the sixty-eight emperors who ruled during the time period the work covers and included some completely unhistorical figures. The major theme is the empire in its political, as well as its social, order, seen in connection with the Church's work for salvation.[6] The good and the evil rulers, whom the prologue mentions, are portrayed to increase wisdom and recognition and to benefit the soul.[7]

The example of a queen accused of adultery provided a useful vehicle to advance the stated goals of the writer. In 887 Queen Richardis, the consort of Charles, was charged with adultery with Bishop Liutward, Charles's closest confidant. These accusations came from powerful figures in the realm who were angered by Charles's concessions to the Normans and Liutward's power and influence over the emperor.[8] Because of his familiarity with Richardis's private affairs, uncontrollable rumors circulated that Liutward and the empress were lovers. In July, 887, an assembly was held at Kirchen in Baden at which the emperor declared that even though he had been married to Richardis for more than ten years, he had never had physical relations with her. She in turn swore that she had never had physical relations with Charles or any other man and offered to clear her name by walking on hot plowshares or through trial by battle. Charles refused this proof, but their joint declarations justified separation, whereupon Richardis retired to a convent at Andlau.[9]

Not until the eleventh century do we hear much about Richardis, but in his Reichenau chronicle the monk Herimann discusses the accusations made against the empress in his entry for the year 887. He writes that her declaration proved that she had remained a virgin, in spite of her twelve-year marriage. His text contains the first mention of an ordeal, though Herimann is not specific about what kind — which would have been difficult, since she never underwent one. His remarks, however, set others to work trying to learn to which ordeal the empress was subjected. In addition, her body was reburied in 1049 with special attention from Pope Leo IX; the enhanced stature her tomb enjoyed made her veneration flourish and aided in the development of the legend that grew up around her, the first German record of which appears in the *Kaiserchronik*.[10]

This historical record was the model for several literary treatments of the same theme: the virtuous queen who redeems her good name through the ordeal.[11] In the *Kaiserchronik* account Richardis chooses a most singular ordeal, that of a burning wax shirt. The association of such an ordeal with the Carolingians is not surprising from an historical point of view, since Charlemagne had placed a new emphasis on the ordeal. During that period there was also a multiplication of types of ordeal, including the ordeal of the cross.[12]

Since the historical records contain ample testimony of the spread of the ordeal in Carolingian times, it is not surprising that the first literary portrayal of an ordeal in medieval German literature comes in this quasi-historical work that includes the Carolingian emperors (ll. 15400–517). Richardis, a model of both feminine and queenly virtues, becomes the target for the slander of a vassal who whispers some alarming news into Charles's ear at a dawn mass (15414–35). Hastening back to his chambers, he upbraids and strikes Richardis (15440–63). Richardis's behavior is described as a matter important not only to the salvation of her soul but also as an affair of state. When Charles accuses his wife of infidelity, he asks how she can be worthy to be the queen of the empire (15463), since adultery on the part of a queen could be met with a charge of treason.

Immediately after Charles accuses her, Richardis states that with God's help she will overcome her troubles (15467) and sends for four bishops to make her confession. Richardis prays, fasts, and gives herself into God's hands (15473–79). She prepares for her ordeal, which she welcomes, with the calm assurance of the innocent, trusting that God will vindicate her (15494–509).[13] After she withstands the trials of the burning wax shirt, she and Charles abdicate the throne (15508–16).

Richardis's survival of the unusual ordeal of the burning wax shirt, impossible to fake, might well be seen as further proof of her sanctity. The exemplary role that she plays means that the main interest of the writer is not the ordeal per se but the edifying value of her withstanding a trial of her faith and remaining constant. Consequently, we cannot expect a detailed factual account of what happened, because the poet's interest lies elsewhere.

An indication of the importance that the writer attached to the ordeal is apparent in the proportion of the episode that deals with it: approximately one-third of the total number of lines concern themselves with the ordeal. Despite the use of the technical term *tägedinch*[14] on the day of Richardis's trial, the account contains few legal or liturgical references. Normally at an assembly such as this one the king or his representative, who could be either a layman or a cleric, would preside. During the time leading up to the performance of the ordeal, Charles is simply not mentioned. Under usual procedure, the charge he leveled in their private rooms (15460–63) would be repeated and a judgment reached. It was the judgment that indicated what was at issue and the means of proof. All of these elements are absent: only the public nature of the assembly receives emphasis.[15] The only figures on center stage during the *tagedinch* are Richardis and the four bishops.

Not only the judgment procedure but also the ordeal process (15494–513) diverges from contemporary historical accounts. Here, too, many important sections of the ritual are missing. While this ordeal uses a burning wax shirt instead of a hot iron, the liturgical procedures that were designed both to discover truth and to protect the innocent would have been basically similar, since the essential process was the ordeal itself and not the kind of ordeal.[16] The *Kaiserchronik* passage has no mention of the blessing of the fire or of the shirt, of the sprinkling of the shirt with holy water, of the *adjuratio*, or of the oath. The focus of the entire scene is on the queen and on others' reaction to her. We know in advance that this queen cannot be guilty: the chronicler praises her virtue at the outset of the passage dealing with her (15404–5). The nobles and prelates present want to stop the proceedings; their blessings beforehand and their hope that God will be gracious to her also indicate that the queen is innocent.

The only section that hints at ordeal liturgy concerns the preparation of the shirt (15497–99). These lines could refer to the impregnation with wax, as well as to the prayers that were said over it. The narrator writes, "They sing and read" (15499); one can assume that that is a reference to the mass that was held immediately before every ordeal.[17] The cry "deo gratias" from those present after the queen successfully underwent the ordeal could also be part of the ceremony.

The saintly figure of Richardis occupies center stage for the *Kaiserchronik* author. The oath, so prominent in our other ordeal scenes, though for different reasons, does not appear here. The impossibility of the queen's guilt has been apparent from the beginning; therefore, the swearing of an oath is superfluous — particularly since there is no secret information that can only be revealed in the oath, as in Ebernand von Erfurt's *Heinrich und Kunegunde*. Unlike the Richardis of the Latin sources, Richardis here never states that she did not have sexual relations with her husband; she simply denies the rumors that she has been unfaithful.[18] Richardis merely asserts immediately before the ordeal that God himself would not want her to wear the crown if people told such tales about what she had done (15489). Richardis's sanctity is apparent to those in authority; it is only through her insistence that the ordeal takes place at all. (Her virtue is so great that the question of rigging the ordeal, so important in the two secular accounts analyzed in this study, never appears.)[19]

The directness and immediacy of the queen's relationship with God and her role as a model worthy of emulation make all around her seem smaller. Perhaps that is one of the reasons that four bishops hear her confession.[20] Just as in the Kunegunde account, there are no mediators between Richardis and God; the accused deals directly with the deity. There are no last chances to confess nor prayers that God render a just examination of whatever is doubtful.[21] The queen's trial seems to be designed not so much to test her faith as to edify her subjects, to make it possible for her to reveal and witness publicly to that faith.

The queen's attackers receive the punishment they asked for if their stories were false (15434–35, 15510–11). The speedy and drastic retribution underscores both the gravity of their offense and Richardis's purity, as well as the political nature of the accusation. Since these men damaged the empire with their false testimony, they deserve death. The swift royal justice that ends their lives also finishes the story of injustice and retribution. The idea that punishment follows perjury is a common motif in legends; here the king acts as the agent of divine wrath.[22]

A later portrayal of an ordeal that has the most similarities with the *Kaiserchronik* account and was apparently influenced by it appears in Ebernand von Erfurt's *Heinrich und Kunegunde,* a legend dealing with the emperor and empress who founded the bishopric of Bamberg. Ebernand seems to have written the work at the urging of a friend, Reimbote, of the Cistercian monastery at Georgenthal, near Erfurt, who had played a role in the canonization of the empress in 1200 (4517–33).[23] At the end of his work Ebernand explains that Reimbot, then a servant in the Bamberg cathedral, had a vision in which the emperor threatened calamity if his queen were not given her rightful place on the altar of the cathedral. He told Reimbot that God would make his feelings for Kunegunde apparent with signs. Church officials mocked Reimbot, but he swore on the emperor's relics that his statement was true; and miracles began to happen at Kunegunde's tomb (4137–275). Her canonization followed.[24]

Ebernand's work of almost 5,000 lines is the first account in German of this popular saint's life. His sources were the Latin accounts of her life; the reports of miracles that had justified her canonization; an addition to the life of Heinrich II written shortly after her elevation to sainthood; oral Bamberg tradition from Reimbot; and probably other sources. The intense devotion to Kunigunde around Bamberg, which sainthood only augmented, would have been reason enough to make the details of her life available in the vernacular — particularly since her popularity in the area soon surpassed that of her husband.[25] Although there is some controversy about the dating of the work, around 1220, between Gottfried's *Tristan* and Stricker's "Das heiße Eisen," seems to find most support.[26] Consequently, it gives us a contemporary version of a saint's life written after the Fourth Lateran Council to use as a comparison with accounts of trial by fire in secular literature written immediately before 1215 and a couple of decades thereafter.

Like the comparable scene in the *Kaiserchronik*, this one treats the ordeal as an agency that can reveal God's judgment and vindicate an unjustly accused woman. The miracle of Kunegunde's unseared feet after her walk on the burning plowshares played a significant role in her elevation to sainthood; but it was not part of the historical record, nor was it noted in the documents surrounding her husband's canonization in 1147, for which the virginal marriage was an important justification.[27] After her husband became a saint, attention began to fall on her, since it takes two to make a chaste marriage. Kunigunde's canonization proceedings were already underway when Lothario di Segni, a student of Peter the Chanter in Paris, became pope as Innocent III in 1198. The bull authorizing her canonization in 1200 included the ordeal as one of the miracles that qualified her for sainthood. Even at this early date in his papacy Innocent had already made his objections to the ordeal clear, but the official position of the Church did not change until 1215.[28]

The ordeal of walking on hot plowshares also appeared during the reign of Charlemagne, when the first reference to it was in the Thuringian law of 802. This earliest allusion specifies that it is to be used for a woman accused of murdering her husband; it was only employed, however, if the woman had no champion to fight for her in battle. There are several points of interest for our consideration in this ordeal's function in the legal code. It only was used for an extremely heinous crime when other means to settle the issue were not available. It may, indeed, have been a Thuringian custom, so it is not surprising that it appears in her vita. Charlemagne seems to have found merit in this ordeal; it appears in Salic law in 803.[29] While it was never as popular as the ordeal of the hot iron, it had an uninterrupted history as a test for those under suspicion of marital infidelity. These two aspects — the exceptional nature of its use and its employment in instances of marital infidelity — have important functions in the legend. The faithful would certainly have been drawn by the drama of this special ordeal that was specifically earmarked for sexual offenses.

The complete trust in the efficacy of the ordeal that manifests itself in this work has its roots in the saintly legends surrounding Heinrich and Kunegunde contemporaneous with the canonization of Heinrich, completed in 1147 by Pope Eugenius III. There would have been a natural reluctance to alter any details in the lives of two saints. One must also keep in mind that for the medieval listener the legend had just as much of a claim to truth as the historical chronicle.[30] Therefore, material such as the ordeal, since it appeared in a legend, would likely be both presented and received differently than if it were the subject of a contemporary secular story. In addition, Ebernand's use of the vernacular shows that he meant his version of the legend to have an effect: an account full of miracles would both strengthen the faith of the laity and provide an example for contemporary rulers in a age that many felt sorely needed imperial paradigms.[31]

Ebernand seemed to see Heinrich and Kunigunde as ideal types of man and woman; certainly the legend of the chaste marriage, which began to appear shortly after the emperor's death, was one of the most prominent traits in the legend material surrounding the two Bamberg saints.[32] Since childlessness in a monarch was frequently seen as a reproach, it is not surprising that efforts were made in the laments composed at Heinrich's death in 1024 to explain this failure to produce an heir as a conscious decision to live a holy life, which led to the belief that he and Kunigunde had had a virginal union that became an important justification for Heinrich's canonization. Since saintly kings and queens were, of course, supposed to have extraordinary strength of character, it was not uncommon for chaste marriages to be attributed to them.[33]

Since the theme of the unconsummated marriage arose after Heinrich's death and was, therefore, not part of the historical record, it becomes especially important to examine this record to see how the historical account influences and shapes the legend. Recent research shows that the story about the chaste marriage most likely does not reflect reality. Detailed study of documents from Heinrich II's reign certainly indicates strong emotional ties between the two and suggests a close physical relationship as well, in spite of bitter, ongoing quarrels between her husband and her family.[34] As the first queen officially crowned and anointed in the German lands, Kunigunde also played a significant political role: she appears as a co-ruler with her husband in an illustration in a liturgical book from around 1011–13, and there is extensive documentation of her influencing the decision-making process, especially when it involved privileges for religious institutions. Her historically attested devotion to the welfare of religious foundations strengthened the case for canonization.[35] However, her role in the empire's affairs did not stop there. She represented Heinrich in border disputes in 1012 and 1016 in Saxony, where she showed such administrative ability and decisiveness that her husband put her in charge of his military campaign in defense of the eastern lands.[36] As we shall see, the legend confirms the close emotional ties between them, as well as Kunigunde's political importance in the empire.

Heinrich, whose subjects gave him the epithet of lame, crippled or the crippled loins, was aware that their marriage would produce no children. He announced in 1007 at the founding of the Bamberg bishopric in Frankfurt that he had lost hope that his marriage to Kunigunde would provide an heir and for this reason was leaving his possessions to the new bishopric. Preparations for the founding of Bamberg began around 1004, so Heinrich must already have been certain at that time that, contrary to the expressed hopes of his subjects, he would have no children.[37] There is some disagreement as to whether or not Heinrich could have followed Germanic custom and divorced a barren wife, but Heinrich apparently kept Kunigunde out of love and because he appreciated her considerable intellectual and spiritual qualities.[38]

The historical background, which confirms their closeness as well as Kunigunde's considerable political role, combines with the legend of the chaste marriage in Ebernand's account. Heinrich's supposed chastity, so important to his canonization, appears early on in the legend in his response to the nobles who urge him to marry and produce a successor; he prefers to have Christ as an heir (755–61). The woman his princes choose for him, Kunegunde, is utterly distraught at the prospect of marriage, since she, too, has made a secret vow of chastity (851–53). Her relief is enormous when she learns that Heinrich shares her views (905–24). On their wedding night the king asks her to make a solemn vow with him (933–51). The word he uses, *geloben* [to solemnly swear or promise], is particularly powerful.[39] In the performance of such promises it was common to involve the hands; here, Heinrich takes her hands in his and asks her to vow chastity in marriage with him; he also promises to give her the full range of authority that would come to her as empress (949–51).[40] Particularly since Kunigunde's legal rights and standing as empress were involved, medieval audiences would have seen Heinrich's gesture, so well known to them from the process of enfeoffment, as a particularly binding one. All oaths involved God as a witness; this one concerns not only promises in regard to temporal power but also promises made directly to God regarding their chaste marriage.[41] This wedding-night vow gives added impact to the apparent faithlessness of Kunegunde.

True to his word, Heinrich involves his wife closely in the affairs of the empire and is utterly devoted to her (1169–84). As proof of their extraordinary virtue, Ebernand cannot resist telling us that though they shared a bed, they remained chaste because of God's protection (1189–94). Only God and Satan knew of this arrangement, which upset the devil mightily, since, according to Ebernand, chastity confused him (1200–202).

The whole ordeal episode is presented as an attempt by the devil to destroy the royal pair through slander, since he could not tempt them to self-destruct through sin (1261–1334). The devil's presence serves to heighten the sanctity of Kunegunde, as well as her importance, and is particularly appropriate in the life of a saint. When the members of court see the devil in the form of a knight leaving her bedchamber on three separate occasions, they react with sorrow, consternation, and in some cases, glee at the prospect of gossip.

The emperor's grief-stricken reaction to the news is to alternate between misery and hope, interviewing those who claimed to be well informed (1335–54). In his distraught behavior he resembles King Mark in Gottfried's *Tristan*, which Ebernand could certainly have known.[42] During a painful interview with her husband Kunegunde suggests the involvement of the princes to repair the damage done to the empire (1388–1416). Her concern for the empire's reputation and well-being, which reflects the historical fact that she played a significant role in the administration of the realm, gives us an insight into the political responsibility she felt she had.[43] Kunegunde is the one who tells Heinrich to invite all of the peers of the realm, from all corners of the empire, lay as well as clerical, to sit in judgment on the matter. Her active involvement in this regard not only reflects her historical role but also serves to anticipate the outcome of the case. She knows that she is innocent (1370–71) and intends to convince those on whom the emperor's power rests: the peers. In her approach to the ordeal and the procedures accompanying it, deep devotion and the knowledge of her innocence combine with a highly developed sense of political acumen. The contrast becomes even more apparent if we compare Kunegunde's behavior to that of Gottfried's Isolde. She certainly did not admonish Mark to bring all of the nobles in to judge her; in contrast, she complained that she could not get a fair trial because she was a foreigner and had no oath helpers.

Ebernand's portrayal of Kunegunde's ordeal could well have been written with two other queens who were forced to make marriage work through a trial by fire in mind: Isolde and Richardis. Baldwin has already noted that the hagiographic account made Kunigunde into an "anti-Queen Iseut."[44] Gottfried's work, which appeared about ten years earlier, certainly made a vernacular version available to Ebernand. Isolde, wishing to appear the pliant penitent, plays a strikingly passive role, except for the formulation of her oath, in comparison with Kunegunde, who also orchestrates things but does so in a manner that opens her to all possible risks in a successful attempt to prove her innocence. The portrayal of Kunigunde in the "Additamentum," one of Ebernand's major sources, does show a queen ready to act and conscious of her political power, but Ebernand makes definite changes that reflect an emphasis on the queen and could contrast her with Isolde. The worldliness of his Kunegunde is apparent in two important scenes: her first interview with Heinrich after he learns of the accusations and her speech before the nobles in advance of the ordeal. While the "Additamentum" Kunigunde tells the emperor she has a plan for removing the dishonor she has caused,[45] Ebernand's Kunegunde reflects a more active and more sagacious character both in rephrasing of passages (italics) and additions (bold):

> sie seite: "hêre, zwâre es sol
> **werden rât über rât:** (I)
> des man mich gezigen hât,
> des weiz mich got unschuldec;
> *hêre, weset geduldec,*
> *gehabet ûch als ein fromer man,* (II)

> den rât ich û noch vinden kan
> **unt harte wol gelêren:** (III)
> daz rîche hat der êren
> harte vil mit mir verlorn,
> **reine hêre wol geborn,**
> **die sult ir mir gewinnen wider!"** (IV)
> . . . . .
> sie sprach: "ir sult besenden
> in dem rîche in allen enden
> die edlen fursten alle
> und lât in her schalle,
> daz sie komen gar ze hove,
> leienfursten, bischove,
> unde sitzet zuo geriht
> unde erteilet dise geschiht,
> wie ûch die fursten lêren:
> diz muget ir tuon mit êren.
> *der diz uber mich verhenget hât,*
> *er ist sô guot, er tuots uns rât:* (V)
> **ezn ist sunder sache niht**
> **geschên ein sô getân geschicht."** (VI)
> (1388–99; 1403–16)

["**Lord, truly a solution is at hand.** What I have been accused of, God knows I am innocent. *Lord, be patient and behave as an honorable man.* I will yet be able to find counsel and **can well instruct you.** The empire has lost much of its reputation because of me; **noble and virtuous lord, you should get it back for me."** . . . "You should send to all the corners of the empire and let all of the noble princes be called here so that they come to the court, lay princes and bishops, and you should sit in judgment on this matter as the peers instruct you. That you may do with honor. *He who has let this happen to me, he is so benevolent that he will help us.* **Such a thing could never have happened without an instigator."**

The first passage in bold, in which Kunegunde announces that a solution is at hand, sets the stance for all of the highlighted sections: a proactive, assertive queen. Passage II includes the imperatives of the Latin passage but omits the phrase entreating the emperor to behave in this manner; Ebernand's Kunegunde tells much more often than she asks. Kunegunde's assertion that she can instruct her husband (III) is missing in the Latin text, as is her charge to him to regain her lost honor for her (IV). While the comparable Latin passage for section V hopes for divine mercy, the Middle High German passage is cast more in terms of God's responsibility (for letting it happen) and his goodness, which will guarantee that he comes to their aid. Kunegunde's keen political sense is apparent in VI, which is not in the Latin text; she knows that such a situation could not have happened without an instigator. Ebernand's adaptations in this passage that emphasize her strength and sagacity appear not only in her speech but also in the characterization of the emperor: the Latin text indicates in indirect discourse that the emperor bade her to sit down and tell him how the matter could be resolved,[46] while Ebernand has Heinrich ask the queen to tell him how this might happen, placing himself in a somewhat subordinate role.

Heinrich continues to figure less prominently in Ebernand's version during the trial scene. While the Latin source contains a lengthy address by the emperor to the assembled peers, Ebernand's version has a terse statement from him, further deemphasizing his role:[47]

> "Ir hêren, es stêt mir vil hô,
> mîn laster hât ir wol vernomen,
> durch daz sît ir zesamen komen.
> *wes sint wert die vrouwen,*
> *die ir man verschouwen*
> *unt die mit huorheit sich erhugent?*
> nû teilet ez, sô rehte ir mugent!" (1432–38)

["My lords, it is a matter of great concern to me, my shame you have heard about, that is the reason you are here. What are ladies worth who hold their husbands in contempt and who give themselves up to whoredom? Now give as just a verdict as you can."]

This passage, approximately 70 percent shorter than the Latin version, contains the briefest of instructions; almost half of it is devoted to a sharper attack on the queen, keeping her in center stage.

Ebernand also stages Kunegunde's appearance before the court somewhat differently than the Latin source does. He notes that the queen came before the princes in a manner befitting her station (1422–24), while the "Additamentum" notes that she serenely entered.[48] In the Latin source she is definitely the queen, but a submissive one; Ebernand's version keeps Kunegunde before the princes, leaving Heinrich out of the picture.[49] Motivated by the peers' reluctance to allow her to clear her name convincingly, Kunegunde asserts her authority before the court more directly than in the Latin source. There she says only that the princes made her husband emperor and asked her to share in his rule, while Ebernand presents her as Heinrich's equal:[50]

> "dô ir kurt den hêren mîn
> ze kunec unt mich ze kunigîn,
> ze hêren wart ir sin vil frô.
> ouch was ich ûwer vrouwe dô;
> dô ir des geruohtet
> und uns ze hêrschaft suohtet,
> do enwas in der werlde dô
> an hêrschaft nieman alsô hô,
> als alle keiser wâren
> vor uns in manegen jâren
> unt die noch nâch uns sullen sîn
> keiser unde keiserîn;
> ez sî mir schade oder gewin,
> wand ich die hôste vrouwe bin,
> ich sol mich ouch des hôsten
> gerihtes getrôsten." (1461–76)

["When you chose my lord as king and me as queen, you were very pleased with my lord, and I was your lady. When you granted us the right to rule over you, there was no one higher in authority in the world, just as all emperors who came before us and those who come after us who will be emperors and empresses. Whether it hurts or benefits me, since I am the highest lady, I should also put my hopes in the highest court."]

The first part of this speech repeats three times that the princes chose both her and Heinrich to rule over them; Kunegunde also places herself in the line of rulers before and after her. This sharp departure from the Latin text certainly corresponds to the historical reality, since she was the first queen in the German lands who was officially crowned and anointed; but it also continues the consistent portrait Ebernand paints of a proactive, politically astute queen concerned for the welfare of the state.

Kunegunde shows a political recognition both of her position as an empress and of the princes' central role. Because she is the highest lady in the land, she should entrust herself to the most rigorous verdict, that of the glowing plowshares (1461–78). Her unshakable determination to proceed naturally reinforces the impression of her innocence, as does her gratitude to those who wished to spare her this misery (1479–86).[51]

The incredible temperature to which the plowshares are heated is enough to satisfy even Kunegunde; Ebernand's vivid description gives added weight to the miracle that occurs (1487–93).[52] Because the clergy is involved, the procedure occurs near the cathedral (1496–97). The innocent queen makes a direct appeal to Christ as judge of the ordeal, asking him to treat her as a faithful servant whose master would help rather than see the servant die

(1501–16). Two of the most worthy bishops accompany her, showing the pre-Fourth Lateran role of the clergy; their status not only foreshadows the outcome but also ratifies the verdict at the highest level (1517–18).

Kunegunde's oath shows a certain similarity to Isolde's in that both swear as to those with whom they have or have not had physical contact. Kunegunde swears that no man, not even her husband, has lain with her. This admission calls forth a distinctly uncourtly gesture from Heinrich, who, unable to silence her to keep this most private aspect of their relationship secret, hits her so hard that blood runs down her face (1555–62). The queen's unqualified statement is in itself a reflection of her innocence; unlike Isolde, Kunegunde did not have to prepare an elaborate ruse or choose her words carefully. The oaths in the legends reflect the process Hans Hattenhauer has described as the Christianization of the oath, which demanded that it be true in reality, not just in appearance.[53]

Other aspects of the account of the ordeal that reflect historically verified proceedings are the removal of Kunegunde's shoes, the sequence of events taking place near a cathedral or in a chapel, and the presence of the clergy. The removal of the shoes was necessary so that the person's flesh could come directly in contact with the hot iron, and it precluded any form of deception. While the latter was not an issue in Kunegunde's case, the fact that this small detail is included shows that her ordeal was completely in order and that she did walk on the plowshares with bare feet. The plowshares have been heated to an extraordinary degree (1488–92), preparing the hearers for the upcoming miracle.[54] She pauses on the twelfth one, just as if she were standing in a morning dew on a soft piece of dough (Ebernand's use of metaphor is frequently more exuberant than eloquent) (1565–75).

Kunegunde's miraculous acquittal immediately receives its legal imprimatur: Ebernand triumphantly announces that the court established justice here (1581); in the legends clerical participation and ratification remain in place. After her successful withstanding of the ordeal, Kunegunde receives homage from her husband, who throws himself at her feet and asks for her *hulde* (1585–89).[55] This gesture parallels hers of sitting at his feet before the trial. Much extravagant praise comes from everyone, including Ebernand, who notes that one of the major results of this ordeal was the revelation of Kunegunde's chastity (1609–16) — yet another indication of where the emphasis lay for him. A major force in this emphasis was the importance at this time of the veneration of Mary, whose virginity was a pillar of her sanctity; naturally, female saints and their hagiographers would have had her as a model. Ebernand repeatedly portrays Kunegunde as a Mary figure; just as Mary was a mother and still a virgin, so Kunegunde was widowed and yet a maiden (3154, 3157). Her closeness to Mary probably accounts for her popularity eclipsing that of her husband.[56] The ordeal scene verifies Kunegunde's chastity, which accounts for the detailed and serious treatment it receives.

The motif and textual parallels between Ebernand's work and the *Kaiserchronik* account of the trial by fire of the saintly Carolingian queen, Richardis, appearing in the vernacular in the in the mid-twelfth century are so striking that influence at some point in the hagiographic tradition, as well as the possibility that Ebernand knew the earlier version, seems highly likely.[57] Kunegunde's ordeal, three times as long as Richardis's, has both important similarities to and differences from the *Kaiserchronik* account. Similarities seem to occur at those points that emphasize the virtue of the women, neither of whom was tempted but both of whose reputations were compromised. Many of the differences arise from Ebernand's emphasis on Kunegunde's virginity, which is not an issue for Richardis in the *Kaiserchronik*. Both women are extraordinarily virtuous, both have husbands who doubt them and hit them, both are falsely accused but trust in God to deliver them, both realize the harm done to the state, and both, convinced of their innocence, demand a trial.[58] Though Richardis is anxious to clear her name, however, and has center stage because of her virtue, she does not take charge in the political way that Kunegunde does in Ebernand's account. In the *Kaiserchronik* Richardis does not appear before a council of peers but goes directly to the ordeal. In contrast, Kunegunde seems to be fully aware of her power base and the need to shore up the assumptions on which it rests, and her appearance before the council gives her the opportunity to do so.

This description does reflect both historical reality and local Bamberg tradition; but Ebernand's repeated references to it may reveal other currents, as well, particularly since he departs from his major Latin source, the "Additamentum," both in expanding Kunegunde's role and diminishing that of Heinrich. A comparison of the three major speeches of Kunegunde — to Heinrich on their first meeting after the accusation becomes known, a second to Heinrich later in that meeting, and her speech before the peers — show the obvious influence of the "Additamentum," but they also strike a distinctly different note. In all three cases Ebernand's account deletes or diminishes the deferential attitude of Kunegunde toward the emperor and substitutes a much more self-assured approach.

Differences arise out of the circumstances surrounding the canonization of both Heinrich and Kunegunde. Their marital chastity, not sexual fidelity, shapes the presentation of the material. In the case of Queen Richardis, the charges arose from an envious ministeriale, while Kunegunde's opponent was none other than the devil in the form of a knight. Since Kunegunde was actually compromised by this handsome devil in her chambers, while Richardis was only slandered, Heinrich's queen has the chance to appear particularly virtuous.

The ordeal procedure itself offers opportunities to emphasize Kunegunde's sanctity. Unlike Richardis, she offers both a prayer, in which she asks Christ to be her judge, and an oath. While Kunegunde's innocence seems as obvious as that of Richardis, who did not offer an oath, Kunegunde's attestation is necessary for the revelation of her chaste marriage. The detailed description of the hot plowshares and her walk on them, as well as the panegyric after her successful completion of the ordeal, all absent from the Richardis account, serve further to establish her credentials as a saint. For medieval people, both the miracle and the ordeal were regarded as a manifestation of divine intervention in human affairs,[59] intervention that resolved intractable human situations. In Kunigunde's case the ordeal served to reveal the *Josephsehe* (chaste marriage), which led to canonization of both her and Heinrich; its results served to give a divine imprimatur to their sanctity.

Notes

[1] Baldwin, *Trial* 16–19 gives a survey of ordeals undergone by accused queens. Their sexual behavior was not only a matter of great political importance but also reflected the predominant use of the ordeal by fire in matters of sexual mores.

[2] The most recent extensive treatment of this topic, Dyan Elliott, *Spiritual Marriage: Sexual Abstinence in Medieval Wedlock* (Princeton: Princeton UP, 1993), does not include the *Kaiserchronik* version of Richardis's trial, though Elliott deals with the chronicle material related to it. She mentions Ebernand's life of Kunigunde in passing (173, note 131), but it does not figure in her detailed discussion of the legend (128–30).

[3] Brundage 5; Brundage's book is an excellent introduction to medieval views on sexuality.

[4] Brundage 6; Elliott 4–9. See also Jo Ann McNamara, "Chaste Marriage and Clerical Celibacy," *Sexual Practices and the Medieval Church*, ed. Vern L. Bullough and James A. Brundage (Buffalo, NY: Prometheus, 1982), 22–33; McNamara, "The *Herrenfrage*: The Restructuring of the Gender System, 1050–1150," *Medieval Masculinities: Regarding Men in the Middle Ages*, ed. Clare Lees (Minneapolis: U of Minnesota P, 1994), 3–29; Pamela Gold, "The Marriage of Mary and Joseph in the Twelfth Century," *Sexual Practices*, ed. Bullough and Brundage 102–17. The marriage of Mary and Joseph may have influenced the proliferation of thirteenth-century spiritual marriages, since the cult of the Virgin expanded during this period (Elliott 176–83). For a discussion of the virgin king and the virgin queen, see Elliott 114–31, 74–83.

[5] Bartlett 16; Baldwin, *Aristocratic Life* 206.

[6] Eberhard Nellmann, "Kaiserchronik," *VF,* vol. 4 (1983) cols. 949–64 (cols. 949, 952–53, 955–57); Ruth Schmidt-Wiegand, "Kaiserchronik," *HWBDR,* vol. 2, cols. 548–52 (col. 549); Helmut de Boor and Richard Newald, *Geschichte der deutschen Literatur von den Anfängen bis zur Gegenwart,* vol. 1 (Munich: Beck, 1949), 223–32; Karl Stackmann, *Mittelalterliche Texte als Aufgabe: Kleine Schriften,* vol. 1 (Göttingen: Vandenhoeck & Ruprecht, 1997): "Erzählstrategie und Sinnvermittlung in der deutschen 'Kaiserchronik'" 51–69 (51–55).

[7] See ll. 12–14, 20–21 of the *Kaiserchronik* prologue, *Kaiserchronik eines regensburger Geistlichen,* ed. Edward Schröder (Berlin: Weidmann, 1964).

[8] See Regino of Prüm, "Chronicon 887," *Monumenta Germaniae historica inde ab anno Christi quingentesimo usque ad annum millesimum et quingentesimum*, vol. 1, ed. G. H. Pertz (Hannover: Hahn, 1876), 596–98, 597.

[9] Folz, *Les saintes reines* 47–48. Folz says that Charles could have been trying to avoid producing an heir with Richardis to favor his bastard Bernard, whom he loved deeply and whom he hoped the pope would make legitimate (45). Dyan Elliot, who does not mention the *Kaiserchronik* version of the trial, sees Charles's worries about succession and Richardis's apparent sterility at the root of the trial (80, 82–83). She notes that after about eleven years of marriage in 873 and no children, Charles said that he wanted to withdraw from the empire and have no sexual relations with his wife. The fact that this statement occurred in the middle of an epileptic fit may account for the irrationality of Charles's solution. In 885 Charles tried unsuccessfully to make his illegitimate son Bernard his heir. Ill in mind and body, Charles brought Richardis to trial in 887. Karl Brunner, *Oppositionelle Gruppen im Karolingerreich* (Vienna, Cologne & Graz: Böhlau, 1979) comments on Liutward and Bernhard (155–56). See Ernst Ludwig Dümmler, *Geschichte des ostfränkischen Reiches*, 3 vols. (Hildesheim: Olms, 1960), III: 243–45 for Bernhard, 282–83 for Liutward, 284–85 for Richardis's accusation and trial; Silvia Konecny, *Die Frauen des karolingischen Königshauses: die politische Bedeutung der Ehe und die Stellung der Frau in der fränkischen Herrscherfamilie vom 7. Bis zum 10. Jahrhundert* (Vienna: VWGÖ, 1976), 141–42; Reynolds provides a description of such an assembly prior to 1140, against which it is useful to compare the *Kaiserchronik* account (25).

[10] *Kaiserchronik* 15400–517. Herimann of Reichenau, "*Chronicon* 887," *Monumenta Germaniae historica inde ab anno Christi quingentesimo usque ad annum millesimum et quingentesimum*, vol. 5, ed. Georg Heinrich Pertz (Hannover: Hahn, 1884; rpt. Leipzig: Hiersemann, 1925), 109; Folz, *Les Saintes Reines* 49–51; Dümmler, III: 285, no. 2.

[11] Bartlett 16–17.

[12] See Bartlett 9–12; Gal 247.

[13] Her comments are echoed in ordeal liturgy. See the ritual blessing of the hot iron from the *Register of Nagyvarad* 1208–35: "Ritus exploranda veritatis," *Regestrum varadinense examinum ferri candentis ordine chronologico digestrum, descripta effigie editionis a. 1550 illustratum, sumptibusque Capituli varadinensis lat. rit.*, ed. Samu Borovszky and János Karácsonyi (Budapest: Hornyánszky Viktor, 1903), 146–52.

[14] Lexer, *MHDHWB*, II, gives a legal meaning, *gerichtstag*, for this word (col. 1387).

[15] "biscove unt herzogen / kômen alle zesamene / und anders volkes ain michel menige" [Bishops and dukes and a large number of other people all came together] (15481–83).

[16] Combridge 97. See also Borovszky and János Karácsonyi 146–52; Elliott believes that the cruelty of this ordeal arose from the fact that affairs of state were involved (90).

[17] The only other possible reflection of ordeal liturgy is the reference to Susanna: "Daniel and Susanna," *The Revised English Bible* 150–52. Combridge, in supplementary texts dealing with other royal ordeals, cites three examples in which Susanna's case appears in ordeal liturgy, two of which are quite similar to the *Kaiser-*

chronik situation (114–16). In one of these cases the slandered Emma prays for God to help her just as he helped Susanna (116); in the third example it appears in the *adjuratio* to the candidate (120). The story of Susanna bears many resemblances to that of Richardis. She, like Susanna, is fair and virtuous (vs. 2). When the falsely accused Susanna is about to be put to death, those around her weep, as do the princes in the Carolingian court (l. 15493). Her trust is in God, as is the queen's (vs. 35, esp. ll. 15467–71) in the *Kaiserchronik*.

[18] In the light of Elliott's comment about the canonization of Kunigunde, "The canonization of Empress Cunegund not only anticipated the return of the spiritual marriage motif to women, but it also signaled the resurfacing of the completely unconsummated marriage as a distinct and well-publicized model of the married state" (266), the fact that the *Kaiserchronik* author omits the historical account of the unconsummated marriage of Richardis and Charles is of great interest and could provide support to Elliott's analysis.

Why did the *Kaiserchronik* author leave out the theme of the unconsummated marriage, particularly since the sanctity of Richardis is a dominant theme? While the clerical compiler of the *Kaiserchronik* finished his work well before the canonization of Kunigunde occurred, he probably came from Regensburg, a short distance from Bamberg, and he would most probably have known about Kunigunde, particularly since he was writing around the time of Henry's elevation to sainthood (see Schmidt-Wiegand, "Kaiserchronik," *HWBDR,* vol. 2, col. 549, for Regensburg origins).

[19] The problem of cheating during an ordeal was a vexing one; many measures were prepared to guard against it, one of which was an imprecation in the liturgy, that is, as in the ordeal liturgy of Nagyvarad: "si hanc praesentem examinationem aliqui aliquod maleficium, aut per herbas, tegere & impedire voluerit. . . ."

[20] Erler, "Gottesurteil," *HWBDR,* vol. 1, col. 1770, notes that if the person undergoing the ordeal were of high rank, one or even two bishops might be present. The participation of four, far beyond actual practice, would, therefore, seem to recognize her high standing.

[21] Nagyvarad: "Te suppliciter exoramus, ut hoc ferru ignitum, ad iustam examinationem cuiuslibet dubietatis faciendum. . . ."

[22] Hattenhauer, *Recht der Heiligen* notes that the idea that punishment follows false statements is a common motif in legends (75–76); here the king acts as the agent of divine wrath.

[23] Helga Schüppert, "Ebernand von Erfurt," *VF,* vol. 2 (Berlin: De Gruyter, 1978) cols. 290–93 (col. 291); Roth no. 13, 7–8. Because of the absence of extensive documentation of Thüringia's literary culture in the early thirteenth century, there is little certain information about Ebernand. There are two candidates in Erfurt documents of the period, one mentioned in 1192, 1193, considered to be the father of the Hebernand mentioned as *iuvenis* in 1212 and 1217, who also appears in 1227. Critical opinion has varied considerably as to whether he was a monk or a layman. Hans-Jürgen Schröpfer, *Heinrich und Kunegunde: Untersuchungen zur Verslegende des Ebernand von Erfurt und zur Geschichte ihres Stoffes* (Göppingen: Kümmerle, 1969) notes the strong monastic tendencies in this work and suggests that he was a member of the middle class who had a late vocation (25, 35–37).

All text references are to Ebernand von Erfurt, *Heinrich und Kunegunde,* ed. Reinhold Bechstein (Amsterdam: Rodopi, 1968).

[24] Roth 12–13; Folz, *Les Saintes Reines* 86–87. Renate Klauser, *Der Heinrichs- und Kunigundenkult im mittelalterlichen Bistum Bamberg* (Bamberg: Bericht des Historischen Vereins für die Pflege der Geschichte des ehemaligen Fürstbistums Bamberg [BHVB], 1957), 64–65, 113–14.

[25] Roth no. 13, 7. Schüppert col. 291; Baldwin, "Crisis" 345–46; Roth 12; Klauser 113–14; Tanja Michalsky, "Imperatrix gloriosa-humilitatis et castitatis exemplum: Das Bild der heiligen Kunigunde," *Kunigunde: Eine Kaiserin an der Jahrtausendwende,* ed. Ingird Baumgärtner (Kassel: Furore, 1997), 187–222 (187). Annegret Wenz-Haubfleisch, "Der Kult der heiligen Kunigunde an der Wende vom 12. Zum 13. Jahrhundert im Spiegel ihrer Mirakelsammlung," *Kunigunde: Eine Kaiserin an der Jahrtausendwende* 157–86 (162–76) discusses the regional popularity of the saint in terms of the number of pilgrims who went to Bamberg seeking cures.

[26] Schüppert col. 291; she suggests dates as early as 1202 and as late as 1240; Roth gives 1220 (7).

[27] Klausner 73–74; Baldwin, "Crisis" 345–46. The detailed ordeal account comes from "Vitae Sancti Heinrici Additamentum," an addition to the life of the emperor, who was canonized in 1147. It was among the miracles that provided grounds for her canonization and was mentioned by Innocent in his authorization of her canonization.

[28] Baldwin, "Crisis" 345–48; John W. Baldwin, *Aristocratic Life* 206–8; Folz, *Les Saintes Reines* discusses the process (86–89) and notes (86–87) that Kunigunde's canonization began late in the reign of Celestine III, some time after 1196, under the instigation of Bishop Thimo of Bamberg. The process slowed because of Celestine's death and also probably because the case did not at that time seem strong enough in Rome. Enthusiasm for her candidacy remained at a high pitch in Bamberg, however. See also Klausner 60–66; Wenz-Haubfleisch 150–60.

[29] Bartlett suggests hagiographic embroidery (10, 17).

[30] See Baldwin, *Aristocratic Life* 206–7; Klausner 69–120. See Schröpfer 22, 131.

[31] See James Walker Scott, "Keisir unde Keisirin by Ebernand von Erfurt. A New Edition" (Diss. Princeton U., 1971), 12, 14.

[32] Stefan Weinfurter, *Heinrich II. (1002–1024): Herrscher am Ende der Zeiten* (Regensburg: Pustet, 1999) notes that the first mention of this marriage occurred in one of the songs of mourning composed in 1024 shortly after the emperor's death. Other accounts followed quickly, in the chronicle of Montecassino, around 1100 and in Frutolf von Michelsberg's *Weltchronik* written around the end of the eleventh century. They formed the basis of the *Vita Heinrici,* written around 1145, shortly before Heinrich's canonization (93). See also Baldwin, *Aristocratic Life* 145.

[33] Weinfurter 93–94; Roth 12; Folz, *Les Saintes Reines* 82–83; Klauser 74–75.

[34] Weinfurter 94–95, 102, 103. Weinfurter carefully analyzes the frequent references by Heinrich that he and Kunigunde are "one flesh." While the biblical origin of this phrase led to a certain amount of formulaic usage, Weinfurter shows that the frequent variations of the biblical phrase could certainly have indicated real feeling on Heinrich's part.

[35] Weinfurter 97–103; Kunigunde was anointed and crowned in Paderborn on August 10, 1002. See also Folz, *Les Saintes Reines* 83; Ingrid Baumgärtner, "Kunigunde: Politische Handlungsspielräume einer Kaiserin," *Kunigunde-eine Kaiserin an der Jahrtausendwende* 11–46 mentions her blood ties to Charlemagne, which justified her joint rule with Heinrich (14–17, 20–24); Eduard Hlawitschka, "Kaiserin Kunigunde," *Frauen des Mittelalters in Lebensbildern,* ed. Karl R. Schnith (Graz: Sytia, 1997), 72–89; Kurt-Ulrich Jäschke, *Notwendige Gefährtinnen: Königinnen der Salierzeit als Herrscherinnen und Ehefrauen im römisch-deutschen Reich des 11. und beginnenden 12. Jahrhunderts* (Saarbrücken-Scheidt: Dadder, 1991), 37–44; Baldwin, "Crisis" 345.

[36] Weinfurter 102; Baumgärtner 20–24.

[37] Weinfurter 159–60; Already in 1001, monks in Tegernsee had indicated to the newly married duke of Bavaria that they hoped he would produce an heir. See also Klaus Guth, *Die Heiligen Heinrich und Kunigunde: Leben, Legende, Kult und Kunst* (Bamberg: St. Otto-Verlag, 1986), 74–75.

[38] Folz, *Les Saintes Reines* 83. Guth disagrees: he says that only adultery and proven inability to produce children on part of the man were grounds to dissolve a marriage (68). Brundage, in his discussion of divorce from the sixth to the eleventh centuries, does not list sterility as grounds for dissolution of a marriage (143–45).

[39] See Lexer, *MHDHWB,* I, col. 822. See also Gerald Buchda, "Gelöbnis," *HWBDR,* vol. q, cols., 1490–94 (cols. 1491–93); Buchda includes in the category of promises those made in the private sphere, such as engagement and *Morgengabe.*

[40] Weinfurter notes that Kunigunde was anointed and crowned as queen on August 10, 1002, and shared in the administration of the kingdom (97–98). Her position is documented pictorially in a liturgical manuscript from around 1011–13, in which she appears in the same size as Heinrich; like him, receives her crown from Christ; and is mentioned in the prayer for the rulers.

[41] Buchda, "Gelöbnis" col. 1491; B. Distelkamp, "Homagium," *HWBDR,* vol. 2, cols. 225–28 (col. 226) describes the process in which the lord/vassal relationship was formalized as one in which the vassal laid his hands in those of the lord, who grasped them. *Geloben* and another form, *loben,* appear three times in this passage: Heinrich uses the word twice (943, 945) and Kunigunde's promise is described with it (952).

[42] Baldwin, "Crisis" says that Kunigunde had become an "anti-Queen Iseut," indicating that the contrast between the Tristan legend and this hagiographic account was unmistakable (347). Since Ebernand's account was most probably written after the Fourth Lateran Council, and, consequently, well after Gottfried's *Tristan,* it certainly could indirectly refer to Isolde.

[43] The frequent references to Kunigunde's joint role in the administration of the empire in this vernacular life find parallels in the sculpture in the Bamberg cathedral, which was done around the time in which Ebernand wrote his account. Michalsky discusses the iconographic significance of Kunigunde as empress in the *Gnadenpforte* (c.1220–5) and the *Adampforte* (before 1237) of the Bamberg cathedral (194–99). In the latter complex Heinrich and Kunigunde, as the imperial Christian couple, stand in a typological relationship to Adam and Eve, for whose sin they try to atone

through their virginal marriage. See Hans Christian Feldmann, *Bamberg und Reims: Die Skulpturen, 1220–50* (Ammersbek bei Hamburg: Verlag an der Lottbek, 1992), 59–62 and Erna Wagner, "Die Gnadepforte am Dom zu Bamberg" (Diss. U of Würzburg, 1965), 6, 24–25, 56.

[44] Baldwin, "Crisis" 347.

[45] "Additamentum" 819. "Conscientia mea munda est, et conscius meus in excelso, quia plane est testis mihi, quia facinus hoc pessimum, quo obiicitur mihi, numquam perpetravi. Obsecro te, domine mi rex, ut viriliter agere et patientiam in me digneris habere. Honor quidem totius imperii per me videtur imminutus, sed volente Deo quantocius per me reformabitur; quod qualiter fieri possit, si sit cum beneplacito vestro, breviter insinuo. . . . Maiestas, . . . vestra, domine, principes universos tam episcopos quam laicos ad curtem regiam convenire iubeat, et presentibus omnibus causa de qua agitur ordine iudicario ventiletur, et quidquid ipsi suggesserint, salvo honore vestro fieri poterit. Spero autem de divina misericordia, quo eripiat nos de luto fecis huius et miseria" [My conscience is clear, and my confidant is in heaven, since he clearly bears witness to the fact that I have never committed this truly wicked deed of which I am accused. I beg you, my lord and king, to play the man and deign to be patient with me. The honor of your whole empire indeed seems to have been undermined by me, but, God willing, it will the more speedily be made good by me; how this can happen I shall shortly explain, if this can be done with your good will. . . . My Lord, Your Majesty should order all the leading men, bishops as well as laity, to gather at his palace, and in the presence of all should air the case now being discussed before a judicial assembly; whatever they suggest to you may be carried out without infringing your honor. I hope however for divine pity to rescue us from this mire and that you too may pity this poor creature].

[46] "Additamentum" 819.

[47] "Additamentum" 819–20. "O dilecti mei principes gloriosi, estimo plane, nequaquam nobilitatem vestram latere, quod per dies aliquot sustinui obprobrium, et operuit confusio faciem meam, propter quod potissimum vos convenire volui, quatenus ab imminentibus incommodis vestre prudentie consilio valeam absolvi. Nunc itaque a vestra dilectione requiro, cuinam sententie matrona debeat subiacere, que contempto coninge legitimo alium ei superducere presumpserit. Obsecro ergo et obsecrando precipio, ut leges et decreta maiorum recolentes, prout iustitia dictaverit, sententiam proferatis" [O my beloved and glorious leaders, I am of the honest opinion that it should on no account be concealed from your nobility that for some days I have been suffering a dishonor, and shame has covered my face. On account of this above all else I wanted you to meet, so that I might be freed from the embarrassment that threatens me by your sensible advice. And so now I request that you tell me, out of your affection for me, what sentence should be applied to a married woman, who despises her legal husband and presumes to take an additional mate. Therefore I beg you, and by begging I order you, to express your opinions in accordance with the dictates of justice, having consideration for the laws and decrees of our ancestors].

[48] "Additamentum" 819.

[49] In the Latin version Kunigunde plays more on the princes' obvious sympathy than she does on her role as empress; the narrator in the Latin version notes that she

sagaciously became aware through their tears at the upcoming ordeal and their various private conversations that they were reluctant to pass judgment on her ("Additamentum" 820). Her speech before the princes concludes with an elaborate compliment to them: "Sed enim serenitati vestre immensas refero gratias, quia mihi parcendo gravem in me ferre sententiam noluit vestra mansuetudo" [And yet I am immeasurably grateful to your fairness, in that by showing me mercy your gentleness was unwilling to pass a heavy sentence on me] ("Additamentum" 820). Ebernand's Kunigunde says only, "'got muoze û lônen, daz ir mîn woldet schônen'" ["God should reward you, since you wanted to spare me"] (1481–82).

[50] "Additamentum" 820: "O principes omni honore digni et mihi delecti, iam duddum vobis complacuit universis, et dominum vel coniugem meum dilectum imperatoria dignitate sublimastis et me participem regni eius esse voluistis, et tam Dei gratia quam vestra constitutione celeris hominibus prestantiores esse videbamur. Quia igitur inter feminas prestantior esse videor, sed iam nunc de pessimo crimine incusor" [O leaders, worthy of all honor and beloved by me, I have for long found favor with you, and you have exalted my lord, or my beloved husband, to the rank of emperor, and you wished me to share in his rule, and we seemed to excel other people as much by God's grace as by your decision. Because therefore I seem to be preeminent among women, but am now arraigned on a terrible charge].

[51] Elliott sees Kunigunde's trial as the result of "masculine efforts to monopolize chastity" and as an expression of enmity towards chaste, spiritual women (129). She notes that Henry presided over the proceedings and implicitly lays the blame for the completion of the ordeal at his feet. In both the "Additamentum" and in Ebernand's text, however, Henry, confronted by the spectacle of the glowing plowshares, asks for the ordeal proceedings to be suspended. It is the queen, not Henry, who insists on the completion of the ordeal to clear her name.

[52] The rigor of the ordeal to which Kunigunde voluntarily subjects herself shows her innate understanding of the importance of gesture in medieval political life. See Gerd Althoff, "Demonstration und Inszenierung: Spielregeln der Kommunikation in mittelalterlicher Offentlichkeit," *Spielregeln der Politik im Mittelalter* 229–57, 230–31, 233.

[53] Hattenhauer, "Der gefälschte Eid," 680–84.

[54] The mention of the degree to which the plowshares were heated is also significant, since recent studies of the ordeal have shown that a certain amount of discretion was possible. (See note no. 46 in the Introduction.) If the community were convinced of the innocence of a candidate for the ordeal, they might well choose not to heat the iron as hot as they would have for a candidate presumed to be guilty. Here Ebernand says that they "made them so hot that there was no human being who would not lose his courage" (1490–92). The degree of heat here does not imply the lady's guilt but, rather, serves to emphasize her miraculous deliverance, as well as her fortitude.

[55] Heinrich's action is, of course, a mark of his deep shame, as well as of his respect for his wife's saintliness and an acknowledgment of her position in the empire. See Althoff, "Hulde" 204–5.

[56] Klauser 107; Schröpfer 141; Folz, *Les Saintes Reines* 90–91, 93; Guth 79.

[57] The *Kaiserchronik* was probably written shortly after the first version of the Vita *Heinrici* (c. 1145) was compiled. It was far and away the most influential German text of the twelfth century, both in literary works and in chronicles. See Nellmann cols. 949, 961–62; Klauser notes that there are obvious parallels but does not examine them (75). The first version of the *Vita Sancti Heinrici* does contain a brief description of the ordeal of the plowshares, occasioned by the Devil's interference (Klauser 75). The "Additamentum," which contains a much fuller account of the ordeal of the glowing plowshares, was written shortly after Kunigunde's canonization to satisfy the increased interest in her life. The content seems to follow oral Bamberg tradition (Baldwin, "Crisis" 346; Klauser 109).

[58] The same technical term *tagedinc,* a day of legal proceedings, is used in both accounts: *Kaiserchronik* 15480 and *Heinrich und Kunigunde* 1510.

[59] See Goodich 149.

Coda: Der Stricker's "Das heisse Eisen" and Conclusion

THE PRECEDING COMMENTARIES on trial by fire in secular literature and legend were all written before or shortly after the Fourth Lateran Council in 1215: in spite of the obvious difference in attitudes toward the ordeal evidenced in *Tristan,* on the one hand, and the legends, on the other, all of these works contain explicit legal and liturgical references to the ordeal and the procedures connected with it, as they deal with the cases of queens caught in a web of accusations of sexual misconduct that had grave implications for the monarchies in question.

The final literary ordeal by fire in this study, Der Stricker's story of the hot iron, written some thirty to forty years after Gottfried's *Tristan,* well after the Lateran Council, differs from *Tristan* and the legends in almost every way, beginning with genre. "Das heisse Eisen" belongs to the tradition of the "märe," short fictitious narratives with comic elements written between approximately 1250 and 1500. Stricker, the first important writer in the genre, is credited with raising the literary level of this type of narrative. The battle of the sexes formed the subject matter of a great many of these works, as it does here, while parody, especially of religious ceremony, was a characteristic element.[1] Stricker's account of the ordeal is a burlesque; it contains neither the theological inferences nor the fieriness of Gottfried's attack nor the vindication of a saintly queen. Stricker's protagonists come from the lower orders, where alleged misconduct has implications only for their own marriage.

Here the ordeal is not a part of a trial but simply an attempt to strengthen a private oath; the ordeal scenario gives Stricker an opportunity to examine some of his favorite themes, stupidity and marital relations.[2] Entertaining literature that mocked the peasantry found a ready audience among the nobility and, probably, the upper bourgeoisie. The generally negative attitude toward the lower orders that characterizes the *märe* provides the context for the references made during the course of the ordeal.[3] Stricker's extensive theological learning appears in the "Hot Iron" in allusions that would have been readily understandable to a mid-thirteenth-century audience but are not so accessible to us.[4]

The events in the story are brief and fast-moving. A woman, perhaps in a capricious mood, wants her husband to prove his fidelity by carrying the hot iron. Specific references to legal terminology are scanty and generally fall together with the demands of the plot: that is, laying the iron in the fire.[5] There is no lengthy preparation. No one is present except the man and wife. The man consents but takes the precaution of slipping a piece of wood into his palm. Of course, he is not burned, and he asks his wife to prove *her* love now. Seized with terror, she gradually confesses to a series of lovers, carries the iron, and is badly burned.

Like Isolde, the woman believes in the ordeal. If Isolde had not respected its power, she would not have thought that she had a chance to survive only if she framed her oath to fit the facts. The errant wife certainly believes in it, or else she would not try to avoid swearing a false oath. Of the three of our artful deceivers, the man's probable attitude toward it is the most problematical.[6] He may provide himself with the wood because he believes he will be burned in any case, guilty or not. It seems more likely that he is just as guilty as she, since he calls on God to show his fidelity, though he has providentially supplied an aid to that end, should God be otherwise occupied or inclined. Since he is sure of the efficacy of his ruse, he does not need to worry about his oath. When the husband turns the tables and demands the same from his wife, he is much more specific than Mark about the oath and demands that it be in the same words as his.

Little remains of the traditional ordeal ceremony in this account; the husband puts the iron in the fire with all the ceremony attendant on a backyard barbecue. There is no *adjuratio*, since no priest is present, but the woman's series of confessions and self-justification are reminiscent of the confession of guilt that could occur after the priest gave the *adjuratio*. She offers several excuses and arguments that allude to certain medieval beliefs and practices. After getting her husband's permission to allow for one lover in her oath, she says that women are weaker than men in sexual matters and, consequently, cannot resist temptations as steadfastly as men can; she blames God for this weakness.[7] Stricker seems to be deliberately twisting around a stereotype in canonical literature so that God has to bear the responsibility for women's lustful natures — a conceit that his hearers no doubt found amusing, coming as it does in a garbled way from an uneducated woman. The wife's third request, that she be permitted to pay her husband a pound for each of the three men she has had, could well be a tacit offer for him to function as a sort of pimp. A man who knew about his wife's adultery and did nothing about it was in the same position legally as a procurer, since it was assumed that that was why he tolerated such behavior.[8]

After the third request the husband tells her that she must undergo the ordeal or he will kill her. As noted in the chapter on *Tristan*, spousal murder because of adultery was extremely rare in the High Middle Ages; Stricker is probably mocking the peasants and making fun of their brutality. The application of a wax bandage was typical of postordeal procedure, but our woman does not need it: her hand is obviously severely burned.[9]

In all four accounts of trial by fire the major interest lies not in the ordeal itself but elsewhere. For that reason these documents are faulty historical accounts, since each leaves out certain details to achieve other ends. In the legends only those sections of ordeal procedure that afford an opportunity to emphasize the saintliness of the women — or, in the case of Kunigunde, to reveal her and Heinrich's vow of chastity in marriage — receive emphasis. In Stricker's tale the ordeal, which was certainly in some degree of disrepute as a contemporary practice even in secular German society, provides the author with a situation against which he can lampoon the garbled understanding of these matters among the peasants; extensive references to ordeal procedure would have undercut his main point. Gottfried's account contains the most specific references to the ordeal procedure itself and to a criticism of it, but, even here, the main focus is on Isolde.

Yet, in spite of the fact that our authors' eyes were fastened on goals other than those of describing ordeal procedure itself, we can, in these four accounts of trial by fire, see important differences in the way ordeals were treated in widely different types of literature and thereby draw tentative conclusions. The ordeal scenes in the *Kaiserchronik* and in *Heinrich und Kunegunde* came from older legendary material whose truthfulness could not be questioned; consequently, the attitude of belief in the ordeal's efficacy remains fixed in a hagiographic amber. Both ordeals involve historical figures; the centuries in which these women lived and those in which the legends were written were largely well disposed toward the ordeal and did not see it as an irrational procedure, a situation that the works reflect.[10] Although the ordeal's presentation does not change, there were certainly differences in the way in which Kunigunde was portrayed, particularly in comparison to Richardis and to the Latin account of her ordeal. Ebernand's Kunegunde differs sharply from Queen Isolde and may be presented in such a way as to make these differences even clearer. The situation is markedly different in the two secular works, written about contemporary people who were certainly not candidates for sainthood: these works could reflect changes in social attitudes.

In both ordeals in *Tristan*, the trial by battle and the ordeal of the hot iron, Gottfried has shown a detailed understanding of legal matters that bespeaks a thorough grounding in the law. His audience would have expected a queen to be tried with some ceremony; Gottfried does not disappoint them. His account is replete with legal terminology and concepts, including a council, types of evidence, and preparations for a public ordeal. We can also assume that Gottfried expected to find, at the very least, tolerance for his savagely sarcastic attack on the ordeal. Had his description of its inner corruption been seen as an attack on the Church, *Tristan* would not have enjoyed the success that it did. It would, perhaps, be fair to conclude that Gottfried expected that his opinions on the ordeal would be at least understood and, in all probability, approved by many, coming, as they did, so close to the official action of the Lateran Council.

By the time of the appearance of Stricker's short verse tale, the controversies surrounding the ordeal had receded, as had the use of all ordeals except trial by battle. Certainly the genre conditioned its presentation, but one must ask if the historical context did not influence it, as well. "Das heisse Eisen" contains the scantiest references of all the works considered to liturgical and legal procedures connected with the ordeal; the parody of the procedure suggests the distance that the intended audience felt from it.[11] Stricker ascribes no supernatural attributes to the ordeal; it is a means for him to lampoon a bawdy, foolish woman, as well as to amuse his hearers by letting the woman twist certain commonly held concepts of canon law in her vain attempt to escape both the heat of her husband's wrath and that of the hot iron.

Since the legends about Kunigunde and Richardis focused on sanctity and sexual purity, the women went to convents; on a political level, however, the ordeal functioned to legitimize their positions as queens, preserving imperial reputations. While the genre of the legend precludes any change in the belief in the ordeal's efficacy, it is possible that, as Baldwin has indicated for the Latin material's relation to the Old French versions of *Tristan*, Ebernand's portrayal of Kunegunde may be an indirect attack, influenced by Gottfried's work, on the manipulation of the ordeal by Isolde. With the secular accounts, the portrayal of the unilateral ordeal in Gottfried and Stricker does seem to reflect attitudes current in the periods in which each work appeared, a nuanced understanding that allows for condemnation or ridicule of the ordeal by fire.

While the ordeal by fire continued to appear as an indication of the queen's saintliness in various versions of the Kunigunde legend during the later Middle Ages, the use of the ordeal as a stock comic element survives in Hans Sachs's sixteenth-century carnival play about the hot iron. Trial by battle, however, shows a different profile. From the supposedly historical trials by battle in *Karl der Grosse* and the *Karlmeinet* to the fictional one in *Tristan*, this study has shown that this ordeal was treated with great seriousness and with definite differences during the period in question, circa 1210 to 1350, in these literary documents, a state of affairs that reflects a contemporary procedure familiar to the writer's audience. In all cases the writers show extensive familiarity with legal procedures, many of which are common to all three accounts, such as the separation of the combatant from the onlookers. In the case of Gottfried and Stricker, both authors give a considerable amount of space to the verbal sparring that preceded the battle, using precise and sophisticated legal arguments. The informed and detailed descriptions of the courtroom scenes and the battles surely rested on an assumption of understanding and interest among the audience.

While these descriptions show a high degree of legal sophistication on the part of the writers and their readers/listeners, they served other functions, as well. In the case of Stricker and the *Karlmeinet* compiler a major function, outside of the dramatic nature of the narrative, was to provide information about Karl as a ruler and as a judge. In both cases these portraits of Karl were meant to serve in an exemplary way to the Germans of the High and late Middle Ages who looked to the great emperor as a sort of political lodestone. The Genelun/Wellis treason trial gave each writer a wonderful opportunity to comment on current issues by placing them in Karl's exemplary reign and resolving them through the legendary monarch. In Stricker's work the differing legal approaches to dispute settlement appear as means of characterization, negative for the feud and positive for the recourse to the courts and the imposition of corporal punishment. In the case of *Karlmeinet* Karl, as the representative of God's justice on earth, presides over a trial and sentencing that tie together late medieval legal practices, such as the increasing use of torture and extreme physical punishments, and currents in the larger society, such as the extensive emphasis on the Passion of Christ and the example of the redeemed thief who died a good death. In this section the *Karlmeinet* compiler seems to try to achieve verbally what artists of the period, in their portrayals of the Passion, did visually and to link himself, to some degree, to the spirit of the Passion narratives. Both writers give readers today a kind of cultural photograph, not only of the symbolic value of Karl in the societies in which these works appeared, but also of contemporary issues and problems for which invocation of the great emperor's name had some relevance.

Notes

[1] See Gerhard Köpf, *Märendichtung* (Stuttgart: Metzler, 1978), 34–47, 52; Hanns Fischer, *Studien zur deutschen Märendichtung* (Tübingen: Niemeyer, 1968), 62–64; Ingrid Strasser, "Und sungen ein liet ze prîse in einer höhen wîse: Zur Frage der höfischen Elemente in den Ehestandmaeren des Stricker." *ABÄG* 15 (1980): 77–107 suggests that this *maere* reaches its comic effects through parody (107).

[2] Otmar Werner, "Entwicklungstendenzen in der mittelhochdeutschen Verserzählung," *ZfdPH* 85 (1966): 369–406 (374); Helmut de Boor and Richard Newald, *Geschichte der deutschen Literatur von den Anfängen bis zur Gegenwart*, vol. 3 (Munich: Beck, 1967), 234–35; Margetts 322.

[3] Fischer 220–45; Köpf 100–101. Margetts believes that a large part of Stricker's audience was always aristocratic but suggests that during the later part of Stricker's career, the period of the *Märe,* it could have included members of the upper bourgeoisie (334–39).

[4] Fischer 146–47. See also Daniel Rocher, "Inwiefern sind Strickers Maeren echte 'contes a rire?'" *Wolfram Studien* 8 (1982):132–43 (137); also see Stephen L.

Wailes, *Studien zur Kleindichtung des Strickers* (Berlin: E. Schmidt, 1981), which deals with Stricker's learning. Wailes does not believe that he was a cleric (249–51).

[5] One specific reference with its background in ordeal procedure was the placing of the hot iron at the man's side. Strasser lists others, such as the degree of heat in the iron, placing it on two stones, and binding the hand in a wax bandage (86–88).

[6] Hattenhauer, in commenting on this story by Stricker, says that this kind of deception belongs to the late Middle Ages, which could no longer respect the magical character of the ordeal ("Der gefälschte Eid" 675).

[7] Brundage 350.

[8] Brundage 467.

[9] Nottarp 260.

[10] See Bartlett 16–17 for information on Richardis and Kunigunde; Davies and Fouracre 221.

[11] See Köpf 103 for remarks about distancing and parody.

Appendix I
Der Stricker, *Karl der Grosse:* Plot Summary

GENELUN'S BETRAYAL OF ROLAND and the ensuing trial for treason has its roots in the council of peers that Karl holds during the campaign against the Muslims in Spain. Marsilie has sent a delegation to the camp of the Franks, offering to convert to Christianity. Karl asks the barons to agree on a common policy. Genelun wants to accept the offer and go home, but other powerful men reject this approach. Both bishops, Turpin and Johann, are against it; Johann suggests sending a messenger to ascertain what Marsilie's real plans are. Roland immediately volunteers to go, but Karl refuses the offer, saying that he cannot do without Roland. Olivier and Bishop Turpin offer their services but are also turned down. Since he himself cannot go, Roland suggests his stepfather, Genelun. He praises the latter's reputation, good judgment, and ability to represent the empire.

Roland has sealed his fate with this speech. Genelun turns white and accuses Roland of trying to get him killed so that he can take Genelun's wealth and deprive Genelun's son Baldwin of his rightful inheritance. Genelun accuses Roland of a lack of fidelity to his half brother and says that Roland will suffer if he returns alive from the mission to the Muslims.

Karl tries to placate Genelun by convincing him that it is an honor to go on such a mission, but Genelun curses Roland publicly. Karl tells him that Genelun is going on the emperor's orders, not on Roland's, and offers Genelun his glove, which Genelun drops. As Genelun realizes that he must go on this mission, he throws himself at Karl's feet and asks Karl, as a brother-in-law, to help him. He is firmly convinced that Roland will plunge his mother and half brother into poverty should he die on this trip. He says that Roland is his enemy, since he arranged Genelun's participation in this trip.

Roland promises publicly not to disinherit his relative. Karl urges Genelun to behave like a man and sets out the terms of the message to Marsilie. The Muslims swear an oath that no harm will come to Genelun. In subsequent conversations with Blanschandiez and Marsilie, Genelun makes the secret agreement through which Roland is betrayed (1705–2883).

When Karl hears Roland blow his horn, he knows immediately that something has gone wrong; but Genelun tells him that Roland is perhaps hunting rabbits. Karl, however, knows that Genelun is responsible and immediately accuses him of having Roland killed. Naymis wants to kill

Genelun on the spot, but Karl wants Genelun to die a death that will disgrace his family for generations.

Genelun is bound, stripped of clothing appropriate to his station, beaten, and put under guard. Karl then goes with the princes to see if they can rescue Roland or any of the others (7110–214).

In a long passage Karl laments Roland's death, with particular emphasis on Roland's value to the maintenance of authority and peace in the empire. Various miracles attest to the virtue of the fallen Franks. Alda, Roland's fiancée, dies on hearing the news of his death (10550–11285).

During the confusion surrounding the death and burial of Alite, Genelun takes the opportunity to escape. He makes his way to the Carolingian lands, where his relatives can help him. On the way he meets twelve merchants, to whom he confesses killing a noble knight who had no reason to declare himself Genelun's enemy. He asks them to tell his pursuers that he is out of their reach.

Soon thereafter, Margrave Otto comes upon the same group of merchants and tells them that he is after a traitor; they assure Otto that he is already six miles away and out of reach. Otto and his men go back to the emperor's camp to give Karl the bad news. Furious, Karl threatens Otto with the loss of privilege, land, and sword if he does not recapture Genelun. In Karl's eyes Otto is a traitor; he has taken away the possibility of Karl's avenging Roland's death.

Although Otto does not believe that he deserves such treatment at Karl's hands, he stops his relatives from declaring a feud against the empire; such an action would be an admission of guilt. Instead, he begs God, who knows that he is innocent of the charges against him, to aid him in the recapture of Genelun. After much hard riding, Otto and his party meet a peasant who directs them to an armed knight sleeping under a tree. After a fierce fight, Otto takes Genelun prisoner.

On their return to court Otto, hoping to regain the emperor's favor, hastens to Karl with the prisoner. Karl restores Otto to his former position, admitting that he has wronged him and telling him there is no retainer more faithful than he. Genelun is to remain in Otto's custody and not stand trial until the retinue arrives at Aachen. Karl wants him convicted in front of all of his relatives.

In Aachen, Karl assembles his court and orders that Genelun be brought before him. Genelun's rich and powerful relatives are there in force and plead that his life be spared. Admitting that Genelun has wronged both the empire and Karl, they promise reparations and guarantee that Genelun will pay them and that they themselves will serve the emperor so well that their service cannot be matched. If Genelun is killed, Karl will lose all of this assistance. Karl replies that all of Arabia's gold would not induce him to spare Genelun's life. Genelun has injured not only him but Christianity.

Speaking in his own defense, Genelun says he did arrange for the deaths of the twelve peers but did not commit murder, since he had declared openly before the council of peers of the realm that he was in a state of feud with Roland. He points out that he also accused Roland openly of injuries perpetrated against him. The peers betrayed him and sent him on a mission that could have ended in his death. For such actions Genelun had to take revenge.

Karl tells the court that now that Genelun has publicly acknowledged that he was responsible for the deaths of the twelve peers, the question for them to decide is what Genelun owes Karl and the empire. Silence reigns; each man fears for his own life if he suggests that Genelun be killed. Stunned, Karl promises rich rewards to any who help him carry out a just sentence. If, however, his nobles do not support him, he will abdicate. Either Genelun receives his just reward, or Karl's reputation is gone.

Genelun's camp is dismayed at this raising of the stakes, since they had hoped, however it might be brought about, to save their relative's life. Now they offer a champion, Pinabel, to defend Genelun's honor in a judicial duel against anyone who might accuse him of murder. Pinabel is an exceedingly strong knight whom others are afraid to challenge. The peers cringe and are silent, except for Dietrich. He grieves for Roland and wants to avenge his relative's death. He accuses Pinabel of dishonesty and says that with God's help he will make Pinabel pay for his faithless defense of his kinsman. While Pinabel relies on his own strength, he, Dietrich, will follow David's example, trusting in God to overcome superior force. God always lets injustice lose, thereby honoring justice. I challenge you to fight before the empire, he tells Pinabel. I certainly am noble enough that you need not be ashamed to do battle with me. God himself must see the battle and do justice to both of us.

Hostages are taken on both sides. If Pinabel loses, all of those who have offered to be hostages for Genelun will also be killed, as they are thereby involved in Genelun's crime. Thirty of his supporters promise freely that they are ready to die if Pinabel loses. Because of Pinabel's superior strength, they are quite confident that they are in no danger.

Before the battle begins, Karl calls for prayers in all the monasteries. A large circle is drawn at the battle scene. As the two combatants prepare for the first blows, the onlookers point out how much smaller Dietrich is and how certain his defeat must be unless God helps him. Karl, however, is firm in his belief that God will provide the victory.

Imprecations against any of Genelun's relatives starting other battles, as well as an order that no one is to step inside the circle on penalty of his life, are made by the officials. The fight is waged with great ferocity. Dietrich carries Roland's sword, Durndart, which is a great comfort to him and saves his life. He wounds Pinabel in the head, causing blood to run into his eyes. Pinabel offers to give Dietrich all of his and Genelun's fiefs and to be subject to him if Dietrich will let Genelun live. Dietrich refuses, telling Pinabel that if he gives up his sword, Dietrich will intercede with Karl for him. Pinabel refuses, and Dietrich tells him that the devil is taking him and his relatives to hell that very day. With Durndart's help, Dietrich wounds Pinabel in the head again, this time so severely that Pinabel gives up. Dietrich beheads him. Genelun and his supporters prepare to die.

Once again the emperor sits in judgment and asks what Genelun owes the empire. Now all speak, begging Karl to protect widows and orphans whose fathers were betrayed by Genelun. Karl should judge the worst man who ever called himself a Christian, as well as those who were hostages for him. Karl asks them what kind of death Genelun owes him.

The peers take counsel among themselves. Since the sin was such a grievous one, they suggest a form of execution for Genelun that is no longer used: he should be torn apart by four horses. They recommend simple beheading for the hostages, against whom they do not feel so much rage. Genelun and Judas were the worst servants that the devil ever obtained. Genelun's relatives will be marked by his crime for the rest of their days.

Appendix II
Karlmeinet: Plot Summary

DURING THE SCENE IN WHICH the mission to Marsilie is discussed, the main lines of events resemble those in Stricker's version. Roland nominates his stepfather — here named Wellis, instead of Genelun — using superlatives to praise his reputation and wisdom. Wellis accuses Roland of sending him to his death among the heathens so that Roland can inherit his wealth and accuses Roland of a lack of fidelity toward his half brother. Wellis tells Roland that he will regret this action if Wellis survives this mission. Karl tells Wellis to calm himself and promises him rich rewards if the mission succeeds. Wellis again issues a general threat against Roland and the twelve peers.

Karl gives Wellis his glove and staff to show that Wellis travels under his protection; Wellis drops the glove. Wellis's angry and threatening speech moves Roland to offer him public assurances that he has no designs on Wellis's wealth and no desire to disadvantage his half brother. Moreover, Karl himself has treated Roland well; Roland has no desire to become a traitor in Karl's eyes by behaving so dishonorably to his mother and Baldwin. Calling Wellis his beloved brother-in-law, Karl prays that the same angel that guided Tobias to protect Wellis on his journey (A432–A443, 4).

Sections A444b, 60–A448b, 68, on Wellis's negotiations with the Muslims, closely follow Konrad's and Stricker's versions.

When the Franks hear Roland's mighty blast on the horn, Karl fears for Roland's safety. Count Names accuses Wellis of having betrayed Roland. Wellis is bound and treated in a manner designed to shame him (A458a, 20–A459, 5).

In the midst of the ensuing battles with the Muslims, Karl visits Runzevalen; here the *Karlmeinet* gives Karl's first extended reaction to Roland's death. Karl laments Roland's loss in terms of his and the empire's needs and Roland's contribution to governing. He mentions the unruly Bavarians and Franks; he cannot now reward Roland for the Saxon and Swabian territories Roland won for him. The *Karlmeinet* version has at this point a lengthy description of Karl's transports of grief and a detailed account of the preparation for burial of the fallen Franks (466b, 44–468, 3).

Unlike Stricker, the *Karlmeinet* leaves out details about the escape of the accused from those responsible for him; the account picks up Wellis on the run (A493, 15 ff.). Otto spots him next to a woods and rides after him, charging him with murder and saying that Wellis is the cause of Otto's troubles with Karl. Otto says that he hopes to regain the emperor's favor through Wellis's capture. Wellis threatening to pay Otto back for his accusations of murder; since Otto has come alone, Wellis hopes to kill him and make his escape. A fierce battle ensues; Otto is getting the worst of it but rallies and takes the fatigued Wellis prisoner, forcing him to give up his sword. Wellis is stripped of his armor, bound, and placed on a horse.

Arriving in Aachen, Otto brings Wellis to Karl, who receives Otto in a friendly manner. The sight of Wellis, however, provokes another outburst on Karl's part; he sends Wellis away to be tortured. Karl restores Otto to his earlier high standing; he apologizes for his treatment of him and offers reparations for the damage he has caused. The *Karlmeinet* Otto responds with a speech that is a model of forbearance and forgiveness; this Otto understands that Karl's anger was necessary. Had Wellis evaded capture, Otto would have died of grief; but God's will and the gravity of Wellis's sin led to his apprehension. For Otto, Karl's goodwill means more than possessions. In a scene that does not exist in Stricker's version, Karl gives a commission to another group of nobles to guard Wellis, telling them that they will suffer the fate reserved for Wellis if they lose him (A493, 12–A496b, 34).

The scene in which Roland's fiancée, Alda, dies on hearing of his death appears after Wellis's recapture by Otto instead of being the occasion for the murderer's escape, as it was in Stricker. Greatly enlarged, this scene includes several repetitions of the accusations against Wellis, threats of corporal punishment, and fresh outpourings of grief as Karl informs Roland and Oliver's relatives of the events leading to their deaths. As Alda journeys to meet the emperor, she has a series of singular dreams about Roland and her brother Oliver and their deaths. Three birds appear to her: a white falcon alights on her head and flies her to a mountain, where he leaves her; an eagle bites and claws her, an attack so severe that Karl comes to her rescue; and a sparrow hawk escapes from her mouth and comes to rest between Roland and Oliver. Bears and lions attack Roland and Oliver in the forest; Roland defends himself with Durndart against one of the lions. In yet another dream Wellis betrays Oliver and Roland, who disappear into the earth. Near the end of the series of dreams Alda is sitting in an undergarment in a dark forest; an elderly man with a gray beard seizes her and carries her to a church on a mountain where Roland and Oliver lie, apparently in death; Wellis is responsible. Karl uses dogs to hunt a stag in the forest. When she sees Roland and Oliver before her, she calls to them, but they do not seem to know who she is and disappear into the earth. Later she sees them in a church, where they once again do not recognize her. Terrified by the dreams, she asks Magnus, the wise man in her retinue, what they mean. He checks the configuration of the stars and realizes that Roland and Olivier are, indeed, dead and that Wellis has betrayed them. When she hears the news that confirms that at which the series of dreams had already hinted, she goes to the cathedral to view the bodies of Oliver and Roland and falls into a faint, in which she hears Oliver tell her that she will soon join him and Roland. Confessing her sins to a bishop, she gazes at the bodies of her brother and intended husband, says goodbye to her family, and dies.

After the burial of Roland, Oliver, and Alda, Karl concentrates on the trial of Wellis. A detailed description is given of Wellis's diminished legal position. The loss of legal rights and property, confirmed by a council of princes, foreshadows Wellis's future. Karl sees Wellis's treason as another aspect of his own failing of his people because of the heavy losses it caused among the Franks in Spain. Asking for the Franks' forgiveness, Karl says that Wellis must die. He visits the shrine of St. Dyonisius immediately before the trial, asking for the saint's help in righting the wrongs perpetrated by Wellis.

As the trial begins, one of the legal rights the princes had taken away from Wellis in the pretrial session — the right to defend himself — becomes a point of dissension. Salomon of Brittany and Otyneir point out that Karl will behave in a manner commensurate with his station, preserving his reputation and authority, if he lets a prince defend himself in court. Though Wellis's rank is mentioned, and his family makes a brief request that he not be killed, there is no real power struggle between Karl and Wellis's relatives. Karl seems firmly in control at all times.

When Wellis begins his defense, one of Karl's nobles, King Gundeluff, accuses him of betraying the Franks for money; Gundeluff has received this information from a Muslim prisoner he captured. According to this informant, Wellis swore an oath to the Muslim king to betray the Franks for silver and gold. To prove the truth of his accusation, Gundeluff challenges Wellis to a judicial duel. Because Gundeluff outranks Wellis, Wellis cannot refuse the challenge. Wellis gives Gundeluff his glove, hostages are offered, and preparations are made for the combat.

Wellis knows that his options are limited. Fighting is out of the question, because Gundeluff's charge is correct; escape is the only possibility, however slim. He pretends to be practicing maneuvers on his horse; but when he gets to the edge of the practice space, he deserts both his relatives and his hostages.

Another heated chase results in another fierce fight and another defeat for Wellis, who is bound and brought to Karl. Karl presents Wellis to the assembly of princes and demands a trial by battle. While the judgment finders are discussing the charges, Pinabel, whose mother is Wellis's sister, arrives with another powerful kinsman, Herffen van Leun, and a small army to defend his relative.

This contingent stops the judicial proceedings as the princes ascertain who Pinabel is; his standing as a prince, plus the 500 armed men, ensure that he will be heard. The narrator concentrates on Pinabel's positive qualities of bravery, generosity, and honor. This Pinabel functions somewhat differently than Stricker's. Through his flight from a judicial duel, Wellis has lost the right to defend himself in court; Pinabel defends him with two legal arguments not present in the earlier versions under consideration in this study: a character defense and an attack on the eligibility of the judgment finders. Wellis has never attempted treason, and there is, according to Pinabel, no evidence for such a charge; moreover, Wellis's rank and reputation excel those of the other members of Karl's court. Pinabel demands to have a part in the judicial proceedings and is prepared to do battle with his small army if the request is not granted.

As in the earlier works, the nobles quail and flinch in the face of force and entreat Karl to acquit Wellis, which he angrily refuses to do. Karl says that he would prefer to fight Wellis himself rather than free him. Names and Oiger offer to challenge Pinabel because of Wellis's treason; Oiger gives an account of Wellis's crimes that is replete with legal terminology. While he is grateful for their support, Karl refuses to let them fight Pinabel, in part because of their age.

An unknighted lad, Dederich Lamp, offers to represent Karl against Pinabel. Unlike his counterparts in the earlier works, he is not related to Roland but is the son of a nobleman, probably a minor one. Dederich does have another connection to Roland that impels him to make this gesture: when Dederich's father died, the young man was in service to Roland, who had planned to knight him at Whitsun — plans that Wellis ruined with his treachery.

Believing that God has sent him this young man, Karl accepts his offer. Pinabel, however, calls him a young fool and promises to give him no quarter when he will surely seek it during the battle. The *Karlmeinet* author now picks up a strain common to the earlier *Karlsepik*, in which Pinabel, through his arrogance in trusting not in God but in his own strength, represents evil. In spite of his youth, Dederich's bearing and speech parallel those of the older peers.

The combatants present gloves for surety and offer hostages, a process to which this author devotes a great deal of consideration. Pinabel sends Wellis, two prominent peers, and others, as Karl wished. Karl swears by his crown that they will suffer the fate of traitors if Pinabel loses.

The site at which the judicial duel takes place is the occasion for a certain amount of dispute. Pinabel wants the battle to occur immediately; but Karl and the nobles move the site to Aachen, so that the German princes, whose loyalty to Karl is unquestioned, can be present. Should general combat break out, Names and Oiger arrange for defensive efforts.

When the battle is ready to occur, Karl himself arms Dederich. In an addition not present in the earlier works, this judicial duel involves the relics of St. Patrick in an oath-swearing scene. God prevents Pinabel, who swears that Dederich is a liar and perjurer, from kissing the relics, but Dederich has no such problem.

The battle officials are nobles of high station who take their place on the smooth green field designated as the legal site. As the judicial duel is ready to begin, Dederich accuses Wellis once more of treason and murder and spurns the offer of a truce. During the battle, the *Karlmeinet* author dwells on the efficacy of Kurtan, Dederich's sword, as well as on specific battle wounds.

In this work Pinabel is not allowed to have the more honorable death of beheading; instead, he is hanged with some of his armor and tied to the gallows with ropes. On Pinabel's death Karl gives a lengthy speech praising God, the highest judge, who cannot tolerate injustice. Once the loser has been appropriately disposed of, Karl turns his attention to rewarding Dederich. Dederich has suffered severe enough wounds in the battle that he is brought to Karl's quarters in the palace in Aachen, where he receives the best medical treatment and much affection from Karl. Karl promises him land and riches.

Prior to the sentencing, Karl goes to mass. When he reaches the court, Wellis makes a speech that has no counterpart in the earlier versions and shows a different side of the man. Wellis admits his guilt, shows some repentance, and hopes to die a good death. When Karl reiterates his crimes — murder, treachery, and the death of Roland — Wellis admits that Roland died because of the evil agreement he made with the Muslims. He understandably shows reluctance to undergo the horrible death destined for traitors. He believes, however, that the severity of the punishment will be good for his soul.

Less concerned with the effect of punishment on the state of Wellis's soul, Karl and his nobles see Wellis's fate as a deterrent to future potential traitors. Unlike earlier versions, the *Karlmeinet* includes a grisly catalog of possible types of execution. For Wellis, who is compared to Judas, a painful punishment that causes fear and misery is appropriate. Five princes describe appropriate punishments in detail: dragging Wellis naked through the kingdom, beaten all the while; burning him alive; turning Karl's lions and vultures loose on him after starving them for several days; imprisoning Wellis for two days, bringing him out on the third and giving him a meal of heavily salted food with nothing to drink, and putting him in an oven where he will die of thirst, as Roland had at Ronceval; and having him pulled apart by four horses, with his flesh being scattered everywhere and devoured by animals. The final punishment is the one chosen.

When Wellis is killed, the horses spread his remains over a wide area — woods, meadows, and rocky areas. Wellis has paid so dearly for his misdeed that his death will be recounted in amazement as a warning example to all Christian people to shun such behavior.

Appendix III
Tristan: Plot Summary

The Duel with Morold

TRISTAN IS KNIGHTED BY HIS UNCLE, King Mark of Cornwall, and goes back to his late father's land of Parmenie, where he transfers power to his foster father Rual's family. Returning to Cornwall, he is greatly distressed to hear that the powerful Irish knight Morold is demanding tribute and threatening war if it is not paid. The tribute has been levied for years by Gurmun of Ireland, who had subjugated Cornwall and England when Mark was a child. Gurmun had married the mighty Duke Morold's sister and benefited greatly from the strength and prowess of his brother-in-law, who acts on his behalf in this matter. At the present time the tribute consists of thirty sons of Cornish nobles and thirty from the English aristocracy; these children, designated for slavery in Ireland, are chosen by lot.

When Tristan arrives in Tintagel, he hears cries of distress from every corner. The barons are all assembled at court, wringing their hands about the loss of their children to Morold. Tristan finds them kneeling at prayer, unashamed of their cowardice. Aghast at their behavior, Tristan addresses Mark, Morold, and the court. He exhorts them to defend their honor and their children against this tribute, particularly since all that is needed is one man to fight a duel with Morold. Fathers should be willing to give their lives for their children; to do otherwise violates God's commandment. He urges them to find a man who is willing to do battle and entrust himself to God's protection against Morold's might.

The barons assure Tristan that no one can best Morold. Amazed, Tristan reminds them of their proud ancestry and tells them that if they can find no one, he himself, with God, will do battle so that they may regain their legal rights. Even if he loses, it will not worsen their legal position vis-à-vis Morold; if he wins, then it was God's will. With God and Right on his side, he has two helpers sure to bring victory, along with his own firm will.

In spite of Tristan's obvious youth, Morold is not at all pleased at the prospect of a duel to settle the legal issue. Tristan gets the permission of the court, but Mark tries in vain to talk his beloved nephew out of his plans. Tristan then confronts Morold, laying out the history of the tribute, the injustice perpetrated on Cornwall, and the necessity of restoring justice in this matter to the land. Cornwall must be compensated for damages, and the noble Cornwall children condemned to servitude in Ireland must be freed — if necessary, by an attack on Ireland itself.

Morold says that Ireland will not give up the tribute that Cornwall owes it by law. He asks Mark and the court if it is, indeed, their will that Tristan represent them in the manner the latter has just described. When they tell him that is so, he accuses them of breaking the treaty. Tristan tells him that that is slander: no one in Cornwall is breaking an oath or the treaty, because the treaty contains within itself the possibility of a judicial duel or war to challenge the tribute. Cornwall is, thus, dealing with Morold in a manner fully consistent with the legal terms of the treaty. Morold must now decide whether he wants a judicial duel or war, because Cornwall will no longer pay tribute.

Morold tells Tristan that the decision is easily made: he came in peace, expecting matters to go according to law and mutual understanding, and, therefore, has only a small contingent of men with him. Now he is confronted with a fight for which he is not prepared. Tristan tells him to go home and get his army; if he does not come back to Cornwall prepared to fight, the Cornish will go to Ireland.

Morold answers this challenge with sarcasm and arrogance, agreeing to Tristan's request for a judicial duel. Tristan offers Morold his glove and makes a speech outlining the legal background and the reasons for the duel so that, as he says, it is clear that he is doing nothing outside the law. Morold remains unmoved, trusting in his own might.

The judicial duel is set for three days later and draws great crowds. Gottfried says that many stories have described Morold's armor in great detail and that this praise is adequate. He then turns his attention to Mark and Tristan. No despairing woman ever agonized more than King Mark about Tristan's participation in the duel. He is convinced that Tristan will die and would gladly have born all pain about the tribute if the battle could have been avoided.

Gottfried describes Tristan's arming in great detail; Mark, with saddened heart, gives him a splendid sword. He wears a crystal helmet with an arrow, the sign of love. His shield has a wild boar. The inner brightness of Tristan's character, however, outshines the splendor of his armor. His horse wears a white cover, which glistens like the armor.

The place of the judicial duel is an island not far from shore, where the battle can easily be viewed from the beach. No one except the two combatants is allowed on the island. The two men sail there in separate boats; Morold arrives first and begins to warm up by putting his horse through its battle paces and himself through an exercise for fighting. Tristan makes his farewell to Mark, putting all his trust in God, who, he hopes, will help bring justice. Many pray for him as he departs.

Arriving at the island, Tristan loosens his boat and lets it float away. Morold, shocked, asks the reason; Tristan replies that only one boat will be needed after the battle. Morold says that if Tristan will assure him that he can keep collecting the tribute, they need not have a duel; he hates to see such a fine young knight die. Tristan declines, telling Morold that if he is so sure he can best him, to go ahead and try.

The battle is fierce, and for awhile Tristan gets the worst of it. Gottfried says that while everyone says that this was a duel, he sees it as a fight between two forces: Morold has the strength of four, while Tristan has God, Justice, himself, and Will on his side. Morold, the devil's man, hits Tristan so often and so fiercely that he holds the shield wrongly and receives a wound that almost kills him. As Tristan's blood flows fiercely onto the island, Morold urges him to give up, because now Tristan's life lies in Morold's hands: Morold has stabbed him with a poisoned sword, and no doctor can heal him except Morold's sister, Queen Isolde of Ireland. If Tristan will acknowledge Morold's right to tribute, he will see to it that his sister heals him. In addition, Morold will grant Tristan's every request. Tristan refuses and makes a mighty charge that ends in Morold's death. Tristan beheads him, but a piece of Tristan's sword remains in Morold's forehead. Tristan says that God has indicated who was in the right in this matter.

Hiding his wound, Tristan returns to the mainland to the wild jubilation of the Cornish.

Isolde's Ordeal by Fire

Marjodoc, Mark's steward, is extremely jealous of Tristan and uses the dwarf Melot to spy on Tristan and Isolde. Tristan is well aware of their duplicity and warns Isolde to be careful in their presence. In addition to seeking out the pair, Marjodoc and Melot insinuated so much about his nephew and his wife to Mark that he again became suspicious.

Marjodoc and Melot advise Mark to have himself, Tristan, and Isolde bled. Afterward, Mark and Melot leave for matins, and Melot strews flour on the floor so that if Tristan approaches Mark's bed, the flow of blood from the reopening of the incision caused by the movement will easily be seen. Brangaene warns Tristan, who leaps from his bed to Mark's without crossing the floor. Unfortunately, his vein opens, and though there is no blood on the floor, there is blood in Mark's bed and in his own after he returns to it. Mark does not know what to think, so he calls his nobles for counsel.

Mark tells the nobles about the rumors and the toll they are taking on his marriage and his reputation. He wants to avoid contact with the queen until he has public proof of her innocence. The nobles advise him to call a council in London and take advantage of the advice of the clerics knowledgeable about canon law.

The meeting takes place in late May after Whitsun and draws many clergy and laity. Mark tells them about the problems the rumors have caused and entreats the council to come up with a solution. After a great deal of talk, the bishop of Thames, a respected and venerable man, gives his opinion. The bishop notes that while Tristan and Isolde are accused of serious offenses, there is no proof. The rumors, however, have reached such an extent that the king and the court are upset. Since that is the case, the queen must be summoned to hear the charges against her.

Isolde appears and listens to the bishop's summary of the case against her. He asks Isolde how she can explain the situation. Isolde answers that she is well aware of the rumors against her; but she is not surprised, since she is a foreigner with no family or friends to defend her and is surrounded by people who would like to believe the worst of her. She offers to do anything she can to prove her innocence. The king accepts her remarks and asks her to undergo the ordeal by fire. The queen agrees to appear in six weeks in Carleon as directed.

Alone, Isolde considers the difficult situation in which she finds herself. The only way to preserve her reputation is to cover up her deceit. She relates her troubles to Christ and thinks of a clever way out that will presume greatly on Christ's courtliness. She sends a letter to Tristan telling him to be at the river when she lands and to look for her.

Tristan comes disguised as a pilgrim with a discolored and blistered face and uncomely body. Isolde, however, immediately recognizes him. As the boat lands, she asks the "pilgrim" to carry her to the shore, because she does not wish to have a knight bear her.

When she is in Tristan's arms, she whispers to him that he is to fall to the bank with her when he is close. Tristan does so and ends up lying in Isolde's arms. The crowd attempts to beat him, but Isolde says that the pilgrim is weak and could not help it. Bantering with the crowd, Isolde says that it might be true that the pilgrim wanted to take his pleasure with her; but, as everyone can see, she cannot truthfully say that Mark is the only man ever to lie in her arms.

The bishops attend to the ritual proceedings before the ordeal, and the iron is made hot. The queen has given away her valuable possessions in the hope that God might overlook her sins.

Isolde arrives dressed in a hair shirt with the sleeves folded back and her ankles exposed. She is the center of attention, and many feel sorry for her. When the relics are brought forward, she has to swear her oath. The content of the oath becomes a matter of dispute. Isolde suggests that she swear that no man knew her or lay in her arms besides the king — and, of course, the wretched pilgrim. This oath satisfies the king and is duly made. Isolde takes the iron in her hand, carries it, and suffers no injury.

Gottfried here offers his famous commentary about the pliant Christ who is just as one wishes.

Appendix IV
Richardis: Plot Summary

WHEN KARL ASCENDS THE THRONE, he marries the beautiful and virtuous Richardis. She is such an exceptional person that many at court become jealous and suspicious of her and attack her with lies. They will come to a bad end because of their jealousy.

Early one morning when the king is at mass, one of his retainers, Sigerat, follows him and tells him that his wife is behaving in a manner that dishonored the king. Karl demands to know whether she has done anything that compromised the honor and reputation of the empire. Sigerat tells the emperor of Richardis's unfaithfulness, suggesting that he be hanged if he is lying.

Karl hastens back to his chambers. When Richardis inquires about his early return from mass, Karl hits her hard. He threatens to kill her if the charges against her are true. Suspecting slander, Richardis asks him what the charges are. Karl tells her, adding that she is not worthy to be the queen of the empire.

Richardis agrees that if she were guilty of such an offense, she should lose her life; but with God's help she will clear herself, just as Susanna did. Richardis sends for four bishops to hear her confession and prays and fasts, putting herself in God's hands.

When the day of her trial arrives, bishops, dukes, and others come to watch the ordeal. The bishops and dukes want to spare her, but Richardis insists on going through the ordeal of the burning wax shirt. It does not harm her.

The emperor orders the slanderers caught and hanged. The queen abdicates and serves God zealously; Karl, too, rules no longer [he died in 888, shortly after the trial].

Appendix V
Ebernand von Erfurt, *Heinrich und Kunegunde:* Translation

THE DEVIL TRIED EVERY MEANS HE COULD to destroy their reputation. He tempted them in many ways, yet he could do nothing against them with his spurious counsel. With his falsity, he then decided to disgrace completely the steadfast couple. God allowed him to perpetrate his evil mockery on the lady. He let himself be seen in the form of a knight as the generous and merciful lady arose in the morning. He did that to disgrace her, making it look as if he had lain with the constant and virtuous queen. The worthless creature then went away. Those who were with the lady at court did not leave the matter undiscussed: they did not know what they should do. The queen was aware of this, as well. It was difficult for all the ladies of the court and their attendants, because such a thing had never been heard about before. They whispered here, they whispered there. The emperor was away.

Alas, the miserable event happened the same way the second morning, when many saw it as well. They talked about it more than ever. What purpose would it serve to pursue this matter longer? The devil went there on the third morning in full view and let himself be seen by all those who wanted to see him. All would have sworn that he was a noble knight whom they recognized, but no one could tell me his name. Everyone was talking about the virtuous Kunegunde, the ladies with the lords, the lesser with the greater. Yet there was much lamenting about the faithful pure maiden because of her great goodness. Kunegunde steadfastly retained her relationship to God. Truly, believe me, she was very patient as she knew she was innocent. She overcame the burden of this suffering very well. She meditated deeply on God; the miraculously pure one knew nothing would hurt her. Yet she did cry about it. Many who were never wronged by her then spoke harshly of her. The good people wept on her account, the bad ones anticipated things in an evil way; later they had to regret it. They said that she had behaved unfaithfully for many a day; the emperor should turn away from her. She behaved as if she were a saint. People talked about the steadfast queen, just as they would do today if such a story about a royal consort were making the rounds.

This news came to the king's attention. He was very unhappy when he heard it. He said, "God forbid, this would be a very grave sin, I don't want to believe it." However, he was miserable; privately he wept over it with the eyes of his heart. However, I believe that his hot tears fell because of the lady's great virtue, as he had never experienced any kind of misbehavior from the pure young queen. His heart told him the same thing, that he had never seen a more chaste person, whether maiden or woman. Full of both hope and fear, he listened to those who wanted to convince him they were telling the truth; one said this, the other that. He thought, "I do not want to see the lady ever again, since she has deceived me in this way with such a grave offense."

Why should I draw this matter out? He rode into Bamberg in misery and in a downcast manner. He behaved in a way inappropriate to his breeding because he refused to see the lady, as he was accustomed to doing. Kunegunde was very upset about this. She thought, "Now it has begun. My lord is now aware of the rumors." Her frame of mind was steady because she had one comfort: she knew she was innocent. She said, "I, miserable Kunegunde, put myself in Christ's hands." She waited an hour while the renowned emperor remained secluded in his private chamber. In considering the matter herself, she had decided to go before the emperor. She received him in a very mannerly way. He did not want to see or greet the dear lady, and he did not want to rise up to welcome her. "My lord, what has happened?" said the virtuous queen. "You are not in a good frame of mind." He said, "You know very well what is the matter." She said, "Lord, truly a solution is at hand. What I have been accused of, God knows I am innocent. Lord, be patient and behave as an honorable man. I will yet be able to find counsel and can set you on a good path. The empire has lost much of its reputation because of me; noble and virtuous lord, you should get it back for me." He said, "Lady, sit down and tell us the way in which that can come to pass." She said, "You should send to all the corners of the empire and let all of the noble princes be called here so that they come to the court, lay princes and bishops, to sit in judgment on this matter as the peers instruct you. That you may do with honor. He who has let this happen to me, he is so benevolent that he will help us. Such a thing could never have happened without an instigator."

Her counsel seemed wise. King Heinrich summoned the princes in the empire, who came there quickly. He presided at court. The queen did not lose her composure, she arrived in a manner befitting her station before the assemblage of princes. There the noble lady sat at the feet of the king. Her mind was free of all taint of shame. She had put herself in God's hands so that He Himself was her representative. The king said, "My lords, it is a matter of great concern to me, my shame you have heard about, that is the reason you are here. What are ladies worth who hold their husbands in contempt and who give themselves up to whoredom? Now give as just a verdict as you can." The princes answered, "We want to make this process shorter for you. If she is found guilty of the deed, then it goes to judgment."

Then the king asked them to get to the point where they could have a fruitful discussion and give him the right verdict. This disturbed many a good nobleman; if they could, they wanted to spare her because of her great virtue.

When that put too much of a strain upon the lady, she stepped before the princes and she asked them to listen to her, for God's sake and because of her request. There was a great silence.

She said, "Lords, all of you together, listen to me, a weak woman. When you granted us the right to rule over you, there was no one higher in authority in the world than all emperors before us, and those who come after us will also be emperors and empresses. Whether it hurts or benefits me, since I am the highest lady, I should also put my hopes in the highest court. There are twelve glowing plowshares, that I tell you truly." Then there was great weeping from many virtuous princes. She said, "God must reward you that you wanted to spare me." After this speech, she sat down.

They talked back and forth: "She is innocent of this deed, since she assigned herself this ordeal." That seemed more than enough to everyone. They carried all twelve plowshares and assiduously made them so glowing hot that no one was so brave that he would not have been afraid. When this was ready, the king asked the dear queen to be brought there, where the judgment was to take place, there by the cathedral. The innocent flower gazed up to heaven from the depths of her soul. She said, "Lord Jesus Christ, who created heaven and earth and who sees all hearts, you call yourself a judge. You are my judge and witness. Show forth your glory on me today, and if you have any worthy female servant on earth, let me be that one today and come to my judgment day as one who had a beloved group of servants whom he would help out of difficulties before he would see them killed. Help me now, my lord, in a manner appropriate to my guilt."

Two bishops brought her, the most worthy ones there at court. The king followed after them until they came to the place where the judgment was to take place. Many a brave man followed him, as well. This all happened in a chapel. When the king saw the plowshares, so glowing and so hot, it began to move him to pity. He thought it was too horrible. He thought, "She will burn herself badly." He spoke to the queen: "You should be released from your word. I do not want to punish you through God." She said, "Those people who talk about me would mock me and say all manner of indecent things about me. For those people I want to undergo a judgment. It will not do me any good at all if I do not allow God to be the judge. Even though this judgment is a harsh one for me, God knows my innocence; I will pull these evil words out of the mouths of people so that they will say other things about Kunegunde and not hate me any more."

She stepped up to the plowshares, which were lying in place, and spoke with a pure disposition: "Dear good Lord, help me today at this time, justly as it is true, look upon this matter with your grace, that this same Heinrich never had me as his spouse, neither he nor any other man." Heinrich wanted in this hour to shut her mouth so as to silence her. Blood flowed from her mouth onto her clothing. Heinrich was immediately remorseful that he had behaved in such an unseemly manner. He went away from her. The noble good queen had her shoes removed. She stepped forth in God's name and walked over eleven plowshares. She stepped on the twelfth and stood there quietly. The lady remained there as coolly as if she were in a dew. Under her feet, the plowshare sank. She stepped on it as if it were dough, so that the lady worthy of God remained standing with her bare feet on the earth. Since it was so hot it was in a molten state, everyone watched that it did not flow over on her. If it had, they would have prevented her from being brought into such danger.

Justice was done here. The lady walked on the plowshares. Each prince saw the great miracle God had performed. The king threw himself at her feet and asked for loving words from her. He said, "I seek your forgiveness, let me be in your favor." She said, "Win God's favor, and rely on his command, you certainly have my good will." He said, "Truly, lady, I should make you forget your suffering." All the princes rejoiced, praise resounded. This story was talked about everywhere. Now the blameless one shines as a noble rose glistens in the midst of the thorns. To the noble, well-born lady was given a much better reputation — all of the world from then on called her a pure maiden.

Appendix VI
Comparison of Parallel Texts from the "Additamentum" and Ebernand von Erfurt

1. Speech of Kunigunde to the Emperor after Accusation

"Additamentum"

"My conscience is clear and my confidant is in heaven, since he clearly bears witness to the fact that I have never committed this truly wicked deed of which I am accused. I beg you, my lord and king, to play the man and deign to be patient with me. The honor of your whole empire indeed seems to have been undermined by me, but, God willing, it will the more speedily be made good by me; how this can happen I shall shortly explain, if this can be done with your good will."

Ebernand

"Lord, truly a solution is at hand. What I have been accused of, God knows I am innocent. Lord, be patient and behave as an honorable man. I will yet be able to find counsel and can set you on a good path. The empire has lost much of its reputation because of me; noble and virtuous lord, you should get it back for me."

2. Recommendation of Kunigunde to the Emperor

"Additamentum"

"My Lord, Your Majesty should order all the leading men, bishops as well as laity to gather at his palace and in the presence of all should air the case now being discussed before a judicial assembly; whatever they suggest to you may be carried out without infringing your honor. I hope however for divine pity to rescue us from this mire, and that you too may pity this poor creature."

Ebernand

"You should send to all the corners of the empire and let all of the noble princes be called here so that they come to the court, lay princes and bishops, to sit in judgment on this matter as the peers instruct you. That you may do with honor. He who has let this happen to me, he is so benevolent that he will help us. Such a thing could never have happened without an instigator."

3. Speech of Kunigunde to the Princes

"Additamentum"

"O leaders, worthy of all honor and beloved by me, I have for long found favor with you, and you have exalted my Lord, or my beloved husband, to the rank of emperor, and you wished me to share in his rule and we seemed to excel other people as much by God's grace as by your decision. Because, therefore, I seem to be preeminent among women but am now arraigned on a terrible charge, I must clear myself of this infamy in your presence before an exceedingly harsh court, consisting, of course, of twelve glowing white plows. And yet I am immeasurably grateful to your fairness, in that by showing me mercy your gentleness was unwilling to pass a heavy sentence on me."

Ebernand

"Lords, all of you together, listen to me, a weak woman. When you granted us the right to rule over you, there was no one higher in authority in the world than all emperors before us and those who come after us will also be emperors and empresses. Whether it hurts or benefits me, since I am the highest lady, I should also put my hopes in the highest court. There are twelve glowing plowshares, that I tell you truly.

"O my beloved and glorious leaders, I am of the honest opinion that it should on no account be concealed from your nobility that for some days I have been suffering a dishonor, and shame has covered my face. On account of this above all else I wanted you to meet, so that I might be freed from the embarrassment that threatens me by your sensible advice. And so now I request that you tell me, out of your affection for me, what sentence should be applied to a married woman, who despises her legal husband and presumes to take an additional mate."

Appendix VII
Der Stricker, "Das heiße Eisen" (The Hot Iron): Translation

A WOMAN SAID TO HER HUSBAND, "Because I made your acquaintance I shall always be happy. God has endowed you so richly in appearance and character and has so fully given to you whatever is most fitting for a man that there is only one worry that threatens my well-being, and it concerns you and other women. If you were so inclined and could convince me that you had no other women, then I would repay you in such a manner that you would affirm, having seen the proof of it, that no woman ever loved her husband so dearly."

He said, "My dear love, I desire no woman but you. You mean more to me than anyone. I would be a faithless thief if I had anyone but you. As God is dear to you, don't accuse me of doing such a thing to you. I love you far too much for that. I'm very willing to give you all the assurance you wish and have you put to the test that I love you above all women."

She said, "If you do that, then no man was ever better treated by his wife than you will be from me. Undergo an ordeal for me, about which I'll instruct you; if you love me, carry the hot iron for me. Then I'll really be able to see what sort of love you have for me, if you actually can survive it without damage I intend to have you go through with it. If you won't perform it for me (such an attitude would be one of lasting hatred), then the only reason you can have is that you love other women and don't care for me at all."

He said, "Such talk is unnecessary. I would rather die than make you hate me. I gladly do everything I can to serve you; I don't want to deny any of your wishes, night or day. I'll carry the iron right now, so that God will show that I love you alone with fidelity and never otherwise desired any other women."

The iron was made glowing hot right away. Two stones were prepared and the iron laid upon them so that it was at his right. She said, "Pick it up and carry it so that I can see how faithful you are." The man bent down. He had earlier placed a suitable piece of wood in his sleeve in such a way that his wife did not find out about it. He now let it fall into his hand and then picked up the iron.

He said, "Now God should make known that neither my body nor my thoughts were ever unfaithful and were always with you in fidelity." He carried the iron more than six steps. As quickly as that was finished, he hid the piece of wood and allowed his hand to be examined. His wife said, "I'll always acknowledge that you have acquitted yourself and stand here without any falseness. Your hand is as beautiful as gold. I will always love you."

He said, "May God reward you for it! Now my request and my command is that you also carry the iron for me. I will not allow you to refuse it. It has to happen on the spot, right now; I want to see your fidelity."

She said, "My darling, I want to be so loving to you that the idea that I would ever desire anyone else would never occur to you. You know well how I feel, that you are a thousand times dearer to me than my own soul."

He said, "Enough talk! You didn't want to spare me the ordeal, truly the same will be done to you. You can't get out of it, you must carry the hot iron right now." Right away he carried it in the fire and got it hot enough and brought it to where it lay before. He said, "Now lift it and carry it while it's still hot!" She said, "Is there no help for it but to carry it?" "No, none at all," he said. "Get up and get over here. You have to carry it as I did."

She said, "My friend, I'd like to ask you for a very small favor, for which I'll repay you as long as I live if you grant it to me. Whatever nice things I have ever done for you, think of that now and do what I ask of you. You know well that a man can deny himself enough things. He has a strong mind and character. But we are weak and easily tempted women who can't restrain ourselves as well. Men are full of strength, they may do one thing and leave another, resisting temptation. That we don't have such fortitude is something that God has done to us. Consequently, no one should think evil of us if we now and then give way. So allow me one man because I never had any more besides you, I'll swear that to God. You will see that in the ordeal." "I want to see it," he said. "Go over and pick up the iron."

She said, "Oh my darling, let me make another request. (I'll treat you in such a way that you'll always be happy you granted it. The heartfelt affection I have for you is always steadfast, with the strength of my great fidelity and love, because you have treated me so well), the request being that you grant me two more men. Since you have been good to me, do something even better — I'll pay you back forever." He said, "So be it. You must go immediately to the iron."

"Dear companion," she said, "I have three pounds of money of which you didn't know even a penny existed. Now do it for God's sake most of all and take these three pounds. If you have ever received any kindness from me, you should think about it now, as precious to you as your soul may be, and allow me three."

He said, "I'll grant you them. But you have talked enough. If you say one more word today, if you don't carry the hot iron for me, then truly I will kill you."

Then she had no choice but to be quiet. She took the iron on her hand and was so badly burned that she cried out with a great deal of expression, "Oh, alas, I've lost my hand!"

He had spread wax and prepared a cloth for it and wanted to wrap her hand. She asked him to stop, saying, "What good is a bandage? My hand is so badly burned that it can never be as useful to me as it was before!"

As he heard and saw that, he said in great anger: "Here your fidelity is apparent. Now you should be very certain that no woman is as disgusting to me as you are; and after this time, everything that makes you miserable is what I will do to you. You've brought on yourself disgrace and disadvantage, which I want to help you increase. I'll reward you for the way in which you have taken your reputation into account."

Bibliography

Abou-El-Haj, Barbara. *The Medieval Cult of Saints: Formations and Transformations.* Cambridge: Cambridge UP, 1997.

Althoff, Gerd. "Colloquium familiare — Colloquium secretum — Colloquium publicum: Beratung im politischen Leben des früheren Mittelalters." *Frühmittelalterliche Studien* 24 (1990): 145–67.

———. "Genugtuung (satisfactio): Zur Eigenart gütlicher Konfliktbeilegung im Mittelalter." *Modernes Mittelalter.* Ed. Joachim Heinzle. Frankfurt am Main & Leipzig: Insel, 1994. 247–65.

———. "Huld: Überlegungen zu einem Zentralbegriff der mittelalterlichen Herrschaftsordnung." *Spielregeln der Politik im Mittelalter: Kommunikation in Frieden und Fehde.* Darmstadt: Primus, 1997. 199–229.

———. "Konfliktverhalten und Rechtsbewußtsein: Die Welfen in der Mitte des 12. Jahrhunderts." *Frühmittelalterliche Studien* 26 (1992): 331–52.

———. "Königsherrschaft und Konfliktbewältigung im 10. und 11. Jahrhundert." *Frühmittelalterliche Studien* 23 (1989): 265–90.

———. "Spielen die Dichter mit den Spielregeln der Gesellschaft." *Mittelalterliche Literatur und Kunst im Spannungsfeld von Hof und Kloster.* Ed. Nigel F. Palmer and Hans-Jochen Schiewer. Tübingen: Niemeyer, 1999. 51–71.

———. *Verwandte, Freunde und Getreue: Zum politischen Stellenwert der Gruppenbindungen im früheren Mittelalter.* Darmstadt: Wissenschaftliche Buchgesellschaft, 1990.

Asmus, Herbert. *Rechtsprobleme des mittelalterlichen Fehdewesens.* Göttingen: Thèse Droit, 1951.

Baist, G. "Der gerichtliche Zweikampf, nach seinem Ursprung und im Rolandslied." *Romanische Forschungen* 5 [Festschrift Konrad Hoffmann zum 70. Geburtstag] (1980): 436–48.

Baldwin, John W. *Aristocratic Life in Medieval France: The Romances of Jean Renart and Gerbert de Montreuil 1190–1250.* Baltimore: Johns Hopkins UP, 2000.

———. "The Crisis of the Ordeal: Literature, Law and Religion around 1200." *Journal of Medieval and Renaissance Studies* 24 (1994): 327–53.

———. "The Intellectual Preparation for the Canon of 1215 against Ordeals." *Speculum* 36 (1961): 613–36.

———. *The Language of Sex: Five Voices from Northern France around 1200*. Chicago: U of Chicago P, 1994.

———. *Masters, Princes, and Merchants: The Social Views of Peter the Chanter & His Circle*. 2 vols. Princeton: Princeton UP, 1970.

Bartlett, Robert. *Trial by Fire and Water*. Oxford: Clarendon P, 1986.

Baumgärtner, Ingrid. "Kunigunde: Politische Handlungsspielräume einer Kaiserin." *Kunigunde: Eine Kaiserin an der Jahrtausendwende*. Ed. Baumgärtner. Kassel: Furore, 1997. 11–46.

Becher, Matthias. *Karl der Grosse*. Munich: Beck, 1999.

Bechstein, R., ed. *Heinrich und Kunegunde von Ebernand von Erfurt*. Amsterdam: Rodopi, 1968.

Beckers, Hartmut. "*Karlmeinet*-Kompilation." *Die deutsche Literatur des Mittelalters: Verfasserslexikon*. Vol. 4. Ed. Wolfgang Stammler, Karl Langosch, and Kurt Ruh. Berlin & New York: De Gruyter, 1983. Cols. 1012–28.

———. "Die *Karlmeinet*-Kompilation: Eine deutsche *vita poetica Karoli Magni* aus dem frühen 14. Jahrhundert." *Cyclification: The Development of Narrative Cycles in the Chansons de Geste and the Arthurian Romances*. ed. Bart Besemusca, Willem P. Gerritsen, Corry Hogetoorn, and Orlanda S. H. Lie. Amsterdam: North-Holland, 1994. 113–17.

Béroul. *The Romance of Tristan by Béroul*. Ed. Stewart Gregory. Amsterdam: Rodopi, 1992.

Bertau, Karl. *Deutsche Literatur im europäischen Mittelalter*. Vol. 1. Munich: Beck, 1972.

Bestul, Thomas. *Texts of the Passion: Latin Devotional Literature and Medieval Society*. Philadelphia: U of Pennsylvania P, 1996.

Betz, Werner. "Gottfried von Straßburg als Kritiker höfischer Kultur und Advokat religiöser Emanzipation." *Festschrift für Konstantin Reichardt*. Ed. Herwig Zauchenberger and Christian Gellinek. Bern & Munich: Francke, 1969. 168–73.

Beumann, Helmut. "Grab und Thron Karls des Großen zu Aachen." *Karl der Grosse*. Vol. 4: *Das Nachleben*. Ed. Wolfgang Braunfels and Percy E. Schramm. Düsseldorf: Schwann, 1967. 9–38.

Beyerle, Konrad. *Von der Gnade im Deutschen Recht*. Göttingen: Vandenhoeck & Ruprecht, 1910.

Bindschedler, M. "Gottfried von Straßburg und die höfische Ethik." *Beiträge* 76 (1954): 1–38.

Bloch, R. Howard. *Etymologies and Genealogies: A Literary Anthropology of the French Middle Ages*. Chicago & London: U of Chicago P, 1983.

Böhm, Sabine. *Der Stricker — ein Dichterprofil anhand seines Gesamtwerkes*. Frankfurt am Main & New York: P. Lang, 1995.

Bonath, Gesa. *Thomas: Tristan*. Munich: Fink, 1985.

Bongert, Yvonne. *Récherches sur les cours laïques du Xè au XIIIe siècle*. Paris: Picard, 1949.

Daniel 3:27. *The Revised English Bible with the Apocrypha*. Oxford: Oxford UP/ Cambridge: Cambridge UP, 1989. 768.

Borovszky, Samu, and János Karácsonyi, eds. "Ritus exploranda veritatis." *Regestrum varadinense examinum ferri candentis ordine chronologico digestrum, descripta effigie editionis a. 1550 illustratum, sumptibusque Capituli varadinensis lat. rit*. Budapest: Hornyánszky Viktor, 1903. 146–52.

Bouchard, Constance Brittain. *Strong of Body, Brave and Noble: Chivalry and Society in Medieval France*. Ithaca, NY: Cornell UP, 1998.

Boulet-Sautel, Marguerite. "Aperçus sur le système des preuves dans la France coutumière du Moyen Age." *La Preuve*. Recueils de la Société Jean Bodin pour l'Histoire Comparative des Institutions, no. 17. Brussels: Editions de la Librairie Encyclopedique, 1965. 275–325.

Boutet, Dominique. *La chanson de geste*. Paris: PU de France, 1993.

———. *Formes littéraires et conscience historique: Aux origins de la literature française*. Paris: PU de France, 1999.

Brandt, Rüdiger. *Erniuwet: Studien zu Art, Grad und Aussagefolgen der Rolandsliedbearbeitung in Strickers "Karl."* Göppingen: Kümmerle, 1981.

Brault, Gerard. *The Song of Roland: An Analytical Edition*. University Park & London: Pennsylvania State UP, 1978.

Brown, Peter. "Society and the Supernatural: A Medieval Change." *Daedalus* 104 (1975): 133–51.

Brundage, James. *Law, Sex and Christian Society in Medieval Europe*. Chicago: U of Chicago P, 1987.

Brunner, Karl. *Oppositionelle Gruppen im Karolingerreich*. Vienna, Cologne & Graz: Böhlau, 1979.

Brunner, Otto. *Land und Herrschaft*. Vienna: Rohrer, 1965. Trans. Howard Kaminsky and James Van Horn Melton as *Land and Lordship: Structures of Governance in Medieval Austria*. Philadelphia: U of Pennsylvania P, 1992.

Buchda, Gerald. "Anklage." *Handwörterbuch zur deutschen Rechtsgeschichte*. 5 vols. Ed. Adalbert Erler, Ekkehard Kaufmann, and Wolfgang Stammler. Berlin: E. Schmidt, 1964–1998. I: cols. 171–75.

———. "Der Beweis im sächsischen Recht." *La Preuve*. Recueils de la Société Jean Bodin pour l'Histoire Comparative des Institutions, no. 17. Brussels: Editions de la Librairie Encyclopedique, 1965. 519–46.

———. "Gelöbnis." *Handwörterbuch zur deutschen Rechtsgeschichte*. 5 vols. Ed. Adalbert Erler, Ekkehard Kaufmann, and Wolfgang Stammler. Berlin: E. Schmidt, 1964–1998. I: cols. 1490–94.

———. "Gerichtsverfahren." *Handwörterbuch zur deutschen Rechtsgeschichte*. 5 vols. Ed. Adalbert Erler, Ekkehard Kaufmann, and Wolfgang Stammler. Berlin: E. Schmidt, 1964–1998. I: cols. 1551–63.

Buschinger, Danielle. "Pouvoir central et principautés territoriales: Perspectives allemandes sur le monde épique à la fin du moyen âge." *Actes du XIe Congrès international de la Société Rencesvals*. Barcelona: Real Academia de Buenas Letras, 1990. 151–64.

Bynum, Caroline Walker. *Holy Feast and Holy Fast: The Religious Significance of Food to Medieval Women*. Berkeley: U of California P, 1987.

———. *The Resurrection of the Body in Western Christianity, 200–1336*. New York: Columbia UP, 1995.

Canisius-Loppnow, Petra. *Recht und Religion im* Rolandslied *des Pfaffen Konrad*. Frankfurt am Main & New York: P. Lang, 1992.

Carbasse, Jean-Marie. "Le duel judicaire dans les coutumes méridionales." *Annales du Midi* 87 (1975): 385–403.

Carlen, L. "Stab." *Handwörterbuch zur deutschen Rechtsgeschichte*. 5 vols. Ed. Adalbert Erler, Ekkehard Kaufmann, and Wolfgang Stammler. Berlin: E. Schmidt, 1964–1998. IV, pt. 2. Cols. 1838–44.

Chinca, Mark. *History, Fiction, Verisimilitude: Studies in the Poetics of Gottfried's Tristan*. London: Modern Humanities Research Association for the Institute of Germanic Studies, U of London, 1993.

Cohen, Esther. *The Crossroads of Justice: Law and Culture in Late Medieval France*. Leiden & New York: Brill, 1993.

———. "Symbols of Culpability and the Universal Language of Justice: The Ritual of Public Executions in Late Medieval Europe." *History of European Ideas* 11 (1989): 407–16.

Colman, Rebecca V. "Reason and Unreason in Early Medieval Law." *Journal of Interdisciplinary History*, vol. 4 (1974): 571–91.

Combridge, Rosemary N. *Das Recht im "Tristan" Gottfrieds von Straßburg*. Berlin: E. Schmidt, 1964.

Conrad, Hermann. *Deutsche Rechtsgeschichte*. Vol. 1. Karlsruhe: Müller, 1962.

———. "Das Gottesurteil in den Konstitutionen von Melfi Friedrichs II von Hohenstaufen (1232)." *Festschrift zum 70. Geburtstag von Walter Schmidt-Rimpler*. Ed. Rechts-und Staatswissenschaftliche Fakultät der Rheinischen Friedrich Wilhelms-Institut. Karlsruhe: Müller, 1957. 9–21.

Cram, Kurt Georg. *Iudicium Belli: Zum Rechtscharakter des Krieges im deutschen Mittelalter*. Münster & Cologne: Böhlau, 1955.

Davies, Wendy, and Paul Fouracre, eds. *The Settlement of Disputes in Early Medieval Europe.* Cambridge: Cambridge UP, 1986.

De Boor, Helmut. "Die Grundauffassung von Gottfrieds Tristan." *Deutsche Vierteljahrsschrift für Literaturwissenschaft und Geistesgeschichte* 18 (1940): 262–306. Rpt. in *Gottfried von Straßburg.* Ed. Alois Wolf. Darmstadt: Wissenschaftliche Buchgesellschaft, 1973. 25–73.

De Boor, Helmut, and Richard Newald. *Geschichte der deutschen Literatur von den Anfängen bis zur Gegenwart.* Vol. 1. Munich: Beck, 1949.

———. *Geschichte der deutschen Literatur von den Anfängen bis zur Gegenwart.* Vol. 2. Munich: Beck, 1966.

———. *Geschichte der deutschen Literatur von den Anfängen bis zur Gegenwart.* Vol. 3. Munich: Beck, 1967.

Deutsches Rechtswörterbuch. Vols. 1–4. Weimar: H. Böhlaus Nachfolger. Vol. 1, 1932; vol. 2, 1935; vol. 3, 1938; vol. 4, 1939.

Deutsches Rechtswörterbuch. Vol. 6. Weimar: H. Böhlaus Nachfolger, 1961.

Deutsches Rechtswörterbuch. Vols. 7–9. Weimar: H. Böhlaus Nachfolger, 1961.

Dickerson, Harold D., Jr. "Language in 'Tristan' as a Key to Gottfried's Conception of God." *Amsterdamer Beiträge zur älteren Germanistik* 3 (1972): 127–45.

Dilcher, G. "Versprechenseide," in "Eid." *Handwörterbuch zur deutschen Rechtsgeschichte.* 5 vols. Ed. Adalbert Erler, U. Kornblum, and G. Dilcher. Berlin: E. Schmidt, 1964–1998. I: cols. 866–70.

Distelkamp, B. "Hulde." *Handwörterbuch zur deutschen Rechtsgeschichte.* 5 vols. Ed. Adalbert Erler, U. Kornblum, and G. Dilcher. Berlin: E. Schmidt, 1964–1998. I: cols. 256–59.

———. "Huldeverlust." *Handwörterbuch zur deutschen Rechtsgeschichte.* 5 vols. Ed. Adalbert Erler, U. Kornblum, and G. Dilcher. Berlin: E. Schmidt, 1964–1998. I: Cols. 259–62.

Dobozy, Maria, trans. *The Saxon Mirror.* Philadelphia: U of Pennsylvania P, 1999.

Duggan, Joseph J. *The Song of Roland: Formulaic Style and Poetic Craft.* Berkeley: U of California P, 1973.

Dümmler, Ernst Ludwig. *Geschichte des ostfränkischen Reiches.* 3 vols. Hildesheim: Olms, 1960.

Ebel, Wilhelm. "Recht und Form: Vom Stilwandel im deutschen Recht." *Probleme der deutschen Rechtsgeschichte.* Göttingen: Schwartz, 1978. 257–79.

Ebernand von Erfurt. *Heinrich und Kunegunde.* Ed. Reinhold Bechstein. Amsterdam: Rodopi, 1968.

Elliott, Dyan. *Spiritual Marriage: Sexual Abstinence in Medieval Wedlock.* Princeton: Princeton UP, 1993.

Erler, Adalbert. "Gottesurteile." *Handwörterbuch zur deutschen Rechtsgeschichte.* 5 vols. Ed. Adalbert Erler, Ekkehard Kaufmann, and Wolfgang Stammler. Berlin: E. Schmidt, 1964–1998. I: cols. 1769–73.

———. "Handschuh." *Handwörterbuch zur deutschen Rechtsgeschichte.* 5 vols. Ed. Adalbert Erler, Ekkehard Kaufmann, and Wolfgang Stammler. Berlin: E. Schmidt, 1964–1998. I: cols. 1975–76.

Erler, Adalbert, U. Kornblum, and G. Dilcher. "Eid." *Handwörterbuch zur deutschen Rechtsgeschichte.* 5 vols. Ed. Adalbert Erler, Ekkehard Kaufmann, and Wolfgang Stammler. Berlin: E. Schmidt, 1964–1998. I: cols. 861–70.

Ernst, Ulrich. "Gottfried von Straßburg in komparatistischer Sicht: Form und Funktion der Allegorese im Tristanepos." *Euphorion* 70 (1976): 1–72.

Farrier, Susan E. *The Medieval Charlemagne Legend: An Annotated Bibliography.* New York: Garland, 1993.

Feistner, Edith. "Karl und Karls Tod: Das 'Rolandslied' im Kontext des sog. 'Karlmeinet': Biographische Zyklik und ihre Implikationen." *Wolfram-Studien XI: Chansons de geste in Deutschland. Schweinfurter Kolloquium 1988.* Ed. Joachim Heinzle, L. Peter Johnson, and Gisela Vollmann-Profe. Berlin: E. Schmidt, 1989. 166–84.

Feldmann, Hans Christian. *Bamberg und Reims: Die Skulpturen, 1220–50.* Ammersbek bei Hamburg: Verlag an der Lottbek, 1992.

Ferrante, Joan. *The Conflict of Love and Honor: The Medieval Tristan Legend in France, Germany and Italy.* The Hague: Mouton, 1973.

Fischer, Hanns. *Studien zur deutschen Märendichtung.* Tübingen: Niemeyer, 1968.

Folz, Robert. "Charlemagne en Allemagne." *Charlemagne et l'Épopée Romane.* Actes du VIIe Congrès International de la Société Rencesvals, vol. 1. Paris: Les Belles Lettres, 1978. 98–101.

———. *Les Saintes Reines du Moyen Age en Occident (VIe–XIIIe siècles).* Brussels: Société des Bollandistes, 1992.

———. *Le souvenir et la légende de Charlemagne dans l'Empire germanique médiéval.* Geneva: Slatkine Reprints, 1973.

Forsyth, Richard D., Margaret H. Kerr, and Michael J. Plyley. "Cold Water and Hot Iron: Trial by Ordeal in England." *Journal of Interdisciplinary History* 22 (1992): 573–95.

Fourquet, Jean. "Der wintschaffene Christ." *La Legende du Tristan au moyen âge.* Ed. Danielle Buschinger. Göppingen: Kümmerle, 1982. 109–11.

Fraher, Richard M. "Preventing Crime in the High Middle Ages: The Medieval Lawyers' Search for Deterrence." *Popes, Teachers and Canon Law in the Middle Ages.* Ed. James Ross Sweeney and Stanley Chodorow. Ithaca, NY: Cornell UP, 1989. 212–33.

Franz, Adolph. *Die kirchlichen Benediktionen im Mittelalter.* Vol. 2. Graz: Akademische Druck- und Verlagsanstalt, 1960.

Freytag, Wiebke. *Das Oxymoron bei Wolfram, Gottfried und anderen Dichtern des Mittelalters.* Munich: Fink, 1972.

Fuhrmann, Horst. *Einladung ins Mittelalter.* Munich: Beck, 1987.

Gal, Alexander. "Der Zweikampf im fränkischen Prozeß." *Zeitschrift der Savigny-Zeitung für Rechtsgeschichte, Germanistiche Abteilung* 28 (1907): 236–89.

Gaudemet, Jean. "Les Ordalies au Moyen Age: Doctrine, Legislation et pratiques canoniques." *La Preuve,* Recueils de la Société Jean Bodin pour l'Histoire Comparative des Institutions, no. 17. Brussels: Editions de la Librairie Encyclopedique, 1965. 99–135.

Geith, Karl-Ernst. *Carolus Magnus: Studien zur Darstellung Karls des Großen in der deutschen Literatur des 12. und 13. Jahrhunderts.* Berlin & Munich: Francke, 1977.

———. "Das deutsche und das französische Rolandslied: Literarische und historisch-politische Bezüge." *Kultureller Austausch und Literaturgeschichte im Mittelalter.* Ed. Ingrid Kasten, Werner Paravicini, and René Pérennec. Sigmaringen: Thorbecke, 1998. 75–84.

Geith, Karl-Ernst, Elke Ukena-Best, and Hans-Joachim Ziegeler. "Der Stricker." *Verfasserslexikon.* Vol. 9. Berlin: De Gruyter, 1993. Cols. 417–49.

Gernhuber, Joachim. *Die Landfriedensbewegung in Deutschland bis zum Mainzer Reichslandfrieden von 1235.* Bonn: Röhrscheid, 1952.

Glogau, Dirk. *Untersuchungen zu einer konstruktivistischen Mediävistik: Tiere und Pflanzen im "Tristan" Gottfrieds von Straßburg und im "Nibelungenlied."* Essen: Item, 1993.

Gold, Pamela. "The Marriage of Mary and Joseph in the Twelfth Century." *Sexual Practices and the Medieval Church.* Ed. Vern L. Bullough and James Brundage. Buffalo, NY: Prometheus, 1982. 101–17.

Goldschmidt-Kunzer, Ruth. *The Tristan of Gottfried von Strassburg: An Ironic Perspective.* Berkeley: U of California P, 1973.

Goodich, Michael. *Violence and Miracle in the Fourteenth Century.* Chicago: U of Chicago P, 1995.

Graus, Frantisek. "Herrschaft und Treue: Betrachtungen zur Lehre von der germanischen Kontinuität." *Historica* 12 (1966): 5–44.

Green, Dennis. *Irony in the Medieval Romance.* Cambridge: Cambridge UP, 1979.

Grimm, Jacob. *Deutsche Rechtsaltertümer.* Vol. 2. Darmstadt: Wissenschaftliche Buchgesellschaft, 1983.

Grimm, Jacob, and Wilhelm Grimm, eds. *Deutsches Wörterbuch*. Vol. 4, Abt. 1, Teil 2. Leipzig: Hirzel, 1897.

———, eds. *Deutsches Wörterbuch*. Vol. 15. Leipzig: Hirzel, 1956.

Grübmüller, Klaus. "'*ir unwarheit warbaeren*': Über den Beitrag des Gottesurteils zur Sinnkonstitution in Gotfrids *Tristan*." *Philologie als Kulturwissenschaft: Studien zur Literatur und Geschichte des Mittelalters. Festschrift für Karl Stackmann*. Göttingen: Vandenhoeck & Ruprecht, 1987. 149–63.

Gudian, Gunter. "Geldstrafrecht und peinliches Strafrecht im späten Mittelalter." *Rechtsgeschichte als Kulturgeschichte: Festschrift für Adalbert Erler zum 70. Geburtstag*. Ed. A. Fink et al. Aalen: Scientia-Verlag, 1976. 273–88.

Guth, Klaus. *Die Heiligen Heinrich und Kunigunde: Leben, Legende, Kult und Kunst*. Bamberg: St. Otto-Verlag, 1986.

Haacke, Dieter. "Konrads Rolandslied und Strickers Karl der Große." *PBB* 81 (1959): 274–94.

Hahn, Gerhard, and Hedda Ragotzky, eds. *Grundlagen des Verstehens mittelalterlicher Literatur*. Stuttgart: Kröner, 1992.

Hattenhauer, Hans. "Der gefälschte Eid." *Fälschungen im Mittelalter*, Teil II: *Gefälschte Rechtstexte: Der bestrafte Fälscher*. Hannover: Hahn, 1988. 661–89.

———. *Das Recht der Heiligen*. Berlin: Duncker & Humblot, 1976.

Haug, Walther. "Âventiure in Gottfried von Straßburgs Tristan." *Festschrift für Hans Eggers zum 65. Geburtstag*. Ed. Hubert Backes. Tübingen: Niemeyer, 1972. 88–125.

Heers, Jacques. *Family Clans in the Middle Ages*. Trans. Barry Herbert. Amsterdam & New York: North-Holland, 1977.

Heinemann, Edward A. "Chansons de Geste." *Dictionary of the Middle Ages*. Vol. 3. New York: Scribner, 1983. 257–62.

Herimann of Reichenau. "*Chronicon* 887." *Monumenta Germaniae historica inde ab anno Christi quingentesimo usque ad annum millesimum et quingentesimum*. Ed. Georg Heinrich Pertz. Vol. 5. Hannover: Hahn, 1884; rpt. Leipzig, 1925.

Hexter, R. J. *Equivocal Oaths and Ordeals in Medieval Literature*. Cambridge, MA.: Harvard UP, 1975.

Hirsch, Hans. *Die hohe Gerichtsbarkeit im deutschen Mittelalter*. Darmstadt: Wissenschaftliche Buchgesellschaft, 1958.

His, Rudolf. *Geschichte des deutschen Strafrechts bis zur Karolina*. Darmstadt: Wissenschaftliche Buchgesellschaft, 1967.

Hlawitschka, Eduard. "Kaiserin Kunigunde." *Frauen des Mittelalters in Lebensbildern*. Ed. Karl R. Schnith. Graz: Styria, 1997. 72–89.

Hoffmann, Werner, and Gottfried Weber. *Gottfried von Straßburg.* Stuttgart: Metzler, 1981. 13–16.

Holger, Eckhardt. *"'Wintschaffen' oder 'tugenthaft'?* Zu Lösungsmethoden werkimmanenter 'Widersprüche' am Beispiel von Gottfrieds Verdikt über Christus." *Neophilologus* 81 (1997): 577–81.

Holzapfel, O. "Holmgangr." *Handwörterbuch zur deutschen Rechtsgeschichte.* 5 vols. Ed. Adalbert Erler, Ekkehard Kaufmann, and Wolfgang Stammler. Berlin: E. Schmidt, 1964–1998. II: col. 219.

Holzhauer, Heinz. "Der gerichtliche Zweikampf." *Sprache und Recht: Beiträge zur Kulturgeschichte des Mittelalters. Festschrift für Ruth Schmidt-Wiegand zum 60. Geburtstag.* Berlin & New York: De Gruyter, 1986. 263–83.

———. "Meineid." *Handwörterbuch zur deutschen Rechtsgeschichte.* Ed. Adalbert Erler, Ekkehard Kaufmann, and Wolfgang Stammler. Vol. 3. Berlin: E. Schmidt, 1984. Cols. 447–58.

———. "Zum Strafgedanken im frühen Mittelalter." *Überlieferung, Bewahrung und Gestaltung in der rechtsgeschichtlichen Forschung.* Ed. Stephan Buchholz, Paul Mikat, and Dieter Werkmüller. Paderborn, Munich, Vienna & Zurich: Schöningh, 1993. 179–92.

Huber, Christoph. *Gottfried von Straßburg: Tristan.* Berlin: E. Schmidt, 2000.

———. *Gottfried von Straßburg: Tristan und Isolde.* Munich: Artemis, 1986.

Hüpper-Dröge, Dagmar. "Der gerichtliche Zweikampf im Spiegel der Bezeichnungen für 'Kampf,' 'Kämpfer,' 'Waffen.'" *Frühmittelalterliche Studien* 18 (1984): 607–61.

Hyams, Paul R., and Colin Morris. "Trial by Ordeal: The Key to Proof in the Early Common Law." *On the Laws and Customs of England: Essays in Honor of Samuel E. Thorne.* Ed. Morris S. Arnold et al. Chapel Hill: U of North Carolina P, 1981. 90–126.

Jackson, W. T. H. *The Anatomy of Love: The Tristan of Gottfried von Strassburg.* New York: Columbia UP, 1971.

Jaeger, C. Stephen. *Medieval Humanism in Gottfried von Straßburg's* Tristan und Isolde. Heidelberg: Winter, 1977.

Jäschke, Kurt-Ulrich. *Notwendige Gefährtinnen: Königinnen der Salierzeit als Herrscherinnen und Ehefrauen im römisch-deutschen Reich des 11. und beginnenden 12. Jahrhunderts.* Saarbrücken-Scheidt: Dadder, 1991.

Jones, Martin H. "The Depiction of Military Combat in Gottfried's Tristan." *Gottfried von Strassburg and the Medieval Tristan Legend.* Cambridge, U.K.: Boydell & Brewer, 1990. 45–66.

Kanzeler, P. "Ueber *Karlmeinet:* Ein Versuch, dieses vor ein Paar Jahren aufgefundene Gedicht einem aachener Verfasser zuzuschreiben." *Annalen des Historischen Vereins für den Niederrhein, insbesondere das Alte Erzbistum Köln* 11–12 (1862): 86–96.

Kaufmann, Ekkehard. "Binden." *Handwörterbuch zur deutschen Rechtsgeschichte.* 5 vols. Ed. Adalbert Erler, Ekkehard Kaufmann, and Wolfgang Stammler. Berlin: E. Schmidt, 1964–1998. I: cols. 437–39.

———. "Buße." *Handwörterbuch zur deutschen Rechtsgeschichte.* 5 vols. Ed. Adalbert Erler, Ekkehard Kaufmann, and Wolfgang Stammler. Berlin: E. Schmidt, 1964–1998. I: cols. 575–77.

———. "Fehde." *Handwörterbuch zur deutschen Rechtsgeschichte.* 5 vols. Ed. Adalbert Erler, Ekkehard Kaufmann, and Wolfgang Stammler. Berlin: E. Schmidt, 1964–1998. I: cols. 1083–93.

———. "Feuerstrafe." *Handwörterbuch zur deutschen Rechtsgeschichte.* 5 vols. Ed. Adalbert Erler, Ekkehard Kaufmann, and Wolfgang Stammler. Berlin: E. Schmidt, 1964–1998. I: cols. 1125–28.

———. "Rache." *Handwörterbuch zur deutschen Rechtsgeschichte.* 5 vols. Ed. Adalbert Erler, Ekkehard Kaufmann, and Wolfgang Stammler. Berlin: E. Schmidt, 1964–1998. IV, pt. 1: cols. 126–27.

———. "Rädern." *Handwörterbuch zur deutschen Rechtsgeschichte.* 5 vols. Ed. Adalbert Erler, Ekkehard Kaufmann, and Wolfgang Stammler. Berlin: E. Schmidt, 1964–1998. IV, pt. 1: cols. 136–38.

———. "Selbsthilfe." *Handwörterbuch zur deutschen Rechtsgeschichte.* 5 vols. Ed. Adalbert Erler, Ekkehard Kaufmann, and Wolfgang Stammler. Berlin: E. Schmidt, 1964–98. IV, pt. 2: cols. 1615–16.

———. "Treue." *Handwörterbuch zur deutschen Rechtsgeschichte* 34. Lieferung. Berlin: E. Schmidt, 1992. Cols. 320–38.

———. "Urteil[rechtlich]." *Handwörterbuch zur deutschen Rechtsgeschichte* 35. 5 vols. Ed. Adalbert Erler, Ekkehard Kaufmann, and Wolfgang Stammler. Berlin: E. Schmidt, 1964–1998. Lieferung. cols. 604–9.

———. "Urteilsfindung — Urteilsschelte." *Handwörterbuch zur deutschen Rechtsgeschichte* 35. 5 vols. Ed. Adalbert Erler, Ekkehard Kaufmann, and Wolfgang Stammler. Berlin: E. Schmidt, 1964–1998. Lieferung, cols. 619–22.

Kay, Sarah. *The Chansons de geste in the Age of Romance.* Oxford: Clarendon P, 1995.

Keller, Adalbert von. *Karl Meinet.* Stuttgart: Litterarischer Verein, 1858; rpt. Amsterdam: Rodopi, 1971.

Kern, Fritz. *Gottesgnadentum und Widerstandsrecht im früheren Mittelalter: Zur Entwicklungsgeschichte der Monarchie.* Münster & Cologne: Böhlau, 1954.

Kerth, T. A. "With God on Her Side." *Colloquia Germanica* 2 (1978): 1–18.

Kieckhefer, Richard. *Unquiet Souls: Fourteenth-Century Saints and Their Religious Milieu*. Chicago: U of Chicago P, 1984.

Klauser, Renate. *Der Heinrichs- und Kunigundenkult im mittelalterlichen Bistum Bamberg*. Bamberg: Bericht des Historischen Vereins für die Pflege der Geschichte des ehemaligen Fürstbistums Bamberg (BHVB), 1957.

Klein, Dorothea. "Strickers 'Karl der Große' oder die Rückkehr zur geistlichen Verbindlichkeit." *Wolfram-Studien* 15 (1998): 299–323.

Klibansky, Erich. *Gerichtsszene und Prozeßform in erzählenden deutschen Dichtungen des 12.–14. Jahrhunderts*. Berlin: Ebering, 1925.

Köbler, Gerhard. *Bilder aus der deutschen Rechtsgeschichte: Von den Anfängen bis zur Gegenwart*. Munich: Beck, 1988.

———. "Land und Landrecht im Frühmittelalter." *Zeitschrift der Savigny-Stiftung für Rechtsgeschichte* 86 (1969): 1–40.

———. "Welches Urteil ist das Gottesurteil des Mittelalters." *Vom mittelalterlichen Recht zur neuzeitlichen Rechtswissenschaft: Bedingungen, Wege und Probleme der europäischen Rechtsgeschichte*. Ed. Norbert Brieskorn, Paul Mikat, Daniela Müller, and Dietmar Willoweit. Paderborn: Schöningh, 1994. 89–108.

Köbler, M. "Hand." *Handwörterbuch zur deutschen Rechtsgeschichte*. 5 vols. Ed. Adalbert Erler, U. Kornblum, and G. Dilcher. Berlin: E. Schmidt, 1964–1998. I: cols. 1927–28.

Kocher, Gernot. "Friede und Recht." *Sprache und Recht: Beiträge zur Kulturgeschichte des Mittelalters. Festschrift für Ruth Schmidt-Wiegand zum 60. Geburtstag*. Berlin & New York: De Gruyter, 1986. 405–16.

———. "Richter." *Handwörterbuch zur deutschen Rechtsgeschichte*. 5 vols. Ed. Adalbert Erler, U. Kornblum, and G. Dilcher. Berlin: E. Schmidt, 1964–1998. IV, pt. 2: cols. 1033–40.

Köhler, Erich. *Ideal und Wirklichkeit in der höfischen Epik: Studien zur Form der frühen Artus- und Graldichtung*. Tübingen: Niemeyer, 1970.

Kolb, Herbert. "Himmlisches und irdisches Gericht in karolingischer Theologie und althochdeutscher Dichtung." *Frühmittelalterliche Studien* 5 (1971): 284–303.

———. "Isoldes Eid: Zu Gottfried von Straßburg, Tristan 15267–15764." *Zeitschrift für deutsche Philologie* 107 (1988): 321–35.

Kölbing, E. *Die nordische Version der Tristram Sage*. Hildesheim: Olms, 1978.

Konecny, Silvia. *Die Frauen des karolingischen Königshauses: Die politische Bedeutung der Ehe und die Stellung der Frau in der fränkischen Herrscherfamilie vom 7. bis zum 10. Jahrhundert*. Vienna: VWGÖ, 1976.

Köpf, Gerhard. *Märendichtung*. Stuttgart: Metzler, 1978.

Köster, Rudolf. *Karl der Große als politische Gestalt in der Dichtung des deutschen Mittelalters*. Hamburg: Hamburger Verlagsanstalt K. Wachholtz, 1939.

Krause, H. "Gnade." *Handwörterbuch zur deutschen Rechtsgeschichte*. 5 vols. Ed. Adalbert Erler, U. Kornblum, and G. Dilcher. Berlin: E. Schmidt, 1964–1998. I: cols. 1714–19.

Krause, Hermann. "Consilio et iudicio: Bedeutungsbreite und Sinngehalt einer mittelalterlichen Formel." *Speculum Historiale: Geschichte im Spiegel von Geschichtsschreibung und Geschichtsdeutung*. Ed. Clemens Bauer, Laetitia Boehm, and Max Mueller. Freiburg & Munich: Alber, 1965. 416–38.

———. "Minne und Recht." *Handwörterbuch zur deutschen Rechtsgeschichte*. 5 vols. Ed. Adalbert Erler, U. Kornblum, and G. Dilcher. Berlin: E. Schmidt, 1964–1998. III: cols. 582–88.

Kroeschell, Karl. *Deutsche Rechtsgeschichte 2 (1250–1550)*. 8th ed. Opladen: Westdeutscher Verlag, 1992.

———. "Recht und Rechtsbegriff im 12. Jahrhundert." *Probleme des 12. Jahrhunderts: Reichenau Vorträge, 1965–67,* Vorträge und Forschungen, vol. 12. Konstanz: Thorbecke, 1968. 309–35.

———. "Die Treue in der deutschen Rechtsgeschichte." *Studi Medievali* 10 (1969): 465–89.

Kross, Renate. "Zum Aachener Karlsschrein." *Karl der Große als vielberufener Vorfahr*. Ed. Lieselotte E. Saurma-Jeltsch. Sigmaringen: Thorbecke, 1994. 49–61.

Kucaba, Kelly. "Höfisch inszenierte Wahrheiten: Zu Isolds Gottesurteil bei Gottfried von Straßburg." *Fremdes wahrnehmen-fremdes Wahrnehmen*. Ed. Wolfgang Harms and C. Stephen Jaeger. Stuttgart: Hirzel, 1997. 73–93.

Kuhn, Hugo. "Allegorie und Erzaehlstruktur." *Formen und Funktionen der Allegorie: Symposion Wolfenbuettel, 1978*. Ed. Walter Haug. Stuttgart: Metzler, 1979. 206–18.

Küsters, Urban. "Liebe zum Hof: Vorstellungen und Erscheinungsformen einer 'höfischen' Lebensordnung in Gottfrieds *Tristan*." *Höfische Literatur, Hofgesellschaft, Höfische Lebensformen um 1200*. Ed. Gert Kaiser and Dirk Müller. Düsseldorf: Droste, 1986. 141–76.

Lacy, Norris. *Early French Tristan Poems* I. Cambridge: D. S. Brewer, 1998.

Lacy, Norris, and Geoffrey Ashe, eds. *The Arthurian Handbook*. New York: Garland, 1988. 92–94, 108, 224, 399–401.

———, eds. *The New Arthurian Encyclopedia*. New York: Garland, 1996. 35–37, 127–28, 206–21, 450–51, 462–65.

LaCroix, Daniel, and Philippe Walter, trans. *Tristan et Iseut: Les poèmes français, la saga norroise*. Paris: Librairie Générale Française, 1989.

Langbein, John H. *Torture and the Law of Proof: Europe and England in the Ancien Régime.* Chicago: U of Chicago P, 1977.

Lanz-Hubmann, Irene. *"Nein unde Jâ": Mehrdeutigkeit im Tristan Gottfrieds von Straßburg: Ein Rezipientenproblem.* Bern: Lang, 1989.

Laufs, A., and K.-P. Schroeder. "Landrecht." *Handwörterbuch zur deutschen Rechtsgeschichte.* 5 vols. Ed. Adalbert Erler, U. Kornblum, and G. Dilcher. Berlin: E. Schmidt, 1964–1998. II: cols. 1527–35.

Lea, Henry Charles. *The Duel and the Oath.* Ed. Edward Peters. Philadelphia: U of Pennsylvania P, 1974.

Legner, Anton. *Reliquien in Kunst und Kult zwischen Antike und Aufklärung.* Darmstadt: Wissenschaftliche Buchgesellschaft, 1995.

Lévy, Jean-Philippe. "L'Evolution des la preuve, des origines à nos jours. Synthèse générale." *La Preuve,* Recueils de la Société Jean Bodin pour l'Histoire Comparative des Institutions, no. 17. Brussels: Editions de la Librairie Encyclopedique, 1965. 9–70.

———. "Le problème de la preuve dans les droits savants du moyen âge." *La Preuve,* Recueils de la Société Jean Bodin pour l'Histoire Comparative des Institutions, no. 17. Brussels: Editions de la Librairie Encyclopedique, 1965. 137–68.

Lexer, Matthias von. *Mitteldeutsches Handwörterbuch.* 3 vols. Leipzig: S. Hirzel, vol. 1, 1872; vol. 2, 1876; vol. 3, 1878.

———. *Mittelhochdeutsches Taschenwörterbuch.* 38th ed. Stuttgart: Hirzel, 1992.

Liermann, Hans. *Die Gottheit im Recht: Ein historisch-dogmatischer Versuch.* Munich: Verlag der Bayerischen Akademie der Wissenschaft; Beck in Kommission, 1969.

Liszka, Thomas R., and Lorna E. M. Walker, eds. *The North Sea World in the Middle Ages: Studies in the Cultural History of North-Western Europe.* Dublin: Four Courts P, 2001.

Loomis, Roger Sherman. *The Development of Arthurian Romance.* Mineola, NY: Dover, 2000.

Lübben, August. *Mittelniederdeutsches Handwörterbuch.* Darmstadt: Wissenschaftliche Buchgesellschaft, 1965.

Mälzer, Marion. *Die Isolde-Gestalten in den mittelalterlichen deutschen Tristan-Dichtungen: Ein Beitrag zum diachronischen Wandel.* Heidelberg: Winter, 1991.

Marchello-Nizia, Christiane, et al., trans. *Tristan et Yseut: Les premières versions européenes.* Paris: Gallimard, 1995.

Margetts, John. "Die erzählende Kleindichtung des Strickers und ihre nichtfeudale orientierte Grundhaltung." *Das Märe: Die mittelhochdeutsche Versnovelle des späten Mittelalters*. Ed. Karl-Heinz Schirmer. Darmstadt: Wissenschaftliche Buchgesellschaft, 1983. 316–43.

Marschall, D. "Hängen." *Handwörterbuch der deutschen Rechtsgeschichte*. 5 vols. Ed. Adalbert Erler, U. Kornblum, and G. Dilcher. Berlin: E. Schmidt, 1964–1998. Vol. 1, cols. 1988–90.

Maurer, Friedrich. *Leid: Studien zur Bedeutungs- und Problemgeschichte*. Munich: Francke, 1969.

McCann, W. J. "Tristan: The Celtic and Oriental Material Re-examined." *Tristan and Isolde: A Casebook*. Ed. Joan Tasker Grimbert. New York & London: Garland, 1995. 3–35.

McNamara, Jo Ann. "Chaste Marriage and Clerical Celibacy." *Sexual Practices and the Medieval Church*. Ed. Vern L Bullough and James A. Brundage. Buffalo, NY: Prometheus, 1982. 22–33.

———. "The *Herrenfrage*: The Restructuring of the Gender System, 1050–1150." *Medieval Masculinities: Regarding Men in the Middle Ages*. Ed. Clare Lees. Minneapolis: U of Minnesota P, 1994. 3–29.

Merback, Mitchell B. *The Thief, the Cross and the Wheel: Pain and the Spectacle of Punishment in Medieval and Renaissance Europe*. Chicago: U of Chicago P, 1999.

Mergell, Bodo. *Tristan und Isolde: Ursprung und Entwicklung der Tristansage des Mittelalters*. Mainz: Kirchheim, 1949.

Meurer, D. "Tötungsdelikte." *Handwörterbuch zur deutschen Rechtsgeschichte*. 34. Lieferung. Berlin: E. Schmidt, 1992. Cols. 286–90.

Michalsky, Tanja. "Imperatrix gloriosa-humilitatis et castitatis exemplum: Das Bild der heiligen Kunigunde." *Kunigunde: Eine Kaiserin an der Jahrtausendwende*. Ed. Ingird Baumgärtner. Kassel: Furore, 1997. 187–222.

Miller, William Ian. *Humiliation and Other Essays on Honor, Social Discomfort, and Violence*. Ithaca, NY: Cornell UP, 1993.

Milsom, S. F. C. *Historical Foundations of the Common Law*. Toronto: Butterworths, 1981.

Mitteis, Heinrich. "Land und Herrschaft: Bemerkungen zu dem gleichnamigen Buch Otto Brunners." *Historische Zeitschrift* 163 (1941): 255–81.

Moignet, Gérard. *La Chanson de Roland*. Paris: Bordas, Larousse, 1969.

Moisan, André. "Le rayonnement de l'épopée de Charlemagne à travers l'Occident." *Cahiers de Civilisation Médiévale Xe–XIIe siècles* 39 (1996): 373–77.

Morris, Colin. "Judicium Dei: The Social and Political Significance of the Ordeal in the Eleventh Century." *Church Society and Politics: Papers Read at the Thirteenth Summer Meeting and the Fourteenth Winter Meeting of the Ecclesiastical History Society.* Ed. Derek Baker. Oxford, 1975. 95–111.

Moss, Claude B. *The Christian Faith: An Introduction to Dogmatic Theology.* London: Society for Promoting Christian Knowledge; New York: Morehouse-Gorham Co., 1961.

Müller, Reinhard. *Studien zum Inzichtverfahren nach bayerischen Quellen.* Leipzig: Weicher, 1939.

Munske, Horst Haider. *Der germanische Rechtswortschatz im Bereich der Missetaten.* Berlin: De Gruyter, 1973.

———. "Meintat." *Handwörterbuch zur deutschen Rechtsgeschichte.* 5 vols. Ed. Adalbert Erler, U. Kornblum, and G. Dilcher. Berlin: E. Schmidt, 1964–1998. III: cols. 458–61.

Munzel-Everling, Dietlinde. "Sachsenspiegel, Kaiserrecht, König Karls Recht? Überschrift und Prolog des Kleinen Kaiserrechtes als Beispiel der Textentwicklung." *Alles was Recht war: Festschrift für Ruth Schmidt-Wiegand zum 70. Geburtstag.* Ed. Hans Höfinghoff. Essen: Item, 1996. 97–111.

Nauen, Hans-Günther. "Die Bedeutung von Religion und Theologie im Tristan Gottfrieds." Diss. U of Marburg, 1947.

Nellmann, Eberhard. "Kaiserchronik." *Verfasserslexikon.* Vol. 4. Berlin: De Gruyter, 1983. Cols. 949–64.

Newstead, H. "The Equivocal Oath in the Tristan Legend." *Mélanges Rita LeJeune.* Vol. 2. Gembloux: J. Duculot, 1969. 1077–85.

Nichols, S. *Formulaic Diction and Thematic Composition in the Chanson de Roland.* U of North Carolina Studies in Romance Languages and Literatures, no. 36. Chapel Hill: U of North Carolina P, 1961.

Nottarp, Hermann. *Gottesurteilstudien.* Munich: Kösel, 1956.

Nussbaum-Kleager, Maria. "'Uzen' and 'Innen': Language and Meaning in Gottfried von Strassburg's Tristan." Diss. SUNY Binghamton, 1987.

Ogris, W. "Geisel." *Handwörterbuch zur deutschen Rechtsgeschichte.* 5 vols. Ed. Adalbert Erler, U. Kornblum, and G. Dilcher. Berlin: E. Schmidt, 1964–1998. I: cols. 1445–51 (col. 1447).

Ohly, Friedrich. "Beiträge zum Rolandslied." *Philologie als Kulturwissenschaft: Studien zur Literatur und Geschichte des Mittelalters. Festschrift für Karl Stackmann zum 65. Geburtstag.* Ed. Ludger Grenzmann, Herbert Herkommer, and Dieter Wuttke. Göttingen: Vandenhoeck & Ruprecht, 1987. 90–135.

———. "Die Legende von Karl und Roland." *Studien zur frühmittelhochdeutschen Literatur*. Ed. L. P. Johnson, H.-H. Steinhoff, and R. A. Wisbey. Cambridge Colloquium 1971. Berlin: E. Schmidt, 1974. 292–343.

———. "Zu den Ursprüngen der Chanson de Roland." *Mediaevalia litteraria: Festschrift für Helmut de Boor*. Munich: Beck, 1971. 135–53.

Okken, Lambertus. *Kommentar zum Tristan Roman Gottfried von Strassburg*. Vol. 1. Amsterdam: Rodopi, 1984.

Ott, Norbert. "Reich und Stadt: Karl der Große in deutschsprachigen Bilderhandschriften." *Karl der Große als vielberufener Vorfahr*. Ed. Lieselotte E. Saurma-Jeltsch. Sigmaringen: Thorbecke, 1994. 87–111.

Ott-Meimberg, Marianne. *"di matteria di ist scone."* Der Zusammenhang von Stoffwahl, Geschichtsbild und Wahrheitsanspruch am Beispiel des deutschen Rolandslileds." *Grundlagen des Verstehens mittelalterlicher Literatur*. Ed. Gerhard Hahn and Hedda Ragotzky, 21. Stuttgart: Kröner, 1992. 17–32.

———. *Kreuzzugsepos oder Staatsroman? Strukturen adeliger Heilsversicherung im deutschen Rolandslied*. Zurich & Munich: Artemis, 1980.

Pappenheim, M. "Über die Anfänge des germanischen Gottesurteils." *Zeitschrift der Savigny-Stiftung für Rechtsgeschichte, Germanistische Abteilung* 48 (1928): 136–75.

Paul, Hermann, Peter Wiehl, and Siegfried Grosse. *Mittelhochdeutsche Grammatik*. Tübingen: Niemeyer, 1989.

Payen, Jean-Charles, trans. *Tristan et Yseut*. Paris: Garnier, 1974.

Pensel, Franzjosef. *Rechtsgeschichtliches und Rechtssprachliches im epischen Werk Hartmann von Aue und im "Tristan" Gottfried's von Straßburg*. Diss., Humboldt Universität Berlin, 1961.

Peters, Edward. *Torture*. Philadelphia: Blackwell, 1996.

Piquet, F. *L'Originalité de Gottfried de Strasbourg dans son poème de Tristan et Isolde*. Lille: Au síege de l'Université, 1905.

Pirenne, Henri. *Histoire du Meurtre de Charles le Bon, Comte de Flandre par Galbert de Bruges*. Paris: Picard, 1891.

Planck, Julius Wilhelm. *Das deutsche Gerichtsverfahren im Mittelalter*. Two vols. in one with separate pagination. Hildesheim & New York: Olms, 1973.

———. *Die Lehre von dem Beweisurtheil*. Göttingen: Dieterich, 1848.

Pötschke, Dieter. "Rolande als Problem der Stadtgeschichtsforschung." *Jahrbuch für die Geschichte Mittel- und Ostdeutschlands* 37 (1988): 4–45.

Preiser, W. "Blutrache." *Handwörterbuch zur deutschen Rechtsgeschichte*. 5 vols. Ed. Adalbert Erler, U. Kornblum, and G. Dilcher. Berlin: E. Schmidt, 1964–1998. I: cols. 459–61.

Priebsch, Robert, ed. *Christi Leiden in einer Vision Geschaut*. Heidelberg: Winter, 1936.

Quinn, Esther. "Beyond Courtly Love: Religious Elements in *Tristan* and *La Queste del Saint Graal*." *In Pursuit of Perfection: Courtly Love in Medieval Literature*. Ed. Joan Ferrante, George D. Economou, and Frederick Goldin. Port Washington, NY: Kennikat P, 1975. 179–219.

Ranke, Friedrich, ed. *Tristan und Isold*. Bern: Francke, 1946.

Rathofer, Johannes. "Der wunderbare Hirsch der Minnegrotte." *Zeitschrift für deutsche Altertum* 95 (1966): 27–40.

Regino of Prüm. "Chronicon 887." *Monumenta Germaniae historica inde ab anno Christi quingentesimo usque ad annum millesimum et quingentesimum*. Vol. 1. Ed. Georg Heinrich Pertz. Hannover: Hahn, 1876.

Reuter, Timothy. "Unruhestiftung, Fehde, Rebellion, Widerstand: Gewalt und Frieden in der Politik der Salierzeit." *Die Salier und das Reich: Gesellschaftlicher und ideengeschichtlicher Wandel im Reich der Salier*. Ed. Stefan Weinfurter and Hubertus Seibert. Sigmaringen: Thorbecke, 1991. 297–325.

Revised English Bible, The. Oxford: Oxford UP / Cambridge: Cambridge UP, 1989. 506.

Reynolds, Susan. *Kingdoms and Communities in Western Europe, 900–1300*. Oxford: Clarendon P, 1984.

Richter, Horst. *Kommentar zum Rolandslied des Pfaffen Konrad, Teil I*. Bern: Herbert Lang, 1972.

Rocher, Daniel. "Hof und christliche Moral: Inhaltliche Konstanten im Oeuvre des Stricker." *Mittelalterliche Literatur und Kunst im Spannungsfeld von Hof und Kloster*. Ed. Nigel F. Palmer and Hans-Jochen Schiewer. Tübingen: Niemeyer, 1999. 99–111.

———. "Inwiefern sind Strickers Maeren echte 'contes a rire?'" *Wolfram Studien* 7 (1981): 132–43.

Rolf, F. Hans. *Der Tod in Mittelhochdeutschen Dichtungen*. Munich: Fink, 1974.

Rossi, Marguerite. "Le duel judiciaire dans les chansons du cycle carolingien: Structure et fonction." *La Chanson de geste et le mythe carolingien: mélanges René Louis*. Vol. 2. Saint-Père-sous-Vézelay: Musée archéologique regional, 1982. 945–60.

Roth, Elizabeth. "Sankt Kunigunde-Legende und Bildaussage." *Historischer Verein für die Pflege der Geschichte des Ehemaligen Fürstbistums zu Bamberg* 123 (1987): 5–68.

Rousset, Paul. "La croyance en la justice immanente à l'époque féodale." *Le Moyen Age* 54 (1948): 225–48.

Rowland, Beryl. *Animals with Human Faces: A Guide to Animal Symbolism*. Knoxville: U of Tennessee P, 1973.

Rychner, Jean. *La Chanson de geste: Essai sur l'art épique des jongleurs*. Geneva: Droz, 1955.

Sachs, Hans. *Werke*. Vol. 9. Stuttgart: Spemann, 1875.

Saurma-Jeltsch, Lieselotte E. "Karl der Große als vielberufener Vorfahr." In *Karl der Große als vielberufener Vorfahr*, ed. Saurma-Jeltsch. Sigmaringen: Thorbecke, 1994.

Saurma-Jeltsch, Lieselotte E., ed. *Karl der Große als vielberufener Vorfahr*. Sigmaringen: Thorbecke, 1994.

Schach, Paul, trans. *The Saga of Tristram and Isönd*. Lincoln: U of Nebraska P, 1973.

Schanze, Frieder. "Kaiser Karls Recht." *Verfasserslexikon*. Vol. 4. Berlin & New York: De Gruyter 1983. Cols. 945–47.

Scheyling, R. "Ehre." *Handwörterbuch zur deutschen Rechtsgeschichte*. 5 vols. Ed. Adalbert Erler, U. Kornblum, and G. Dilcher. Berlin: E. Schmidt, 1964–1998. Vol. 1, cols. 846–49.

———. "Eideshelfer." *Handwörterbuch zur deutschen Rechtsgeschichte*. 5 vols. Ed. Adalbert Erler, U. Kornblum, and G. Dilcher. Berlin: E. Schmidt, 1964–1998. I: cols. 870–72.

Schild, Wolfgang. *Alte Gerichtsbarkeit: Vom Gottesurteil bis zum Beginn der modernen Rechtsprechung*. Munich: Callwey, 1985.

———. *Die Geschichte der Gerichtsbarkeit vom Gottesurteil bis zum Beginn der modernen Rechtssprechung*. Hamburg: Nikol-Verlag Gesellschaft, 1997.

———. "Das Gottesurteil der Isolde: Zugleich eine Überlegung zum Verhältnis von Rechtsdenken und Dichtung." *Alles was Recht war: Rechtsliteratur und literarisches Recht. Festschrift für Ruth Schmidt-Wiegand zum 70. Geburtstag*. Ed. Hans Höfinghoff. Essen: Item, 1996. 55–75.

———. "Verbrennen." *Handwörterbuch zur deutschen Rechtsgeschichte*. 5 vols. Ed. Adalbert Erler, U. Kornblum, and G. Dilcher. Berlin: E. Schmidt, 1964–1998. 35. Überlieferung. Cols. 673–80.

Schleissner, Margaret. "Animal Images in Gottfried von Strassburg's *Tristan*: Structure and Meaning of Metaphor." *The Medieval World of Nature: A Book of Essays*. Ed. Joyce E. Salisbury. New York & London: Garland, 1993. 77–90.

Schlosser, H. "Inzichtverfahren." *Handwörterbuch zur deutschen Rechtsgeschichte*. 5 vols. Ed. Adalbert Erler, U. Kornblum, and G. Dilcher. Berlin: E. Schmidt, 1964–1998. II: cols. 413–15.

Schmidt, Eberhard. *Einführung in die Geschichte der deutschen Strafrechtspflege*. Göttingen: Vandenhoeck & Ruprecht, 1965.

Schmidt-Lornsen, Jutta. "Der Griff an den Bart-wikingerzeitliche Bildzeugnisse zu einer bekräftigenden Gebärde." *Sprache und Recht: Beiträge zur Kulturgeschichte des Mittelalters. Festschrift für Ruth Schmidt-Wiegand zum 60. Geburtstag*. Berlin & New York: De Gruyter, 1986. 363–79.

Schmidt-Wiegand, Ruth. "Eid und Gelöbnis, Formel und Formular im mittelalterlichen Recht." *Recht und Schrift im Mittelalter*. Ed. Peter Classen. Vorträge und Forschungen, vol. 8. Sigmaringen: Thorbecke, 1977. 55–90.

———. "Gebärdensprache im mittelalterlichen Recht." *Frühmittelalterliche Studien* 16 (1981): 363–79.

———. "Kaiserchronik." *Handwörterbuch zur deutschen Rechtsgeschichte*. 5 vols. Ed. Adalbert Erler, U. Kornblum, and G. Dilcher. Berlin: E. Schmidt, 1964–1998. II: cols. 548–52.

———. "Mord (Sprachlich)." *Handwörterbuch zur deutschen Rechtsgeschichte*. 5 vols. Ed. Adalbert Erler, U. Kornblum, and G. Dilcher. Berlin: E. Schmidt, 1964–1998. III: cols. 473–75.

———. "Mord und Totschlag in der älteren deutschen Rechtssprache." *Forschungen zur Rechtsarchäologie und Rechtlichen Volkskunde*, vol. 10. Zurich: Schulthess, Polygraphischer Verlag, 1989. 47–84.

———. "Prozeß Ganelons (Geneluns)." *Handwörterbuch zur deutschen Rechtsgeschichte*. 5 vols. Ed. Adalbert Erler, U. Kornblum, and G. Dilcher. Berlin: E. Schmidt, 1964–1998. IV, pt. 1: col. 20.

———. "Prozeßform und Prozeßverlauf im 'Rolandslied' des Pfaffen Konrad." *Recht, Gericht, Genossenschaft und Policey: Studien zu Grundbegriffen der germanistischen Rechtshistorie. Symposion für Adalbert Erler*. Ed. Gerhard Dilcher and Bernhard Diestelkamp. Berlin: E. Schmidt, 1986. 1–12.

———. "Urkunde." *Handwörterbuch zur deutschen Rechtsgeschichte*. 5 vols. Ed. Adalbert Erler, U. Kornblum, and G. Dilcher. Berlin: E. Schmidt, 1964–1998. Cols. 566–77.

Schmitz, Wolfgang. *Der Teufelsprozeß vor dem Weltgericht nach Ulrich Tenngler's Neuer Layenspiegel von 1511 (Ausgabe von 1512)*. Cologne: Wienand, 1980.

Schnell, Rüdiger. "Rechtsgeschichte, Mentalitäten und Gattungsgeschichte." *Literarische Interessenbildung im Mittelalter*. Ed. Joachim Heinzle. Stuttgart & Weimar: Metzler, 1993. 401–30.

———. "Rechtsgeschichte und Literaturgeschichte: Isoldes Gottesurteil." *Akten des VI. Internationalen Germanisten-Kongresses Basel 1980*. Ed. Heinz Rupp and Hans-Gert Roloff, part 4. *Jahrbüch für internationale Germanistik 8*. Bern, Frankfurt am Main & Las Vegas: P. Lang, 1980. 307–19.

———. "Strickers 'Karl der Große': Literarische Tradition und politische Wirklichkeit." *Zeitschrift für deutsche Philologie* 93, Sonderheft (1974): 50–80.

———. *Suche nach Wahrheit: Gottfrieds "Tristan und Isold" als erkenntnisreicher Roman*. Tübingen: Niemeyer, 1992.

Schoepperle, Gertrude. *Tristan and Isolt: A Study of the Sources of the Romance*. 2 vols. New York: B. Franklin, 1960.

Schröder, Edward, ed. *Kaiserchronik* prologue. *Kaiserchronik eines regensburger Geistlichen*. Berlin: Weidmann, 1964.

Schröder, Richard, and Eberhard von Künßberg. *Lehrbuch der deutschen Rechtsgeschichte*. Berlin: De Gruyter, 1932.

Schröder, Werner. *Text and Interpretation: Das Gottesurteil im Tristan Gottfrieds von Straßburg*. Sitzungsberichte der wissenschaftlichen Gesellschaft an der Johann Wolfgang Goethe Universität Frankfurt/Main. Wiesbaden: Steiner, 1979.

Schröpfer, Hans-Jürgen. *"Heinrich und Kunegunde": Untersuchungen zur Verslegende des Ebernand von Erfurt und zur Geschichte ihres Stoffes*. Göppingen: Kümmerle, 1969.

Schulz, Monika. "'Was beduerfen wir nu rede mêre?' Bemerkungen zur Gerichtsszene im 'Rolandslied.'" *Amsterdamer Beiträge zur Älteren Germanistik* 50 (1998): 47–72.

Schüppert, Helga. "Ebernand von Erfurt." *Verfasserslexikon*. Vol. 2. Berlin: De Gruyter, 1978. Cols. 290–93, 877–79.

Schwab, D. "Eigen." *Handwörterbuch zur deutschen Rechtsgeschichte*. 5 vols. Ed. Adalbert Erler, U. Kornblum, and G. Dilcher. Berlin: E. Schmidt, 1964–1998. I: cols. 877–79.

Schwab, Ute. "Die Zweikämpfer von Monkwearmouth." *Iconologia Sacra: Mythos, Bildkunst, und Dichtung in der Religions-und Sozialgeschichte Alteuropas [Festschrift für Karl Hauck.]* Ed. Hagen Keller and Nikolaus Staubach. Berlin & New York: De Gruyter, 1994. 496–518.

Schwarz, W. *Gottfrieds von Strassburg* Tristan und Isolde. Groningen: Wolters, 1955.

Schwinekörper, Berent. *Der Handschuh im Recht, Ämterwesen, Brauch, und Volksglauben*. Sigmaringen: Thorbecke, 1981.

Schwentner, Bernhard. "Die Stellung der Kirche zum Zweikampfe bis zu den Dekretalen Gregors IX." *Theologische Quartalschrift* 3 (1930): 190–234.

Schwob, Anton. *"fride unde reht sint sêre wunt:* Historiographen und Dichter der Stauferzeit über die Wahrung von Frieden und Recht." *Sprache und Recht: Beiträge zur Kulturgeschichte des Mittelalters* Vol. 2. Berlin & New York: De Gruyter, 1986. 846–68.

Scott, James Walker. "Keisir unde Keisirin by Ebernand von Erfurt. A New Edition." Diss., Princeton University, 1971.

Sellert, W. "Leumund." *Handwörterbuch zur deutschen Rechtsgeschichte*. 5 vols. Ed. Adalbert Erler, U. Kornblum, and G. Dilcher. Berlin: E. Schmidt, 1964–98. II: cols. 1856–58.

Shaw, Frank. "Karl der Große und die schottischen Heiligen." *Verfasserslexikon*. Vol. 4. Berlin & New York: De Gruyter, 1983. Cols. 1004–6.

———, ed. *Karl der Grosse und die schottischen Heiligen*. Berlin: Akademie-Verlag, 1981.

Spahr, Blake Lee. "Tristan versus Morolt: Allegory against Reality?" *Helen Adolf Festschrift*. Ed. Sheema Z. Buehne, James L. Hodge, and Lucille B. Pinto. New York: Ungar, 1968. 72–85.

Spierenburg, Pieter. *The Spectacle of Suffering: Executions and the Evolution of Repression*. Cambridge & New York: Cambridge UP, 1984.

Spieß, Karl-Heinz. "Lehn(s)recht, Lehnswesen." *Handwörterbuch zur deutschen Rechtsgeschichte*. 5 vols. Ed. Adalbert Erler, U. Kornblum, and G. Dilcher. Berlin: E. Schmidt, 1964–1998. II: cols. 1725–41.

Spiewok, Wolfgang. "Karl der Grosse als Maezen und Literarische Figur." *Das Rolandslied des Konrad: Gesammelte Aufsaetze von Danielle Buschinger und Wolfgang Spiewok*. Greifswald: Reineke, 1996. 1–13.

Stacey, Robin Chapman. "Law and Order in the *Very* Old West: England and Ireland in the Early Middle Ages." *Crossed Paths: Methodological Approaches to the Celtic Aspect of the European Middle Ages*. Ed. Benjamin Hudson and Vickie Ziegler. Penn State Proceedings in Medieval Studies, no. 1. Lanham, MD: UP of America, 1991. 39–60.

Stackmann, Karl. "Karl und Genelun: Das Thema des Verrats im Rolandslied des Pfaffen Konrad und seine Bearbeitungen." *Poetica* 8 (1976): 258–80.

———. *Mittelalterliche Texte als Aufgabe: Kleine Schriften*. Vol. 1. Göttingen: Vandenhoeck & Ruprecht, 1997.

Steger, Hugo. *David Rex et Propheta*. Nuremberg: Carl, 1961.

Stein, Peter K. "Tristan." *Epische Stoffe des Mittelalters*. Ed. Volker Mertens and Ulrich Müller. Stuttgart: Kröner, 1984. 365–94.

———. "Tristans Schwertleite: Zur Einschätzung ritterlich-höfischen Dichtung durch Gottfried von Straßburg." *Deutsche Vierteljahrsschrift für Literaturgeschichte und Geistesgeschichte* 51 (1977): 300–352.

Stengel, Edmund. *Abhandlungen und Untersuchungen zur Geschichte des Kaisergedankens im Mittelalter*. Graz: Böhlau, 1965.

Strasser, Ingrid. "Und sungen ein liet ze prîse in einer hôhen wîse: Zur Frage der höfischen Elemente in den Ehestandmaeren des Stricker." *Amsterdamer Beiträge zur älteren Germanistik* 15 (1980). 77–107.

Stratz, H.-W. "Konzil." *Handwörterbuch zur deutschen Rechtsgeschichte*. 5 vols. Ed. Adalbert Erler, U. Kornblum, and G. Dilcher. Berlin: E. Schmidt, 1964–1998. II: cols. 1132–36.

Stricker, Der. *Karl der Grosse von dem Stricker*. Ed. Karl Bartsch. Berlin: De Gruyter, 1965.

———. *Verserzählungen I*. Ed. Johannes Janota. Tübingen: Niemeyer, 1979.

Tax, Petrus. *Wort, Sinnbild, Zahl im Tristanroman*. Berlin: E. Schmidt, 1961.

Theuerkauf, G. "Felonie." *Handwörterbuch zur deutschen Rechtsgeschichte*. 5 vols. Ed. Adalbert Erler, U. Kornblum, and G. Dilcher. Berlin: E. Schmidt, 1964–1998. I: cols. 1098–99.

Thomas. *Les Fragments du roman de Tristan, poème du XII siècle: Edités avec un commentaire*. Ed. Bartina H. Wind. Geneva: Droz / Paris: Minard, 1960.

———. "Un nouveau fragment du *Tristan* de Thomas." Trans. Michael Benskin, Tony Hunt, and Ian Short. *Romania* 113 (1992–95): 289–319.

Tomasek, Tomas. *Die Utopie im "Tristan" Gotfrids von Straßburg*. Tübingen: Niemeyer, 1985. 76–78.

Trusen, Winfried. "Das Verbot der Gottesurteile und der Inquisitionsprozeß." *Sozialer Wandel im Mittelalter: Wahrnehmungsformen, Erklärungsmuster, Regelungmechanismen*. Ed. Jürgen Miethke and Klaus Schreiner. Sigmaringen: Thorbecke, 1994. 235–47.

Tyssens, Madeleine. *La Geste de Guillaume d'Orange dans les manuscrits cycliques*. Paris: Société d'édition "Les Belles Lettres," 1967.

Uitti, Karl D. *Story, Myth and Celebration in Old French Narrative Poetry, 1050–1200*. Princeton: Princeton UP, 1973.

van Caenegem, Raoul C. "Law in the Medieval World." *Tijdschrift voor rechtsgeschiedenis* 49 (1981): 13–46.

———. "Methods of Proof in Western Medieval Law." *Mededelingen von de Koninklijke Academie voor Wetenschappen, Letteren en Schone Kunsten von België, Klasse der Letteren* 45 (1983). 83–127.

———. "La Preuve dans le droit du moyen âge occidental-Rapport de synthèse." *La Preuve*, Recueils de la Société Jean Bodin pour l'Histoire Comparative des Institutions, no. 17. Brussels: Editions de la Librairie Encyclopedique, 1965. 691–753.

Van Stockum, Theodor C. "Die Problematik des Gottesbegriffs im 'Tristan' des Gottfried von Strassburg." *Koninklijke Nederlandse Akademie von Wetenschappen. Afd. Letterkunde. Verslagen en mededeelingen, nieuwe reeks* (deel 26, no. 9, 1963): 3–27.

von den Steinen, Wolfram. "Karl und die Dichter." *Karl der Grosse: Lebenswerk und Nachleben*. Ed. Wolfgang Braunfels. Vol. 2. Düsseldorf: Schwann, 1967. 63–94.

von der Burg, Udo. "Konrads *Rolandslied* und das *Rolandslied* des *Karlmeinet*." *Rheinische Vierteljahrsblätter* 39 (1975): 321–41.

———. *Strickers Karl der Grosse als Bearbeitung des Rolandsliedes*. Göppingen: Kümmerle, 1974.

von Pfeil, Sigurd Graf. "Karl der Grosse in der deutschen Sage." *Karl der Grosse*, vol. 4: *Das Nachleben*. Ed. Wolfgang Braunfels and Percy E. Schramm. Düsseldorf: Schwann, 1967.

Wagner, Erna. "Die Gnadenpforte am Dom zu Bamberg." Diss. U of Würzburg, 1965.

Wailes, Stephen L. *Studien zur Kleindichtung des Strickers*. Berlin: E. Schmidt, 1981.

Waitz, Georg, ed. "Vitae Sancti Heinrici Additamentum." *Monumenta Germaniae historica inde ab anno Christi quingentesimo usque ad annum millesimum et quingentesimum. Legum.* 5 vols. Ed. Georg Heinrich Pertz. Hannover: Hahn, 1835–1889. IV: 819–20.

Weber, Gottfried. *Gottfrieds von Straßburg: Tristan und die Krise des hochmittelalterlichen Weltbildes um 1200*. 2 vols. Stuttgart: Metzler, 1953.

Weber, Gottfried, and Werner Hoffmann. *Gottfried von Straßburg*. Stuttgart: Metzler, 1981.

Wehrli, Max. "Der Tristan Gottfrieds von Straßburg." *Trivium* 4 (1946): 81–117. Rpt. in *Gottfried von Straßburg*. Ed. Alois Wolf. Darmstadt: Wissenschaftliche Buchgesellschaft, 1973. 97–134.

Weinfurter, Stefan. *Heinrich II. (1002–1024): Herrscher am Ende der Zeiten*. Regensburg: Pustet, 1999.

Wenz-Haubfleisch, Annegret. "Der Kult der heiligen Kunigunde an der Wende vom 12. Zum 13. Jahrhundert im Spiegel ihrer Mirakelsammlung." *Kunigunde: Eine Kaiserin an der Jahrtausendwende*. Ed. Ingrid Baumgärtner. Kassel: Furore, 1997. 162–76.

Werkmüller, Dieter. "Handhafte Tat." *Handwörterbuch zur deutschen Rechtsgeschichte*. 5 vols. Ed. Adalbert Erler, U. Kornblum, and G. Dilcher. Berlin: E. Schmidt, 1964–1998. I: cols. 1965–73.

Werner, Otmar. "Entwicklungstendenzen in der mittelhochdeutschen Verserzählung." *Zeitschrift für deutsche Philologie* 85 (1966): 369–406.

Wesle, Carl, ed. *Das Rolandslied des Pfaffen Konrad*. 2nd ed. Ed. Peter Wapnewski. Tübingen: Niemeyer, 1967.

White, Stephen D. "Proposing the Ordeal and Avoiding It: Strategy and Power in Western French Litigation, 1050–1110." *Cultures of Power: Lordship, Status and Process in Twelfth-Century Europe*. Ed. Thomas N. Bisson. Philadelphia: U of Pennsylvania P, 1995. 89–123.

Whitman, Jon. *Allegory: The Dynamics of an Ancient and Medieval Technique.* Oxford: Clarendon P, 1986.

Widmaier, Sigrid. *Das Recht im "Reinhart Fuchs."* Berlin: De Gruyter, 1993.

Willoweit, Dietmar. "Gewalt und Verbrechen, Strafe und Sühne im alten Würzburg-Offene Probleme der deutschen strafrechtsgeschichtlichen Forschung." *Die Entstehung des öffentlichen Strafrechts: Bestandaufnahme eines europäischen Forschungsproblems.* Ed. Willoweit. Cologne, Weimar & Vienna: Böhlau, 1999. 215–33.

Willson, H. B. "The Old and the New Law in Gottfried's Tristan." *Modern Language Review* 60 (1965). 212–24.

Wolf, A. *Gottfried von Straßburg und die Mythe von Tristan und Isolde.* Darmstadt: Wissenschaftliche Buchgesellschaft, 1989.

Wood, Ian. "Disputes in Late Fifth- and Sixth-Century Gaul: Some Problems." *The Settlement of Disputes in Early Medieval Europe.* Cambridge & New York: Cambridge UP, 1986. 7–22.

York, E. C. "Isolt's Ordeal: English Legal Customs in the Medieval Tristan Legend." *Studies in Philology* 68 (1971): 1–9.

Zacharias, Rainer. "Die Blutrache im deutschen Mittelalter." *Zeitschrift für deutsche Altertum* 91 (1962): 167–201.

Zagolla, R. *Der Karlmeinet und seine Fassung vom Rolandslied des Pfaffen Konrad.* Göppingen: Kümmerle, 1988.

Zandt, Gertrud J. "Bemerkungen zu einer Neuausgabe einiger Abschnitte des Rolandteils aus der *Karlmeinet*-Kompilation." *Amsterdamer Beiträge zur Älteren Germanistik* 30 (1990): 151–58.

———. "Zur Karlmeinet Kompilation." In *Cyclification: The Development of Narrative Cycles in the Chansons de Geste and the Arthurian Romances,* ed. Bart Besemusca, Willem P. Gerritsen, Corry Hogetoorn, and Orlanda S. H. Lie. Amsterdam: North-Holland, 1994.

Zender, Matthias. "Die Verehrung des Hl. Karl im Gebiet des mittelalterlichen Reiches." *Karl der Große: Lebenswerk und Nachleben.* Vol. 4. Düsseldorf: Schwann, 1967. 100–112.

Ziegler, Vickie L. "Points of Law at the Point of a Sword: Tristan's Duel with Morolt in the North Sea World." *The North Sea World in the Middle Ages.* Ed. Thomas R. Liszka and Lorna E. M. Walker. Dublin: Four Courts P, 2001. 33–51.

Zips, Manfred. "Tristan und die Ebersymbolik." *Beiträge zur Geschichte der deutschen Sprache und Literatur* 94 (1972): 134–52.

Index

Aachen, 102, 103, 107, 110, 111, 176, 180, 182
Abou-El-Haj, Barbara, 111
accusation, 3, 5, 6, 7, 8, 9, 13, 27, 28, 33, 36, 41, 45, 54, 56, 58, 59, 60, 61, 85, 89, 95, 105, 108, 123, 124, 125, 126, 127, 142, 146, 147, 150, 154, 159, 161, 168, 180, 181, 193
adjuratio, 127, 149, 162, 169
adultery, ix, x, 6, 7, 16, 114, 116, 123, 124, 127, 141, 146, 147, 148, 164, 169
Alcuin, 102, 103, 107, 110, 111, 176, 180, 182
Alda, 57, 58, 81, 106, 107, 176, 180, 181. See also Alite
Alite, 57, 176
allegory, 122, 123, 135, 136, 139, 140
Althoff, Gerd, 19, 83, 84, 86, 89, 90, 91, 92, 93, 96, 97, 98, 100, 103, 136, 166
ansprache, 142. See also accusation
antwort, 142. See also defense
antwürte, 142
Ashe, Geoffrey, 132
Asmus, Herbert, 95, 96
aspersio, 127

Baist, G., 100
Baldwin, John W., xi, 12, 13, 14, 16, 18, 19, 141, 144, 145, 146, 154, 160, 163, 164, 165, 167, 171
Baligan, Baligain, 33, 109
Bartlett, Robert, 11, 12, 13, 14, 15, 16, 17, 18, 19, 137, 138, 139, 142, 144, 145, 160, 161, 163, 173
Baumgärtner, Ingrid, 163, 164
bears, 93, 107, 180
Becher, Matthias, 79, 80
Bechstein, R., 137, 163
Beckers, Hartmut, 81, 102, 103
begrüezen, 106
beheading, 68, 102, 108, 178, 183. See also decapitation; execution
Béroul, 114, 115, 132, 133
Bertau, Karl, 79, 80
Bestul, Thomas, 74, 75, 106, 107, 113
Betz, Werner, 134
Beumann, Helmut, 79
Beyerle, Konrad, 89, 90
bezîhen, 142
Bible, Revised English, 15, 113, 139, 161
Binabel, 34, 46, 47, 99, 100. See also Pinabel
binding, bound, 3, 5, 34, 39, 49, 50, 55, 56, 61, 71, 73, 86, 87, 89, 94, 100, 105, 108, 153, 173, 176, 179, 180, 181
Bindschedler, M., 133
birds, 106, 180: eagle, 106, 180; sparrow hawk, 106, 180; white falcon, 106, 180
Blanschandiez, Blantschadis, 42, 97, 175
Bloch, R. Howard, 78
blood revenge, 35, 83, 86, 93, 106
boar, 122, 140, 185
boessen, buoze, 34, 37, 93, 106

Böhm, Sabine, 82, 90, 99
Book of Daniel, 6, 15, 82, 132, 161, 172
Bonath, Gesa, 144
Bongert, Yvonne, 13, 16, 17, 18, 138
Borovsky, Samu, 161
Bouchard, Constance Brittain, 18, 85, 86, 87
Boulet-Sautel, Marguerite, 18, 19, 141, 142
Boutet, Dominique, 77, 78
Brandt, Rüdiger, 82, 90, 94, 95, 96, 98, 103
Brault, Gerard, 77, 78, 96
Brother Robert, 115, 126, 132, 135, 137, 144
Brown, Peter, 11, 19
Brundage, James, 16, 141, 160, 164, 173
Brunner, Karl, 161
Brunner, Otto, 82, 83, 84, 86, 90, 92, 93, 95, 96, 97, 98, 99, 102, 103
Buchda, Gerald, 85, 92, 136, 164
Buschinger, Danielle, 79, 134
Bynum, Caroline Walker, 112, 113

Canisius-Loppnow, Petra, 28, 79, 80, 82, 86, 87, 89, 93, 94, 95, 96, 97, 99, 100, 101, 103, 104
Carbasse, Jean-Marie, 17, 18, 137
Carlen, L., 103
Carolingians, 1, 21, 22, 25, 148
Celestin III, 4, 163
census, 117
champion, 8, 12, 18, 52, 62, 65, 99, 100, 118, 119, 151, 177
Chanson de Rolan (Turoldus), x, 21, 22, 23, 39, 42, 48, 77, 78, 82, 92, 99. *See also Rolandslied* and *Song of Roland*
Charlemagne, i, x, xi, 10, 21, 22, 25, 27, 64, 78, 79, 81, 92, 98, 102, 103, 114, 120, 122, 148, 151, 164. For listings as character in Der Stricker's *Karl der Grosse, see also* Karl
Chinca, Mark, 135
chivalry, 116, 119
Christi Leiden in einer Vision Geschaut, 74, 113. *See also* passion narratives
Cohen, Esther, 103, 112, 113
Colman, Rebecca V., 19
Combridge, Rosemary N., 133, 135, 137, 140, 141, 142, 143, 144, 161
compensation, 57, 60, 93, 97, 106
compurgation, 109
compurgator, 4, 5, 14, 15
concilje, 124
confession, 9, 12, 58, 70, 106, 111, 148, 150, 169, 188
Conrad, Hermann, 17, 94
Cornwall, 115, 116, 117, 118, 120, 137, 184, 185
council, i, 1, 10, 18, 41, 48, 57, 59, 66, 70, 74, 84, 86, 95, 124, 126, 128, 130, 141, 142, 151, 159, 164, 168, 170, 171, 175, 177, 181, 186, 187
Council of Clermont, 18
Cram, Kurt Georg, 17, 137
crucifixion, 72, 73, 74, 75, 112

Daniel 3:27, 15
David, King David, 27, 47, 48, 54, 78, 85, 99, 109, 121, 131, 135, 139, 177
Davis, Wendy, 13, 14, 173
De Boor, Helmut, 80, 133, 135, 139, 160, 172
decapitation, 73.
    See also beheading; executions
Dederich, 64, 65, 66, 67, 68, 109, 110, 182, 183
Der Stricker, i, x, 5, 11, 15, 19, 21, 23, 24, 25, 26, 27, 28, 29, 30, 31, 32, 33, 34, 35, 36, 37,

38, 39, 40, 41, 42, 44, 45, 46,
47, 48, 49, 50, 51, 52, 53, 54,
55, 56, 57, 58, 59, 60, 61, 63,
64, 65, 66, 67, 68, 70, 71, 72,
75, 76, 77, 78, 79, 81, 82, 84,
85, 86, 87, 88, 89, 90, 91, 93,
94, 95, 96, 97, 98, 99, 100,
101, 102, 103, 104, 105, 106,
108, 109, 110, 121, 150, 168,
169, 170, 171, 172, 173, 175,
177, 179, 180, 182, 195, 197
Der Stricker, works by: "Das
heisse Eisen," 168, 171, 195;
Karl der Grosse, x, xiii, 5, 10,
15, 21, 23, 24, 26, 27, 37, 39,
40, 41, 43, 47, 49, 54, 55, 57,
71, 78, 84, 89, 121, 171, 175
devil, 33, 44, 49, 67, 97, 101, 104,
107, 110, 122, 123, 131, 140,
153, 159, 167, 178, 186, 189
Diarmaid, 114
Dickerson, Harold D., Jr., 136,
144
Dietrich, 27, 33, 34, 47, 48, 49,
65, 67, 68, 76, 99, 101, 109,
131, 139, 177, 178
diffidatio, 40
Dilcher, G., 12, 14, 81, 91, 92,
100, 107, 136, 137
dismemberment, 113
dispute settlement, x, 7, 11, 25,
172
Distelkamp, B., 89, 90, 102, 164
Dobozy, 12, 14, 107
Duggan, Joseph J., 78
Dümmler, Ernst Ludwig, 161
Durndart, 27, 49, 67, 99, 101,
104, 107, 177, 178, 180
Dyonisius, 59, 181

Ebel, Wilhelm, 14, 15
Ebernand von Erfurt, x, 137, 142,
149–60, 162, 163, 164, 166,
189, 193, 194

Ebernand von Erfurt, works by:
Heinrich und Kunegunde, x,
137, 142, 149–60, 162, 163,
164, 166; translation, 190–92
eigen, 31, 89, 90
Eilhart von Oberg, 114, 115
Einhard, 22, 23, 78, 99
eit, 117, 118, 129, 136
Elliot, Dyan, 160, 161, 162, 166
Engelhard, Archbishop of
Cologne, 3
England, 9, 12, 16, 19, 110, 120,
184
Entscheidungseid, 13
êre, 28, 30, 85, 86
erkennen, 64
Erler, Adalbert, 12, 13, 15, 16,
17, 81, 91, 92, 100, 103, 107,
136, 138, 143, 162
Ernst, Ulrich, 135, 139
Eugenius III, 151
execution, 28, 50, 53, 70, 71, 72,
73, 75, 77, 94, 102, 103, 111,
112, 113, 178, 183; by
beheading, 68, 102, 108, 178,
183; by burning, 19, 73, 98,
148, 149, 151, 183, 188; by
hanging, 32, 73, 102, 108,
111, 112; involving animals,
71, 72, 73, 105, 106, 107, 183

family, 6, 25, 26, 28, 29, 30, 32,
36, 38, 45, 46, 47, 48, 50, 51,
52, 53, 54, 55, 56, 58, 60, 61,
62, 63, 65, 66, 73, 76, 84, 87,
88, 93, 96, 98, 99, 102, 104,
109, 126, 152, 176, 181, 184,
187
Farrier, Susan E., 81, 102, 103
Fastnachtsspiel, 10
Feistner, Edith, 81
Feldmann, Hans Christian, 165
Ferrante, Joan, 142, 145
feud, *Fehde,* i, 10, 11, 21, 22, 24,
25, 26, 31, 32, 35, 38, 39, 40,

41, 42, 43, 44, 46, 47, 51, 52, 53, 56, 60, 61, 62, 63, 69, 70, 76, 82, 83, 84, 86, 91, 92, 93, 94, 95, 96, 97, 98, 99, 102, 103, 105, 109, 112, 172, 176, 177
fidelity, 7, 27, 34, 35, 50, 84, 85, 89, 93, 97, 110, 115, 117, 124, 129, 146, 159, 168, 169, 175, 179, 195, 196, 197
Fischer, Hanns, 134, 172
Folz, Robert, 78, 79, 92, 102, 103, 161, 163, 164, 166
Forsyth, Richard D., 16
Fouracre, Paul, 13, 14, 173
Fourquet, Jean, 134
Fourth Lateran Council, i, 1, 10, 18, 48, 70, 74, 130, 151, 164, 168
Fraher, Richard M., 136
France, 12, 13, 18, 59, 77, 78, 98, 103, 141, 142
Francis, Saint, 73
Franks, 18, 22, 25, 55, 56, 60, 61, 101, 104, 105, 108, 175, 176, 179, 181
Franks, Salian, 18, 25
Franz, Adolph, 19, 142, 143
Frederick I [Barbarossa], 23
Frederick II, 8, 23
Freytag, Wiebke, 134, 144
Friedensordnungen, 30
Friederich, Count of Altena, 97
Fuhrmann, Horst, 80

Gal, Alexander, 15, 17, 137, 161
Ganelon, x, 11, 18, 21, 42, 87
Genelun, x, 5, 11, 14, 22, 23, 24, 25, 26, 27, 28, 29, 30, 31, 32, 33, 34, 35, 36, 37, 38, 39, 40, 41, 42, 43, 44, 45, 46, 47, 48, 49, 50, 51, 52, 53, 54, 56, 57, 60, 62, 65, 68, 69, 70, 71, 75, 76, 80, 82, 84, 85, 86, 87, 88, 89, 90, 91, 92, 93, 94, 95, 96, 97, 98, 99, 100, 101, 102, 104, 105, 106, 107, 109, 111, 112, 120, 121, 122, 172, 175, 176, 177, 178, 179
Gaudemet, Jean, 12, 19, 142
Geith, Karl-Ernst, 79, 80, 81, 82, 89, 90, 99
geloben, 153, 164
gelübede, 117, 126
gelüppet, 131, 140, 144
Gerbert, 12, 18
Gerbert, works by: *Violette*, 18, 19
Gerhart, 71
gerihte, 36, 90, 110, 142, 143, 157
Gernhuber, Joachim, 84, 103
Gesta Karoli (Notker der Stammler), 23
gewißheit, 143
giluppi, 144
Glogau, Dirk, 140
glove, 53, 61, 65, 101, 103, 110, 120, 175, 179, 181, 182, 185
Goliath, 47, 48, 99, 109, 121, 131
Gold, Pamela, 160
Goldschmidt-Kunzer, Ruth, 134
Goodich, Michael, 13, 106, 111, 112, 167
gotes reht, 124
Gottfried von Straßburg, x, 10, 114, 115, 116, 118, 119, 120, 121, 122, 123, 124, 125, 126, 127, 128, 129, 130, 131, 132, 133, 134, 135, 136, 137, 138, 139, 140, 142, 143, 144, 170, 171, 185, 186, 187
Gottfried von Straßburg, works by: *Tristan und Isold*, 132, 133, 134, 140
Grainne, 114
Graus, Frantisek, 87
Green, Dennis, 116, 134, 137, 138
Grimm, Jacob, 136, 140, 144
Grimm, Wilhelm, 136, 140
Grosse, Siegfried, 107

Grübmüller, Klaus, 134
guilt, 1, 6, 9, 18, 25, 31, 32, 33, 36, 37, 38, 39, 45, 49, 57, 58, 60, 68, 69, 70, 84, 91, 100, 107, 120, 121, 125, 136, 149, 166, 169, 176, 183, 191
Gudian, Gunter, 94
Gundeluff, 60, 108, 181
Guth, Klaus, 164, 166

Haacke, Dieter, 81
Hahn, Gerhard, 80
hanging, 32, 73, 102, 108, 111, 112
Hattenhauer, Hans, 13, 14, 15, 17, 111, 136, 140, 143, 144, 158, 162, 166, 173
Haug, Walther, 134, 137, 138, 140
Heers, Jacques, 98
Heilsgeschichte, 22
Heinemann, Edward A., 77, 78, 206
Heinrich II, Heinrich, 83, 84, 98, 123, 125, 137, 142, 146, 147, 148, 149, 150, 151, 152, 153, 154, 155, 156, 157, 158, 159, 160, 161, 162, 163, 164, 165, 166, 167, 170, 189, 190, 191, 192
heresy, 6
Herimann of Reichenau, 147, 161
Hexter, R. J., 15, 144
Hirsch, Hans, 85, 86, 87, 88, 89, 90, 93, 94, 95, 99, 101, 140
His, Rudolf, 83, 90, 92, 94, 95, 102, 105, 112
Hlawitschka, Eduard, 164
Hoffmann, Werner, 132, 133
Holger, Eckhardt, 143
holmgangr, 138
Holzapfel, O., 138
Holzhauer, Heinz, 13, 14, 16, 17, 83, 84, 99, 100, 101, 136, 138, 143

hostages, 22, 48, 50, 61, 65, 66, 100, 102, 112, 177, 178, 181, 182
Hruodland, 24
Huber, Christoph, 132, 133, 134, 135, 139
hulde, 31, 32, 50, 89, 91, 93, 102, 158, 166
Huldeverlust, 31, 32, 89, 90
Hüpper-Dröge, Dagmar, 18, 100, 101
Hyams, Paul R., 11, 12, 13, 18, 142, 143

Iceland, 138, 139
Innocent II, 15
Innocent III, 15, 93, 144, 151, 163
inquests, 1, 2
inquisition, 9, 19
inziht, 125, 141, 142
Iseut, 115, 132, 154, 164
Isold, Isolde, x, xi, 5, 6, 7, 15, 16, 114, 115, 116, 119, 120, 123, 124, 125, 126, 127, 128, 129, 130, 131, 132, 133, 134, 135, 140, 141, 142, 143, 144, 146, 154, 158, 164, 169, 170, 171, 186, 187
Isönd, 126, 133, 142

Jackson, W. T. H., 116, 132, 133, 134, 135, 143
Jaeger, C. Stephen, 140
Jäschke, Kurt-Ulrich, 164
Jones, Martin H., 138
Judas, 54, 71, 72, 76, 97, 104, 112, 113, 178, 183
judgment of God/*judicium Dei*, 2, 7, 8, 9, 14, 28, 87, 118, 127, 135, 137, 151, 191
judicial duel, ix, 8, 9, 12, 17, 18, 21, 27, 28, 36, 45, 46, 47, 52, 60, 61, 63, 65, 66, 67, 68, 77, 81, 82, 87, 97, 98, 99, 100,

108, 109, 110, 116, 117, 118,
120, 121, 122, 123, 124, 129,
130, 131, 134, 135, 136, 137,
138, 177, 181, 182, 183, 185
jury, juries, ix, 9, 13, 177
justice, 2, 3, 7, 11, 14, 17, 23,
25, 26, 28, 29, 34, 44, 45, 46,
47, 49, 51, 52, 53, 68, 72, 76,
77, 78, 84, 86, 90, 97, 98, 99,
103, 112, 113, 116, 119, 121,
123, 137, 138, 150, 158, 165,
172, 177, 184, 185, 186, 192;
compensatory, 11, 25, 38, 52,
101; immanent, 2, 14

Kaiserchronik, x, 78, 80, 88, 123,
137, 146, 147, 148, 149, 150,
151, 159, 160, 161, 162, 167,
170
kamp, 109
Kanzeler, P., 102
Karácsonyi, János, 161
Karl (character in Stricker's *Karl der Grosse*), x, 5, 14, 22, 23, 24, 25, 26, 27, 28, 29, 30, 31, 32, 33, 34, 35, 36, 38, 39, 40, 42, 43, 44, 45, 46, 47, 48, 49, 50, 51, 52, 53, 54, 55, 56, 57, 58, 59, 60, 61, 62, 63, 64, 65, 66, 67, 68, 70, 71, 75, 76, 77, 78, 79, 80, 84, 85, 86, 87, 88, 89, 90, 91, 92, 93, 94, 95, 96, 97, 98, 99, 100, 101, 102, 104, 105, 106, 107, 108, 109, 110, 111, 119, 172, 175, 176, 177, 178, 179, 180, 181, 182, 183, 188
Karl der Grosse (Der Stricker), i, x, xiii, 5, 10, 15, 21, 23, 24, 26, 27, 37, 39, 40, 41, 43, 47, 49, 54, 55, 57, 59, 71, 78, 79, 81, 82, 84, 88, 89, 121, 171, 175
Karl der Große und die schottischen Heiligen (ed. Frank Shaw), 110
karles reht, 23

Karlmeinet, i, x, 10, 11, 21, 23, 24, 31, 50, 51, 52, 53, 54, 55, 56, 57, 58, 61, 62, 63, 64, 65, 66, 67, 68, 69, 70, 71, 72, 73, 74, 75, 76, 77, 81, 84, 102, 103, 171, 172, 179, 180, 182, 183
Karlsepik, 10, 18, 21, 23, 64, 66, 71, 111, 131, 132, 135, 139, 182
Kaufmann, Ekkehard, 83, 84, 91, 92, 94, 95, 97, 99, 103, 105, 108, 111, 113, 136
Kay, Sarah, 77
Keller, Adalbert von, 84, 102, 103
Kern, Fritz, 80
Kerr, Margaret H., 16
Kerth, T. A., 134
Kieckhefer, Richard, 112, 113
klagen, 41, 95
Klauser, Renate, 163, 166, 167
Klein, Dorothea, 81, 86, 89, 97, 104
Klibansky, Erich, 94
Köbler, Gerhard, 11, 13, 14, 109, 137
Köbler, M., 103
Kocher, Gernot, 91, 92, 101
Köhler, Erich, 78
Kolb, Herbert, 13, 18, 134, 141, 142, 143
Kölbing, E., 138
Konecny, Sylvia, 161
Konrad von Würzburg, 93, 98
Konstantin, Emperor, 99
Konzil, 141, 220
Köpf, Gerhard, 172, 173
Kornblum, U., 12, 14, 15, 91, 92, 100, 103, 107
Köster, Rudolf, 82
Krause, H., 89
Krause, Hermann, 137
Kroeschell, Karl, 14, 78, 87, 88, 92, 137
Kross, Renate, 79

Kucaba, Kelly, 134
Kuhn, Hugo, 139
Kunegunde, Kunigunde, i, x, 6, 7, 19, 49, 58, 117, 119, 123, 124, 125, 126, 131, 132, 137, 142, 146, 147, 148, 149, 150, 151, 152, 153, 154, 155, 156, 157, 158, 159, 160, 161, 162, 163, 164, 165, 166, 167, 170, 171, 173, 189, 190, 191, 193, 194
Künßberg, Eberhard von, 94
Kurtan, 67, 110, 183
Küsters, Urban, 135, 137

Lacy, Norris, 132, 133
LaCroix, Daniel, 132
landes reht, lantrecht, 59, 63, 118
Landfrieden, 26, 83, 96, 97; Mainzer, 26, 83
Langbein, John H., 19
lant, 55, 59, 68, 69, 88, 107, 137
lant unde reht, 137
Lanz-Hubmann, Irene, 135
laster, 32, 62, 90, 109, 156
Laufs, A., 107, 137
law, ix, x, xi, xii, 1, 3, 5, 6, 7, 9, 10, 11, 13, 14, 17, 18, 23, 24, 25, 26, 32, 33, 34, 35, 43, 44, 45, 46, 47, 49, 50, 51, 52, 53, 58, 61, 63, 64, 74, 77, 78, 79, 80, 81, 83, 84, 88, 90, 91, 92, 96, 97, 99, 101, 104, 106, 108, 111, 112, 117, 118, 119, 120, 123, 124, 128, 134, 135, 137, 138, 141, 143, 151, 165, 170, 171, 185, 186; natural, 6; Roman, 1, 9, 13, 74, 106, 111, 117, 123
Lea, Henry Charles, 14, 15, 17, 18, 137, 138, 142
legends, i, ix, x, 6, 10, 14, 19, 22, 23, 79, 80, 81, 99, 102, 110, 111, 113, 116, 119, 121, 122, 124, 125, 126, 127, 131, 132, 134, 135, 138, 142, 144, 146, 147, 148, 150, 151, 152, 153, 158, 160, 162, 164, 168, 170, 171
Legner, Anton, 111
lehen, 31, 89, 90
Lehnsgericht, 32
leit, 37, 40, 41, 42, 96, 143
lên, 107
Lévy, Jean-Philippe, 19
Lex Gundobad, 7
Lexer, Matthias von, 89, 90, 91, 92, 95, 96, 101, 104, 106, 107, 109, 110, 111, 136, 140, 141, 142, 143, 161, 164
Liermann, Hans, 144
lions, 71, 99, 107, 180, 183
Liszka, Thomas R., 133
liument, 125, 141, 142
Liutprand, 18
Loomis, Roger Sherman, 132
Louis the Pious, 11
Lübben, August, 104, 106, 108, 109, 110, 111
lüppe, 140
lüppen, luppen, 140, 144

Mainz, 26, 83, 84, 103, 133
Mälzer, Marion, 134, 142, 143
mannes reht, 108
manslaughter, 45, 84, 95
Marchello-Nizia, Christiane, 132, 133
märe, 168, 172
Margetts, John, 82, 172
marital relations, 168
Mark, King, 115, 118, 120, 121, 122, 124, 125, 126, 127, 128, 135, 136, 138, 141, 142, 143, 153, 154, 169, 184, 185, 186, 187
marriage, 16, 57, 61, 115, 141, 143, 146, 147, 151, 152, 153, 154, 160, 161, 162, 163, 164, 165, 168, 170, 176; chaste,

unconsummated, 146, 151, 152, 153, 160, 162, 165
Marschall, D., 111
Marsilie, 40, 42, 45, 69, 93, 95, 97, 101, 175, 179
Mary, 102, 158, 160
Maurer, Friedrich, 133, 135
McCann, W. J., 132
McNamara, Jo Ann, 160
Meineid, meyne eyde, 111, 143, 144. *See also* perjury
Merback, Mitchell B., 106, 107, 108, 111, 112, 113
Mergell, Bodo, 133
Meurer, D., 94
Michalsky, Tanja, 163, 164
Miller, William Ian, 94
Milsom, S. F. C., 12, 13
miracle, 12, 150, 151, 152, 157, 158, 160, 163, 176, 192
missedait, missedat, missetat, mis-dôn, 60, 90, 111
Mitteis, Heinrich, 84, 96, 103
Moignet, Gérard, 77, 78
Moisan, André, 79, 110
Morold, Morolt, x, 115, 116, 117, 118, 119, 120, 121, 122, 123, 124, 125, 129, 131, 133, 135, 136, 137, 138, 139, 140, 141, 144, 184, 185, 186
Morris, Colin, 11, 12, 13, 18, 142, 143
mort, 35, 39, 40, 92, 94, 97, 99, 109, 110
Moss, Claude B., 144
Müller, Reinhard, 141
Munske, Horst Haider, 90, 91, 143
Munzel-Everling, Dietlinde, 79
murder, 6, 8, 30, 36, 39, 40, 41, 45, 46, 50, 58, 65, 67, 68, 84, 92, 93, 94, 95, 96, 97, 98, 99, 100, 105, 109, 110, 114, 169, 177, 179, 180, 183

Muslims, 21, 22, 85, 95, 96, 104, 175, 179, 181, 183

Nauen, Hans-Günther, 144
Naymis, Names, 28, 55, 94, 110, 179, 182
Nellman, Eberhard, 160, 167
Newald, Richard, 80, 160, 172
Newstead, H., 134
Nichols, S., 78
Notker der Stammler, 23
Notker der Stammler, works by: *Gesta Karoli*, 23
Nottarp, Hermann, 11, 12, 17, 18, 19, 101, 137, 173
nudity, 112
Nussbaum-Kleager, Maria, 135

oath breaking, 5, 117, 185
oath helpers, oath helping, 2, 3, 6, 14, 126, 142, 154
oaths, x, 1, 2, 3, 4, 5, 6, 7, 8, 12, 13, 14, 15, 17, 22, 33, 42, 48, 50, 60, 61, 66, 67, 68, 97, 100, 108, 115, 116, 117, 118, 119, 120, 123, 125, 126, 127, 128, 129, 130, 131, 134, 136, 137, 142, 144, 149, 153, 154, 158, 159, 160, 168, 169, 175, 181, 182, 185, 187; promissory, 117, 136; purgative, 117
Ogris, W., 100
Ohly, Friedrich, 80, 81, 82, 97, 102, 104, 113
Okken, Lambertus, 138, 139, 140, 143
Old Norse, 121, 126, 132, 135, 138
Oliver, 55, 58, 106, 107, 180, 181
ordeal, i, ix, x, xi, 1, 2, 3, 4, 6, 7, 8, 9, 10, 11, 12, 13, 14, 15, 16, 17, 18, 19, 24, 34, 36, 46, 47, 48, 49, 61, 65, 74, 75, 76, 93, 101, 110, 114, 115, 116, 117, 118, 119, 120, 121, 122, 123,

124, 125, 126, 127, 128, 129, 130, 131, 132, 133, 134, 135, 136, 138, 141, 142, 143, 144, 145, 146, 147, 148, 149, 150, 151, 153, 154, 157, 158, 159, 160, 161, 162, 163, 166, 167, 168, 169, 170, 171, 173, 186, 187, 188, 191, 195, 196; by battle, i, iv, ix, x, xii, 1, 3, 6, 7, 8, 9, 10, 11, 12, 13, 16, 17, 18, 19, 21, 28, 34, 38, 42, 47, 48, 49, 55, 56, 61, 63, 64, 65, 66, 67, 75, 87, 88, 96, 99, 100, 101, 104, 107, 109, 110, 114, 115, 116, 117, 118, 119, 120, 121, 122, 123, 127, 130, 131, 133, 135, 136, 138, 139, 140, 147, 151, 168, 170, 171, 177, 179, 180, 181, 182, 183, 184, 185, 186; bilateral, 1, 10, 117, 130, 131, 135; of the cross, 1, 4, 11, 134; demise of, 1, 12, 75, 144; by fire, i, iv, ix, x, xi, xii, 1, 6, 7, 10, 15, 16, 19, 114, 115, 116, 118, 119, 123, 125, 127, 128, 130, 131, 133, 135, 143, 146, 149, 151, 154, 159, 160, 168, 169, 170, 171, 186, 187, 196; unilateral, 1, 9, 10, 12, 117, 130, 131, 135, 144, 171; by water, 1, 7, 12, 16, 17, 18, 149
Ott, Norbert, 78, 82
Ott-Meimberg, Marianne, 78, 79, 80, 81
Otto: character in Stricker's *Karl der Grosse,* 26, 28, 31, 32, 33, 34, 35, 44, 57, 79, 88, 89, 90, 91, 93, 106, 107, 176; character in *Karlmeinet,* 56, 57, 105, 106, 109, 179, 180
Otto III, 23
Ottonians, 35
Oyger, Ogier, 66, 71, 110, 113

Pappenheim, M., 11
passion narratives, 74, 75, 113
Patrick, Saint, 66, 67, 68, 77, 110, 111, 182
Paul, Hermann, 107
Payen, Jean-Charles, 132
Pensel, Franzjosef, 136
perjury, 3, 4, 5, 7, 14, 15, 67, 100, 117, 119, 128, 150
Peter the Chanter, 12, 129, 151
Peters, Edward, 14, 15, 17, 18, 19, 106
Philipp von Schwaben, 98
Pinabel, 33, 45, 46, 47, 48, 49, 52, 60, 62, 63, 64, 65, 67, 68, 99, 100, 109, 110, 111, 121, 122, 131, 177, 178, 181, 182, 183. *See also* Binabel
Piquet, F., 133, 135, 137, 144
Planck, Julius Wilhelm, 13, 17, 85, 91, 92, 93, 94, 108, 137, 138, 139, 142
pledge, 8
plowshares, 7, 19, 147, 151, 157, 158, 160, 166, 167, 191, 192, 194
Plyley, Michael J., 16
poison, 115, 119, 123, 129, 130, 131, 140, 144, 186
Pötschke, Dieter, 101
Prague, 23
Preiser, W., 92
Priebsch, Robert, 113
Priest Konrad, Pfaffe Konrad, Konrad, x, 9, 14, 22, 23, 24, 27, 29, 30, 36, 37, 38, 40, 41, 46, 47, 48, 49, 50, 52, 53, 55, 64, 67, 72, 77, 79, 80, 81, 82, 84, 87, 89, 94, 95, 97, 99, 100, 101, 103, 104, 108, 120, 179
primus inter pares, 141
proof, i, ix, 1, 2, 5, 6, 9, 13, 17, 34, 38, 47, 58, 62, 70, 81, 91, 105, 106, 110, 113, 125, 126, 131, 136, 137, 142, 147, 148,

149, 153, 186, 187, 195;
irrational, 1, 2; rational, 2, 6, 9
property disputes, 18

Quinn, Esther, 145

rache, wrach, 69, 70, 92, 111
Ragotzky, Hedda, 80
Ranke, Friedrich, 132
Regensburg, 80, 110, 147, 162
Regino of Prüm, 161
reht, 23, 33, 47, 50, 88, 89, 93, 99, 101, 118, 124, 129, 137, 136
Reimbot, 150
Reinigungseid, 13
relics, saints', 3, 6, 8, 66, 67, 68, 77, 80, 110, 111, 128, 150, 182, 183, 187
reparations, 34, 36, 37, 39, 43, 45, 51, 52, 56, 76, 93, 180
Reuter, Timothy, 83, 84, 86, 97, 98
Richardis, i, x, 49, 58, 119, 124, 131, 146, 147, 148, 149, 150, 154, 159, 160, 161, 162, 170, 171, 173, 188
Richter, Horst, 80, 103, 104
rihten, 35
Rocher, Daniel, 82, 172
Roland, i, 10, 11, 21, 22, 23, 24, 25, 26, 27, 28, 29, 30, 31, 32, 33, 34, 36, 38, 39, 41, 42, 43, 44, 45, 46, 47, 49, 50, 51, 52, 53, 54, 55, 57, 58, 60, 62, 63, 64, 65, 66, 68, 69, 71, 76, 82, 84, 85, 86, 87, 88, 93, 94, 95, 96, 98, 101, 102, 103, 104, 105, 106, 107, 109, 121, 175, 176, 177, 179, 180, 181, 182, 183. *See also* Hruodland, Rolant
Rolandslied, x, 9, 22, 23, 24, 27, 28, 31, 35, 36, 37, 38, 39, 40, 41, 42, 45, 47, 49, 51, 53, 54, 55, 57, 71. *See also Chanson de Roland* and *Song of Roland*

Rolant, 55, 69
Rolf, F. Hans, 144
Rossi, Marguerite, 82, 92, 93, 98
Roth, Elizabeth, 19, 162, 163
Rousset, Paul, 14, 17
Rowland, Beryl, 107
Rudolf von Habsburg, 13
rules of combat, 12
Rychner, Jean, 78

Sachs, Hans, 10, 19, 171
Sachsenspiegel, 12, 50, 79, 89, 94, 108, 118
sacrament, 12
sagas, 138, 139, 147
Salic Law, 151
Saurma, Jeltsch, Lieselotte E., 79, 99
Schach, Paul, 133, 137, 142, 144
Schanze, Frieder, 78
Scheyling, R., 142
Schild, Wolfgang, 16, 102, 113, 134, 135, 142, 145
Schleissner, Margaret, 140
Schlosser, H., 141
Schmidt, Eberhard, 83, 93, 94, 97, 98, 99, 102
Schmidt-Lornsen, Jutta, 14
Schmidt-Wiegand, Ruth, 14, 78, 81, 83, 85, 91, 92, 93, 94, 95, 98, 101, 112, 136, 160
Schmitz, Wolfgang, 112
Schnell, Rüdiger, 82, 85, 100, 101, 102, 117, 133, 134, 135, 136, 137, 139, 142, 143, 144
Schoepperle, Gertrude, 132
Schröder, Edward, 137, 160
Schröder, Richard, 94
Schröder, Werner, 134
Schroeder, K. P., 107, 137
Schröpfer, Hans-Jürgen, 162, 163, 166
Schulz, Monika, 80, 82, 92, 94, 112
Schüppert, Helga, 162, 163

Schwab, D., 89
Schwab, Ute, 16
Schwarz, W., 16
Schwentner, Bernhard, 18
Schwinekörper, Berent, 103, 138
Schwob, Anton, 88
Scott, James Walker, 163
Sebastian, Saint, 112
di Segni, Lothario, 151
Sellert, W., 141
sexual offenses, 6, 16, 151
Shaw, Frank, 110
sicherheit, 117, 136
Song of Roland, 10, 77, 120, 131.
  See also *Chanson de Roland* and
  Rolandslied
Spahr, Blake Lee, 135, 136, 138,
  140
Spierenburg, Pieter, 94, 97, 103,
  113
Spieß, Karl-Heinz, 90
Spiewok, Wolfgang, 79, 82, 108
Stacey, Robin Chapman, 16
Stackmann, Karl, 89, 90, 97, 134,
  160
Stammesrecht, 109
stealth, 6, 39, 95, 102
Steger, Hugo, 85
Stein, Peter K., 116, 132, 134,
  138
Stengel, Edmund, 88
Strasser, Ingrid, 172, 173
Stratz, H. W., 141
Stricker, Der. *See* Der Stricker
suone, 43, 93
Susanna, 161, 162, 188
swert, 31, 88
swords, i, ix, 34, 47, 49, 56, 62,
  67, 101, 104, 110, 115, 119,
  122, 123, 129, 131, 139, 176,
  177, 178, 180, 183, 185, 186;
  poisoned, 115, 123, 129, 186

tägedinch, 148
Tax, Petrus, 133, 135, 140

theft, 5, 6, 95
Theodulf, 23
Theuerkauf, G., 90
thief, thieves, 40, 73, 102, 113,
  172, 195
Thimo, Bishop of Bamberg, 163
Thomas of Britain, 114, 115,
  126, 132, 138, 144
Thuringian Law of, 802, 151
Tirrich, 47, 67, 99, 100, 101, 111
Tobias, 54, 104, 179
Tomasek, Tomas, 134, 135, 143
torture, 9, 56, 70, 73, 74, 75, 77,
  100, 106, 113, 122, 172, 180
Totschlagssühne, 38, 93
totslac, 39, 94
treachery, 22, 25, 28, 34, 35, 36,
  54, 58, 64, 68, 84, 85, 93, 95,
  104, 182, 183
treason, i, ix, x, 6, 8, 10, 21, 23,
  24, 31, 32, 33, 46, 50, 51, 52,
  59, 60, 63, 64, 65, 67, 71, 75,
  76, 81, 85, 93, 97, 100, 111,
  114, 123, 138, 148, 172, 175,
  181, 182, 183
treaties, 119
trial by battle, i, x, 1, 3, 7, 8, 9,
  10, 11, 12, 13, 17, 18, 28, 38,
  42, 49, 61, 64, 65, 75, 87, 96,
  100, 107, 114, 116, 119, 123,
  137, 130, 131, 135, 147, 170,
  171, 181. *See also* ordeal;
  judgment of God/*judicium Dei*
Tristan, x, 15, 114, 115, 116,
  117, 118, 119, 120, 121, 122,
  123, 124, 125, 126, 127, 128,
  129, 131, 132, 134, 135, 136,
  137, 138, 139, 140, 141, 142,
  143, 164, 184, 185, 186, 187
Tristan (Gottfried von Straßburg),
  i, x, 1, 3, 6, 10, 15, 18, 116, 118,
  123, 128, 129, 131, 132, 135,
  136, 137, 143, 144, 150, 153,
  164, 168, 169, 170, 171, 184
Tristramssaga, 126, 142, 144

triuwe, 29, 84, 85, 87, 117, 118, 136
triwe, 33
Trusen, Winfried, 19
truwen, 53
Turoldus, 21
Turoldus, works by: *Chanson de Roland,* x, 21, 22, 23, 39, 42, 48, 77, 78, 82, 92, 99
Tyssens, Madeleine, 78

überseit, 124, 141
Uitti, Karl D., 77
Ukena-Best, Elke, 81
ungenade, 62, 99
ungetat, 90
unreht, 34, 47
untriuwe, 28, 54, 89
urkünde, 34
urliuge, 32
urtaile, urteil, 35, 87, 92, 109
urteilsschelte, 99

Van Caenegem, Raoul C., 11, 12, 14, 18, 19
Van Stockum, Theodor C., 133, 135, 145
vassals, 25, 30, 31, 32, 56, 84, 85, 88, 89, 90, 100, 111, 114, 122, 148, 164
vechten, 108, 109
verdeilen, verdeylen, verteilen, 59, 64, 107, 110, 111
versagen, 34, 86
vient, 31, 35, 41, 42, 96
von den Steinen, Wolfram, 99
von der Burg, Udo, 81
von Pfeil, Sigurd Graf, 78
vreden, 53, 104
Vulcan, 122

Wagner, Erna, 165
Wailes, Stephen L., 173
Waitz, Georg, 78, 142
Walker, Lorna E. M., 133

Walter, Philippe, 132
Weber, Gottfried, 132, 133
Wehrli, Max, 133
Weinfurter, Stefan, 83, 163, 164
Weistümer, 30
Wellis (character in *Karlmeinet*), 24, 28, 51, 52, 53, 54, 55, 56, 57, 58, 59, 60, 61, 62, 63, 64, 65, 66, 67, 68, 69, 70, 71, 72, 73, 75, 76, 77, 96, 104, 105, 106, 107, 108, 109, 112, 172, 179, 180, 181, 182, 183
Wenzel, King of Bohemia, 23
Wenz-Haubfleisch, Annegret, 163
wergeld, 39, 97
Werkmüller, Dieter, 17, 89, 91, 93, 94, 105
Werner, Otmar, 172
Wesle, Carl, 84
White, Stephen D., 13, 16, 93
Whitman, Jon, 140
widersagen, 41, 95
Widmaier, Sigrid, 87, 90, 91, 92, 94
Wiehl, Peter, 107
Willoweit, Dietmar, 11, 83, 84, 93, 98
Willson, H. B., 143
Wolf, Alois, 133, 134
Wood, Ian, 13, 14
Würzburg, Konrad von, 93, 98
Würzburg, Konrad von, works by: *Engelhard,* 3

York, E. C., 134, 142

Zacharias, Rainer, 99
Zagolla, R., 81, 104
Zender, Matthias, 79
Ziegeler, Hans-Joachim, 81
Ziegler, Vickie L., i, 16, 133
zins, 117, 137
Zips, Manfred, 140